Lecture Notes in Computer Science 8639

Commenced Publication in 1973
Founding and Former Series Editors:
Gerhard Goos, Juris Hartmanis, and Jan van Leeuwen

T0212708

Maki Yoshida   Koichi Mouri (Eds.)

Advances in Information and Computer Security

9th International Workshop on Security, IWSEC 2014
Hirosaki, Japan, August 27-29, 2014
Proceedings

 Springer

Volume Editors

Maki Yoshida
National Institute of Information and Communications Technology (NICT)
Network Security Research Institute
4-2-1 Nukui-Kitamachi, Koganei
Tokyo 184-8795, Japan
E-mail: maki-yos@nict.go.jp

Koichi Mouri
Ritsumeikan University
College of Information Science and Engineering
1-1-1 Nojihigashi, Kusatsu
Shiga 525-8577, Japan
E-mail: mouri@cs.ritsumei.ac.jp

ISSN 0302-9743   e-ISSN 1611-3349
ISBN 978-3-319-09842-5   e-ISBN 978-3-319-09843-2
DOI 10.1007/978-3-319-09843-2
Springer Cham Heidelberg New York Dordrecht London

Library of Congress Control Number: 2014945125

LNCS Sublibrary: SL 4 – Security and Cryptology

Typesetting: Camera-ready by author, data conversion by Scientific Publishing Services, Chennai, India

Printed on acid-free paper

Springer is part of Springer Science+Business Media (www.springer.com)

Preface

The 9th International Workshop on Security (IWSEC 2014) was held at Hakkoda Hall, Hirosaki University, in Hirosaki, Japan, during August 27–29, 2014. The workshop was co-organized by ISEC in ESS of IEICE (Technical Committee on Information Security in Engineering Sciences Society of the Institute of Electronics, Information and Communication Engineers) and CSEC of IPSJ (Special Interest Group on Computer Security of Information Processing Society of Japan).

This year, the workshop received 55 submissions. Finally, 13 papers were accepted as regular papers, and 8 papers were accepted as short papers. Each submission was anonymously reviewed by at least three reviewers, and these proceedings contain the revised versions of the accepted papers. In addition to the presentations of the papers, the workshop also featured a poster session and two keynote speeches. The keynote speeches were given by Reihaneh (Rei) Safavi-Naini, and by Yasuhiko Taniwaki.

The best student paper award was given to "Cheater Identifiable Secret Sharing Schemes Via Multi-Receiver Authentication" by Rui Xu, Kirill Morozov and Tsuyoshi Takagi.

A number of people contributed to the success of IWSEC 2014. We would like to thank the authors for submitting their papers to the workshop. The selection of the papers was a challenging and dedicated task, and we are deeply grateful to the members of Program Committee and the external reviewers for their in-depth reviews and detailed discussions. We are also grateful to Andrei Voronkov for developing EasyChair, which was used for the paper submission, reviews, discussions, and preparation of these proceedings.

Last but not least, we would like to thank the general co-chairs, Kouichi Sakurai and Masakatsu Nishigaki, for leading the Local Organizing Committee, and we also would like to thank the members of the Local Organizing Committee for their efforts to ensure the smooth running of the workshop.

June 2014

Maki Yoshida
Koichi Mouri

IWSEC 2014
9th International Workshop on Security

Hirosaki, Japan, August 27–29, 2014

Co-organized by

ISEC in ESS of IEICE

(Technical Committee on Information Security in Engineering Sciences Society of the Institute of Electronics, Information and Communication Engineers)

and

CSEC of IPSJ

(Special Interest Group on Computer Security of Information Processing Society of Japan)

General Co-chairs

Kouichi Sakurai   Kyushu University, Japan
Masakatsu Nishigaki   Shizuoka University, Japan

Advisory Committee

Hideki Imai   Chuo University, Japan
Kwangjo Kim   Korea Advanced Institute of Science and
                                        Technology, South Korea
Günter Müeller   University of Freiburg, Germany
Yuko Murayama   Iwate Prefectural University, Japan
Koji Nakao   National Institute of Information and
                                        Communications Technology, Japan
Eiji Okamoto   University of Tsukuba, Japan
C. Pandu Rangan   Indian Institute of Technology, India
Ryoichi Sasaki   Tokyo Denki University, Japan

Program Co-chairs

Maki Yoshida   National Institute of Information and
                                        Communications Technology, Japan
Koichi Mouri   Ritsumeikan University, Japan

Poster Chair

Yuji Suga   Internet Initiative Japan Inc., Japan

Local Organizing Committee

Yuki Ashino   NEC Corporation, Japan
Keita Emura   National Institute of Information and
                           Communications Technology, Japan
Yu-ichi Hayashi   Tohoku University, Japan
Masaki Inamura   Tokyo Denki University, Japan
Masaki Kamizono   SecureBrain Corporation, Japan
Akira Kanaoka   Toho University, Japan
Yuichi Komano   Toshiba Corporation, Japan
Takashi Matsunaka   KDDI R&D Laboratories Inc., Japan
Tomoyuki Nagase   Hirosaki University, Japan
Yukiyasu Tsunoo   NEC Corporation, Japan

Program Committee

Rafael Accorsi   University of Freiburg, Germany
Toru Akishita   Sony Corporation, Japan
Claudio Agostino Ardagna   Università degli Studi di Milano, Italy
Nuttapong Attrapadung   AIST, Japan
Reza Azarderakhsh   Rochester Institute of Technology, USA
Sabrina De Capitani
  di Vimercati   Università degli Studi di Milano, Italy
Isao Echizen   National Institute of Informatics, Japan
Sebastian Faust   EPFL, Switzerland
Eiichiro Fujisaki   NTT, Japan
David Galindo   LORIA, France
Dieter Gollmann   Hamburg University of Technology, Germany
Goichiro Hanaoka   AIST, Japan
Yoshikazu Hanatani   Toshiba Corporation, Japan
Swee-Huay Heng   Multimedia University, Malaysia
Takato Hirano   Mitsubishi Electric Corporation, Japan
Mitsugu Iwamoto   The University of Electro-Communications,
                           Japan
Tetsu Iwata   Nagoya University, Japan
Akinori Kawachi   Tokyo Institute of Technology, Japan
Angelos Keromytis   Columbia University, USA
Hiroaki Kikuchi   Meiji University, Japan
Hyung Chan Kim   ETRI, South Korea
Takeshi Koshiba   Saitama University, Japan
Kenichi Kourai   Kyushu Institute of Technology, Japan
Noboru Kunihiro   The University of Tokyo, Japan
Kwok-Yan Lam   National University of Singapore, Singapore
Kanta Matsuura   The University of Tokyo, Japan
Ken Naganuma   Hitachi, Japan

External Reviewers

Table of Contents

Foundation

Encryption

Privacy-Friendly Access Control
Based on Personal Attributes

Jan Hajny[1], Lukas Malina[1], and Ondrej Tethal[2]

[1] Cryptology Research Group
Brno University of Technology
Czech Republic
{hajny,malina}@feec.vutbr.cz
[2] OKsystem
Czech Republic
tethal@oksystem.cz

Abstract. In attribute-based access control systems, the attribute ownership instead of identity is verified before an access to private services or areas is granted. This approach allows more privacy-friendly verification of users since only individual attributes (such as age, citizenship or ticket ownership) are disclosed to service providers, not the complete identity. Unfortunately, there are very few cryptographic systems allowing practical attribute-based access control system implementations. The lack of cryptographic schemes is caused by the fact that the good balance between privacy and accountability is very difficult to achieve. In this paper, the first implementation of the HM12 attribute-based scheme and a practical choice of its security parameters are presented. The cryptographic scheme is implemented on off-the-shelf hardware, namely on MultOS programmable smart-cards and, experimentally, on Android devices. Finally, the results from our pilot deployment of the access-control system and the obtained user feedback are presented.

Keywords: Access Control, Anonymity, Smart-Cards, Privacy, Attributes, Security, Cryptography.

1 Introduction

The attribute-based access control is usually realized by using cryptographic schemes called anonymous attribute-based credentials. The cryptographic foundations for attribute-based credentials (ABCs) started to appear in the late 1990s. Since then, the technologies now known as U-Prove [27] or Idemix [10] have been developed. Their purpose is to provide more privacy and digital identity protection for the process of electronic user verification. In the first place, the cryptographic schemes are designed to provide users with the ability to give anonymous proofs of the ownership of personal attributes, such as age, group membership or citizenship. With anonymous proofs, the digital identity of Internet users, as well as real identity of citizens with electronic ID cards (eIDs), would be better protected. Furthermore, unauthorized tracing of people and behavioral profiling would be much more difficult due to advanced features such as

M. Yoshida and K. Mouri (Eds.): IWSEC 2014, LNCS 8639, pp. 1–16, 2014.

the unlinkability of verification sessions or untraceability. But despite the cryptographic technologies having been known for over a decade, there are only very few practical implementations of these technologies.

The first reason why the cryptographic ABCs are so hard to implement is their very high complexity. In most schemes, the advanced zero-knowledge protocols [15], or their lightweight variant Σ-protocols [14], are employed. These protocols involve computationally demanding operations such as modular multiplication and exponentiation with big numbers. While these operations are fast enough on computers, they are currently very difficult to run on highly resource-limited devices such as smart-cards. Unfortunately, smart-cards are the most preferred devices for user verification as they can be used in mass transportation, building access-control systems or as national eIDs.

The second reason why there are so few practical implementations of ABCs might be the missing important features. Although the research into privacy-enhancing ABCs has been running since the late 1990s, some features are still very difficult to achieve. In particular, it is very difficult to provide practical revocation of users if all necessary privacy protection features are supported. In ABC systems, where all user sessions are anonymous, unlinkable and untraceable, it is very difficult to exclude one particular user from the system once they have been let in. It is even more difficult to do so if all users use an offline device such as the smart-card, where no information can be updated after the card has been issued.

In this paper, we present the first implementation and the practical pilot deployment of the HM12 scheme, which was fully cryptographically described at the CARDIS conference in 2012 [20]. In contrast to similar implementations of related schemes like U-Prove or Idemix (as shown in the Related Work section), we implement all phases necessary for a practical deployment, namely the attribute issuance phase, the anonymous attribute verification phase and the offline revocation phase. All protocols involving a user were implemented on programmable smart-cards with the MultOS ML-3 operating system. The protocols were parameterized to run in a reasonable, practical time and we succeeded in supporting all privacy-enhancing features together with offline revocation features.

1.1   Related Work

First, we briefly analyze the existing schemes from the cryptography perspective. There are two main cryptographic designs of ABCs available, the U-Prove by Stefan Brands and Microsoft [27] and the Idemix by IBM [10]. Both schemes allow users to anonymously prove their attributes to electronic verifiers. Both schemes support the untraceability feature where the issuer of attributes cannot trace users while they use their credentials to prove their attributes. The U-Prove has the drawback of lacking unlinkability of verification sessions. In practice, the verifier (or any eavesdropper) can trace or even deanonymize the user by linking all the verification sessions to a single profile. This is possible due to a unique user ID which is present in all user's transactions. The Idemix has the drawback of unresolved revocation process. The users can be revoked either by the expiry of their credentials after their life time is out [11] or by a blacklisting or whitelisting method based on accumulators [23]. The latter method is impossible when offline devices are used, the first method if fast revocation is required. Both U-Prove and Idemix were originally designed for computers but can be implemented on smart-cards too. The HM12 scheme [20] is a scheme initially designed for offline smart-cards. The scheme supports all privacy-enhancing features such as anonymous attribute proofs, the untraceability of users, the unlinkability of verification sessions. But in addition, HM12 includes a practical offline revocation method. Using the method in HM12, the users can be revoked immediately without revealing their identity and without the need to contact any other remaining users. Thus, the revocation in HM12 is available even if completely offline devices like smart-cards are used for user verification. This type of revocation is called verifier-local revocation (VLR) [8]. The drawback of the HM12 scheme is that it relies on the tamper-resistance of the smart-card to prevent collusion attacks. Thus, the scheme better suits scenarios where the benefits of creating a new fake user are not higher than the effort needed to break the protection of a set of modern smart-cards.

With all the above ABC schemes having stronger and weaker aspects and fitting different implementation scenarios, it is impossible to choose one that fits all situations. Thus, we analyze existing implementations of all schemes.

We start with the U-Prove scheme which was first published by Stephan Brands and Credentica in 2000 [9] and implemented on PC and phones in Java in 2007 [1]. After acquisition by Microsoft, the protocol specification, test vectors and SDK [27] were released. The implementation on JavaCard programmable smart-cards was described in 2009 [28]. Using this implementation, the time necessary for attribute ownership verification exceeds 5 s for 2 attributes and 9 s for 4 attributes. The implementation on MultOS programmable smart-cards was described in 2012 [25]. In this implementation, the MultOS device is the preferred user device for all scheme protocols, in contrast to Microsoft's implementation where PC is preferred. On MultOS, the user is able to prove their attribute in less than 1 s.

The first version of the IBM's Idemix scheme was first described in 2002 [13], based on foundations published in [24]. The first implementations used the JavaCard smart-card platform. The implementation from 2007 [16] needs around 10 s to prove attribute ownership and the improved implementation from 2009 [7] needs ca 7.4 s. Considering the usage of ABC in everyday situations for access control or mass public transportation, a proof generation time of over 5 s is impractical. Thus, Idemix was also implemented on the MultOS smart-card platform, with ca 1.5 s needed to generate the attribute proof. The main weakness of all existing implementations of Idemix is that they do not include a revocation mechanism that would be able to exclude invalid cards (users) from the systems. The inclusion of such a revocation mechanism increases the system complexity very significantly. Therefore, the above shown times of attribute proofs might be misleading since any system lacking the revocation feature would be useless in practice. Recently, pilot projects for Idemix were launched. The IRMA (I Reveal My Attributes) project pilot [3] started in December 2013 and two ABC4Trust pilot deployments have been running since 2013 [6,4], with the expected evaluation at the end of 2014.

The HM12 scheme published in 2012 [20] has not been fully implemented until now. The implementation of the primitives [20,21] indicated that the time of proof generation can be around 2 s, including revocation mechanisms. The full implementation on MultOS ML-3 cards, performance and the evaluation of pilot deployment results are presented in this paper.

1.2   Our Contribution

We present the first implementation of an ABC scheme which supports all privacy-enhancing features, has practical execution times on offline smart-cards and, most importantly, provides functional VLR revocation mechanisms. We describe protocols of the scheme, describe our choice of security parameters, show our implementation and present the resulting system. We describe the results of our pilot deployment in which the scheme was used to control students' access to university laboratories during standard semester operation.

1.3   Notation

For various proofs of knowledge or representation, we use the efficient notation introduced by Camenisch and Stadler [12]. The protocol for proving the knowledge of discrete logarithm of c with respect to g is denoted as $PK\{\alpha : c = g^\alpha\}$. The proof of discrete log equivalence with respect to different generators g_1, g_2 is denoted as $PK\{\alpha : c_1 = g_1^\alpha \wedge c_2 = g_2^\alpha\}$. A signature by a traditional PKI (e.g., RSA) scheme of a user U on some data is denoted as $Sig_U(data)$. The scheme selection, key certification, key distribution, etc., are out of the scope of this paper. The symbol ":" means "such that", "|" means "divides", "$|x|$" is the bitlength of x and "$x \in_R \{0,1\}^l$" is a randomly chosen bitstring of maximum length l.

2   Scheme Description

The HM12 scheme [20] allows a *User* to apply for an attribute at the *Issuer*. The attribute can represent any personal information, the possession of a driving license, for instance. If the Issuer agrees with the attribute issuance, they sign User's application for the attribute. Then, the user can activate their attribute at the *Revocation Referee*. The Revocation Referee is a privacy protection guarantee who decides about revocation or deanonymization in cases where system rules are violated by the User. The attribute is activated to the User by granting an attribute key. After the attribute issuance is completed, a User can anonymously prove their attribute ownership to *Verifiers*. All proofs will remain anonymous, untraceable and unlinkable if the user adheres to the rules. In the case of rule violation, the attribute ownership proof can be de-anonymized, but only by a joint procedure done by the Issuer and Revocation Referee. The roles in the HM12 scheme are the following:

- *Issuer (I)*: validates the applications for attributes, issues attributes to Users.
- *User (U)*: gets issued an attribute from Issuers and anonymously proves its possession to Verifiers.
- *Verifier (V)*: receives the attribute ownership proof generated by the User, verifies its validity. In the case of disputes, initiates the revocation or de-anonymization process.
- *Revocation Referee (RR)*: activates the attributes to Users, decides about the legitimacy of revocation or deanonymization requests by Verifiers.

The interaction among entities is described by the protocols. They are the Setup protocol, IssueAtt protocol, ProveAtt protocol and Revoke protocol, as shown in Figure 1.

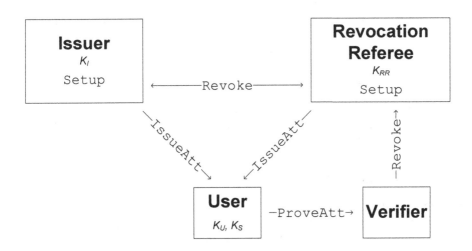

Fig. 1. Architecture of HM12 Scheme

A full cryptographic description of the protocols is presented in the original paper [20]. The purpose of protocols is the following:

- $(params, K_{RR}, K_I) \leftarrow \texttt{Setup}(k, l, m)$: this algorithm is run by RR and Issuer. Setup inputs security parameters (k, l, m) and outputs system parameters $params$. RR's private output of the protocol is the K_{RR} key and I's private output is the K_I key.
- $K_U \leftarrow \texttt{IssueAtt}(params, K_I, K_{RR})$: the protocol outputs User's master key K_U. The master key is needed by the User to create the attribute ownership proof in the ProveAtt protocol. By using advanced cryptographic techniques,

the K_U is generated in such a way that only User's smart-card learns it although both RR and Issuer must contribute data and collaborate on K_U creation.

- $proof$ ←ProveAtt($params, K_U$): using public system parameters and the K_U generated by the IssueAtt protocol, it is possible to build an attribute $proof$ using the ProveAtt. For each $proof$, a unique session key K_S is generated by the User. The proof is anonymized and randomized by K_S. The protocol runs between the Verifier and User's smart-card. By ProveAtt, the User proves their ownership of attributes.

- rev ←Revoke($params, proof, K_{RR}, K_I$): in special cases (e.g., smart-card loss, theft or damage), the issued attributes can be revoked or the malicious Users can even be de-anonymized. In that case, the $proof$ transcript is sent by the Verifier to the RR with adequate evidence for revocation. RR evaluates the evidence and opens the $proof$ transcript using their K_{RR}. Depending on the type of revocation chosen by RR, the RR can either blacklist the attribute by publishing anonymous revocation information rev on a public blacklist or provide the Issuer with information necessary for User identification. The Issuer is then able to identify and charge the malicious User.

3   Scheme Implementation

This section contains information regarding our choice of security parameters, development environment and implementation aspects, and the description of server and user applications.

3.1   Choice of Security Parameters

The scheme contains three key security parameters k, l, m. They are the inputs to the Setup protocol and significantly affect the generation of all system variables. Their meaning and the values, we use as follows:

- k - is the bitlength of the output of the hash function used in the Fiat-Shamir heuristics [17] used in the non-interactive zero-knowledge proofs. We used the SHA-1 function which is available on MultOS smart-card, thus $k = 160$.
- l - is closely related to the length of the user key. The user key consists of two parts, of length l and $2l$. Since keys represent the discrete logarithm in groups where discrete logarithm is hard to compute, we adhered to the NIST recommendation for minimal 160 b keys and chose $l = 80$ for a faster variant and $l = 160$ for a slower variant of our implementation.
- m - is the verification error parameter. We chose $m = 80$. In the non-interactive zero-knowledge protocols, the probability of error is then 2^{-80}, see [5] for details.

The HM12 scheme is based on two multiplicative groups where discrete logarithm is hard to compute. Namely, the DSA group modulo prime p [18] and the Okamoto-Uchiyama group modulo composite $n = r^2 s$ [26] are used. Due to the computational restriction of the smart-card, we chose 1024 bit and 1392 bit groups for our pilot implementation. Our choice of cryptographic parameters for two versions of the implementations are summarized in Table 1.

Table 1. Specification of cryptographic parameters used in the implementation

Parameter	Faster Variant	Slower Variant
$|p|$	1024	1392
$|n|$	1024	1392
k	160	160
l	80	160
m	80	80

3.2 Architecture

The implementation environment contains servers, terminals, smart-cards and mobile phones, see Figure 2.

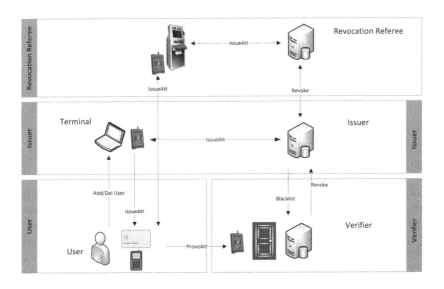

Fig. 2. Implementation Environment of Proposed Scheme

The Revocation Referee, Issuer and Verifier entities were implemented as server applications. The Java SE environment [19] and the Spring framework [22] were used. For data storage, the SQLite database was selected. The communication is based on the Java Remote Method Invocation (RMI). Although the

servers run as services most of the time, a graphic user interface is needed for
a new User registration and for their deletion. The Swing technology is used to
provide the graphic interface. Both `IssueAtt` and `ProveAtt` run on the smart-
card on the User's side. Remote terminals with smart-card readers are used to
forward the communication between User's smart-card and Issuer's and RR's
servers. The communication with smart-card readers is provided by the Java
Smart Card I/O API. Apache Maven [2] is used for building the software. The
classes for cryptographic keys are shown in Figure 3, the designation respects
the notation used in the original paper [20].

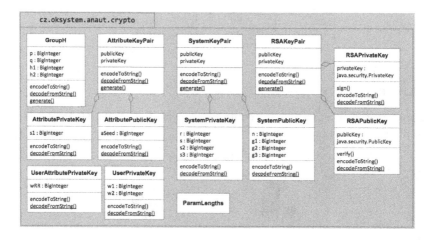

Fig. 3. Diagram of Cryptographic Key Classes

3.3   Smart-Card Application

The `IssueAtt` and the `ProveAtt` protocols run on the smart-card. This allows
the user to securely generate and use their cryptographic keys without leaving
the hardware-protected storage. On the other hand, the protocols can use only
very limited hardware resources shown in the specification of the smart-card in
Table 2, in particular a very low RAM. The original `IssueAtt` and `ProveAtt`
had to be split into multiple parts, the specification of both protocols is in the
Appendix A.

Application Life Cycle. The life cycle of the application is defined by a state
machine (see Figure 4). The current state determines which values are considered
valid and the set of allowed commands.

Table 2. Hardware specification of the MultOS ML-3 cards used

Hardware Specification	
Chip	SLE78CLXxxxPM
CPU	16 bit
Int./Ext. clock	33 MHz/7.5 MHz
RAM Memory	1088+960 B
ROM/EEPROM	280 kB/60 kB
Modular API	Yes

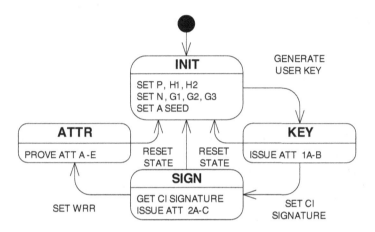

Fig. 4. Smart-Card State Diagram

The INIT, KEY and SIGN states are used during card and attribute issuance (system parameters are set, user key is generated, the IssueAtt protocol is performed). In the last state, ATTR, the card is able to prove the possession of the attribute via the ProveAtt protocol.

- INIT: The initial state of the application. The card does not have any valid values. In this state, the system parameters are set using the Setup protocol. After generating the user private key using the GENERATE USER KEY command the card changes its state to KEY.
- KEY: The card contains the system parameters and user private key (w_1, w_2). None of these components can be changed. The IssueAtt 1 protocol (between the card and the issuer) is performed. After obtaining the issuer's signature of the commitment $Sig_I(C_I)$ using the SET CI SIGNATURE command the card changes its state to SIGN.
- SIGN: The card contains the system parameters, user private key (w_1, w_2) and commitment signature $Sig_I(C_I)$. None of these components can be changed. The IssueAtt 2 protocol (between the card and the revocation referee) is performed. After obtaining the user attribute private key (w_{RR}) using the SET WRR command the card changes its state to ATTR.

- ATTR: In this state, the card has all the necessary parameters to prove the possession of the attribute A_{seed} using the ProveAtt protocol. No value can be changed.

Protocols

This section describes the cryptographic protocols implemented on the smart card:

- Setup: performed by the User and the Issuer.
- IssueAtt 1: performed by the User and the Issuer
- IssueAtt 2: performed by the User and the Revocation Referee
- ProveAtt: performed by the User and the Verifier

Setup

This protocol is performed by the issuer for the values of the system parameters to be written onto the card. At the end of the protocol, the user private key (w_1, w_2) is generated.

IssueAtt 1

This protocol is performed by the user and the issuer. During this protocol, the issuer obtains the user's commitment $C_I = h_1^{w_1} h_2^{w_2} \bmod p$ and the user proves the knowledge of the corresponding values w_1 and w_2. The issuer then signs the commitment and sends the signature $Sig_I(C_I)$ to the card.

The protocol is executed in the KEY state to ensure that the system parameters (in this case p, h_1 and h_2) have been set and the user key (w_1, w_2) has been generated.

IssueAtt 2

This protocol is performed by the user and the revocation referee. During this protocol, the revocation referee obtains the user's commitment $C_I = h_1^{w_1} h_2^{w_2} \bmod p$, $A'_{seed} = g_1^{w_1} g_2^{w_2} \bmod n$, and the issuer's signature of the commitment $Sig_I(C_I)$. The user proves the knowledge of the corresponding values w_1 and w_2. After checking the commitment signature, the revocation referee computes w_{RR} : $A_{seed} = g_1^{w_1} g_2^{w_2} g_3^{w_{RR}} \bmod n$ and sends it to the card.

The protocol is executed in the SIGN state to ensure that the system parameters (in this case p, h_1 and h_2) have been set, the user key (w_1 and w_2) has been generated and the card has obtained $Sig_I(C_I)$ from the issuer.

ProveAtt

The ProveAtt protocol is the main feature of the ACard application. In this protocol, the card (representing the user) proves to the verifier that it owns the attribute A_{seed}, i.e. that it knows $(w_1, w_2, w_{RR}) : A_{seed} = g_1^{w_1} g_2^{w_2} g_3^{w_{RR}} \bmod n$.

The protocol is executed in the ATTR state to ensure that all the necessary parameters have been set.

The protocols are invoked by sending APDU commands. The list of supported APDU commands, their name, description and state in which they operate can be found in Appendix B.

3.4   Android Application

Now only experimentally, we implemented the `ProveAtt` protocol also on Android devices. Both the User's and the Verifier's side of the protocol were implemented. Using these applications, Users can generate their attribute proofs on their mobile phones using the User app, and Verifiers can use mobile phones or tablets to check the proofs using the Verifier app.

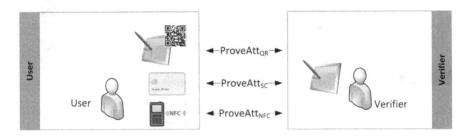

Fig. 5. Verification with Three Types of Communication Interfaces

The Verifier application supports three types of communication interfaces, see Figure 5. The first option is to use QR codes to transfer the attribute proof data. In that case, the QR code containing cryptographic proof data is scanned by the camera of the Verifier device, e.g. a phone or tablet. This option is ideal for devices lacking other simple communication interfaces, like iPhone or iPad. The second option is to use the NFC (Near Field Communication) interface. In that case, the cryptographic proof is transferred by attaching two NFC-enabled devices close to each other. The NFC interface is ideal for situations where both the User and the Verifier applications are running on NFC-enabled devices, like Android phones or tablets. The third option is to use the standard smart-card with the application as described in previous section 3.3 and read the attribute proof by using the RFID (Radio Frequency IDentification, ISO/IEC 14443) technology. Since NFC and RFID in smart-cards are compatible, the Verifier mobile application can be also used to read proofs generated by standard smart-cards. Therefore, our smart-cards can be read either by standard terminals or mobile devices interchangeably without any modifications.

To take advantage of new interfaces, namely NFC and QR codes, we also developed User applications which are able to generate attribute proofs according to the ProveAtt protocol and transfer the cryptographic data via QR or NFC. With these applications available, Users can choose whether they prefer standard smart-cards or mobile devices for the verification of their attribute ownership. The Verifier application with scanned QR code from the User application is depicted in Figure 6.

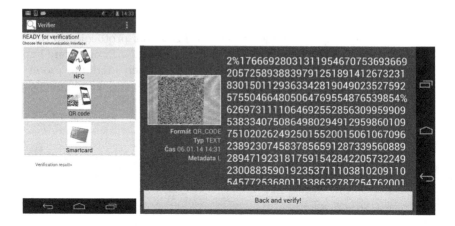

Fig. 6. Verifier Application during Verification of a QR Code - Two Screen Captures

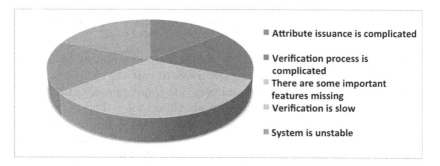

Fig. 7. Evaluation Results - Weak Aspects Selected by Evaluators in Questionnaire (at least 1 weakness had to be selected)

4   Pilot Deployment

The attribute-based credential system has been experimentally deployed at the university during the fall semester of 2013. The goal of the pilot deployment was to verify, whether the attribute-based credentials can be practically deployed for privacy-enabled access control. An attribute indicating student group membership has been issued to 30 smart-cards. Then, the students used the smart-cards to gain access to university laboratories. In this pilot deployment, the students remained anonymous and untraceable while the university had the ability to control access to its premises.

The attribute issuance phase is represented by the IssueAtt protocol and is realized via communication between the student's smart-card and the issuance terminal. The attribute issuance took around 4.5 s, including the time necessary for user key generation and data transfer. The operation needs to be done only once in a lifetime. After attribute issuance, the students were able to use the smart-card to access laboratories. The access was granted after successful completion of the ProveAtt protocol. The attribute proof generation and verification took around 2.9 s, including the time necessary for session randomization, revocation check and data transfer. The 1024 b variant was used.

After completion, the attribute-based system was anonymously evaluated by the students. The general results can be seen in Figure 7, indicating that the speed of attribute verification is the main aspect to be improved by future optimization. The speed improvement might be easily achieved by using smartphones instead of smart-cards for attribute proof generation. In our pilot deployment, only smart-cards were used as User devices.

5   Conclusion

We presented the first practical implementation of the HM12 scheme for anonymous attribute-based credentials (ABCs). We presented the complete implementation of all protocols, namely the attribute issuance protocol, the attribute verification protocol and the revocation protocol. In particular, the practical VLR revocation protocol has been missing in existing ABCs implementations until now. All protocols were implemented on the MultOS ML3 smart-cards with only 16 b CPU and 2 kB of RAM available. We showed the results of our pilot deployment and presented the applications for mobile devices. Our future plan is to modify the `ProveAtt` protocol in order to get rid of the need for device tamper-resistance, which is the known weakness of the HM12 scheme. That will allow easier deployment on Android and iOS mobile devices.

Acknowledgment. This research work is funded by the Technology Agency of the Czech Republic project TA02011260 "Cryptographic system for the protection of electronic identity", the project SIX CZ.1.05/2.1.00/03.007 and the Czech Science Foundation project 14-25298P.

References

1. U-prove sdk overview. White paper. Tech. rep., Credentica Inc. (2007), http://www.credentica.com/GovOnline.pdf
2. Apache maven project (2014), http://maven.apache.org
3. I reveal my attributes, irma (2014), https://www.irmacard.org
4. Abendroth, J., Liagkou, V., Pyrgelis, A., Raptopoulos, C., et al.: D7. 1 application description for students. Technical report, ABC4Trust (2012)
5. Bao, F.: An efficient verifiable encryption scheme for encryption of discrete logarithms. In: Quisquater, J.-J., Schneier, B. (eds.) CARDIS 2000. LNCS, vol. 1820, pp. 213–220. Springer, Heidelberg (2000)
6. Bcheri, S., Goetze, N., Orski, M., Zwingelberg, H.: D6. 1 application description for the school deployment. Technical report, ABC4Trust (2012)
7. Bichsel, P., Camenisch, J., Gro, T., Shoup, V.: Anonymous credentials on a standard java card. In: Proceedings of the 16th ACM Conference on Computer and Communications Security, CCS 2009, pp. 600–610. ACM Press (2009)
8. Boneh, D., Boyen, X., Shacham, H.: Short group signatures. In: Franklin, M. (ed.) CRYPTO 2004. LNCS, vol. 3152, pp. 41–55. Springer, Heidelberg (2004)
9. Brands, S.A.: Rethinking public key infrastructures and digital certificates. MIT Press (c2000)

10. Camenisch, J., et al.: Specification of the identity mixer cryptographic library, Tech. rep. (2010)
11. Camenisch, J., Kohlweiss, M., Soriente, C.: Solving revocation with efficient update of anonymous credentials. In: Garay, J.A., De Prisco, R. (eds.) SCN 2010. LNCS, vol. 6280, pp. 454–471. Springer, Heidelberg (2010)
12. Camenisch, J., Stadler, M.: Proof systems for general statements about discrete logarithms. Tech. rep. (1997)
13. Camenisch, J., Van Herreweghen, E.: Design and implementation of the idemix anonymous credential system. In: Proceedings of the 9th ACM Conference on Computer and Communications Security, CCS 2002, pp. 21–30. ACM, New York (2002)
14. Cramer, R.: Modular Design of Secure, yet Practical Cryptographic Protocols. Ph.D. thesis, University of Amsterdam (1996)
15. Cramer, R., Damgård, I., MacKenzie, P.: Efficient zero-knowledge proofs of knowledge without intractability assumptions. In: Imai, H., Zheng, Y. (eds.) PKC 2000. LNCS, vol. 1751, pp. 354–373. Springer, Heidelberg (2000)
16. Danes, L.: Smart card integration in the pseudonym system idemix. Master's thesis, University of Groningen (2007)
17. Fiat, A., Shamir, A.: How to prove yourself: Practical solutions to identification and signature problems. In: Odlyzko, A.M. (ed.) CRYPTO 1986. LNCS, vol. 263, pp. 186–194. Springer, Heidelberg (1987)
18. Gallagher, P., Kerry, C.: Fips pub 186-4: Digital signature standard, dss (2013), http://nvlpubs.nist.gov/nistpubs/FIPS/NIST.FIPS.186-4.pdf
19. Gosling, J., et al.: The java language specification, java se 7 edition (2013)
20. Hajny, J., Malina, L.: Unlinkable attribute-based credentials with practical revocation on smart-cards. In: Mangard, S. (ed.) CARDIS 2012. LNCS, vol. 7771, pp. 62–76. Springer, Heidelberg (2013)
21. Hajny, J., Malina, L., Martinasek, Z., Tethal, O.: Performance evaluation of primitives for privacy-enhancing cryptography on current smart-cards and smart-phones. In: Garcia-Alfaro, J., Lioudakis, G., Cuppens-Boulahia, N., Foley, S., Fitzgerald, W.M. (eds.) DPM 2013 and SETOP 2013. LNCS, vol. 8247, pp. 17–33. Springer, Heidelberg (2014)
22. Johnson, R., et al.: The spring framework - reference documentation, version 2.5.6 (2008)
23. Lapon, J., Kohlweiss, M., De Decker, B., Naessens, V.: Performance analysis of accumulator-based revocation mechanisms. In: Rannenberg, K., Varadharajan, V., Weber, C. (eds.) SEC 2010. IFIP AICT, vol. 330, pp. 289–301. Springer, Heidelberg (2010)
24. Camenisch, J., Lysyanskaya, A.: An efficient system for non-transferable anonymous credentials with optional anonymity revocation. In: Pfitzmann, B. (ed.) EUROCRYPT 2001. LNCS, vol. 2045, pp. 93–118. Springer, Heidelberg (2001)
25. Mostowski, W., Vullers, P.: Efficient U-prove implementation for anonymous credentials on smart cards. In: Rajarajan, M., Piper, F., Wang, H., Kesidis, G. (eds.) SecureComm 2011. LNICST, vol. 96, pp. 243–260. Springer, Heidelberg (2012)
26. Okamoto, T., Uchiyama, S.: A new public-key cryptosystem as secure as factoring. In: Nyberg, K. (ed.) EUROCRYPT 1998. LNCS, vol. 1403, pp. 308–318. Springer, Heidelberg (1998)
27. Paquin, C.: U-prove cryptographic specification v1.1, Tech. rep. (2011)
28. Tews, H., Jacobs, B.: Performance issues of selective disclosure and blinded issuing protocols on java card. In: Markowitch, O., Bilas, A., Hoepman, J.-H., Mitchell, C.J., Quisquater, J.-J. (eds.) WISTP 2009. LNCS, vol. 5746, pp. 95–111. Springer, Heidelberg (2009)

Appendix A: Cryptographic Specification of Implemented Protocols

The IssueAtt protocol for issuing new attributes implemented on the ML3 smart-card is depicted in Figure 8, using the CS notation [12].

RR   **User**   **Issuer**

$$w_1 \in_R \{0,1\}^{2l-1}, \; w_2 \in_R \{0,1\}^{l-1}$$
$$C_I = commit(w_1, w_2) = h_1^{w_1} h_2^{w_2} \bmod p$$

$$\underline{PK\{w_1, w_2 : C_I = h_1^{w_1} h_2^{w_2}\}, Sig_U(C_I)} \rightarrow$$

Store $(C_I, Sig_U(C_I))$

$$\xleftarrow{\quad Sig_I(C_I) \quad}$$

$$A'_{seed} = g_1^{w_1} g_2^{w_2} \bmod n$$

$$\xleftarrow{\begin{array}{c} A'_{seed}, C_I, Sig_I(C_I), \\ PK\{(w_1, w_2) : C_I = h_1^{w_1} h_2^{w_2} \wedge A'_{seed} = g_1^{w_1} g_2^{w_2}\} \end{array}}$$

$$\xrightarrow{\quad w_{RR} : A_{seed} = g_1^{w_1} g_2^{w_2} g_3^{w_{RR}} \bmod n \quad}$$

User master key for A_{seed}: $K_U = (w_1, w_2, w_{RR})$

Fig. 8. IssueAtt Protocol in Camenisch-Stadler Notation

The ProveAtt protocol for verifying attributes implemented on the ML3 smart-card is depicted in Figure 9, using the CS notation [12].

User   **Verifier**

$$A_{seed} = g_1^{w_1} g_2^{w_2} g_3^{w_{RR}} \bmod n$$
$$K_S \in_R \{0,1\}^l$$
$$A = A_{seed}^{K_S} \bmod n$$
$$C_1 = g_3^{K_S w_{RR}} \bmod n$$
$$C_2 = g_3^{K_S} \bmod n$$

$$\begin{array}{l} PK\{(K_S, K_S w_1, K_S w_2, K_S w_{RR}) : A = g_1^{K_S w_1} g_2^{K_S w_2} g_3^{K_S w_{RR}} \\ \wedge A = A_{seed}^{K_S} \wedge C_1 = g_3^{K_S w_{RR}} \wedge C_2 = g_3^{K_S}\} \end{array} \longrightarrow$$

Fig. 9. ProveAtt Protocol in Camenisch-Stadler Notation

Appendix B: List of Smart-Card APDU Commands

Table 3. List of APDU commands

INS Name	Description	State
0Eh RESET STATE	Sets state to INIT	ANY
10h SET P	Sets p	INIT
12h SET H1	Sets h_1	INIT
14h SET H2	Sets h_2	INIT
16h SET N	Sets n	INIT
18h SET G1	Sets g_1	INIT
1Ah SET G2	Sets g_2	INIT
1Ch SET G3	Sets g_3	INIT
1Eh SET A SEED	Sets A_{seed}	INIT
20h GENERATE USER KEY	Generates w_1, w_2	INIT
22h ISSUE ATT 1A	Phase A of IssueAtt 1	KEY
24h ISSUE ATT 1B	Phase B of IssueAtt 1	KEY
26h SET CI SIGNATURE	Stores $Sig_I(C_I)$	KEY
28h GET CI SIGNATURE	Returns $Sig_I(C_I)$	SIGN
2Ah ISSUE ATT 2A	Phase A of IssueAtt 2	SIGN
2Ch ISSUE ATT 2B	Phase B of IssueAtt 2	SIGN
2Eh ISSUE ATT 2C	Phase C of IssueAtt 2	SIGN
30h SET WRR	Sets w_{RR}	SIGN
32h PROVE ATT A	Phase A of ProveAtt	ATTR
34h PROVE ATT B	Phase B of ProveAtt	ATTR
36h PROVE ATT C	Phase C of ProveAtt	ATTR
38h PROVE ATT D	Phase D of ProveAtt	ATTR
3Ah PROVE ATT E	Phase E of ProveAtt	ATTR

Are You Threatening My Hazards?

Marina Krotofil[1] and Jason Larsen[2]

[1] Hamburg University of Technology, Hamburg, Germany
[2] IOActive, Inc., Seattle, WA 98104, USA

Abstract. This paper presents a framework for discussing security in cyber-physical systems, built on a simple mental model of the relationship between security and safety that has protection flows at its core. We explain their separation of concerns and outline security issues which can yield a violation of the protection flow, supporting the discussion with real world examples. We conclude the paper with a discussion on matters which are beyond our control, subjected to contradictory requirements, or do not have easy solutions. We also identify novel research challenges in the emerging field of cyber-physical security.

1 Introduction

Advances in computing and networking have rendered possible the addition of new capabilities to physical systems that could not be feasibly added before. This led to the emergence of engineering systems called cyber-physical systems (CPS): collaborative environments consisting of computational and communication elements controlling physical entities with the help of sensors and actuators. Aircrafts, robots, utilities, chemical and food plants are examples of such systems. Some cyber-physical systems are termed critical infrastructures because their functionality is critical to modern society.

While "cyberfication" contributes to improving the efficiency of physical processes, it is also a source of concerns about vulnerabilities to both random cyber failures and security attacks. On one hand embedded computers have enabled the governing of physical applications to achieve desired outcomes. On the other hand physical systems can be instructed in the same way to perform actions that are not intended. As a result software code which does not inherently possess tangible force can potentially acquire destructive capacity through the ability to instruct physical systems to malfunction. Cyber attacks on physical systems are correspondingly called *cyber-physical attacks*. The implications of this class of cyber attacks (the ability to inflict physical damage) is the main difference between cyber-physical and conventional cyber attacks. What is not always understood is that breaking into the cyber-physical system and taking over its component(s) is not enough to carry out an attack. Actually abusing the system requires additional knowledge such as a good understanding of mechanics, physics, signal processing, control principles, etc. Moreover, different types of CPS are subjected to fundamentally dissimilar failure modes which first need to be discovered.

M. Yoshida and K. Mouri (Eds.): IWSEC 2014, LNCS 8639, pp. 17–32, 2014.

In the context of CPS, safety systems have the critical function of detecting dangerous or hazardous conditions and taking actions to prevent catastrophic consequences on the users and the environment. The industrial control community has substantial experience in identifying and addressing potential hazards and operational problems in terms of plant design and human error, used to minimize the effects of atypical situations and to achieve a safe outcome from a situation that could have resulted in a major accident. However, the evolution of safety systems is largely built on the ability to interconnect systems and to automate notifications and alarms in the event of safety breaches. As a result, safety systems became vulnerable to cyber attacks. In the past the relationship between safety and security was studied in the context of dependable computing (Fig. 1). Compared to previous work on determining common approaches to safety and security, which had its focus on IT or system-design, see e.g. [24], [18], we also include the underlying physical processes in our considerations.

Fig. 1. Dependability and security attributes, based on [5]

Both cyber security and safety have distinct histories and have developed their own bodies of work. In both disciplines basic concepts have developed into a language that can be used to describe best practices. However, the current efforts to secure critical infrastructure have used the language of cyber security drawing little from the language of safety. Architectures are most often described in terms of security boundaries and not in terms of hazards. This cyber-oriented view of the world has been codified into standards and regulations governing process control.

One regulation illustrating this point are the NERC CIP standards [22]. Under this regulation a control system is broken down into a set of "control centers". The communications between control centers and to outside entities defines an electronic security perimeter (ESP). Not all control centers are required to be defended. Simple tests are used to determine whether a particular control center is required to be defended in compliance with the standard. However, most of the tests are cyber-oriented. The only safety-oriented test is that the control system should have the ability to shed 300 MW of load. All other hazards such as bringing a generator out of phase [29] or energizing a line during maintenance work are ignored by the standard.

The NIST 800-53a standard has a similar flavor [23]. Its general hardening recommendations such as password lengths are applied broadly to the devices used in process control. The standard is meant to be applied to all industrial processes without any modification for the specific product being manufactured.

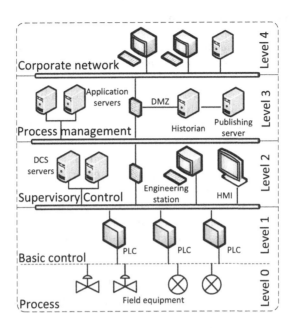

Fig. 2. ICS reference architecture

In both cases, there is no need for the implementer to understand the inherent hazards of the system. Hazards are simply part of the nameless devices represented by the lowest level of the Industrial Control Systems (ICS) architecture (Fig. 2) whereas cyber security exists as a barrier on top of those devices (predominantly in the form of the firewalls). One of the key dangers of this style of thinking is that all parts of the process can be grouped together into a single security compartment without any regard to how the parts of the process interact with each other and, specifically, how those interactions are key parts of the safety of the process.

The purpose of this paper is threefold. First, we propose an easily comprehensible mental model of the relationship between safety and security in cyber-physical systems. We explain the most important differences between the protective roles of safety and security and justify concerns about the violations of the direction of the protection flow. Second, we show that cyber-physical systems cannot be secured only by the means of canonical IT security approaches; the physical world of the CPS needs to be taken into consideration. In this respect the cyber-part of a cyber-physical system should not be seen as an infrastructure that needs protection from attacks in cyberspace as this leads to losing view of what is happening in the physical world and whether the system remains safe. Third, we identify novel research challenges which require solutions for improving the security posture of cyber-physical systems.

2   Disassembling the Safety and Security Nexus

'Take care of the sense and the sounds will take care of themselves.'
-Lewis Carroll, Alice's Adventures in Wonderland (1865)

In the physical world safety is a primary concern. Even before somebody is allowed to visit a plant, they usually watch a safety training video. Many industrial companies have a large screen displaying the number of days elapsed since the last safety accident. Very few, if any, companies address cyber security concerns in the same way. Security is still traditionally seen as an IT-issue, predominately concerned with protecting emails and the data on the enterprise servers. Security is often accompanied with the term privacy reflecting its information-centric approach.

Connection of safety systems has allowed processes to become more efficient and has become de facto a component of a facility's infrastructure. The growing body of regulations and standards is a direct result of the importance being placed on safety. Safety systems are not just reactive alert systems responding to a crisis, but also a proactive and predictive way of avoiding disastrous situations. It is unthinkable that these systems may fail to alert when the need arises. However software intense industrial systems and communication technologies have opened up pathways for external security threats to impact the safety of the system. Physical systems can now be attacked through cyberspace and cyberspace can be attacked though physical devices. In order to meet the challenge of securing cyber-physical systems, the security community needs to develop an understanding of safety and security that is not wholly derived from either computer science or safety engineering. It should, in fact, evolve into a new discipline which merges the fundamental concepts from each and inject new ideas of its own.

Safety and security are sometimes described as two sides of the same coin [9]. If the attacker can compromise safety systems through cyberspace and prevent them from performing their intended protection function, a security incident may lead directly to a catastrophic event. Security and safety are interconnected but both have different missions and employ different vocabularies. In order to understand their "separation of concerns" we examine the purpose and the properties of both security and safety.

2.1   Safety

Safety measures are intended to protect against *hazards*, while security measures protect against *threats*. In the safety field, hazards present a risk to a tangible entities such as human health, environment and machinery. Hazards are closely related to the concept of energy release or its change. The energy might be mechanical, chemical, electrical, thermal, kinetic, etc. An incident develops when an uncontrolled energy hits a human body, environment or material assets. Hazardous situations are generally assumed to be random events caused by natural conditions such as mechanical or human failures or as a result of disturbances to the environment. Due to the assumption of independent failures, the safety field employs statistical methods used in reliability engineering. Once the system is in a safe state, it stays so if untouched.

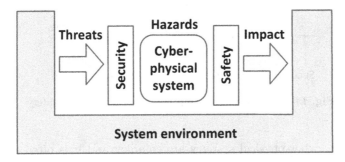

Fig. 3. Relationship between security and safety

2.2   Security

In contrast to hazards, IT security threats are directed at data and the supporting communication infrastructure, and do not present a direct risk of physical damage. Threats can always be traced back to humans and their will to perform a certain action. Threats may be further divided into external (e.g., hackers) and insider threats (e.g., employees of an organization). Most security incidents are caused by deliberate acts[1]. The purpose of a deliberate malicious act is forcing and incident to happen with the desire of a beneficial outcome for the attacker. It is impossible to control security threats (where, when and how an attack happens) but an organization can apply its best effort in protecting itself. Security depends on continuous updates to counter the current threats. Based on the above discussion the relationship between security and safety can be summarized in the simple model depicted in Fig. 3.

2.3   Protection Flow

The direction of the arrows in Fig. 3 represents the ideal protection flow. If security measures fail and a security incident occurs, safety precautions kick in to prevent major losses (Fig. 4). A real-life example which demonstrates accordance with the intended flow of protection is an accident at the Hatch nuclear power plant [12]. The plant was forced into an emergency shutdown for 48 hours after an engineer applied a software update to a single computer on the plant's business network. The computer was used to collect diagnostic data from the process control network and the update was designed to synchronize data between both networks. When the engineer rebooted the computer, the synchronization program reset the data on the control network. The control systems interpreted the reset as a sudden drop in the reactor's water reservoirs and triggered an automatic shutdown. The nuclear plant's emergency systems performed as designed, and the cyber incident did not endanger the safety of the nuclear facility.

---

[1] Security also deals with unintended incidents, but the methods of preventing accidental security violations are the same as dealing with deliberate violations.

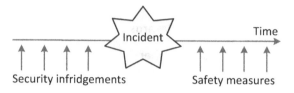

Fig. 4. Temporal relationship between security and safety

In practice, cyber-physical systems are complex and it is often not easy to draw a distinct line between the protective boundaries of safety and security. The physical layer can expose digital systems to cyber attacks. For example a frame relay link to a remote substation exposes the control layer to third party manipulation. The cyber layer also directly influences the safety of the physical layer. For example an interlock that stops a generator from starting when its oil pump is off is necessary for the physical protection of a generator. The field of cyber-physical security is concerned with these interdisciplinary cases. In the following sections we will discuss issues which can violate the flow of protection as well as identify interesting research problems.

3   Violations of the Model

'If everybody minded their own business, the world would go around a great deal faster than it does.'
-Lewis Carroll, Alice's Adventures in Wonderland (1865)

As safety systems were integrated into common infrastructures, it became essential to examine the way in which safety-critical data flows as it is collected, transferred, and shared. Manipulations of data may have a domino effect on the rest of the of the system from that point onward. Control data flow from the cyber systems towards the physical systems. Status and measurement data flow in the reverse direction, giving another opportunity for an attacker to impact the safety of a process. Once a cyber-physical system is created, an attacker may use it to impact the veracity, integrity, or availability of the data (Fig. 5).

3.1   Veracity

The standard armory in network security such as firewalls, secure tunnels, digital signatures, and access control provide no defense if sensor readings were manipulated before reading. When false data is submitted to the cyber infrastructure, false data will be delivered securely to the intended application. In the context of cyber-physical systems process data originates in the physical space and no canonical IT security solution can guarantee that the inputs from a sensor faithfully capture reality. The identification of a hazardous situation depends on the measurements of physical phenomena. If the attacker manages to manipulate

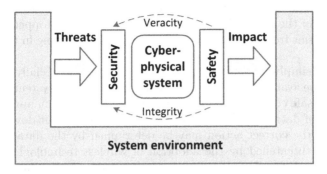

Fig. 5. Violation of the protection flow

sensor signals, e.g. through the manipulation of the surrounding environment or through sensor miscalibration, safety systems will not take over in a critical situation. Such an attack would violate one crucial but predominantly overlooked security property of information called trustworthiness or *veracity* [11]. To give an example, an explosion at BP Texas City Refinery killed 15 people and injured another 180 [27]. The root cause of the tragedy was critical alarms and control instrumentation providing false indications. Due to calibration errors the splitter tower level indicator showed that the tower level was declining when it was actually overfilling with flammable liquid hydrocarbons. As a result the operator kept filling in the tower. This chain of events eventually led to an explosion.

3.2 Integrity and Availability

At any point in the processing or transmission of a critical data, the integrity of that data can be compromised. In a cyber-physical system, this starts from the first point that a measurement is converted into digital form. Certain pieces of the process data must be accurate at all times in order to maintain the safety of the process. For example if a value is manipulated an interlock designed to protect the equipment may not engage. A common design in sensors is to vary the voltage or amperage in response to a physical phenomenon. The analog signal is then converted into a digital number by the controller. While a sensor can be purely analog, it is now more common for a microcontroller to be embedded into the sensor itself [21]. That microcontroller then produces a separate signal which is consumed by the controller. In all cases, the analog signal must be calibrated and scaled to transform it into a useful unit of measurement. This represents the first step where malicious actors may manipulate the data. The scaled data is then transmitted to a controller that uses it to make process control decisions. Data may be processed and combined with other data and transferred as inputs to yet additional controllers. Understanding the data source and its pathway is essential to understanding how an attacker might cause a negative outcome. The Stuxnet worm masked its destructive operation by invading a Siemens controller and hijacking a read function. When an outside computer asked for the state of the system, the malware returned pre-recorded well-behaved process data. Such violation of the integrity property of the process data stopped higher level safety mechanisms from shutting down the centrifuges resulting in their physical damage [13].

Data can be simply missing instead of being incorrect. Especially where safety is concerned, the availability of the data is important. Safety system are designed to *detect* an unsafe condition and then *respond* to the condition appropriately. If there is a loss of data, the process can be programmed to shut down safely, but in many cases the correct action may be determined by the data. Availability is particularly threatened by the adoption of wireless technologies by process control vendors. Even if a third party cannot understand or manipulate the data, interfering with a radio transmission is simple and often done by accident.

3.3 Hidden Impact Data

A hazard is usually contained within a particular cyber-physical system. In order to determine the scope of the infrastructure that must be protected to mitigate a particular hazard, the extent of the cyber-physical systems that contains the hazard must be defined. A granular definition of a cyber-physical system can be defined by starting with the physical equipment that embodies the hazard and working back through the data flows and the logic that are required for the cyber-physical system to operate. If this analysis is done with sufficient fidelity, the cyber-physical system will be bounded to a specific set of devices, the logic that is contained within those devices, the specific pieces of data the logic operates on, and finally the communications infrastructure that transmits the data from one device to another.

Any nontrivial process will be composed of more than one cyber-physical system operating on a connected set of equipments. A cyber-physical system as defined above does not operate independently. The physics of the process connect a cyber-physical system to other cyber-physical systems. For example one cyber-physical system may generate steam and another will use that steam to produce electricity. That physical connection between two cyber-physical systems is a dependency relationship and can be seen as a data flow. This hidden data flow can lead to an improperly described cyber-physical system.

When the logic of a cyber-physical system operates on a particular datum, that datum may actually be an *aggregate* of other data even if that value was directly measured from the process. In such case the unseen data may have a negative impact on the cyber-physical system. Consider as an example a process unit that produces ammonia in which a pressure in a vessel is maintained with a pump. Maintaining the right ammonia pressure is critical to the financial health of the plant. Another pump is responsible for the outflow of the ammonia from the vessel but is not considered critical to the economy of the plant. It may be possible to set up a standing wave between the two pumps that has a direct impact on the ability of the first pump to perform its function. In that case the state of the non-critical pump can be considered *hidden impact data* for the CPS that contains the critical pump. The unseen state of the second pump is critical to the functionality of the first pump even though there are no data flows between the two control loops. Controlling for these types of resonances is part of the standard training for process control engineers and may be obvious to them, but if the cyber-physical system was defined by tracing its electronic data flows, the state of the second pump would not be identified.

Narrowly defining a cyber-physical system may lead to cases where each individual system is protected but the system-of-systems is improperly protected. The best way to identify hidden impact data has not been investigated and may be a topic of future research.

3.4   Wireless Communication

Major vendors are adopting short range wireless networks in their product lines. This represents a major shift in both the architecture and the security of cyber-physical systems. Davis [10] showed that a practical worm could be created to attack electric power meters. The worm used the wireless interface on the meters to spread from device to device eventually giving control of the remote disconnect switches on the meters over a wide geographic area. In this case the field equipment was the source and the target of the attack. The wireless interfaces allowed the attacker to completely bypass the outer layers of security and approach the hazards directly. Wireless sensors hope to use encryption to protect the communication between nodes. History suggest that flaws will be found in these new wireless protocols [2].

While the wireless protocol certainly differ, many of them are based on the IEEE 802.15.4 standard. Mobile phones and other gadgets are already collecting data on nearby wireless networks as they travel including those based on 802.15 antennas. The databases are designed to map wireless devices that are only in close proximity periodically. This is sometimes referred to as "device social networks". The wireless sensors used in cyber-physical systems may be first mapped by a mobile device and then later attacked by it. This would be a logical extension to the work done by Leverett [16] to identify SCADA targets using the popular device search engine Shodan [20]. Encryption has long promised to make wireless hops as secure as physically wired devices, but have always fallen short of perfect security.

While this may still seem far in the future, cell phone makers are already adding software to collect proximity data of wireless devices [1]. Google will soon know that a doctor rides a bus with an industrial control technician every day even if they never interact with each other. The attackers cannot be far behind. In a recent case, the pumping stations in Oslo were converted to bluetooth for control adding a wireless component to this particular CPS [8]. In the very near future, it will be possible to plan attacks that use the antenna on the doctor's phone to compromise the technician's phone and then compromise the pumping station. These new pathways completely bypass the known and understood security boundaries in place to stop cyber attacks.

4   Preserving Flow of Protection

'My dear, here we must run as fast as we can, just to stay in place. And if you wish to go anywhere you must run twice as fast as that.'
-Lewis Carroll, Through the Looking-Glass (1871)

The model suggests that control is meant to flow from the cyber systems to the physical system. In cyber-physical systems backwards data flows give the opportunity for attackers to impact the process. Minimizing or eliminating those backward flows hardens the process in respect to cyber attacks.

Logically commands come from the operator and then instruct the field equipment to perform some action. Data then flows from the field equipment back to the operator. When data is consumed by a computing device that then issues a command based on that data, a cyber-physical system has been created. These loops are the basis of modern process control. The scope of a cyber-physical system is bounded by those flows. The system contains every device, wire, and physical actuator that is involved in these flows. That would include the networking gear that carries the data as well as the valve that controls flow.

It is important to note that CPSs are fractal in structure. Consider the feedback mechanisms in a smart valve. A feedback loop is performed between the pressure sensor and the air controller to ensure the valve closes at the correct speed. The valve on the other hand is seen as a single element in a larger subcomponent of a factory. The scope of a CPS depends greatly on the definition of the "system". The choices made in designing a communications architecture can quickly add a large number of devices to a CPS, as a common infrastructure is used in the control of individual systems. A properly defined CPS should include all of the devices that can be used to manipulate it. Under this definition an attacker must interact with some part of the CPS to achieve her goals.

4.1   Ensuring Veracity

At the lowest level a physical measurement is turned into data. Veracity can be achieved in two ways. First, if the environment warrants a sufficient degree of physical protection tamper-resistant sensors can be deployed which protect the physical sensor. Second, if the environment cannot be easily controlled, countermeasures can take the form of consistency or plausibility checks on received sensor inputs [11]. Sensor readings can be false on purpose (due to attack) or by accident (e.g. wrong calibration of sensor). Although this distinction does not matter for the application, it matters for the design of the countermeasures. Redundancy and consistency checks such as majority voting have been used for detecting accidental sensor failures. With intentional attacks defenses cannot be built on the basis of statistical independencies and may take the form of plausibility checks. In this case the models of the physical space under observation are used to judge to which extent individual sensor readings [19] are consistent with the overall state of the system derived from all the readings. It is possible to further model the relationship between different aspects of the physical process (e.g. temperature and pressure) in order to detect impossible sensor readings and flag them as suspicious. Changes in the plant configuration are not required to implement such countermeasures which make make them more practical.

4.2 Security Zones

As noted above, a granular architecture can be created by tracing specific hazards back through a cyber-physical system matching specific devices and specific pieces of data with the hazard. When the components involved have been identified, the maximum impact of an attack can be determined by examining the hazards assigned to the compromised components. If the hazard may potentially lead to a loss of life, the components should be protected more vigorously than those relating to a hazard that only results in financial loss. Components related to similar negative outcomes can be placed within a common security boundary. A new network diagram might detail a "loss-of-life security boundary" and a "financial-damage security boundary". Such boundaries would be much more useful to all parties than the traditional boundary between the "Process Control LAN" and the "Business Network".

What constitutes a hazard depends on where the boundaries of a system are drawn. The boundaries will determine which conditions and components are considered as part of the hazard. As suggested in [18] the most useful way to define the boundaries is to draw them to include the conditions related to the accident over which a system engineer has some control. This will allow to avoid the accident through eliminating or controlling the hazard.

As an example consider a robotic arm installed in an automotive factory. The robotic arm is used to paint cars on an assembly line. It poses both a chemical hazard to plant personnel (painting them) and a physical hazard (knocking them on the head). The painting chamber has a door sensor that powers off the robot if a human enters the room maintaining the safety of the system. The whole control system for the robot is complex containing multiple computers and an array of optical equipment used to automate the painting process. In contrast, the actual equipment needed to protect human life is a much smaller subset. The door sensor must accurately detect a human, the communications infrastructure must transmit the door status to the controller, and the controller logic must instruct the power relay to power off the robot. This control circuit is simple, concise, and easy to understand. Only these parts of equipment need to be secured from cyber attacks to mitigate these particular hazards.

This model has the additional utility that it immediately alerts the maintainers to the risks associated with modifications of the system. As in the above example, if the devices necessary for the protection of human life are within a separate boundary, it is inherently obvious that adding a new function to those devices may impact human safety. If the entire robotic system is contained within the same boundary, a small change vital to safety may go overlooked. Such granular security zoning facilitates better harmonization of safety and security life cycles. Whereas security relies on frequent updates such as installing patches, upgrading firmware or adding new firewall rules, any such change in software or operational practices must be followed by a cumbersome safety revision. Failing to do so can result in casualties. Thus, after update of the SAP-based maintenance software at DuPont (without review), an alarm notifying on a hose change due date "disappeared". As a result, a hose used to transfer phosgene from a cylinder to a process wore out and catastrophically failed spraying a worker in the face and resulting in his death [26].

Once a process is analyzed there will be a number of security zones ranging from "public safety hazards" to "public relations problems". A process could be designed from the start to separate those hazards into different equipment, but in most situations individual devices will have multiple hazards associated with them. A single controller could be involved in a hazard to human life and a catastrophic financial event. In the robot painting example a single controller is likely responsible for painting the automobiles and for powering off the robot. The logical choice would be to place that controller into the most risky category namely hazards to human life. Small changes to the design of the process could be used to "downgrade" the controller from human life to financial loss. If the function of shutting down the robot was moved to a separate controller, the rest of the robot network is only a threat to the financial resources of the company. The new controller and its communications could then be more conservatively protected.

Greater protection often leads to greater costs and less flexibility. Identifying the hazards tied to each individual piece of equipment can be used to reduce costs and increase flexibility. In the original case, the entire painting network needs to be aggressively protected. Installing a vendor VPN to streamline support would open the possibility for an outside entity to endanger human life. Understanding the hazards and separating them into zones allows greater flexibility for the rest of the network. If the greatest harm from the VPN is merely financial, a simple cost/benefit argument could be made when sizing the defenses.

Even with the additional costs caused by adding and maintaining an additional device, the solution could end up being more cost effective for the implementer. Cyber security resources are scarce and expensive. More complex systems take greater resources. Being able to allocate more resources to protecting higher risk but simpler devices could result in an overall cost savings to the implementer. Also, better protected security zones, assuming that they are not invaded by an attacker, can be used for the detection of cyber-physical attacks as proposed in [3].

4.3   Eliminating Cyber-Physical Systems

Hazards with particularly severe negative outcomes can be mitigated by removing them from digital control entirely. As an example the petroleum refining industry has a requirement that remotely operated valves be present to interrupt fuel supplies during a jet fire. The valves must be remotely operated since it is too hazardous for a human to approach a burning column of petroleum [28]. This example illustrates a key conflict. The valves need to be remotely controlled for safety, but the critical nature of the valves makes them a target for an attacker. In these cases, the remote valve could be replaced with a non-digital circuit to perform the same function. If there is no digital circuitry there is no chance for disruption via cyber means.

The U.S. Nuclear Regulator Commission is investigating the use of field-programmable gate arrays (FPGA) for critical controls [6]. Traditionally a Programmable Logic Controller (PLC) or other logic controller is used in the safety systems that protect critical hazards within a plant. The use of digital systems is flexible allowing the mitigation to be updated as the plant changes and hazards are more completely understood. It also opens up those critical controls to potential cyber attack. At some time in the near future, those controller may be replaced with FPGAs running a very discrete set of logic embodying the safety requirement. If the safety logic needs to be updated, the FPGA can be updated without the need to build and test new physics-based mitigations. This approach may provide a middle ground between purely analog systems and digital systems.

5 Discussion

'It would be so nice if something made sense for a change.'
-Lewis Carroll, Alice's Adventures in Wonderland (1865)

Even in the formal world of process control, there can be competing goals. Some conflicts are obvious. During a cyber attack, a compromised device cannot simply be unplugged. Disconnecting a part of a cyber-physical system does not guarantee that the system will eventually enter a safe state. For example a chemical reaction does not stop simply because its controller is no longer regulating the temperature. Larsen [14] has shown that a full attack payload can be miniaturized to fit into a small microcontroller located directly on the field equipment. Shutting down a controller does not guarantee that code execution stops on all the attached field devices. In addition, shutting down a cyber-physical system in response to a cyber event results in a loss-of-control for the operator. The desire to stop the attack and the desire to control the process are in conflict. Leverett [17] has shown that an attacker can gain code execution on an PLC which may be used to modify the state of an operator's display. It follows that the operator cannot rely on her displays during a cyber event. There is no consensus answer about the best course of action during such an event.

These competing goals exist at the macro level as well. The safe state for a nuclear reactor is to shut down. Nearly all the logic in a reactor control system is used to detect an unsafe condition and perform a controlled shutdown. If that same reactor is considered as a part of the larger electric grid the correct action become less clear. First consider the reactor's role during a severe winter snowstorm. If the state of the grid is already unstable and the reactor goes offline, a blackout will occur resulting in a loss of life [4] and other externalities [25]. Second consider the same reactor during the East coast blackout. During that event reactor operators were slow to shut down even though excessive generation had resulted in the frequency of the grid had rising to 63.4Hz eventually resulting in additional outages.

Without knowledge of the state of the larger system, the safe course of action may not be known. If the state of the larger system is used as part of the safety logic, it must be imported from an external and therefore untrusted connection. If the connection is untrusted, how can it be used as part of a critical safety decision? This is an area for further study.

Currently there is no way for attackers to remotely analyze a cyber-physical system using the physics of the process. This is an area wide open for research. Although preliminary research has been already done [15], the full potential of a cyber-physical system to affect the physical world has not been explored yet. Bratus [7] has defined security violations as "unexpected computations" that can be described by so called *weird machines*. This has lead to exploitation techniques that use everything from ELF (Executable and Linkable Format) loaders to cryptographic validators to invade cyber systems. No such abstraction exists for cyber-physical systems.

Just as in the early days of cyber exploitation, it is clear that unexpected results can come from manipulating the controls of a process. If these unexpected results can be predicted and chained together, an attacker may be able to achieve heretofore unexplored results. What is lacking is an equivalent set of primitives for cyber-physical systems. In the future those primitives may be chained together to produce "unexpected physics".

6   Conclusions

Securing cyber-physical systems is challenging in the sense that they are all very dissimilar and most security problems (and solutions) exist only in a particular context. Nevertheless, we should start studying them trying to identify common patterns so that we can investigate unified solutions to address those patterns.

References

1. Configure access points with Google Location Service,
   https://support.google.com/maps/answer/1725632?hl=en
2. Project KillerBee, https://code.google.com/p/killerbee/
3. Safety securing approach against cyber-attacks for process control system. Computers & Chemical Engineering 57, 181–186 (2013)
4. Anderson, G., Bell, M.L.: Lights Out: Impact of the Power Outage on Mortality in New York August 2003. Epidemiology 23(2), 189–193 (2012)
5. Avizienis, A., Laprie, J.C., Randell, B., Landwehr, C.: Basic concepts and taxonomy of dependable and secure computing. IEEE Transactions on Dependable and Secure Computing 1, 11–33 (2004)
6. Bobrek, M., Bouldin, D., Holcomb, D., Killough, S., Smith, S., Ward, C., Wood, R.: Review Guidelines for Field-Programmable Gate Arrays in Nuclear Power Plant Safety Systems. U.S.RNC (2010)

7. Bratus, S., Locasto, M., Patterson, M.L., Sassaman, L., Shubina, A.: Exploit Programming: From Buffer Overflows to 'Weird Machines' and Theory of Computation. USENIX; Login 36(6), 13–21 (2011)
8. connectBlue: Bluetooth Technology in Oslo Pump Stations (2011),
   http://www.connectblue.com/fileadmin/Connectblue/Web2006/Documents/References/ABB_Norway.pdf
9. Cusimano, J., Byres, E.: Safety and Security: Two Sides of the Same Coin. ControlGlobal (2010)
10. Davis, M.: SmartGrid Device Security: Adventures in a new medium. Black Hat USA (2011)
11. Gollmann, D.: Veracity, plausibility, and reputation. In: Askoxylakis, I., Pöhls, H.C., Posegga, J. (eds.) WISTP 2012. LNCS, vol. 7322, pp. 20–28. Springer, Heidelberg (2012)
12. Kesler, B.: The vulnerability of nuclear facilities to cyber attack. Strategic Insights 10(1), 15–25 (2011)
13. Langner, R.: To kill a centrifuge. Tech. rep., Langner Communications (2013)
14. Larsen, J.: Going Small When Attacking a Process,
   http://vimeopro.com/s42012/s4x14/video/84632472
15. Larsen, J.: Breakage. Black Hat USA (2008)
16. Leverett, É.P.: Quantitatively Assessing and Visualising Industrial System Attack Surfaces. Master's thesis, University of Cambridge, UK (2011)
17. Leverett, É.P., Wightman, R.: Vulnerability Inheritance Programmable Logic Controllers. In: The 2nd International Symposium on Research in Grey-Hat Hacking, GreHack (2013)
18. Leveson, N.G.: Engineering a Safer World: Systems Thinking Applied to Safety. The MIT Press (2012)
19. Linda, O., Manic, M., McQueen, M.: Improving control system cyber-state awareness using known secure sensor measurements. In: Hämmerli, B.M., Kalstad Svendsen, N., Lopez, J. (eds.) CRITIS 2012. LNCS, vol. 7722, pp. 46–58. Springer, Heidelberg (2013)
20. Matherly, J.C.: SHODAN (2009), http://www.shodanhq.com/
21. McIntyre, C.: Using Smart Instrumentation. Plant Engineering: online magazine (2011), http://www.controleng.com/single-article/using-smart-instrumentation/a0ec350155bb86c8f65377ba66e59df8.html (retrieved: December 2013)
22. NERC: Critical Infrastructure Protection Standards,
   http://www.nerc.com/pa/Stand/Pages/CIPStandards.aspx
23. NIST: Guide for Assessing the Security Controls in Federal Information Systems and Organizations (2010)
24. Novak, T., Gerstinger, A.: Safety- and Security-Critical Services in Building Automation and Control Systems. IEEE Transactions on Industrial Electronics 57(11), 3614–3621 (2010)
25. Rinaldi, S., Peerenboom, J., Kelly, T.: Identifying, understanding, and analyzing critical infrastructure interdependencies. IEEE Control Systems 21(6), 11–25 (2001)
26. U.S. Chemical Safety and Hazard Investigation Board: DuPont Corporation Toxic Chemical Releases: Investigation Report. Tech. rep., U.S. Chemical Safety Board (CSB) (20011)

27. U.S. Chemical Safety and Hazard Investigation Board: Bp America Refinery Explosion: Final Investigation Report. Tech. rep., U.S. Chemical Safety Board (CSB) (2007)
28. U.S. Chemical Safety and Hazard Investigation Board: LPG Fire ar Valero–McKee Refinery: Final Investigation Report. Tech. rep., U.S. Chemical Safety Board (CSB) (2007)
29. Zeller, M.: Myth or reality - does the Aurora vulnerability pose a risk to my generator? In: 2011 64th Annual Conference for Protective Relay Engineers, pp. 130–136 (2011)

Complicating Process Identification
by Replacing Process Information for Attack Avoidance

Masaya Sato and Toshihiro Yamauchi

Graduate School of Natural Science and Technology, Okayama University,
3-1-1 Tsushima-naka, Kita-ku, Okayama, 700-8530 Japan
m-sato@swlab.cs.okayama-u.ac.jp, yamauchi@cs.okayama-u.ac.jp

Abstract. Security-critical software is open to attacks by adversaries that disable its functionality. To decrease the risk, we propose an attack avoidance method for complicating process identification. The proposed method complicates identification based on process information by dynamically replacing the information held by a kernel with dummy information. Replacing process information makes identifying the attack target difficult because adversaries cannot find the attack target by seeking the process information. Implementation of the proposed method with a virtual machine monitor enhances the security of the mechanism itself. Further, by implementing the proposed method with a virtual machine monitor, modification to operating systems and application programs are unnecessary.

Keywords: Attack avoidance, process information, virtual machine.

1 Introduction

Attacks exploiting vulnerabilities in programs to illegally control computers are increasing. Therefore, software is developed to prevent such attacks and mitigate their effects. However, attacks still succeed when they are able to deactivate such software. For instance, Agobot [1] has the functionality to stop anti-virus software. T0rnkit [2] and Dica [3] stop log collectors in order to hide the installation process of malware from the system administrator of a target computer. The risk of damages to target computers increases when protective software (essential services) is deactivated. Therefore, it is an important challenge to detect and prevent attacks on programs such as anti-virus software and log collector to reduce damage to a computer, and to avoid the attack.

To prevent attacks on essential services, methods using a virtual machine monitor (VMM) have been proposed [4], [5]. These methods prevent the essential services from being affected by isolating them from the target computer using virtualization technology. Research [4] reveals a method for offloading the intrusion detection system (IDS) from one virtual machine (VM) to another. Moreover, Jiang et al. proposed a method for malware detection using a VMM [5]. However, these methods do not utilize existing essential services and software already installed and operational. Research [6] has proposed a method to prevent anti-virus software from being terminated

M. Yoshida and K. Mouri (Eds.): IWSEC 2014, LNCS 8639, pp. 33–47, 2014.
© Springer International Publishing Switzerland 2014

without the consciousness of the anti-virus software users. This method monitors Windows APIs by SSDT hooking and filter out hazardous API calls that will terminate anti-virus software. This method is effective for termination of anti-virus software using API calls. However, this method is vulnerable to SSDT (System Service Descriptor Table) patching commonly used by rootkits because this method replaces some SSDT entries to their handlers. Protecting the system from kernel-level malware is a challenging problem.

To address these problems, this paper proposes an attack avoidance method to complicate process identification for adversarial software. The proposed method complicates the identification of an essential service by replacing the process information with a dummy. Specifically, this method detects context switches and replaces the original process information with dummy process information when a process is not running. Once the process is dispatched, the original information is restored. The process information of the essential service is replaced without disturbing its functionality. Adversaries cannot detect and identify a target for attack because the process information of the target is replaced. For security and adaptability, the proposed method is implemented using a VMM. Because of its design, a VMM is more difficult to attack than an operating system (OS). Furthermore, implementation with modification to a VMM can reduce the costs involved in modifying existing software.

The contributions made in this paper are as follows:

— We propose an attack avoidance method complicating process identification from adversaries. Because adversaries identify and attack a target process using process information, replacing the process information complicates the identification of an attack target.
— We design a system for replacing the process information of essential processes with a VMM. Because the proposed system is designed with modifications to the VMM along with an additional application program (AP) on a manager VM, the proposed system requires no modification to OSes and APs on a VM providing essential services.
— An evaluation using a prototype of the proposed system shows the effectiveness of the method for attack avoidance.

2   Background

2.1   Attacks for Anti-virus Software

Agobot is malware that attacks anti-virus software. Agobot installs backdoor to Windows hosts. The malware seeks target processes by searching out the name from the process list in order to disable it. An investigation on August 8th, 2013, revealed that Agobot included 579 targeted process names. When anti-virus software is disabled by malware such as Agobot, the risk of damage to the computer system increases.

T0rnkit and Dica are malware for disabling a logging program. T0rnkit is a rootkit that aims to install a backdoor for concealing their location. Its target system is Linux. When installing programs used by T0rnkit, the malware stops the syslog daemon, thus hiding the installation process from a system administrator. Consequently, the system administrator cannot detect the installation or even the existence of other malware.

Some malware stops or disables software that prohibits their activity on the computer. If essential services are stopped or disabled, the risk of damage to the system increases. For this reason, detection, prevention, moderation of damages, and avoidance of attacks for an essential services are required.

2.2   Existing Countermeasures for Attacks

Research into an offloading host-based intrusion detection system (IDS) with a VMM is proposed in VMwatcher [4]. Implementing an IDS by modifying a VMM makes it difficult to attack the IDS. In a same manner, NICKLE [5], which prevents the execution of a kernel-level rootkit, has been proposed. Because it monitors the execution of kernel code with a VMM, only authorized code can be executed. These methods help to prevent attacks that are difficult for existing methods without a VMM to detect and prevent.

2.3   Problems with Existing Methods

Existing methods cannot use essential services without modifying them. Furthermore, these methods are effective only when they are not themselves attacked. If these methods are themselves attacked by adversaries, a system administrator cannot utilize those services to avoid attack. The methods described in Section 2.2 are advantageous given that attacks on a VMM are more difficult than attacks on an OS. However, porting the functions from existing software to a VMM is difficult and expensive. The IDS offload method without modification is an effective approach. However, it is difficult to apply to general application because the method involves the emulation of each system call. To completely offload the IDS, it is necessary to emulate all system calls. However, complete emulation is difficult to implement.

Even though effective VMM-based methods have been proposed, many of them cannot use existing software without modification. Moreover, exporting existing functions used by anti-virus software to a VMM is difficult. Further, the information collected by existing application programs (APs) and kernel is different from the information a VMM collects. This semantic gap makes it difficult to port functions from existing software to a VMM.

3   Attack Avoidance Method for Complication of Process Identification

3.1   Purpose

The following explains the purposes of our research:

1. Purpose 1) Avoidance of attacks to essential services
2. Purpose 2) Use of existing software without modification

It is difficult to handle various attacks with existing methods. Therefore, we aim not to protect but to avoid such attacks. Even if offloading the functionality of existing services is considerably effective, the cost of doing so is high. Thus, it is preferable to avoid attacks without modifying existing software.

3.2   Basic Idea

To achieve the purposes outlined in Section 3.1, we propose complicating process identification to avoid attacks by replacing the process information for essential processes providing the security services. Because adversaries identify a target to attack, we propose replacing the original process information of the target process with dummy process information. Moreover, by implementing our method in a VMM, the existence of our system is difficult to identify. Because of this, an attack on the proposed method itself is difficult and unlikely.

Because a VMM is developed only for providing VMs, interfaces for accessing it are limited and the total amount of source codes involved is far less than in a normal OS. Thus, attacking the VMM is more difficult than attacking the OS. Moreover, implementing the proposed method does not necessitate modifications to the source code of the guest OS or its essential services. With this feature, existing software resources are utilized efficiently. For these reasons, we utilize a VMM with the proposed method.

3.3   Hiding Process Information of Essential Processes

The complication of process identification consists of the following:

1. Limiting access to the process information
2. Replacing the process information

Figure 1 provides an overview of the procedure for limiting access to the process information. With this method, the kernel text area, which can access process infor- mation, is pre-defined. Access to the page that includes process information is set as forbidden. When an access violation to that page occurs, the method returns a dummy value when the subject is not included in the pre-defined area. If the subject is in- cluded in the pre-defined area, the method returns the original content. With this ap- proach, the original process information is invisible from adversaries because only legitimate functions in the kernel text are permitted to access process information.

In replacing the process information, process information for the essential processes must first be replaced. When an essential process is running, the original process in- formation is restored. The overall procedure for replacing the process information is shown in Figure 2. Here, we define normal processes as all processes excluding essen- tial processes. When a context switch from an essential process to a normal process occurs, the method exchanges the original process information with a dummy. Alterna- tively, when a context switch from a normal process to an essential process occurs, the method restores the original process information. With this approach, the original process information for the essential processes is invisible from other processes. This method does not disturb the execution of essential processes. The replacement of process information is described in detail in Section 4.

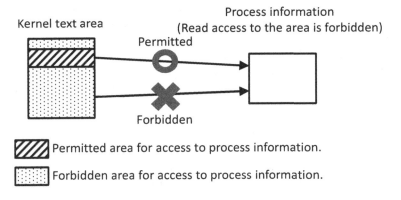

Fig. 1. Access control to process information

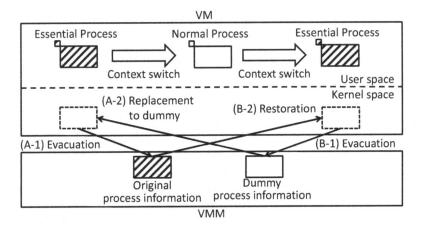

Fig. 2. Replacement of process information between essential process and normal process

3.4   Method for Identifying Essential Processes and Countermeasures

Identification Method. Adversaries can stop or disable essential processes if they detect the existence of the proposed system and identifying the essential process. Thus, it is necessary to make it difficult for adversaries to judge whether a process is an essential process or not.

Adversaries can identify an essential process by comparing the processing time of the context switch between an essential process and a normal process or by continuously monitoring the process information. With the proposed system, the process information of the essential process is replaced. Thus, the time for essential process context switches is longer than with a normal process. Given this difference, adversaries can identify which process is an essential one.

Adversaries can identify the essential process by continuously monitoring the process information for each process to determine whether the process information has changed during a context switch. If a process is an essential process, its process information is replaced during a context switch whereas the process information for a normal process is remains unchanged. Therefore, if part of the process information has changed, even though given a normal context switch it would not, adversaries can identify that process as an essential process.

Countermeasures. To conceal the difference in the processing times of context switches, it might suffice to apply the same processing time to normal processes. This done, the difference in the processing times of context switches between the essential processes and the others becomes meaningless. However, the performance of the entire system degrades.

As an alternative, a time controlling function is effective. This function is used in malware analysis. Some malware detect the presence of debuggers by measuring the processing time and respond by changing their behavior to avoid analysis. To prevent this from happening, a time controlling function is proposed. This function stops a virtual CPUs allocated for malware. When the CPU is stopped, the debugger analyzes malware and resumes the CPUs when the analysis is complete. This function enables us to evade the detection of the proposed system by adversaries.

To prevent detection by continuous monitoring of process information, a combination of access control and process information replacement is effective. Here, we assume an adversary who continuously monitors process information with a loadable kernel module in Linux. At first, the VMM forbids read access to areas containing process information from kernel codes. This is done to prepare for avoiding attacks. The area containing kernel code without kernel modules must be pre-defined. In this situation, if an access violation to the designated area occurs, the VMM determines whether the access is acceptable or not by following the procedure shown in Figure 3. If an instruction pointer is out of range from the designated area, the VMM returns the dummy value to the guest. If not, the VMM traces back the kernel stack and collects the virtual addresses of each function. If all the addresses are contained within the designated area, the VMM emulates the read access and returns an original value. If not, the VMM returns the dummy value.

Because this access control model depends on an integrity of the guest kernel, an attack patches a kernel text must be considered. DKSM attack is one of an attack patching kernel text area [7]. To patch kernel text area, manipulation of CR0 is required. Because kernel text area is write protected ordinarily, adversaries manipulate CR0 to remove write protect of kernel text area. In fully virtualized environment with VT-x, access to control registers causes VM exit. Therefore, the VMM can detect patching of kernel text area by monitoring access to CR0. This monitoring ensures kernel code integrity and functionality of above access control model.

With this procedure, even if adversaries continuously monitoring process information, identifying an essential process is impossible.

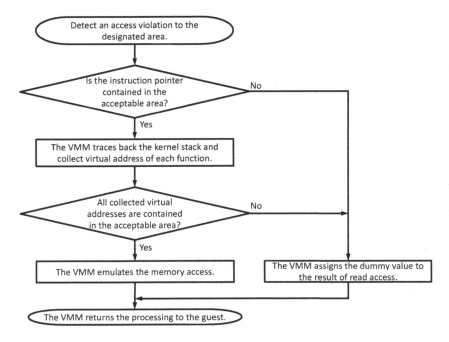

Fig. 3. Determination procedure for access to process information

3.5   Structure of the Proposed System

The overview of the proposed system is shown in Figure 4. The proposed system consists of a process information manager, replacing process information and

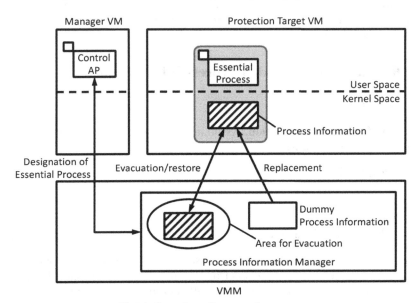

Fig. 4. Overview of proposed system

controlling access to process information. The process information manager monitors context switches in the target VM. The process information manager exchanges essential process information with dummy information, and in legitimate case, restores the original. The original process information is evacuated from the VM and stored in an area allocated in the VMM. The area is allocated and managed by the VMM for each VM. A variety of dummy process information is prepared in advance and the system determines what information is paired with each process when a context switch occurs.

In the proposed system, the Control AP designates which process is an essential process. Thus, a security administrator responsible for the protection of the target VM must communicate to the VMM manager in advance which processes are essential.

3.6   Limitations

Because the proposed method only makes process identification difficult, the essential processes are visible from adversaries. Therefore, if an adversary stops a process at random, it is possible that an essential process will be stopped. To prevent attacks on essential processes, regulating access control to process information is effective. However, because attack prevention diverges from our stated purpose, we do not discuss strategies in attack prevention.

Because the proposed methods replace the legitimate process information of an essential process with dummy information, a security administrator tasked with protecting the target VM cannot control the essential process. This is inconvenient for the administrator. We assume that the essential process is a kind of resident programs. Thus, the scope for the application of the proposed method is restricted to resident programs. We do not assume this method will feasibly apply to other programs. To do so, an additional interface would be needed for the security administrator to communicate with the process information manager. However, this addition would expose vulnerabilities. Thus, we do not consider implementing any additional communication interface to the VMM.

4   Replacement Method of Process Information

4.1   Replacement Target

Definition of Process Information. Assuming Linux for x86 or x64, we defined the following as process information:

(1)   Process control block
(2)   Kernel stack
(3)   Hardware context
(4)   Page tables
(5)   Memory used by a process

Hiding all of the above information is necessary to make the process completely invisible. However, identifying a process from (3), (4), and (5) is considerably difficult. On the other hand, (1) and (2) include especially helpful information for process identification. For these reasons, we treat (1) and (2) as process information.

The following describes the process information in detail:

Process Control Block (task_struct)

The process control block contains information that is effective for process identification including the *PID* (Process ID), the *TGID* (Thread Group ID), the executable file name, and the PID of the parent process. In Linux, the process control block is given as *task_struct* structure, and it is generated for each process or thread.

Kernel Stack and thread_info Structure

Both the kernel stack and *thread_info* structure are allocated in a union, named *thread_union*. A *thread_union* is allocated for each *task_struct*. A kernel stack contains the address, arguments, and return value of functions called in the kernel space. The *thread_union* and *task_struct* are linked to one another.

Replacement Target. The process information defined above includes information used with a kernel when a process is not running. For example, a kernel schedules processes or delivers signals by reference to the process information for each process. For this reason, process scheduling and signal delivery would be obstructed were all process information replaced. Thus, two policies are considered for replacing process information.

Policy (1).   Replace as much process information as possible, with the exception of information used by a kernel while the process is not dispatched.

Policy (2).   Replace only information helpful to adversaries for identifying processes.

When replacing process information under Policy (1), processes are more difficult to identify than under Policy (2). However, replacement under Policy (1) requires many more replacement copies leading to overall performance degradation. Replacement under Policy (2) results in less overhead than Policy (1). However, the strategy suggested under Policy (2) requires that we survey what information is used by malware for identifying the attack target.

Understood merely as a countermeasure to adversarial attack, replacement under Policy (1) is preferable. However, practical utility requires the efficient suppression of any superfluous performance overhead. Therefore, in this paper, we employ Policy (2) for a replacement strategy.

Information Used for Process Identification. We turn now to a discussion of the information used by malware to identify an attack target process. Agobot, developed for Windows, searches the name of a program from a process list in a target computer. If a name matches an entry in the list, Agobot issues the *TerminateProcess()* function to stop the process and all threads within the process. Dica, developed for Linux, stops *syslogd* with the *killall* command. The *killall* command acquires the process PID to suspend processes by searching the name of the attack target from the *proc filesystem*. After acquisition, the command invokes a *kill* system call to stop the process.

Whereas it is not un-common to find malware that stop processes, many of these programs discern the target process with the name of the program. Therefore, it is effective to replace the process name as well.

Adequate Dummy Information. To hide the existence of essential processes, dummy information should be chosen properly. For instance, to hide a process, the process name should be replaced with a name of a common program, running on common servers. If the name of an essential process is replaced with a common name, it will be more difficult for adversaries to detect the existence of the essential process. Additionally, the name should be chosen randomly. It would be easy to detect the existence of the proposed method were the dummy information always the same.

4.2   Trigger for Replacement of Process Information

To replace the process information, it is necessary to determine whether or not a process-switch *from* and a process-switch *to* are replacement targets. For this mechanism, the detection of context switches in a VM from a VMM is required.

In fully virtualized environments, a guest OS works in VMX non-root mode and a VMM works in VMX root mode. Some instructions in non-root mode cause a VM exit and the processing is switched to the software running in the VMX root mode. Instructions not permitted in VMX non-root mode contain write to CR3 register. In an OS supporting multiple virtual address spaces, write to CR3 occurs when context switching to change address space because CR3 contains a beginning address of a page directory. Therefore, a context switch in a VM can be detected by monitoring VM exits caused by writes to CR3.

4.3   Acquisition of Process Information in Guest OS

Acquisition of Process Information of Current Process. As shown in Figure 5, *thread_info* and *task_struct* can be acquired by calculating the address from the RSP register with the VMM. Because the beginning address of a *thread_info* can be calculated from the RSP register and a task member of the *thread_info* indicates the beginning address of a *task_struct*, the VMM can acquire the process information in a guest OS from the RSP register. In this regard, the VMM must hold the definitions for each structure beforehand.

Acquisition of Next-process Information. The method for acquiring the process information stated above is not effective for any processes set to run next (i.e. for the next-process). Therefore, another method is needed. What is about to be written to the CR3 register is usable information for the acquisition of process information concerning the next-process. Considering this, there are three methods for identifying the next-process to acquire its process information.

- Scanning method: this method scans the process list of the protection target VM to determine the next process.
- List-based method: With this method, the VMM holds a list, containing the CR3 value and the address of the *task_struct* for each essential process. This method searches the value for what is going to be written to the CR3 register to identify the next-process.

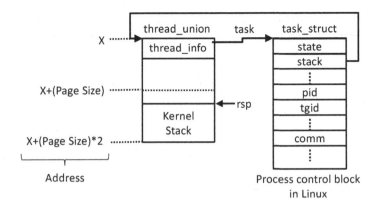

Fig. 5. Relation between *thread_union* and *task_struct*

- Trigger-insertion method: This method inserts a trigger, switching execution from the protection target VM to the VMM, in the kernel of the protection target VM for the identification of the next-process. For example, inserting the *INT3* instruction in the kernel memory area is effective. The trigger must be inserted in the place where the proposed method can acquire the process information concerning the next-process.

The advantages and limitations for each method are shown in Table 1. The scanning method is easy to implement because it requires only a look-up of the next process from the process list of the protection target VM. However, this method creates debilitating performance overhead because the method scans the process list after each context switch on the protection target VM. By contrast, the list-based method and the trigger insertion method do not require significant performance overhead. The list-based method uses a VM exit, which occurs unconditionally in a fully virtualized environment. Because unnecessary VM exits do not occur using the list-based method, performance overhead is minimal in above three methods. With the trigger-insertion method, unnecessary VM exits occur. Thus, from a viewpoint of performance, the list-based method is considered best. Even though the list-based method is disadvantageous in terms of amount of memory usage, it can be estimated as sufficiently small. The amount of memory used by the list-based method can be estimated as under 100 bytes given that an entry in the list created by the method averages at nearly 10 bytes. Memory used by Xen [8] one of the more popular VMM is about 182 megabytes. The amount of memory used by the list-based method is therefore sufficiently small relative to Xen. One disadvantage to the trigger-insertion method is the limitation to the number of triggers. The use of debug registers and the insertion of the *INT3* instruction are pertinent triggers with the method. Using debug registers is faster than inserting *INT3* instruction. However, the number of debug registers is limited. For these reasons, we employ the list-based method.

Table 1. Pros and cons of identification methods of next process

Methods	Pros	Cons
Scanning method	Ease of implementation.	Large performance overhead.
List-based method	Performance overhead is small.	Total amount of memory usage increases.
Trigger-insertion method	Performance overhead is small.	Number of triggers is limited.

4.4   Designation of Essential Process

The proposed method requires the Control AP to designate the essential processes prior to replace their process information. Because of the structure of the proposed method, it is necessary for the administrator of the protection target VM to provide the essential process information to the administrator of the manager VM via e-mail, or by other means. The proposed method does not provide a notification mechanism because additional interfaces to the VMM must be kept at a minimum. Such additions of the VMM interface risk exposing it to vulnerabilities. Before the program initiates, the administrator for the protection target VM must provide ether the full path of the essential process's executable file or a command name. The administrator of the manager VM takes that information and provides it in the process information manager. The exchange is implemented with an event channel a mechanism for VMs to communicate with a Xen hypervisor. When the process information manager receives the information, it can monitor the name of the process running on the protection target VM. If it detects that the process with the designated name is scheduled, the process information manager replaces the process information of that process on the protection target VM. Because the procedure for designating essential processes is conducted as described above, the information must be exchanged before the essential process initializes on the protection target VM.

4.5   Handling Multi-core Processors

We shall here assume an environment with multi-core processors. When an essential process is running on one CPU core, other processes might be running simultaneously on the other CPU cores if multiple CPU cores are allocated to a VM. In this situation, a process running on one CPU core is able to refer to the process information of essential processes running on other CPU cores because the original process information is restored when the process is dispatched.

To address this problem, we prohibit running normal processes while essential processes are running. This is accomplished by suspending all virtual CPUs except the virtual CPU used by an essential process. Therefore, any reference to essential process information by normal processes is restricted.

5   Evaluation

5.1   Environment for Evaluation

The environment for evaluation is shown in Table 2. We evaluated the proposed system with an Intel Core i7-2600. The protection target VM is fully virtualized by Intel VT-x.

Table 2. Environment for evaluation

VMM	Xen 4.2.0
OS (Manager VM)	Debian 7.3 (Linux 3.2.0 64-bit)
OS (Protection target VM)	Debian 7.3 (Linux 3.2.0 64-bit)

5.2   Purpose and Evaluation Method

The purpose of the evaluation is to confirm effectiveness of the proposed method to attacks. In our experiment, we examined whether the name of an essential process was replaced when the proposed method was applied to the essential processes. We assumed the *killall* command as a tool used by adversaries. The *killall* command searches the name of a program from the *proc filesystem* to determine the PID of the attack target. In this experiment, we examined whether or not the original name of the essential process is listed under a *ps* command. These commands refer to the same information inside a kernel. To evaluate the proposed method, we assumed *syslogd* as an essential process and changed its name to *apache2*.

5.3   Evaluation Results

On the protection target VM, we listed the names for all processes. The list did not contain *syslogd*. Instead, *apache2* was listed in its place. This result shows that the name of the essential process was successfully changed—thus concealing it. The results also show that adversaries basing their attacks on the process name can be avoided using the proposed method.

6   Related Work

Some researchers have proposed methods for preventing the illegal alteration of memory contents [9], [10]. While these researches methods are indeed useful in preventing attacks, the proposed method avoids them. Even if these methods succeed in preventing an attack, the existence of essential services is still detectable to adversaries. When adversaries detect essential services, they can nonetheless disable them to avoid detection. Because our method complicates process identification, adversaries will find it difficult to avoid detection by essential services hidden with the proposed method.

SecVisor employs a similar approach for access control using a hypervisor [11]. While SecVisor protects kernel codes, the proposed method focuses on the data area of the guest kernel. Our system is similar to the approach found in Sentry [12]. Sentry protects data inside the user VM by partitioning the data structure of the kernel. Our method, however, is advantageous in that it does not require any modification to the data structure.

ANSS [6] is effective for protecting anti-virus software from termination. ANSS intercepts and monitors some API calls with parameters that will stop or suspend anti-virus software to filter out malicious calls. Even though ANSS is effective, it is vulnerable to malware patching SSDT entries. The paper proposing ANSS stated working with the anti-hooking mechanism is effective. Our method is tolerant to attacks patching tables in kernel space because the VMM restores the original process information when essential processes are running. Moreover, our method has possibilities to avoid unknown attacks as long as they rely on the process information.

7   Conclusion

We proposed the replacement of process information for essential process with a VMM to complicate process identification by adversaries. Because adversaries identify an attack target process with available process information, a replacement of that process information by our system is effective in avoiding attacks of that kind. The proposed method is implemented by modifying the VMM and with a Control AP on the manager VM. Modification to guest OSes and APs on each VM is unnecessary.

An experiment using a prototype of the proposed system based on the Xen hypervisor showed that an essential process name was successfully replaced with a dummy name. This result indicates that attacks based on the process name are avoidable with the proposed method.

Future work shall include the implementation of tan access control function to the process information, evaluation with real-world malware, and extensive performance analysis of the proposed method.

References

1. F-Secure: Agobot, http://www.f-secure.com/v-descs/agobot.shtml
2. F-Secure: Tornkit, http://www.f-secure.com/v-descs/torn.shtml
3. Packetstorm: dica.tgz, http://packetstormsecurity.com/files/26243/dica.tgz.html
4. Jiang, X., Wang, X., Xu, D.: Stealthy Malware Detection Through VMM-Based "Out-of-the-Box" Semantic View Reconstruction. In: Proc. 14th ACM Conference on Computer and Communications Security (CCS 2007), pp. 128–138 (2007)
5. Riley, R., Jiang, X., Xu, D.: Guest-Transparent Prevention of Kernel Rootkits with VMM-Based Memory Shadowing. In: Lippmann, R., Kirda, E., Trachtenberg, A. (eds.) RAID 2008. LNCS, vol. 5230, pp. 1–20. Springer, Heidelberg (2008)
6. Fu-Hau, H., Min-Hao, W., Chang-Kuo, T., Chi-Hsien, H., Chieh-Wen, C.: Antivirus Software Shield Against Antivirus Terminators. IEEE Transactions on Information Forensics and Security 7(5), 1439–1447 (2012)

7. Bahram, S., Jiang, X., Wang, Z., Grace, M., Li, J., Srinivasan, D., Rhee, J., Xu, D.: DKSM: Subverting Virtual Machine Introspection for Fun and Profit. In: 29th IEEE Symposium on Reliable Distributed Systems, pp. 82–91 (2010)

8. Barham, P., Dragovic, B., Fraser, K., Hand, S., Harris, T., Ho, A., Neugebauer, R., Pratt, I., Warfield, A.: Xen and the Art of Virtualization. SIGOPS Opr. Syst. Rev. 37(5), 164–177 (2003)

9. Dewan, P., Durham, D., Khosravi, H., Long, M., Nagabhushan, G.: A Hypervisor-Based System for Protecting Software Runtime Memory and Persistent Storage. In: Proc. 2008 Spring Simulation Multiconference (SpringSim 2008), pp. 828–835 (2008)

10. McCune, J.M., Yanlin, L., Nung, Q., Zongwei, Z., Datta, A., Gligor, V., Perrig, A.: TrustVisor: Efficient TCB Reduction and Attestation. In: Proc. 2010 IEEE Symposium on Security and Privacy, pp. 143–158 (2010)

11. Seshadri, A., Luk, M., Qu, N., Perrig, A.: SecVisor: A Tiny Hypervisor to Provide Lifetime Kernel Code Integrity for Commodity OSes. In: Proc. 21st ACM SIGOPS Symposium on Operating System Principles, pp. 335–350 (2007)

12. Srivastava, A., Giffin, J.: Efficient Protection of Kernel Data Structures via Object Partitioning. In: Proc. 28th Annual Computer Security Application Conference (ACSAC 2012), pp. 429–438 (2012)

Kernel Memory Protection by an Insertable Hypervisor Which Has VM Introspection and Stealth Breakpoints

Kuniyasu Suzaki[1], Toshiki Yagi[1], Kazukuni Kobara[1], and Toshiaki Ishiyama[2]

[1] National Institute of Advanced Industrial Science and Technology, Japan
{k.suzaki,yagi-toshiki,k-kobara}@aist.go.jp
[2] FFRI, Inc., Japan
ishiyama@ffri.jp

Abstract. Recent device drivers are under threat of targeted attack called Advanced Persistent Threat (APT) since some device drivers handle industrial infrastructure systems and/or contain sensitive data e.g., secret keys for disk encryption and passwords for authentication. Even if attacks are found in these systems, it is not easy to update device drivers since these systems are required to be non-stop operation and these attacks are based on zero-day attacks. DriverGuard is developed to mitigate such problems. It is a light weight hypervisor and can be inserted into pre-installed OS (Windows) from USB memory at boot time. The memory regions for sensitive data in a Windows kernel are protected by VM introspection and stealth breakpoints in the hypervisor. The hypervisor recognizes memory structure of guest OS by VM introspection and manipulates a page table entry (PTE) using stealth breakpoints technique. DriverGuard prevents malicious write-access to code region that causes Blue Screen of Death of Windows, and malicious read and write access to data region which causes information leakage. Current implementation is applied on pre-installed Windows7 and increases security of device drivers from outside of OS.

Keywords: Computer Security, Information Leakage, Virtual Machine Introspection, Stealth Breakpoints.

1 Introduction

Device drivers are key components on current operating systems since they bridge between logical space of the operating system and physical space of devices. As current device drivers are flexible and intelligent, most of them are loaded after booting and plugged-in to a kernel. They are stackable to an existing device driver and add intelligent functions. The feature enables to add access control, encryption, and compression on an existing device driver. The intelligent functions include sensitive data in a device driver (e.g., secret keys for disk encryption, passwords for authentication, tables of access control, etc).

Device drivers were thought to be safe since they run in privilege mode. However, device drivers become a target of attacks as the importance is increased, and the

M. Yoshida and K. Mouri (Eds.): IWSEC 2014, LNCS 8639, pp. 48–61, 2014.

vulnerability is revealed. For example, Stuxnet[5] and Duqu[3] are famous attacks for device drivers. These attacks use vulnerabilities of device drivers in a commodity operating system as a steppingstone of attacks on a real device (e.g., nuclear reactor, chemical plant, etc). They are targeted attacks and called Advanced Persistent Threat (APT). Most of them are zero-day attacks and signature based security tools cannot detect these attacks. Furthermore if the target is a critical infrastructure or an industrial control system, the availability is important. The countermeasures must be taken without stopping the operating system.

In order to mitigate the problems, we propose DriverGuard which is a light weight and insertable hypervisor to a pre-installed OS (Windows). DriverGuard has a function of VM introspection[6,7,9], and recognizes the data structure of Windows7. It also has stealth breakpoints technique[14] which manipulates page table entries (PTE) on a shadow page table of hypervisor. The combination of VM introspection and stealth breakpoints in an insertable hypervisor prevents malicious write-access to code region which causes Blue Screen of Death of Windows, and malicious read and write access to data region which causes information leakage.

This paper is organized as follows. Section 2 briefs related works and Section 3 introduces threat model for DriverGuard. Section 4 reviews countermeasures for the threats. Section 5 describes the design of DriverGuard. Section 6 reports the current implementation. Section 7 discusses some issues for DriverGuard, and Section 8 summarizes our conclusions.

2   Relates Work

Device drivers are recognized as a weak point in kernel space, and many protecting methods have been proposed.

Nooks[13] is a famous research for protecting device drivers. Nooks offers reliable subsystem that isolates a kernel from device drivers. It uses special memory management system to limit access to the device driver. The limitation of access resembles DriverGuard, but the aim of Nooks is to enhance OS reliability from failures. The limitation of accesses on Nooks is also used for security, but Nooks does not prevent information leakage from device drivers.

OS2, which is developed by IBM and Microsoft in 90s, uses protection rings architecture of IA-32 that offers one more privilege level for device drivers. It can increase the security level, but it requires operating system to recognize the ring levels and makes difficult to develop a device driver.

Instead of protection ring architecture, virtualization architecture (e.g., Intel VT or AMD SVM) is developed and used widely. It offers a mode for virtualization that is independent of OS and makes easy to make a hypervisor. Some hypervisors have a function to recognize behavior of OS, called to VM introspection[6,7,9]. It also makes possible to manipulate device drivers and prevent attacks on them.

HUKO[15] is a hypervisor-based integrity protection system designed to protect commodity OS kernel from untrusted device drivers. HUKO manipulates CR3 register of IA-32 architecture which manages page table entry (PTE), and separates virtual memory space between the kernel and device drivers. The device drivers use isolated virtual memory space from the kernel. On the other hand, DriverGurad manipulates PTE contents, and the access to the memory for sensitive data is protected by Stealth Breakpoints technique [14]. DriverGurad does not require additional virtual memory space for device drivers.

SecVisor [10] is a hypervisor that ensures code integrity for OS kernels. It protects the kernel against code injection attacks, which works as same to DriverGuard. Furthermore, SecVisor uses the IO Memory Management Unit (IOMMU) to protect kernel code from Direct Memory Access (DMA) access, which is more progressive than DriverGuard. However, SecVisor requires to add 2 hypercalls in a target OS kernel. The feature is not accepted our target because DriverGuard treats Window7 which does not allow to customize the kernel. DriverGuard detects the code and data region using VM Introspection. It requires small customization to allocate sensitive data, but the customization is trivial because it only changes memory allocation method with normal Windows' function. In addition, SecVisor requires customization on bootstrap code in Linux because SecVisor has to be loaded as a part of Linux kernel. On the other hand, DriverGuard is insertable hypervisor which uses chain-loader of GRUB and does not require the change of the existing boot procedure.

Taint tracking technique is useful to prevent information leakage. The technique tracks data flow and finds illegal usage of data. Some hypervisors integrate taint tracking mechanism and are used to find information leakage dynamically. For examples, TTAnalyze [1], TEMU[12], V2E[16] and Ether[4] are developed on open source hypervisor Xen or QEMU. They are used to analyze malware behavior because they can avoid anti-debugger mechanism in a malware. Unfortunately, they take much time to track data flows because they have to monitor data flows aside from the original processing. Heavy overhead is not accepted to prevent sensitive data at normal operation. Fortunately, DriverGuard does not need to track data flow because DriverGuad knows the region of sensitive data and only have to prevent malicious access to there. It does not cause extra overhead to track data flow.

3   Threat Model

We assume two types of threat model for DriverGuard. One of the threats is code injection attack to a device driver's code, and the other is information leakage from the device driver's data. Most of them are zero-day attacks, and security patch and security signature are not available.

The aim of code injection attack is to take control and run malware. The attack re-writes an existing code on memory and passes control to the malware. Even if the attack cannot get the full control, failure is enough for attackers on an infrastructure system because the aim is to stop or runaway the system. Therefore, security systems for infrastructure have to prevent Blue Screen of Death (BSoD) on Windows, even if the system is shrunk.

The other threat is stealing or re-writing sensitive data of device driver's data region memory. Current device drivers are intelligent and have some sensitive data.

Attackers try to read or write the sensitive data with some techniques (e.g., buffer overflow). The access to the sensitive data should be limited to the legitimate device driver's code only.

4   Requirement for Countermeasures

DriverGuard is used for protecting device drivers in industrial infrastructure systems. These systems have already established and security features must be added on the systems. Furthermore, some attacks to device drivers exploit a previously unknown vulnerability in the operating system and cannot be protected by the operating system itself. As a countermeasure of zero-day attack, anomaly behavior detection is one approach, but it cannot avoid false-negative.

DriverGuard offers a white-list approach. The user must notify the hypervisor identifications of device drivers. The identifications are used to find the region of legitimate code when the drivers are loaded. The device drivers also must notify the hypervisor the memory region for sensitive data. After the setup of DriverGuard, the code region of device driver is not re-written, and sensitive data region is accessed by legitimate code of device driver only. The accesses to protected regions are monitored by the hypervisor of DriverGuard, which works as a small Trusted Computing Base (TCB).

In order to satisfy the requests, DriverGuard uses insertable hypervisor which has VM introspection and stealth breakpoints.

4.1   Hypervisor for an Existing OS

The hypervisor has to offer full virtualization in order to boot pre-installed OS as a guest OS. The hypervisor should be as light as possible to make a small impact on pre-installed OS. Current popular hypervisors (e.g., KVM, Xen, VMware) require a control OS (host OS), even if the hypervisor is type I (Bare-metal hypervisor. The example is Xen.) or type II (Hypervisor hosted by an OS. The example is KVM). A control OS requires much memory and storage. It is not suitable for our purpose. In order to solve the problem, we build DriverGuard on the hypervisor called BitVisor[11] which does not require a control OS.

Furthermore, most hypervisor has a fixed device model (QEMU-Device model on KVM and Xen). The device model requires remapping from pseudo devices on a VM to real devices. Even if these hypervisors allows to boot a pre-installed OS, they require to install device drivers for pseudo devices on a pre-installed OS, which is not acceptable for our purpose. BitVisor has a para-passthrough mechanism which offers bare-metal devices to a guest OS and does not require any change of pre-installed OS.

A pre-installed OS is stored on a real hard disk and users do not want to change the contents. It means hypervisor is requested to be inserted from other devices at boot time.

4.2   VM Introspection

The hypervisor for DriverGuard has to recognize the memory map and behavior of the guest OS since it needs to know the memory region for code and sensitive data. The function is called VM introspection [6,7,9]. Unfortunately, most hypervisors do not have the function because they have to solve semantic gaps between guest OS and hypervisor.

BitVisor also has no function for VM introspection. Fortunately we can use GreenKiller [8] which offers VM introspection on top of BitVisor. GreenKiller recognizes the memory map of Windows and hooks some system calls. We build DriverGuard on GreenKiller.

4.3   Stealth Breakpoints

Debugger is a fundamental tool to analyze a malware. It places a breakpoint on an instruction, where the control goes to a debugger from the targeted code. The targeted instruction is replaced with an instruction of software interrupt. On IA-32 architecture, INT 3H (0xCC) instruction is used.

Breakpoints are useful for debugging, but they are detected by some type of malware. If the malware finds break points (INT 3H instructions) on its code region, it recognizes that it is analyzed. The function is called Anti-Debugger. The malware with Anti-Debugger changes its behavior in order to prevent the analysis.

Stealth breakpoints technique[14] is used to solve this drawback. The technique manipulates page table entry (PTE) which indicates the address of the page. The PTE content is changed in order to cause a page fault, when an access is issued to the page. The page fault is carried to stealth breakpoints as a break point. Stealth breakpoints changes the status of PTE and allows the access to the page. After that, stealth breakpoints sets single step mode and returns control to the original code. The original code causes an exception of the single step, which is carried to stealth breakpoints again. At the exception handler of the single step, stealth breakpoints disables the page in order to work as breakpoint again, and releases single step mode. Then, the control is returned the original code.

Stealth breakpoints works as normal break point and countermeasure for Anti-Debugger of malware. However, the cost is heavy because page fault is slower than software interrupt. Furthermore, stealth breakpoints hooks accesses to the region which is outside of the region for sensitive data in the protected page. It will make performance degradation when it applied on code region, which accessed frequently. DriverGuard avoids this problem by applying stealth breakpoints on heap region which includes sensitive data only.

5   Driverguard

DriverGuard is build on top of GreenKiller[8] which has VM introspection. GreenKiller is based on BitVisor[11] which is a thin hypervisor with para-passthrough. BitVisor offers bare-metal devices to guest OS and does not require any changes on a pre-install OS. Current target OS is pre-installed Windows7. This section describes key features of DriverGuard.

5.1   Inserting DriverGuard in an Pre-installed Windows

In order to load DriverGuard before booting Windows, we used USB boot and chain-loader. It does not require any change on the hard disk. Figure 1 show the steps.

Most current BIOS can select USB storage as a boot device. DriverGuard is loaded from the GRUB bootloader on the MBR of USB storage. DriverGuard occupies the VMX root mode of Intel VT and remains on the memory. After that, DriverGuard returns the control to the MBR of the booted device (USB memory). The GRUB has a function called chain-loader which sends the control to another bootloader. The control goes to the MBR of hard disk which includes bootloader of pre-installed Windows. The bootloader boots Windows besides DriverGuard hypervisor.

The kernel of Windows7 has a security function of ASLR (Address Space Layout Randomization) It allocates the starting address of the kernel at random and prevents buffer overflow attacks. DriverGuard must find the starting address for VM introspection. Current implementation detects the starting address by linear search technique. A MD5 hash of beginning contents of the kernel is used as an identifier, which is passed to the DriverGuard as a parameter of bootloader GRUB. The DriverGuard searches the starting address with the MD5 when the kernel is loaded. MD5 hash is used instead of SHA-1 because GRUB has a size limitation of arguments and must pass some other identifiers mentioned in the next section.

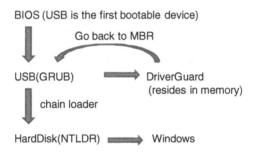

Fig. 1. Method to insert DriverGuard before booting Windows

5.2   Set Up DriverGuard

DriverGuard has to recognize which device drivers are protected and where are the protected memory regions. The setting up of DriverGuard has three steps, which are illustrated in Figure 2.

The first step is identification of device driver protected by DriverGuard. Identification is based on MD5 hash value of a binary of device driver. The identification is passed as parameters of bootloader GRUB.

The second step is to recognize the code region of the protected device drivers. DriverGuard still knows the identifications, but does not know when and where the codes of device drivers are loaded. DriverGuard uses a mechanism of VM introspection which comes from GreenKiller.

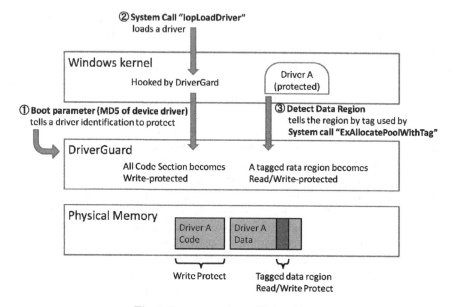

Fig. 2. Setup procedure of DriverGuard

DriverGuard hooks "IopLoadDriver" system call to recognize the protected device drivers. IopLoadDriver is an internal function of ntkrnlpa.exe, which inserts a device driver to the kernel space. DriverGuard recognizes the memory map of Windows7 and replaces an instruction of IopLoadDriver with INT 3H (0xCC) instruction as a break point of debugger. When IopLoadDriver is called, the break point causes an exception and switches to DriverGuard. The DriverGuard analyzes the data structure of the created process using identification (MD5 hash value), which allows to detect a protected device driver and know the code region. After the analysis, DriverGuard returns the control to the break point with the replaced original instruction.

The third step is to recognize protected region for sensitive data. Current implementation requires to customize the device driver to tell the region of sensitive data. The region must be allocated dynamically with a "tag" caused by "ExAllocatePoolWithTag" function. The VM introspection of DriverGuard detects memory region using the tag caused by ExAllocatePoolWithTag. The pages which used by tagged memory are protected by DriverGuard.

DriverGuard recognizes that the request comes from the code of legitimate device driver and registers the memory region to be prohibited from read and write accesses of other code. The code region is detected by VM Introspection when the driver is installed by IopLoadDriver. After the setting up DriverGuard, the code and sensitive data region are protected from malicious accesses.

5.3   Protecting Code Region

DriverGuard protects the code of device drivers from write-access, but the code region is mapped as read-only by Windows7 already. Therefore, DriverGuard does not need to change the permission in general. However, when a write-access is issued to the read-only memory, the exception handler is called as a Bug Check Code (0xBE: ATTEMPTED_WRITE_TO_READONLY_MEMORY), which causes Blue Screen of Death (BSoD) of Windows. If an attacker wants to stop the Windows, the attack means a success.

In order to prevent an attack, DriverGuard hooks the exception handler and causes an infinite loop. The infinite loop runs as low Interrupt ReQuest Level (IRQL) and causes high CPU load on Windows7. However, it is interrupted by other higher IRQL, the user can cope with the situation.

5.4   Protecting Data Region

DriverGuard allows memory accesses on the protected region from processes that officially use the registered device drivers. The processes loads registered .sys files only. The other processes which loads registered .sys files with others are recognized as malicious processes by DriverGuard.

The region of sensitive data is informed by a protected device driver as mentioned in Section 5.2. DriverGuard protects the memory region using stealth breakpoints technique on shadow page table. Shadow page table is pseudo page table that offers a virtual memory on a virtual machine. The management unit is 4KB page, and the protected region is rounded to the 4KB unit.

Figure 3 shows the data protection that uses stealth breakpoints. Each process has its own page directory and a set of page table entries (PTE), which are virtualized as shadow page table by DriverGuard. A PTE has two addresses for virtual memory and physical memory in order to map them. The address of page directory is in CR3 (page directory register) when the process is running. The PTEs are set by the operating system.

DriverGuard manages page table entries and changes the P-bit (persistent bit). P-bit is used for swapping and indicates that the page exists in the memory or swaps out. The P-bit for a page table entry for a protected page is set to 0 by DriverGuard. It means all access to the page causes a page fault. The page fault is hooked by DriverGuard and analyze whether the access comes from legitimate code or not. If an access comes from non-legitimate code (process B in Figure3), the access is failed. The DriverGuard decides it as malicious access and brings to an infinite loop with low IRQL. Even if an access comes from legitimate code and is allowed, a page fault occurs.

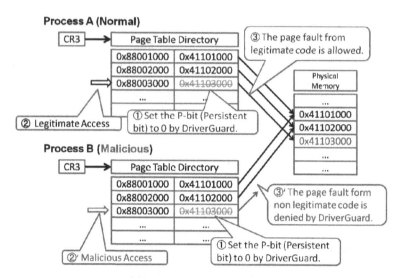

Fig. 3. Data protection mechanism of DriverGuard. P-bit (persistent bit) of page table entry on shadow page table is set to 0 to cause page fault for any accesses. DriverGuard investigates all page faults at the page, and malicious access to the sensitive data is denied.

Figure 4 shows the procedure of stealth breakpoints in DriverGuard. A protected driver runs on VMX non-root mode and DriverGuard runs on VMX root mode. When an access is issued to the sensitive data, the access causes a page fault because the P-bit for the page table entry is set to 0. It causes VMEnter to change the VMX root mode and invokes DriverGuard. DriverGuard investigates the address of instruction that cased the page fault. If the address does not come from the legitimate code, DriverGuard decides it as malicious access and bring to an infinite loop with low IRQL.

When the access comes from the legitimate code, DriverGuard goes to the procedure of stealth breakpoints. It sets a hardware break point to the next instruction. DriverGuard sets P-bit 1 and allows the access. After that DriverGuard cause VMExit to bring the control back to the driver. The driver can access to the sensitive data. After the access, the next instruction is trapped immediately by hardware breakpoint and causes VMEnter to invoke DriverGuard. DriverGuard clear the hardware breakpoint and sets the P-bit set 0 again. After that DriverGuard causes VMExit and returns the control to the driver.

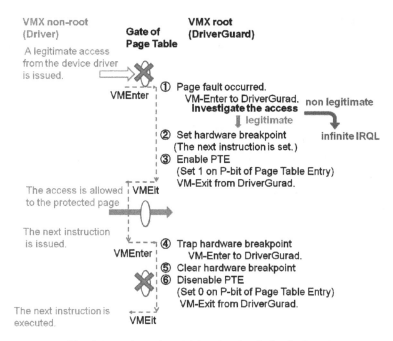

Fig. 4. Procedure of stealth breakpoints in DrvierGuard

The implantation of stealth breakpoints in DriverGuard is different from the Original. Original stealth breakpoints uses single step mode to hook the next instruction, but stealth breakpoints in DriverGuard uses hardware break point. Original stealth breakpoints is designed to hide hardware break point from a malware, but DriverGuard does not need to care about detection from a malware. Furthermore, the implementation is easy, because DriverGuard can use the information which is recorded at VMEner. VMEnter uses VMCS (Virtual Machine Control Structure) to record the status information of VMX mode. The information includes the instruction which causes VMEnter, and DriverGurad know the address of the next instruction. DriverGuard easily sets a hardware break point to the next instruction. It makes easy to implement.

Page fault occurred by stealth breakpoints does not cause access to a disk, which is quicker than normal page fault. Normal page fault takes milli-second to get data from the disk, but page fault of stealth breakpoints takes micro-second order. The real performance is showed in the next section.

6   Implementation

This section reports current implementation issues on hardware, guest OS, and the performance.

6.1   Limitation

DriverGuard requires a CPU which has Intel VT since DriverGuard depends on hardware virtualization assists. The VMX root mode on the CPU is occupied by DriverGuard and another hypervisor cannot use the mode.

The guest OS cannot use page size extension (PSE) since a unit of page size becomes 4MB. It is too large to protect sensitive data. 4KB page is common page size for many operating systems and good for DriverGuard.

The guest OS is limited to Windows7 ServicePack1 since the VM introspection of DriverGuard is design for the OS. Other Windows may be applied by DriverGuard, but we have not tested yet.

Swapping page mechanism must be disabled since current DriverGuard cannot follow the swapped-out pages. Hibernation is also unsupported.

Some device drivers are loaded at the boot time, but DriverGuard cannot recognize them since they do not use IopLoadDriver system call. Some of device drivers are necessary to boot Windows (e.g., storage driver for root file system and video card driver), and they are recognized as parts of Windows kernel. Therefore, current DriverGuard does not care them.

6.2   Performance

We measured the performance of DriverGuard on Lenovo ThinkCentre (Intel Core2 Duo E6850 3.0GHz, 2 GB memory). The size of current DriverGuard is 16.2 MB. It is not significant because it includes VM introspection for Windows7.

The DriverGuard is inserted at boot time. The insertion of DriverGuard took about 6 seconds, which excludes the loading time of the GRUB. The boot time of Windows7 on DriverGuard took 40 seconds while the boot time of original Windows7 took 17 seconds. The overhead was caused by setup OS, which was pressure on a hypervisor. However, we did not feel any stress to use the Windows 7 on DriverGuard after the booting.

The Windows7 on DriverGuard recognized 1.83GB memory while the normal Windows7 recognized 2.00GB memory. The difference size of memory (about 170MB) was used by DriverGuard. The size is not big as a hypervisor which has VM introspection. When another hypervisor requires host OS for VM introspection, much more memory will be used.

We made a pseudo malware to attack a device driver and confirmed that the malicious write-access to sensitive data was detected and went to an infinite loop at low IRQL. The CPU load on Windows 7 went to 100%, but the keyboard and mouse were active and we could control the windows7.

Figure 5 shows the procedure for stealth breakpoints in DriverGuard, and the elapsed time which took on Core2 Duo E6850. The time is measured by the function equipped in BitVisor and the resolution is 1 micro-second. There were no time difference for read and write accesses.

The elapsed time between page fault and enabling PTE took 5 micro-seconds. The elapsed time by trapping hardware breakpoint took 18 micro-seconds. It took 22 micro-seconds by the end of stealth breakpoints in DriverGuard. The measurement was achieved in DrvierGurad and did not include the time for the first VMEnter and the last VMExit.

The time is heavy for one access to normal memory, but the region includes sensitive data. The overhead is acceptable for sensitive data which are used a few times, for example, sensitive data for authentication.

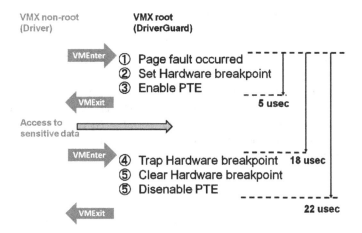

Fig. 5. Performance in DriverGuard

The most part of the elapsed time was spent between enabling PTE and trapping hardware breakpoints, which includes 2 switches between VMX root mode and VMX non-root mode. It causes VMEnter and VMExit which spend thousands of CPU cycles on Core2 Duo. Furthermore, DriverGuard uses shadow page table and takes time to manage it. If the time for the switches becomes short, DriverGurad can improve the performance. This issue is discussed in Section 7.

7   Discussions

Current implementation assumes that DriverGuard is inserted at boot time securely. There is, however, no method to verify the procedure. We have a plan to include trusted boot which records the procedure in a secure chip; Trusted Platform Module (TPM). The recorded data in the TPM is tamper-proof, and can be sent to a trusted third party so that the receiver can verify the boot procedure. When the data is exported from a TPM, the data is digitally signed with a secret key in the TPM and is verified with the public key of the TPM. If DriverGuard utilizes this mechanism, the integrity is confirmed.

Return oriented programming (ROP) is not prevented by DriverGuard since it reads loaded code only and does not require write-access to the code. In order to prevent such attacks, we have a plan to improve DriverGuard to protect read access from malicious processes.

DriverGuard employs white-list approach. The granularity of it can be categorized as middle since the unit of white-list is application software. The smallest granularity is a system call offered by Korset[2]. Korset analyzes the source code of an application and makes control flow graphs (CGF) of system calls in order to trace the behavior. If the behavior of the process does not follow the CFG, Korset alerts that the process is intruded by malware. It offers very strict white-list and can detect any intrusions. We are studying how to introduce the same idea to DriverGuard.

Current implementation uses shadow page table that is virtual memory emulated by software, and does not utilize hardware assist for memory virtualization called nested page table. Current X86 architecture CPUs have the function, for examples, Intel's EPT (Extended Page Table) or AMD's NPT (Nested Page Table). Some reports show the performance improvement caused by Intel EPT and AMD NPT. In order to receive the benefit, DriverGuared have to change the code. Fortunately, SecVisor[10], which modifies page table entry as DriverGuared does, shows two implementations on shadow page table and AMD's NPT. We will refer the implementation of SecVisor and revise DriverGuard. It will improve the performance of DriverGuard and make more useful for yours.

8 Conclusions

Current device drivers are under threat of targeted attack since they include sensitive data and control industrial control systems. The operations must be non-stop and protected from attacks without change after booting. We proposed DriverGuard to prevent malicious access to the device driver's memory. It is a light weight hypervisor based on GreenKiller and BitVisor. DriverGuard inherits para-passthrough and can be inserted from USB to a pre-installed OS at boot time. DriverGuard recognizes the memory structure of Guest OS (Windows7) and hooks some system calls by VM introspection of GreenKiller.

DriverGuard prevents malicious write-access to code region, and read and write-access to data region of protected device drivers. The code region is set as read-only by Windows, and it causes Blue Screen of Death when a write access is issued on the region, which is a kind of death attack. DriverGuard hooks the exception handler and prevents to go to Blue Screen of Death. The control hooked by DriverGuard is brought to an infinite loop of Low Interrupt ReQuest Level (IRQL). It caused an overhead on the guest OS, but the user still control the OS. This feature is useful for infrastructure systems and industrial control systems.

The protection on data region is based on stealth breakpoints technique and manipulates page table entries of shadow page table. Read and write accesses to the protected data region is also hooked and investigated the address of the instruction which cause the page fault. If the instruction is not a part of the legitimate device driver's code, the access is brought to an infinite loop of IRQL. When the instruction is in the legitimate code, the access is allowed by the treatment of stealth breakpoints. The implementation uses hardware breaking point.

The implementation was applied on pre-installed Windows7 and the performance was measured. Most part of the overhead of stealth breakpoints is estimated to the operation of VMExit and VMEnter. The result shows that DriverGuard is acceptable for operation which accesses sensitive data a few times, such as authentication. It increases security of device drivers from outside of OS.

Acknowledgement. This work was in part supported by the Strategic Information and Communications R&D Promotion Programme (SCOPE) of the Ministry of Internal Affairs and Communications, Japan.

References

[1] Bayer, U., Kruegel, C., Kirda, E.: TTAnalyze: A Tool for Analyzing Malware. In: 15th European Institute for Computer Antivirus Research, EICAR (2006)

[2] Ben-Cohen, O., Wool, A.: Korset: Automated, Zero False-Alarm Intrusion Detection for Linux. In: Linux Symposium (2008)

[3] Bencsáth, B., Pék, G., Buttyán, L., Félegyházi, M.: Duqu: Analysis, Detection, and Lessons Learned. In: European Workshop on System Security, EuroSec (2012)

[4] Dinaburg, A., Royal, P., Sharif, M., Lee, W.: Ether: Malware Analysis via Hardware Virtualization Extensions. In: ACM Conference on Computer and Communications Security, CCS (2008)

[5] Falliere, N., Murchu, L.O., Chien, E.: W32.Stuxnet Dossier, Symantec Security Response (2011)

[6] Garfinkel, T., Rosenblum, M.: A Virtual Machine Introspection Based Architecture for Intrusion Detection. In: 10th Annual Network & Distributed System Security Symposium, NDSS (2003)

[7] King, S.T., Dunlap, G.W., Chen, P.M.: Operating System Support for Virtual Machines. USENIX Annual Tech. (2003)

[8] Murakami, J.: FFR GreenKiller - Automatic kernel-mode malware analysis system. In: 12th Associates of Anti-Virus Asia Reserachers International Conference (2009)
http://www.fourteenforty.jp/research/research_papers/
avar-2009-murakami.pdf

[9] Nance, K., Bishop, M., Hay, B.: Virtual Machine Introspection: Observation or Interference? IEEE Security and Privacy 6(5) (2008)

[10] Seshadri, A., Luk, M., Qu, N., Perrig, A.: SecVisor: A Tiny Hypervisor to Provide Lifetime Kernel Code Integrity for Commodity OSes. In: The 21st ACM Symposium on Operating Systems Principles, SOSP (2007)

[11] Shinagawa, T., et al.: BitVisor: A Thin Hypervisor for Enforcing I/O Device Security, Virtual Execution Environments, VEE (2009)

[12] Song, D., Brumley, D., Yin, H., Caballero, J., Jager, I., Kang, M.G., Liang, Z., Newsome, J., Poosankam, P., Saxena, P.: BitBlaze: A New Approach to Computer Security via Binary Analysis. In: International Conference on Information Systems Security, ICISS (2008)

[13] Swift, M.M., Bershad, B.N., Levy, H.M.: Improving the Reliability of Commodity Operating Systems. In: 19th ACM Symposium on Operating Systems Principles, SOSP (2003)

[14] Vasudevan, A., Yerraballi, R.: Stealth Breakpoints. In: 21st Annual Computer Security Applications Conference, ACSAC (2005)

[15] Xiong, X., Tian, D., Liu, P.: Practical Protection of Kernel Integrity for Commodity OS from Untrusted Extension. In: 18th Annual Network & Distributed System Security Symposium, NDSS (2011)

[16] Yan, L., Jayachandra, M., Zhang, M., Yin, H.: V2E: combining hardware virtualization and softwareemulation for transparent and extensible malware analysis, Virtual Execution Environments, VEE (2012)

Key Management for Onion Routing in a True Peer to Peer Setting

Paolo Palmieri and Johan Pouwelse

Parallel and Distributed Systems, Delft University of Technology
Mekelweg 4, 2628 CD Delft, The Netherlands
p.palmieri@tudelft.nl, peer2peer@gmail.com

Abstract. Onion routing is a technique for anonymous and privacy preserving communication at the base of popular Internet anonymity tools such as Tor. In onion routing, traffic is relayed by a number of intermediary nodes (called relays) before it reaches the intended destination. To guarantee privacy and prevent tampering, each packet is encrypted multiple times in a layered manner, using the public keys of the relays. Therefore, this mechanism makes two important assumptions: first, that the relays are able to communicate with each other; second, that the user knows the list of available relays and their respective public keys. Tor implements therefore a distributed directory listing the relays and their keys. When a user is not able to communicate with relays directly, he has to use special bridge servers to connect to the onion network.

This construction, however, does not work in a fully peer to peer setting, where each peer only knows a limited number of other peers and may not be able to communicate with some of them due, for instance, to NAT or firewalls. In this paper we propose a key management scheme for onion routing that overcomes these problems. The proposed solution does not need a directory system and does not imply knowledge of all active relays, while it guarantees the secure distribution of public keys. We also present an alternative strategy for building circuit of relays based on bloom filters. The proposed construction overcomes some of the structural inefficiencies of the Tor design, and opens the way for implementing onion routing over a true peer to peer overlay network.

Keywords: Key Management, Onion Routing, Peer to Peer.

1 Introduction

At the beginning of its diffusion to the general public, Internet was perceived by most users as a private or even anonymous medium of communication [19]. However, this perception has changed over the years, and the lack of online privacy is becoming more and more evident (and for some worrisome) to the users. Anonymous communication over the Internet is thus receiving increased interest and attention. A particular kind of application whose users are particularly concerned about privacy is that of peer to peer (p2p) systems. However, most peer to peer applications currently lack effective measures to protect the privacy of their

M. Yoshida and K. Mouri (Eds.): IWSEC 2014, LNCS 8639, pp. 62–71, 2014.

users. Those that do attempt at building privacy-preserving and anonymous p2p networks, such as Freenet [6] or GNUnet [3,2], have often found scarce adoption, mostly due to the relatively difficult operation of such software by inexperienced users and (paradoxically) to the small existing user-base, which makes them unattractive to new users. The first software for private and censorship-resistant communication to receive widespread attention by non specialized users was Tor (The Onion Router) [7], who now counts millions of active users. Tor can be used to connect to existing Internet services in an anonymous manner, but it is not designed for peer to peer: users are actually actively discouraged from running p2p software such as Bittorrent over its network. Likewise most tools for achieving anonymity over the Internet, Tor relies on a multiple relay setup, in which communication between the originator (the user) and the destination (the web service) is tunneled through a number of proxies, called relays. Tor uses a specific approach to the relaying of messages, called Onion Routing (OR) [20]. In onion routing, messages are repeatedly encrypted: each relay removes a layer of encryption, and then forwards the message to the next relay, where this is repeated. This prevents intermediary hops from learning the contents, origin and destination of any message that passes through them. In the Tor setup, relays are publicly disclosed and organized in a directory system, which allows users to locate active relays and retrieve their public key information. The directory is especially needed for one reason: clients communicate only with the first relay in a circuit, and rely on its services to talk to relays further down the chain in order to preserve their privacy. This prevents them from contacting directly other relays to obtain their public key, and makes the directory necessary to prevent the first node from impersonating other relays in the circuit. However, while the directory is distributed among several "trusted" nodes, this scenario is far from a real peer to peer setting, in which we can not assume peers to have a full view of the network, or even be able to connect to all nodes (due to NATs, firewalls, etc.). Therefore, if we are to implement an onion routing mechanism over a true peer to peer setting, we need a key distribution and management mechanism that takes into account the critical peculiarities of peer to peer systems.

1.1 Contribution

In this paper, we discuss why the directory infrastructure used by Tor for key distribution is not applicable to a peer to peer setting, where peers are at the same time clients and relays, they do not know the full list of other relays or the network topology and may not even be able to connect to part of the peer list known to them. While key management schemes for peer to peer settings already exist in literature, none of them addresses the specific needs of distributed onion routing systems, and in particular the impossibility of challenging peers directly to confirm their identity or obtain their keys. Existing peer to peer designs based on anonymizing relays, on the other hand, do not implement a Tor-like onion routing, which, due to the resilience to attacks proved by the Tor network, is believed to be a reliable privacy-preserving mechanism. We address these issues by proposing a novel scheme implementing a Tor-like secure key distribution and management mechanism based on a true peer to peer overlay. The solution presented in this paper allows the secure retrieval of temporary onion keys, and their validation against the long-term identity key for each relay, while not requiring a directory structure based on trusted known nodes. In the design of our solution we also provide an innovative mechanism for selecting relays during circuit creation based on bloom filters, which might be of independent interest.

1.2 Related Works

While no established peer to peer software uses onion routing, its adoption has been proposed in various theoretical designs [14]. However, the lack of a distributed Tor-like key management solution imposed to deviate from the standard onion routing paradigm. ShadowWalker [15] constructs circuits based on a random walk over a redundant structured topology, while Saboori and Mohammadi propose a design relying on supernodes so that no peer can identify the communicating parties with certainty [18]. Landsiedel et al. instead extend onion routing by allowing the first half of the path to be selected by the sender and the second half by the receiver of the packet [9]. A sizable part of relevant literature focuses instead on a way to perform secure and anonymous lookups (in this context, useful for retrieving the public keys) [21]. Torsk [12], in particular, utilizes a combination of two p2p lookup mechanisms, in order to preserve the confidentiality and integrity of lookups. On the other hand, distributed key management schemes based on the concept of distributed hash table have been proposed in the past [17,22,11]. These mechanisms present solutions for a number of different purposes: among them, multimedia streaming services, where the goal of distributed key management is to safeguard content security [17,16], mobile ad-hoc networks [13], or (heterogeneous) wireless sensor networks [10,5].

2   Onion Routing and Key Management in Tor

The concept of onion routing was first proposed by Syverson, Goldschlag and Reed in 1997 [20], but it was only in 2002 that Dingledine, Mathewson and again Syverson refined the paradigm and finally implemented it as the Tor software [7]. The aim of onion routing is to protect the identity and network activity of its users from surveillance and traffic analysis. This goal is achieved by concealing to external observers both the content and routing information of the user's traffic, which is forwarded through a virtual circuit composed of three successive relays. Each relay only knows the preceding and following node: this guarantees sender's anonymity to all relays except the first and the secrecy of the destination to all relays except the last. At the same time, communication is repeatedly encrypted with a public key encryption scheme in a layered manner, using in inverse order the public keys of all the relays in the circuit. Traffic going back to the user from the destination is similarly encrypted and routed from the last to the first relay, and on to the user. In general, Tor allows users to connect to any Internet service independently of the protocol, as long as the software supports Socks proxying.

Tor uses a number of different encryption keys, for three different purposes: encryption of traffic, verifying the identity of the relays, and making sure that all clients know the same set of relays. Encryption is performed on all connections within the Tor network. Tor uses TLS link encryption, which guarantees that observers can not learn which circuit a given packet is intended for. Furthermore, Tor clients establish a session key with each relay in the circuit. This extra layer of encryption ensures that only the exit relay can read outbound packets, and only the users can decrypt inbound traffic. Both sides discard the session keys when the circuit is disposed of, achieving forward secrecy. Every Tor relay generates regularly (once a week) a public and private key pair called *onion key*. When a Tor client establishes a circuit, at each step it challenges the Tor relay to prove knowledge of its onion key, to prevent spoofing. Since the Tor client chooses the path independently, circuits are based on the concept of *distributed trust*: no single relay can learn both the client address and the traffic destination. The list of relays and their keys are shared through a distributed *directory*. Fast and stable servers are selected for the task directly by the Tor developers, and locations and public keys for each directory authority (a relay hosting the directory service) are hard-coded into the Tor client software. Each relay has a long-term signing key pair called *identity key*. Each directory authority additionally has a *directory key*. The directory authorities provide a list of all known relays signed with its directory key. The list also contains the onion key for each relay (signed with their identity key).

3   Distributed Hash Table (DHT) Networks

Large decentralized, distributed systems are notoriously difficult to design and implement. Successful designs are often based on simple primitives, such as the *distributed hash table* (DHT). A DHT can be used to efficiently store and retrieve data (for instance, files) in a distributed manner, while respecting the three main properties of peer to peer systems: operating without central coordination; being able to accommodate nodes joining, leaving, or failing without disruption of service; and functioning efficiently for any number of peers. Over the years, many different DHT's have been proposed in literature, but only a subset has found widespread usage. A notable example is Mainline DHT, introduced by the developers of peer to peer software Azureus and then incorporated in a slightly modified version in the BitTorrent protocol, used daily by millions of users. In general, DHT are nowadays regarded as one of the most stable and efficient setups for peer to peer network [1]. Given the growing interest in privacy preserving techniques for DHT networks [8], we base our scheme on this network structure.

A DHT is built over a *keyspace*[1], usually defined by a hash function: an example is the set of all strings of length 160 bits output by SHA-1. A partitioning scheme for the keyspace is used to divide responsibility for the keyspace among

---

[1] We use the term keyspace for consistency with the relevant literature, bit it is important to clarify that the keyspace of a DHT has no relation to the keyspace of the PKC schemes we use for the purposes of onion routing in the following.

the peers participating in the network. This is achieved by defining function measuring the *distance* between two values in the keyspace, and by assigning to each peer a value in the keyspace called *identifier*: the peer is then responsible for the subset of values that have less than a predefined distance from his identifier value. Finally, an overlay network connecting the peers is generated. Each peer maintains a connection to a number of other peers, called *neighbors*. Neighbors are selected according to a certain structure, known as the network topology, which, together with the hash and distance functions, defines the specific DHT. Once a DHT is established, peers are able to find peers responsible for any given value in the keyspace. While the design of our key management scheme is independent of the specific DHT, we assume the DHT to specify: a keyspace K of size s; a hash functions h mapping information that can be retrieved through the network (files, etc.) to values in the keyspace; a function f_{dist} for determining the distance between two values of the keyspace; and the distance d within which a peer is responsible for keys in the keyspace. We also assume the keyspace to be two-dimensional: given a distance d, a function f_{dist}, and a value v in the keyspace, there are exactly two values v^+ and v^- for which

$$f_{dist}\left(v^+\right) = f_{dist}\left(v^-\right) = d \ . \tag{1}$$

The distance d should be calibrated over the number of peers in the network: if the value is too high, each peer has to store too much information, while if d is too low information is spread too thin and may be difficult or impossible to retrieve. For this reason, some DHT constructions adjust this value during operation of the network. The key management scheme for onion routing we propose in the following is therefore able to accommodate for a varying d.

4   Onion Routing Key Management over a DHT Network

In the following we propose a key management mechanism for achieving onion routing over an existing DHT peer to peer network. In particular, we imagine a scenario in which peers in the network communicate and transmit information according to the employed DHT construction, but also want to preserve their privacy by using onion routing in the communication within the peer to peer overlay. Therefore, when retrieving information (such as files) over the peer to peer network, peers relay the communication through a number of other peers, following the onion routing principles described in Section 2.

Being a peer to peer scenario, we assume that each peer in the network acts as both a regular user and as a relay, as opposed to the Tor implementation in which most relays are dedicated servers and most users do not relay traffic. In order to be able to act as a relay, a peer creates during bootstrap an *identity key* pair, using a public key encryption scheme. Identity keys, similarly to the key management of Tor, are kept by the peers indefinitely. Additionally, the peer also creates a temporary *onion key* pair, which expires after a predetermined amount of time and is then replaced by a new pair. The two different key pairs serve different purposes: the identity key is used prove the identity of the peer and sign information regarding it, so that other peers can verify it as legitimate. The onion key, instead, is used for actual communication during the creation of onion circuits, and specifically before the generation of the symmetric session key with which the peer encrypts traffic for the relays and vice versa. In order to participate in the network, a peer needs to distribute the public keys of both his identity and onion pairs. In the following, we describe how the different keys are spread across the network, and which peers are responsible for storing and distributing the keys. We say that a peer *owns* a key (whether it is an identity or an onion key) if he generated the key himself, while we say that a peer is *responsible* for a key if he stores the key and distributes it to other peers requesting it. The novel key distribution scheme we propose still relies on the underlying DHT structure for the actual transmission of the information: keys are transmitted over the network in the same way files are, following the specific DHT protocol employed. We assume the number of relays in a circuit to be 3.

Identity Keys Distribution. The peers responsible for the identity key of a peer are determined by hashing the identifier for the peer using the hash function employed by the DHT scheme, similarly to any information shared in the network. As defined in the previous section, a peer X is responsible for the identity key $i_P \in K$ of the peer P if: $f_{dist}(X - h(P)) < d$. This defines a subset I_B of size $2d$ of the keyspace K. The peer owning the key is responsible for initiating the distribution of its identity key to the peers responsible for storing it. This is done using the information retrieval algorithm of the underlying DHT scheme. Should d increase during operation, peers already responsible for the key distribute it to the new peers in I_P. Should d decrease, instead, peers that are no longer in I_P just drop the key and stop distributing it.

Onion Keys Lifetime. Similarly to the Tor design, we require onion keys to be replaced after a number of hours t. Tor uses a time interval of one week, but in our peer to peer design we leave the decision on the interval duration to the protocol implementation, depending on the specific needs of the network. In order to prevent flooding of the network at the end of each validity interval, when all onion keys expire at the same time, we divide the peers into subgroups, and we assign to each subgroup a different time offset from the reference expiration time. We determine the time offset according to the identifier of the peer owning the onion key: we consider the first n bits of the identifier value in order to have 2^n different expiration times. For instance, given a reference time, all peers with the first n bits of the identifier having value 0 have no offset (their key expires at the reference time), those with value 1 have a positive offset of one hour (their key expires one hour after the reference time) and so on. Assuming identifiers are chosen uniformly in the keyspace, this divides equally the peers. Moreover, if the identifier of a peer is known, so are the expiration times of his onion keys.

Onion Keys Distribution. Temporary onion keys are stored within the DHT network similarly to identity keys. However, peers responsible for storing the identity key of a peer will never be responsible for his onion keys too. Moreover, a peer responsible for the onion key of a peer for the current time interval, will not be responsible for a key of the same peer for a number of following time intervals. We achieve this using the following distribution scheme. For each peer P and his identifier $i_P \in K$, we divide the keyspace (and hence the other peers in the network) into $u = \frac{s}{2d}$ partitions of size $2d$, such that one such partition coincides with I_P, as defined above. Peers in each partition except I_P cyclically store the current onion key for P. The arbitrary function

$$f_{on} : \quad K \to \{\text{all possible partitions of } K \text{ of size } 2d\}, \qquad (2)$$

defines the partitions. It takes an identifier $i \in K$ as input and outputs the set of partitions $\{O_1, \ldots, O_{u-1}\}$, such that $O_1, \ldots, O_{u-1}$ are disjoint subsets of K of equal size and $O_1 \cup \ldots \cup O_{u-1} = K \smallsetminus \{I_P\}$. In any $u - 1$ contiguous time intervals, each available partition is selected once for storing the onion key of the peer, starting with O_1 and proceeding in ascending order till O_{u-1}. The peer owning the key is responsible for the distribution of the next key to the peers in the appropriate partition O_n before the current key expires. Should d change, the partitions are adjusted from the next time interval. When a peer is queried for onion keys he is responsible for, he always reply with all of them: that is, queries are not made for retrieving a specific key, but for retrieving all keys under the responsibility of one peer.

4.1   Building an Onion Circuit

The process of building an onion circuit is more complex in a peer to peer setting than it is for Tor, as peers have only a partial view of the network. In building a circuit, this means that two consecutive relays may not able to communicate with each other, thus causing the circuit to fail. This issue may be addressed by letting the first relay in a circuit decide the second, and so on. However, if the user stumbles on a first relay that is malicious, then the whole circuit will be likely composed of malicious nodes. Therefore, we decide to keep the circuit creation and relay selection under the user's direct control, and we propose the use of bloom filters to let the user identify which relays can connect to each other.[2] In particular, we require each peer to attach to his public onion key a bloom filter where the neighbors of the peer have been encoded, called *neighbor bloom filter* and built over the neighbors' identifiers. The filter, as well as the onion key, must be signed by the peer with his identity key, and is stored and distributed together with the onion key. The neighbor filter lets us construct circuits in which the relays can communicate to each other: the peer building the circuit can in fact calculate the intersection of the filters of the potential first and last relays to identify whether they have a common neighbor that can be used as middle relay. But the bloom filter does more than that: it also allows us to evaluate the relatedness of relays, based on the number of common neighbors.

---

[2] Bloom filters (BF) are space-efficient data structures representing a set. A BF generated for a set allows to determine, without knowledge of the set itself, whether an element is in the set or not. In the following we assume knowledge of the bloom filter definition and properties: the interested reader can find a thorough discussion in [4].

We may want, for instance, to build a circuit in which the first and third relays are not neighbors, nor have more than n common neighbors, in order to diversify the circuit and reduce its locality (for a security discussion, see Section 5).

Considering that all peers are responsible, at some point in time, for an onion (or identity) key for all other peers, due to the distribution mechanism described above, all peers are naturally aware of most of other peers (the exception being the peers that entered the network later than $u - 1$ time intervals before the current one). No further step is therefore necessary for a peer to discover new peers prior to building a circuit, as the identifiers of (most) other peers are known. A circuit is built as follows:

1. The peer selects a potential first relay among his neighbors, and acquires his onion key and neighbor filter through the DHT (and not directly from the neighbor himself).
2. Once the relay information for the first relay has been acquired, the peer identifies potential third relays by calculating the intersection between their neighbor filter b_3 and the one of the first relay b_1. The peer queries peers through the DHT to acquire additional relay information if necessary. Then he selects a third relay satisfying the following requirements: not being a neighbor of the first one nor the peer; and having a number of common neighbors with the first relay within the range defined as acceptable by the peer. Once the third relay is selected, the peer sends to the first relay the intersection filter $b_i = b_1 \cap b_3$. Then, the peer instructs the first relay to build a circuit with one of his own neighbors whose identifier satisfies b_i.
3. The peer communicates to the second relay through the first one in an encrypted manner (following the onion routing scheme), and instructs him to extend the circuit to the selected third relay. The second relay is a neighbor of both the first and third relay minus the false positive probability of the intersection bloom filter. In case the second relay is unable to communicate to the third one, the peer starts again from step 2.

5   Security Analysis

In this section we analyze the security of the proposed key management scheme.

Distributed Trust No single relay in the circuit should be aware of both the initiating peer and the traffic destination. We achieve this by letting the peer select independently the first and last relay, and by not disclosing to the first relay the identity of the third one. This is possible thanks to the use of the intersection of neighbor filters, as explained in step 2 of the circuit building protocol. This, in turn, allows the first relay to extend the circuit to a neighbor able to communicate with the third relay without knowledge of his identity. It is important to note here that the first relay does learn the list of potential third relays, as this is the same list as the list of neighbors of the second relays. However, since relays can only communicate with their neighbors, this issue is impossible to prevent in a peer to peer setting.

Information Leakage when Querying Relay Information When a peer queries other relays through the DHT for retrieving relay information, he somehow reveals his willingness to build a circuit with one of those relays. Calibrating the onion key lifetime and increasing the number of queries performed by a peer during each time interval is however sufficient to prevent potentially identifying information from being leaked: computing a correlation is possible only if the queries recover relay information for a limited number of peers only.

Identity Key Verification The identity key of each peer is verified directly by the peers responsible for its distribution through a challenge. When the challenge can not be accomplished (for example, if the peer responsible for the key is unable to contact the owner), the peer responsible for the key does not distribute that key. Having a subset of peers distributing the identity keys makes an attack possible if at least a majority of those peers collude in order to reply with a fake key instead of the real one. However, we note here that the peer building the circuit obtains onion keys from a different set of peers, and is also aware of the partition of peers in the network responsible for that specific identity key. The attack is therefore limited to preventing a peer from using the selected peer as relay, as the onion key can not be verified against the (fake) identity key. Moreover, should a subset of peers be responsible for a statistically relevant number of un-verifying keys, the peer building the circuit can choose to discard keys from that subset entirely.

Onion Key Verification The onion key for the current time interval is verified by the peer directly with the relay through the circuit, by asking the relay to reply a challenge in the same way Tor does.

6   Conclusions

In this paper, we propose a key management scheme for the distribution of onion keys over a DHT peer to peer network. Achieving onion routing in a true peer to peer setting is in fact a complex task, as no participating peer can be assumed to be able to connect to any other peer. This, in turn, makes the creation of a distributed relay directory similar to the one implemented by Tor impossible. The key distribution scheme we propose addresses this problem by distributing the onion encryption keys among the peers in an decentralized manner. We enable peers to select circuits without knowledge of the full list of relays, and we ensure that selected relays are able to communicate with each other without disclosing their identity by using a bloom filter structure indexing each relay's neighbors. The proposed construction allows the implementation of onion routing over peer to peer application used every day by millions of users, and finally provides and answer to these user's increasing demand for privacy.

References

1. Balakrishnan, H., Kaashoek, M.F., Karger, D.R., Morris, R., Stoica, I.: Looking up data in p2p systems. Commun. ACM 46(2), 43–48 (2003)

2. Bennett, K., Grothoff, C., Horozov, T., Patrascu, I.: Efficient sharing of encrypted data. In: Batten, L.M., Seberry, J. (eds.) ACISP 2002. LNCS, vol. 2384, pp. 107–120. Springer, Heidelberg (2002)
3. Bennett, K., Grothoff, C., Horozov, T., Patrascu, I., Stef, T.: The GNet whitepaper. Tech. rep., Purdue University (2002)
4. Bloom, B.H.: Space/time trade-offs in hash coding with allowable errors. Commun. ACM 13(7), 422–426 (1970)
5. Chung, K.-I., Sohn, K., Yung, M. (eds.): WISA 2008. LNCS, vol. 5379. Springer, Heidelberg (2009)
6. Clarke, I., Sandberg, O., Wiley, B., Hong, T.W.: Freenet: A distributed anonymous information storage and retrieval system. In: Federrath, H. (ed.) Anonymity 2000. LNCS, vol. 2009, pp. 46–66. Springer, Heidelberg (2001)
7. Dingledine, R., Mathewson, N., Syverson, P.F.: Tor: The second-generation onion router. In: USENIX Security Symposium, pp. 303–320. USENIX (2004)
8. Isdal, T., Piatek, M., Krishnamurthy, A., Anderson, T.E.: Privacy-preserving p2p data sharing with oneswarm. In: SIGCOMM, pp. 111–122. ACM (2010)
9. Landsiedel, O., Pimenidis, L., Wehrle, K., Niedermayer, H., Carle, G.: Dynamic multipath onion routing in anonymous peer-to-peer overlay networks. In: GLOBE-COM, pp. 64–69. IEEE (2007)
10. Lu, K., Qian, Y., Guizani, M., Chen, H.H.: A framework for a distributed key management scheme in heterogeneous wireless sensor networks. IEEE Transactions on Wireless Communications 7(2), 639–647 (2008)
11. Luo, Z., Li, Z., Cai, B.: A self-organized public-key certificate system in p2p network. Journal of Networks 6(10), 1437–1443 (2011)
12. McLachlan, J., Tran, A., Hopper, N., Kim, Y.: Scalable onion routing with torsk. In: ACM CCS, pp. 590–599 (2009)
13. van der Merwe, J., Dawoud, D.S., McDonald, S.: A survey on peer-to-peer key management for mobile ad hoc networks. ACM Comput. Surv. 39(1) (2007)
14. Michéle, B.: Using Onion Routing in Well-Established P2P Networks to Provide Anonymity. Master's thesis, Technische Universität Berlin (December 2008)
15. Mittal, P., Borisov, N.: Shadowwalker: peer-to-peer anonymous communication using redundant structured topologies. In: ACM CCS, pp. 161–172 (2009)
16. Naranjo, J.A.M., López-Ramos, J.A., Casado, L.G.: Key management schemes for peer-to-peer multimedia streaming overlay networks. In: Markowitch, O., Bilas, A., Hoepman, J.-H., Mitchell, C.J., Quisquater, J.-J. (eds.) WISTP 2009. LNCS, vol. 5746, pp. 128–142. Springer, Heidelberg (2009)
17. Qiu, F., Lin, C., Yin, H.: EKM: An efficient key management scheme for large-scale peer-to-peer media streaming. In: Zhuang, Y., Yang, S.-Q., Rui, Y., He, Q. (eds.) PCM 2006. LNCS, vol. 4261, pp. 395–404. Springer, Heidelberg (2006)
18. Saboori, E., Mohammadi, S.: Anonymous communication in peer-to-peer networks for providing more privacy and security. CoRR abs/1208.3192 (2012)
19. Sheehan, K.: Toward a typology of internet users and online privacy concerns. Inf. Soc. 18(1), 21–32 (2002)
20. Syverson, P.F., Goldschlag, D.M., Reed, M.G.: Anonymous connections and onion routing. In: IEEE Symposium on Security and Privacy, pp. 44–54. IEEE (1997)
21. Wang, Q., Mittal, P., Borisov, N.: In search of an anonymous and secure lookup: attacks on structured peer-to-peer anonymous communication systems. In: ACM CCS, pp. 308–318. ACM (2010)
22. Wen, Z., Zhang Niu, S., Cheng Zou, J.: A Key Management Mechanism for DHT Networks. In: IIH-MSP, pp. 339–342. IEEE (2012)

Cheater Identifiable Secret Sharing Schemes via Multi-Receiver Authentication

Rui Xu[1], Kirill Morozov[2], and Tsuyoshi Takagi[2]

[1] Graduate School of Mathematics, Kyushu University, Japan
r-xu@math.kyushu-u.ac.jp
[2] Institute of Mathematics for Industry, Kyushu University, Japan
{morozov,takagi}@imi.kyushu-u.ac.jp

Abstract. We introduce two publicly cheater identifiable secret sharing (CISS) schemes with efficient reconstruction, tolerating $t < k/2$ cheaters. Our constructions are based on (k, n) threshold Shamir scheme, and they feature a novel application of multi-receiver authentication codes to ensure integrity of shares.

The first scheme, which tolerates rushing cheaters, has the share size $|S|(n-t)^{n+t+2}/\epsilon^{n+t+2}$ in the general case, that can be ultimately reduced to $|S|(k-t)^{k+t+2}/\epsilon^{k+t+2}$ assuming that all the t cheaters are among the k reconstructing players. The second scheme, which tolerates non-rushing cheaters, has the share size $|S|(n-t)^{2t+2}/\epsilon^{2t+2}$. These two constructions have the smallest share size among the existing CISS schemes of the same category, when the secret is a single field element.

In addition, we point out that an improvement in the share size to $|S|/\epsilon^{n-\lfloor (k-1)/3 \rfloor +1}$ can be achieved for a CISS tolerating $t < k/3$ rushing cheaters presented by Xu et al. at IWSEC 2013.

Keywords: Cheater identifiable secret sharing, multi-receiver authentication code, Shamir secret sharing, rushing adversary.

1 Introduction

We consider cheater identifiable secret sharing (CISS) which is an upgrade of (k, n)-threshold secret sharing schemes [1, 13] that can tolerate up to t actively corrupt participants. The dealer in CISS is assumed to be honest. The goal in this scenario is to identify cheaters from the threshold k number of players, and to recover a correct secret whenever possible. In this work, we focus on *public* cheater identification, where reconstruction of the secret and cheater identification can be performed by a third party who collects shares from a threshold of players. Note that an honest majority, i.e. $t < k/2$, is necessary in this case, otherwise the dishonest majority of cheaters might simply generate a new consistent set of (authenticated) shares and submit it at the reconstruction. We will consider, in particular, *rushing* cheaters who are allowed to decide their messages (in every round) upon seeing the messages of honest parties.

M. Yoshida and K. Mouri (Eds.): IWSEC 2014, LNCS 8639, pp. 72–87, 2014.

1.1 Related Works

The observation of McEliece and Sarwate [8] on a connection between the Shamir scheme [13] and the Reed-Solomon codes [11] allowed for identification of cheaters, however redundant shares (i.e., more than k of them) were required. The first CISS scheme came from a related area of robust secret sharing (where the secret is always reconstructed from n shares, while no cheater identification is required) when Rabin and Ben-Or [10] proposed to use unconditional authentication codes for enforcing the integrity of shares. Then, a number of proposals for CISS schemes followed where the efforts were directed at achieving efficient reconstruction against maximal number of cheaters, while reducing the share size. We refer the reader to the survey of Martin [7] for the history of this subject.

Recently, Obana [9] proposed a CISS scheme that is secure against $t < k/2$ non-rushing cheaters but has inefficient reconstruction algorithm (the computation complexity is exponential in the number of cheaters). Choudhury [2] presented a CISS scheme secure against $t < k/2$ rushing cheaters with efficient reconstruction. The share size of his scheme is optimal $O(|S|/\epsilon)$ provided that the size of the secret is $\Omega(n)$, where $|S|$ denotes the size of the secret and ϵ is the cheater success probability. In this work, we focus on the scenario where the secret is "short", i.e., it is represented by a single field element – the same scenario as in [9]. In this case, the share size of Choudhury's scheme is far from optimal.

Under assumption of having $t < k/3$ non-rushing cheaters, Obana [9] presented a CISS scheme with nearly optimal share size $|S|/\epsilon$. Xu et al. [15] upgraded the above scheme to security against rushing cheaters for the price of increasing the share size to $|S|/\epsilon^{n-t+1}$.

1.2 Our Contribution

We present two new CISS schemes tolerating up to $t < k/2$ cheaters, which are based on multi-receiver authentication codes [4, 12]. These schemes are introduced below as Proposals 1 and 2.

Proposal 1: Our scheme tolerating rushing cheaters has the share size $|S|(n - t)^{n+t+2}/\epsilon^{n+t+2}$ in the general case. However, if the number of shares presented at the reconstruction is restricted to k, then the share size can be made equal to $|S|(k - t)^{k+2t+1}/\epsilon^{k+2t+1}$. In other words, when restricting the number of reconstructing players, the share size can be reduced. This is an interesting point in the sense that generally, redundant information is used to identify cheaters. However, in this particular case, we observe that some redundant information can be beneficial to the cheaters. In fact, the share size can be reduced even further to $|S|(k - t)^{k+t+2}/\epsilon^{k+t+2}$, under assumption that all the corrupt players always participate in the reconstruction.

Proposal 2: Our scheme tolerating non-rushing cheaters has the share size $|S|(n - t)^{2t+2}/\epsilon^{2t+2}$. Our proposal has smaller share size as compared to $|V_i| = |S|(t + 1)^{3n}/\epsilon^{3n}$ in Choudhury scheme [2]. We emphasize that the work [2] presents a scheme tolerating non-rushing adversaries, but it is trivial to extend it to the rushing case, such that the share size is the same in both cases.

Table 1. Comparison of Our Proposals to Existing CISS schemes

Scheme	Assumption	Share Size	Adversary
Choudhury [2]*	$t < k/2$	$|V_i| = |S|(t+1)^{3n}/\epsilon^{3n}$	Rushing
Our Proposal 1**	$t < k/2$	$|V_i| = |S|(k-t)^{k+t+2}/\epsilon^{k+t+2}$	Rushing
Obana [9]***	$t < k/2$	$|V_i| \approx |S|(nt \cdot 2^{3t})^2/\epsilon^2$	Non-Rushing
Our Proposal 2	$t < k/2$	$|V_i| = |S|(n-t)^{2t+2}/\epsilon^{2t+2}$	Non-Rushing
Obana [9]	$t < k/3$	$|V_i| = |S|/\epsilon$	Non-Rushing
Xu et al. [15]	$t < k/3$	$|V_i| = |S|/\epsilon^{n-t+1}$	Rushing
Our Proposal 3	$t < k/3$	$|V_i| = |S|/\epsilon^{n-\lfloor(k-1)/3\rfloor+1}$	Rushing

*   When the secret is a single field element.

**   The smallest share size, when restricting to k reconstructing parties such that only these ones can be actively corrupt.

*** The reconstruction needs $\binom{3t}{t+2}$ Lagrange interpolations. For comparison, each of our Proposals 1 and 2 needs one Lagrange interpolation and k polynomial evaluations.

Proposal 3: Under assumption that $t < k/3$, we improve the share size of the scheme [15] from $|S|/\epsilon^{n-t+1}$ to $|S|/\epsilon^{n-\lfloor(k-1)/3\rfloor+1}$ by eliminating some encryption keys in their construction.

Our contributions and the related works are summarized in Table 1.

Remark 1. We emphasize that the main contribution to the share size typically comes from the factor $1/\epsilon$, since one expects the cheating probability ϵ to be made negligible, while the parameters n, k, and t are some constants. Consequently, the major efforts in reducing the share size are made towards reducing the degree of the factor $1/\epsilon$.

2   Preliminaries

Set $[n] = \{1, 2, \ldots, n\}$. The cardinality of the set X is denoted by $|X|$. Let $\mathbb{F}_p$ be a Galois field of a prime order p satisfying $p > n$. Let $\phi(\cdot, \cdot) : \mathbb{F}_p \times [n] \to \mathbb{F}_q$ be a injective function ($q > np$ is a prime power). All computation is done in the specified Galois fields.

2.1   Shamir Secret Sharing

We describe the k-out-of-n threshold secret sharing scheme by Shamir [13]. Such the secret sharing scheme involves a dealer D and n participants $\{R_1, \ldots, R_n\}$, and consists of two algorithms: **ShareGen** and **Reconst**. The **ShareGen** algorithm takes a secret $s \in \mathbb{F}_p$ as input and then outputs a list $(\sigma_1, \ldots, \sigma_n)$. Each σ_i

is respectively distributed to participant R_i and called her share. The algorithm **Reconst** takes a list $(\sigma_1, \ldots, \sigma_m)$ as input and outputs the secret s if $m \geq k$. Otherwise, the **Reconst** outputs $\perp$. Formally, the properties of *correctness* and *perfect secrecy* hold:

1. Correctness: If $m \geq k$, then $\Pr[\mathbf{Reconst}(\sigma_1, \ldots, \sigma_m) = s] = 1$;
2. Perfect secrecy: If $m < k$, then $\Pr[S = s | (V_1 = \sigma_1, \ldots, V_m = \sigma_m)] = \Pr[S = s]$ for any $s \in S$.

In the Shamir scheme, the above mentioned algorithms proceed as follows:

ShareGen

1. For a given secret $s \in \mathbb{F}_p$, the dealer D chooses a random polynomial $f(x) \in \mathbb{F}_p[X]$ with degree at most $k - 1$ and $f(0) = s$.
2. For $i \in [n]$, compute $\sigma_i = f(x_i)$ for fixed, public and distinct $x_i \in \mathbb{F}_p$ (where x_i can be seen as a unique identifier for R_i) and send σ_i privately to participant R_i.

Reconst

If $m \geq k$ then output the secret s using the Lagrange interpolation formula, otherwise output $\perp$.

2.2   Cheater Identifiable Secret Sharing

We will focus on cheater identifiable secret sharing that is based on the Shamir scheme. In CISS, we require that the reconstruction algorithm **Reconst** both computes the secret and identifies incorrect shares, which point at cheaters among the involved participants. The output of **Reconst** algorithm is a tuple (s', L), where s' is the reconstructed secret and L is the set of cheaters. If the secret cannot be reconstructed because there are not enough of honest players, it is set to be $\perp$. When $s' \neq \perp$, $s' = s$ except with negligible probability.

The following definitions are developed using those by Choudhury [2] and Xu et al. [15].

Communication Model: We assume that the participants $\mathcal{R} = \{R_1, \ldots, R_n\}$ are connected with the dealer D by private and authenticated channels, and in addition, a broadcast channel is available to every entity. The communication network is assumed to be synchronous and the adversary can be *rushing* or not [5]. In synchronous network the protocols proceed in rounds: the current round is known to all parties, and messages sent in some round are delivered by the beginning of the next round. The term "rushing" refers to allowing the corrupted parties to learn the messages sent by the uncorrupted parties in each round, before sending their own messages for this round.

Adversary Model: There exist two adaptive, computationally unbounded adversaries $\mathcal{A}_{listen}$ and $\mathcal{A}_{cheat}$. The listening adversary $\mathcal{A}_{listen}$ can passively control any $k - 1$ parties in $\mathcal{R}$. The cheating adversary $\mathcal{A}_{cheat}$ can adaptively choose to control any t parties in $\mathcal{R}$ in the malicious manner. Additionally, we assume that $\mathcal{A}_{listen}$ and $\mathcal{A}_{cheat}$ do not collude. This implies that $\mathcal{A}_{cheat}$ will not get any information about the computation and communication of the parties, which are under the control of $\mathcal{A}_{listen}$ (but not $\mathcal{A}_{cheat}$) and vice-versa. Intuitively, security against $\mathcal{A}_{listen}$ implies the standard (perfect) secrecy of (k,n)-threshold secret sharing, while security against $\mathcal{A}_{cheat}$ implies protection against active cheaters intending to disrupt the reconstruction of a correct secret. As usual in CISS schemes, we assume that adversaries cannot corrupt the dealer D.

Definition 1 ([15]). A cheater identifiable secret sharing scheme Σ is a tuple $(n, k, S, V, \mathbf{ShareGen}, \mathbf{Reconst})$ consisting of:

- A positive integer n called the number of players;
- A positive integer k denoting the number of honest shares from which the original secret can be reconstructed;
- A finite set S with $|S| \geq 2$, whose elements are called secrets;
- A finite set $V = \{V_1, \ldots, V_n\}$, where V_i is the set of player R_i's shares;
- An algorithm **ShareGen**, that takes as input a secret $s \in S$, and outputs a vector of n shares $(\sigma_1, \ldots, \sigma_n) \in V_1 \times \cdots \times V_n$; and
- An algorithm **Reconst**, that takes as input a vector $(\sigma'_{i_1}, \ldots, \sigma'_{i_m}) \in V_{i_1} \times \cdots \times V_{i_m}$, and outputs a tuple (s', L), where s' is the reconstructed secret and L is the set of identified cheaters.

Recall that the cheating adversary can corrupt at most t players. Denote by $(R_{i_1}, \ldots, R_{i_t})$ the t cheaters under the control of $\mathcal{A}_{cheat}$ and by $\sigma'_{i_1}, \ldots, \sigma'_{i_t}$ their possibly corrupt shares. We define the successful cheating probability to be the probability that *the cheater is not identified when she provided a forged share (thus resulting in a corrupt secret) at the reconstruction.*

Definition 2. For some $s' \neq s$, the successful cheating probability of player R_{i_j} under the control of $\mathcal{A}_{cheat}$ against the cheater identifiable secret sharing scheme $\Sigma = (n, k, S, V, \mathbf{ShareGen}, \mathbf{Reconst})$ is defined as

$$\begin{aligned}
&\epsilon(\Sigma, R_{i_j}, \mathcal{A}_{cheat}) \\
&= \max_{\sigma'_{i_j} \neq \sigma_{i_j}} \Pr[(s', L) \leftarrow \mathbf{Reconst}(\sigma'_{i_1}, \ldots, \sigma'_{i_t}, \sigma_{i_{t+1}}, \ldots, \sigma_{i_k}) \wedge R_{i_j} \notin L], \quad (1)
\end{aligned}$$

where the probability is taken over the distribution of S, and the random coins of **ShareGen** and $\mathcal{A}_{cheat}$.

Henceforth, we will write the above probability as $\epsilon(\Sigma, R_{i_j})$, for short.

Remark 2. For simplicity of our analysis – and similarly to the previous works – we estimate the success probability for a *single* cheater. The overall success probability for the cheating adversary can be estimated using the union bound.

Definition 3. A CISS scheme $\Sigma = (n, k, S, V, \mathbf{ShareGen}, \mathbf{Reconst})$ is called (t, ϵ)-CISS scheme if the following properties hold:

1. Perfect secrecy: At the end of the algorithm **ShareGen**, $\mathcal{A}_{listen}$ has no information about the secret s.
2. $(1 - \epsilon)$-correctness: $\epsilon(\Sigma, R_i) \leq \epsilon$ for any cheater R_i under the control of $\mathcal{A}_{cheat}$.

2.3 Unconditional Multi-Receiver Authentication Codes

In the traditional setting of unconditional authentication codes [3], there are three participants: a transmitter, a receiver and an opponent. The task of authentication codes is to prevent the opponent from deceiving the receiver by impersonation attacks and substitution attacks. Desmedt, Frankel and Yung [4] proposed a generalized notion of authentication called unconditional multi-receiver authentication (MRA). An MRA code involves one transmitter, one opponent and n receivers. When authenticating a source, the transmitter broadcasts a message to n receivers and each receiver verifies the authenticity of the message based on their own keys. If an MRA code ensures that neither the outside opponent nor the coalition of t receivers can deceive any other honest player, it is called a (t, n) MRA code.

Desmedt et al. constructed a (t, n) MRA code capable of authenticating a single message. Safavi-Naini and Wang [12] generalized Desmedt et al.'s construction to allow multiple messages to be authenticated with the same key. We will call it a (t, n) MRA code with multiple messages. We briefly describe Safavi-Naini and Wang's construction in Algorithm 1.

Let $Poly_t$ be the set of all polynomials of degree at most t over the finite filed $\mathbb{F}_q$. Define a map $f : \mathbb{F}_q \times Poly_t^{w+1} \to Poly_t$ with $f(s, P_0(x), \ldots, P_w(x)) = P_0(x) + sP_1(x) + \cdots + s^w P_w(x)$, where $P_i(x) \in Poly_t$ for $i = 0, \ldots, w$. For the ease of presentation, set $e = (P_0(x), \ldots, P_w(x))$ and express f as $f_e(s) = A_s(x)$. We also denote by $e_i = (P_0(x_i), \ldots, P_w(x_i))$ the verification key for Player R_i.

Algorithm 1 ((t, n) MRA with w messages)

Assume that $q \geq w$, where w is the number of possible messages, and that $q \geq n$. The system consists of the following steps:

1. **Key distribution:** The key distribution center (KDC) randomly generates $w + 1$ polynomials $e = (P_0(x), P_1(x), \ldots, P_w(x))$, each of degree at most t and chooses n distinct elements $x_1, x_2, \ldots, x_n$ of $\mathbb{F}_q$. KDC makes all x_i public and sends privately $(P_0(x), \ldots, P_w(x))$ to the sender T as her authentication key, and $e_i = (P_0(x_i), \ldots, P_w(x_i))$ to the receiver R_i as her verification key.
2. **Broadcast:** For a message s, T computes $A_s(x) = f_e(s) = P_0(x) + sP_1(x) + \cdots + s^w P_w(x)$ and broadcasts $(s, A_s(x))$.
3. **Verification:** R_i accepts $(s, A_s(x))$ as authentic if $A_s(x_i) = P_0(x_i) + sP_1(x_i) + \cdots + s^w P_w(x_i)$.

It is proven by Safavi-Naini and Wang that Algorithm 1 is a (t, n) MRA code in which each key can be used to authenticate up to w messages with both impersonation and substitution probability $1/q$.

Formally, we have the following property:

Property 1. The probability that t corrupt receivers and/or the outside opponent succeed in deceiving any receiver R_i is at most

$$\Pr[R_i \text{ accepts } (s_{w+1}, A_{s_{w+1}}(x)) | f_e(s_1) = A_{s_1}(x), \ldots, f_e(s_w) = A_{s_w}(x);$$
$$e_{i_1}, \ldots, e_{i_t}] = 1/q. \tag{2}$$

for any choice of $(s_{w+1}, A_{s_{w+1}}(x))$ with $s_{w+1} \neq s_i$ for $i = 1, \ldots, w$; for any choice of $(P_0(x), \ldots, P_w(x)) \in Poly_t^{w+1}$, and for any $[i_1, \ldots, i_t] \subseteq [n] \setminus \{i\}$.

3   CISS Against Rushing Adversary

In this section, we propose two CISS schemes against a rushing active adversary, $\mathcal{A}_{cheat}$, who can corrupt at most t players provided $t < k/2$. The first one restricts the number of reconstructing players to be exactly k which allows us to achieve a smaller share size compared to the case of allowing more than k players to join the reconstruction. The second one extends to general situation where the number of reconstructing players can be any value m with $k \leq m \leq n$. Since in both schemes $\mathcal{A}_{cheat}$ can corrupt at most t players, the fact that the second scheme requires larger share size implies that the higher ratio of honest players benefits the adversary. This may seem counter-intuitive, but the reason for this is that the adversary is rushing so that more honest players provide more information to her. We will emphasize this point in the proof of security.

3.1   Overview

The basic idea of our proposal is to follow the paradigm of Rabin and Ben-Or [10] that is to use unconditional authentication codes for pairwise authentication and to use the majority voting to identify cheaters. The twist of our scheme is to employ *multi-receiver* authentication codes [4,12], instead of ordinary ones. More specifically, the dealer D generates Shamir shares, denoted $v_{s,i}$, for player R_i and authenticates it using MRA codes. Then the dealer sends $v_{s,i}$, its authentication tag $v_{c,i}(x)$ (note that it is a polynomial), and the verification key to player R_i privately. Reconstruction of the secret is performed in two rounds. In the first round, each player broadcasts her share and authentication tag $(v_{s,i}, v_{c,i}(x))$. In the second round, each player broadcasts her verification key (we emphasize that in MRA each player holds different verification key). After receiving all the above information, the players vote for correctly authenticated shares, and then identify cheaters as the players who did not get enough approvals.

3.2   CISS with Restriction on Reconstructing Players

The following scheme restricts the number of reconstructing players to be exactly the threshold k.

Protocol 1 (ShareGen)
Public parameters: $x_i \in \mathbb{F}_p$ as player R_i's identifier for $i = 1, \ldots, n$.
Input: Secret $s \in \mathbb{F}_p$.
Output: A list of n shares $\sigma_1, \sigma_2, \ldots, \sigma_n$.
A dealer D performs the following:

1. Generate a random degree-$(k-1)$ polynomial $f_s(x)$ over $\mathbb{F}_p$, such that $f_s(0) = s$. Compute $v_{s,i} = f_s(x_i)$, for $i \in [n]$.

2. Uniformly at random, generate $e = (P_0(x), \ldots, P_{k+t_{max}}(x))$ that is an authentication key for a (t, n) MRA code with $k + t_{max}$ messages, where $t_{max} = min\{t - 1, n - k\}$, and $P_i(x) \in Poly_t$ is a polynomial of degree at most t over $\mathbb{F}_q$.

3. For $i \in [n]$, compute $v_{c,i}(x) = f_e(\phi(v_{s,i}, i))$ as the authentication tag for $v_{s,i}$. Note that $v_{c,i}(x) \in Poly_t$ is a polynomial of degree at most t over $\mathbb{F}_q$.

4. For $i \in [n]$, set $\sigma_i = \{v_{s,i}, v_{c,i}(x), P_0(x_i), \ldots, P_{k+t_{max}}(x_i)\}$ and distribute it privately to player R_i.

Remark 3. Note that in Step 3, we combine player's share $v_{s,i}$ with her identifier i before authentication. This is because Shamir scheme does not guarantee that each player gets distinct shares. Therefore, a cheater may simply re-use the share and authentication information submitted by any honest player – naturally it would be accepted as authentic. In order to prevent that from happening, we use the injective function $\phi(\cdot, \cdot)$ to make sure that the entities to be authenticated will be distinct for every player even if they received the same share.

Without loss of generality, assume that the first k players want to recover the secret. Moreover, let $\sigma'_i = \{v'_{s,i}, v'_{c,i}(x), P'_0(x_i), \ldots, P'_{k+t_{max}}(x_i)\}$ be the (possibly corrupt) share for player R_i.

Protocol 2 (Reconst)

Input: A list of k shares $(\sigma'_1, \ldots, \sigma'_k)$.
Output: Either $(\perp, L)$ or (s', L), where L is the list of cheaters.

Communication rounds performed by each player $i \in [k]$:
    Round 1: Announce $(v'_{s,i}, v'_{c,i}(x))$.
    Round 2: Announce $(P'_0(x_i), \ldots, P'_{k+t_{max}}(x_i))$.

Computation by players in $[k]$:

1. For $i \in [k]$, do:
   a) Use the verification key $(P'_0(x_j), \ldots, P'_{k+t_{max}}(x_j))$ to verify the authenticity of $(v'_{s,i}, v'_{c,i}(x))$, for $j \in [k]$.
   b) If less than $t + 1$ keys verify $(v'_{s,i}, v'_{c,i}(x))$ as authentic, then player R_i is put into the cheater list L.
2. If $L = \emptyset$, reconstruct $f'_s(x)$ from k shares $v'_{s,i}$ using Lagrange interpolation and output $(f'_s(0), L)$. Otherwise output $(\perp, L)$.

Remark 4. It is easy to check that in Round 2, the players can broadcast their votes regarding each player's share, instead of their verification keys. Precisely, the player R_i can use her verification key $(P_0(x_i), \ldots, P_{k+t_{max}}(x_i))$ to verify the share $(v'_{s,j}, v'_{c,j}(x))$ announced by player R_j. After verifying all the shares, R_i broadcasts a binary vector of length k indicating her votes against all the k players. Broadcasting every player's votes instead of her verification key can reduce the communication cost of **Reconst** protocol. However, this does not affect the share size.

Theorem 1. *If $t < k/2$ then the scheme described above is a (t,ϵ)-CISS against rushing adversary such that*

$$|S| = p, \quad \epsilon = \frac{k-t}{q}, \quad q \geq n \cdot p, \quad |V_i| = p \cdot q^{k+2t+1} = \frac{|S|(k-t)^{k+2t+1}}{\epsilon^{k+2t+1}}. \quad (3)$$

For proving Theorem 1, we will use the following two lemmas.

Lemma 1. *The above (k,n)-CISS has perfect secrecy, i.e. $\mathcal{A}_{listen}$ has no information about the secret s at the end of **ShareGen**.*

Proof. We can assume w.l.o.g. that the passive adversary $\mathcal{A}_{listen}$ corrupts the first $k-1$ players after **ShareGen**. $\mathcal{A}_{listen}$ will know $k-1$ Shamir shares $(v_{s,1}, \ldots, v_{s,k-1})$ from which she can get no information about the secret s due to perfect secrecy of Shamir scheme. Besides the Shamir shares, $\mathcal{A}_{listen}$ also knows the verification keys for $k-1$ players and the $k-1$ authentication tags. But the authentication key $e = (P_0(x), \ldots, P_{k+t_{max}}(x))$ is randomly generated independently of the secret s, and it decides the verification key for each player. So the verification keys leak no information about s. Moreover, the authentication tags are decided by the Shamir shares and the authentication key, they also do not give any information on the secret s. Thus we have proven that after **ShareGen**, $\mathcal{A}_{listen}$ gets no information about the secret s. □

Lemma 2. *In the above CISS, $\epsilon(\Sigma, R_i) \leq \frac{k-t}{q}$ for any player R_i under control of $\mathcal{A}_{cheat}$.*

Proof. We divide all the n players into the following two groups: The *active* group $(R_1, \ldots, R_k)$ who take part in the reconstruction phase; and the *inactive* group $(R_{k+1}, \ldots, R_n)$ who just hold their shares. Recall that $\mathcal{A}_{cheat}$ can corrupt at most t players. Assume $\mathcal{A}_{cheat}$ corrupts t' players in the active group and t'' players in the inactive group such that $t' + t'' = t$. Note that $t' \geq 1$ (which implies $t'' \leq t-1$), since $\mathcal{A}_{cheat}$ has to corrupt at least one player in the active group in order to cheat the honest players. Combining this observation with $t'' \leq n - k$, we get $t'' \leq t_{max} = min\{t-1, n-k\}$. Suppose w.l.o.g. that $\mathcal{A}_{cheat}$ corrupts $R_1, \ldots, R_{t'}$ in the active group and $R_{k+1}, \ldots, R_{k+t''}$ in the inactive group. Remember that since the adversary $\mathcal{A}_{cheat}$ is rushing, she can see all the communication of honest players during each round, prior to deciding her own messages. Denote the verification key for R_i by $e_i = (P_0(x_i), \ldots, P_{k+t_{max}}(x_i))$. We summarize the view of the adversary in Table 2.

Suppose w.l.o.g. that player R_1 under control of $\mathcal{A}_{cheat}$ submits a forged share $\sigma'_1 = \{v'_{s,1}, v'_{c,1}(x), e'_1\}$. If R_1 is not identified as a cheater, then at least one honest player will accept $(v'_{s,1}, v'_{c,1}(x))$ as authentic. At the end of the first round R_1 has to submit $(v'_{s,1}, v'_{c,1}(x))$ with $v'_{s,1} \neq v_{s,1}$. At that time, she can see $(v_{s,1}, \ldots, v_{s,k+t''})$, $(v_{c,1}(x), \ldots, v_{c,k+t''}(x))$, and $(e_1, \ldots, e_{t'})$, $(e_{k+1}, \ldots, e_{k+t''})$. From the $t'+t'' = t$ verification keys and the $k+t''$ authentication tags R_1 cannot generate a new authentication tag for $\phi(v'_{s,1}, x_1)$. This is because $t'' \leq t_{max}$, so $k + t'' \leq k + t_{max}$. Recall that we use (t,n) MRA with $k + t_{max}$ messages in the **ShareGen** Protocol. At the end of round 1, $\mathcal{A}_{cheat}$ has seen at most $k + t_{max}$

Table 2. View of $\mathcal{A}_{cheat}$ in **Reconst**

First round	Second round
$(v_{s,1}, v_{c,1}(x), e_1)$	$(v_{s,1}, v_{c,1}(x), e_1)$
$\dots$	$\dots$
$(v_{s,t'}, v_{c,t'}(x), e_{t'})$	$(v_{s,t'}, v_{c,t'}(x), e_{t'})$
$(v_{s,t'+1}, v_{c,t'+1}(x))$	$(v_{s,t'+1}, v_{c,t'+1}(x), e_{t'+1})$
$\dots$	$\dots$
$(v_{s,k}, v_{c,k}(x))$	$(v_{s,k}, v_{c,k}(x), e_k)$
$(v_{s,k+1}, v_{c,k+1}(x), e_{k+1})$	$(v_{s,k+1}, v_{c,k+1}(x), e_{k+1})$
$\dots$	$\dots$
$(v_{s,k+t''}, v_{c,k+t''}(x), e_{k+t''})$	$(v_{s,k+t''}, v_{c,k+t''}(x), e_{k+t''})$

authentication tags and knows t verification keys. By Equation (2) in Property 1 we have for any honest player R_j where $j \in [k] \setminus [t']$,

$$\Pr[R_j \text{ accepts } (v'_{s,1}, v'_{c,1}(x))| \text{ the view of } \mathcal{A}_{cheat}] = 1/q.$$

The probability that one honest player accepts R_1's fake share is $1/q$. Now we consider the optimal strategy for the adversary $\mathcal{A}_{cheat}$. Given the construction of the CISS scheme, especially the use of (t, n) MRA code with $k + t_{max}$ messages, no matter how the adversary distributes his corruption between the active group and inactive group, he can not get advantage over the MRA code. Thus the optimal choice for $\mathcal{A}_{cheat}$ is to corrupt t players in the active group so that any cheater under her control only needs to get one vote of support from the honest players (since the cheaters will surely support each other). Then, there are $k - t$ honest players whom R_1 can cheat. By the union bound, the probability that R_1 will not be identified as a cheater is at most $(k - t)/q$, which concludes the proof. □

Proof of Theorem 1: Combining Lemmas 1 and 2, it is easy to see that the above scheme is a (t, ϵ)-CISS with $t < k/2$ and $\epsilon = \frac{k-t}{q}$. Let us now calculate the share size. Each player gets her share $\sigma_i = (v_{s_i}, v_{c_i}(x), e_i)$, where $v_{s_i} \in \mathbb{F}_p$, $v_{c_i}(x) \in Poly_t$ and $e_i \in \mathbb{F}_q^{k+t_{max}+1}$. So the share size is $|V_i| = p \cdot q^{t+1+k+t_{max}+1} = pq^{k+t+t_{max}+2}$. Taking $p = |S|$, $q = \frac{k-t}{\epsilon}$ and $t_{max} = min\{t - 1, n - k\}$, one gets the desired results in Theorem 1. Note that for the ease of presentation, we take $t_{max} = t - 1$. □

Remark 5. The restriction on the number of shares present at the reconstruction can be achieved even if more than k players are present. Trivially, the players can decide that only some (e.g., k randomly chosen) shares should be input into the reconstruction algorithm, while the rest of the players never disclose their shares. A problem of this solution is that even a single cheater will be able to disrupt the reconstruction.

If we assume that the active adversary $\mathcal{A}_{cheat}$ can only corrupt the players in the active group (i.e., the players who participate in the reconstruction phase), then we can use a (t, n) MRA code with k messages and get a scheme with even smaller share size. We summarize this observation in Theorem 2.

Theorem 2. *Under the assumption that $\mathcal{A}_{cheat}$ can only corrupt the players in the active group and $t < k/2$, we get a (t,ϵ)-CISS against rushing adversary such that*

$$|S| = p, \ \epsilon = \frac{k-t}{q}, \ q \geq n \cdot p, \ |V_i| = p \cdot q^{k+t+2} = \frac{|S|(k-t)^{k+t+2}}{\epsilon^{k+t+2}}. \qquad (4)$$

We note that the later CISS scheme has the smallest known share size among existing CISS schemes in the same category.

3.3 (k, n)-CISS without Restriction on Reconstructing Players

In the general case, we may not be able to restrict the number of shares appearing at the reconstruction. Moreover, we may encounter a problem mentioned in Remark 5. Therefore, we extend the construction of the previous subsection to fit a general setting where the number of reconstructing players m can be any value between (and including) k and n.

The general scheme is almost identical to the restricted version in the last subsection except that we use the MRA code capable of authenticating n messages, thus increases the share size slightly. For completeness, we provide the scheme below.

As before, all the players are divided into active group $(R_1, \ldots, R_m)$ and inactive group $(R_{m+1}, \ldots, R_n)$.

CISS scheme with $k \leq m \leq n$ reconstructing players.

Protocol 3 (ShareGen-General)

Public parameter: $x_i \in \mathbb{F}_p$ as player R_i's identifier for $i = 1, \ldots, n$.

Input: Secret $s \in \mathbb{F}_p$.

Output: A list of n shares $\sigma_1, \sigma_2, \ldots, \sigma_n$.

A dealer D performs the following:

1. Generate a random degree-$(k-1)$ polynomial $f_s(x)$ over $\mathbb{F}_p$, such that $f_s(0) = s$. Compute $v_{s,i} = f_s(x_i)$, for $i \in [n]$.
2. Uniformly at random, generate authentication key $e = (P_0(x), \ldots, P_n(x))$ for a (t, n) MRA code with n messages, where $P_i(x) \in Poly_t$ is a polynomial of degree at most t over $\mathbb{F}_q$.
3. For $i \in [n]$, compute $v_{c,i}(x) = f_e(\phi(v_{s,i}, i))$ as the authentication tag for $v_{s,i}$, where $v_{c,i}(x) \in Poly_t$ is a polynomial of degree at most t over $\mathbb{F}_q$.
4. For $i \in [n]$, set $\sigma_i = (v_{s,i}, v_{c,i}(x), e_i)$ and distribute it privately to player R_i, where $e_i = (P_0(x_i), \ldots, P_n(x_i))$ is the verification key of R_i.

Protocol 4 (Reconst-General)

Input: A list of m shares $(\sigma'_1, \ldots, \sigma'_m)$.
Output: Either $(\perp, L)$ or (s', L), where L is the list of cheaters.

Communication rounds performed by each player $i \in [m]$:
    Round 1: Announce $(v'_{s,i}, v'_{c,i}(x))$.
    Round 2: Announce e'_i.

Computation by players in $[m]$:

1. For $i \in [m]$, do:
    a) Use the verification key e_j to verify the authenticity of $(v'_{s,i}, v'_{c,i}(x))$, for $j \in [m]$.
    b) If less than $t + 1$ verification keys accept $(v'_{s,i}, v'_{c,i}(x))$ as authentic, then player R_i is put into the cheater list L.
2. If $m - |L| \geq k$, reconstruct $f'_s(x)$ from $m - |L|$ shares $v'_{s,i}$ using the Lagrange interpolation
    a) If degree of $f'_s(x)$ is at most k, output $(f'_s(0), L)$.
    b) Otherwise output $(\perp, L)$.
3. If $m - |L| < k$, output $(\perp, L)$.

Theorem 3. *If $t < k/2$ then the scheme described above is a (t, ϵ)-CISS against rushing adversary (with no restriction on the number of reconstructing players) such that*

$$|S| = p, \quad \epsilon = \frac{n - t}{q}, \quad q \geq n \cdot p, \quad |V_i| = p \cdot q^{n+t+2} = \frac{|S|(n-t)^{n+t+2}}{\epsilon^{n+t+2}}. \quad (5)$$

Proof (sketch). Perfect secrecy is shown by the same argument as in the proof of Lemma 1.

For $(1 - \epsilon)$-correctness, note that the rushing adversary $\mathcal{A}_{cheat}$ can observe at most n authentication tags after Round 1 of **Reconst-General**. Since $\mathcal{A}_{cheat}$ can corrupt at most t players, clearly she can get the verification keys of at most t players. Since **ShareGen-General** uses (t, n) MRA code with n messages to authenticate the shares, the argument for $(1 - \epsilon)$-correctness follows from that of Lemma 2. An important difference is that this time, there are at most $m - t$ honest players whom $\mathcal{A}_{cheat}$ can cheat. So that the upper bound of cheating probability is $\epsilon = \frac{n-t}{q}$ which is computed for the case when all the players appear at the reconstruction phase.

The remaining task is just to evaluate the share size. Again, we have got $\sigma_i = (v_{s,i}, v_{c,i}(x), e_i)$, where $v_{s,i} \in \mathbb{F}_p$, $v_{c,i}(x) \in Poly_t$ and $e_i \in \mathbb{F}_q^{n+1}$. Therefore, the share size is $|V_i| = p \cdot q^{t+1+n+1} = pq^{n+t+2}$. Taking $p = |S|$ and $q = (n - t)/\epsilon$, we get the results claimed in Theorem 3. □

Remark 6. From the above proof, we can see that the higher ratio of honest players leaks more information to the rushing adversary and provides more targets for the adversary to attack. Thus, it is not surprising that our general scheme requires larger share size than its restricted version. We also note that the proof of Choundury [2] did not pay attention to this phenomenon and the failure probability and share size in their proposal is written incorrectly. The correct share size should be $|V_i| = |S|(n-t)^{3n}/\epsilon^{3n}$ for a single secret rather than $|V_i| = |S|(t+1)^{3n}/\epsilon^{3n}$. However, this does not affect the performance of his scheme in the asymptotic case, since one usually takes $n << 1/\epsilon$.

4   CISS against Non-Rushing Adversary

Our proposal follows the same pattern as the two previous schemes, but now we can perform reconstruction in a single round. Also, we only need to take care of t shares available to the adversary A_{cheat}. This allows us to reduce the share size, as compared to the previous schemes. For completeness, we provide a description of our protocol below.

Protocol 5 (ShareGen-NR)

Public parameter: $x_i \in \mathbb{F}_p$ as player R_i's identifier for $i = 1, \ldots, n$.

Input: Secret $s \in \mathbb{F}_p$.

Output: A list of n shares $\sigma_1, \sigma_2, \ldots, \sigma_n$.

A dealer D performs the following:

1. Generate a random degree-$(k-1)$ polynomial $f_s(x)$ over $\mathbb{F}_p$, such that $f_s(0) = s$. Compute $v_{s,i} = f_s(x_i)$, for $i \in [n]$.
2. Randomly and uniformly generate authentication key $e = (P_0(x), \ldots, P_t(x))$ for a (t, n) MRA code with t messages, where $P_i(x) \in Poly_t$ is a polynomial of degree at most t over $\mathbb{F}_q$.
3. For $i \in [n]$, compute $v_{c,i}(x) = f_e(\phi(v_{s,i}, i))$ as the authentication tag for $v_{s,i}$, where $v_{c,i}(x) \in Poly_t$ is a polynomial of degree at most t over $\mathbb{F}_q$.
4. For $i \in [n]$, set $\sigma_i = \{v_{s,i}, v_{c,i}(x), P_0(x_i), \ldots, P_t(x_i)\}$ and distribute it privately to player R_i.

Without loss of generality, assume that the first $m \geq k$ players want to recover the secret.

Protocol 6 (Reconst-NR)

Input: A list of m shares $(\sigma_1', \ldots, \sigma_m')$.

Output: Either $(\perp, L)$ or (s', L), where L is the list of cheaters.

Communication rounds performed by each player $i \in [m]$:

Round 1: Announce $(v_{s,i}', v_{c,i}'(x), P_0'(x_i), \ldots, P_t'(x_i))$.

Computation by players in $[m]$:

1. For $i \in [m]$, do:
   a) Use the verification key $(P_0'(x_j), \ldots, P_t'(x_j))$ to verify the authenticity of $(v_{s,i}', v_{c,i}'(x))$, for $j \in [m]$.
   b) If less than $t + 1$ verification keys accept $(v_{s,i}', v_{c,i}'(x))$ as authentic, then player R_i is put into the cheater list L.

2. If $m - |L| \geq k$, reconstruct $f'_s(x)$ from $m - |L|$ shares $v'_{s,i}$ using Lagrange interpolation
   a) If degree of $f'_s(x)$ is at most k, output $(f'_s(0), L)$.
   b) Otherwise output $(\perp, L)$.
3. If $m - |L| < k$, output $(\perp, L)$.

Theorem 4. *If $t < k/2$ then the scheme described above is a (t,ϵ)-CISS against non-rushing adversary such that*

$$|S| = p, \quad \epsilon = \frac{n-t}{q}, \quad q \geq n \cdot p, \quad |V_i| = p \cdot q^{2t+2} = \frac{|S|(n-t)^{2t+2}}{\epsilon^{2t+2}}. \tag{6}$$

Proof (sketch). Perfect secrecy is easy to show similarly to the proof of Lemma 1.

Note that now the active adversary $\mathcal{A}_{cheat}$ is non-rushing. So that she can get the view of at most t players. Since the above scheme uses (t, n) MRA codes with t messages, the adversary can successfully generate a fake share and its authentication tag with probability $1/q$. When all players get involved in the reconstruction phase, there are at most $n - t$ honest players for $\mathcal{A}_{cheat}$ to cheat. Thus, the cheating probability for a cheater is $\epsilon = (n - t)/q$, and the share size follows easily.   □

Remark 7. Assume that a trusted third party (usually called a reconstructor) collects the shares from the players, and then runs the reconstruction algorithm on them. If we assume in addition that the parties submit their shares to the reconstructor over point-to-point private channels, then the rushing adversary has exactly the same power as the non-rushing one.

5   Improvement of IWSEC 2013 Scheme

Xu et al. [15] presented a (t, ϵ)-CISS scheme capable of identifying $t < k/3$ rushing cheaters with share size $|V_i| = \frac{|S|}{\epsilon^{n-t+1}}$. We make a proposal to improve the share size of their scheme to $|V_i| = \frac{|S|}{\epsilon^{n-\lfloor(k-1)/3\rfloor+1}}$. The intuition for the improvement comes from a somewhat counter-intuitive property that the larger number of cheaters t require the smaller share size. Therefore, replacing it with a maximum possible value will lead to improving the share size for any t.

Next, we briefly describe the **ShareGen** protocol by Xu et al.

1. For a secret $s \in \mathbb{F}_p$, the dealer D generates Shamir share $v_{s,i}$ for each player R_i.
2. The dealer D generates a random polynomial $g(x) \in Poly_t$ over $\mathbb{F}_q$ as the authentication key.
3. The dealer authenticates each share $v_{s,i}$ using $g(x)$ and the corresponding tag is $v_{c,i} = g(\phi(v_{s,i}, i))$, where x_i is the public identifier for player R_i and $\phi(\cdot, \cdot)$ is an injective function.
4. For $i \in [t]$, set $\overline{v}_{c,i} = v_{c,i}$; for $i \in [n] \setminus [t]$, set $\overline{v}_{c,i} = v_{c,i} + k_i$ where k_i is the one-time pad key.

5. For $i \in [n] \setminus [t]$ share the key k_i among the n players using a $(t+1, n)$ Shamir secret sharing scheme. Each player R_j's share for k_i is denoted $k_{j,i}$.
   6. The share for player R_i is $\sigma = (v_{s,i}, \bar{v}_{c,i}, k_{i,t+1}, \ldots, k_{i,n})$.

Player R_i's share consists of $v_{s,i} \in \mathbb{F}_p$, $\bar{v}_{c,i} \in \mathbb{F}_q$ and $n - t$ shares for the one-time pad keys. So the share size is $|V_i| = p \cdot q^{n-t+1}$. As we mentioned above, the share size increases while the number of cheaters decreases. For example, when there is only one cheater, the share size will get to its maximum $|V_i| = p \cdot q^n$.

Therefore, instead of generating a polynomial of degree at most t, the dealer must always generate a polynomial $g(x)$ of degree at most $\lfloor k-1/3 \rfloor$ to authenticate the Shamir shares in the above step 2. Then, the $\lfloor k-1/3 \rfloor$ of the authentication tags do not need to be encrypted since the polynomial $g(x)$ serves as strongly universal$_{\lfloor k-1/3 \rfloor + 1}$ hash function (see the detailed explanation in [15]). Therefore, the number of encryption keys will be reduced to $n - \lfloor k-1/3 \rfloor$. Correspondingly, the share size in Xu et al.'s scheme can be reduced to $|V_i| = |S|/\epsilon^{n - \lfloor (k-1)/3 \rfloor + 1}$ that does not depend on the number of cheaters.

6   Conclusion

We presented CISS schemes tolerating $t < k/2$ cheaters, which utilize the properties of multi-receiver authentication codes to reduce the share size, as compared to the existing constructions based on traditional message authentication codes. From our CISS against rushing adversary, we get a somewhat counter-intuitive observation that higher ratio of honest players benefits the rushing adversary. On the one hand, this is true because the rushing adversary gets more information and more targets to attack. On the other hand, this problem might be circumvented by more sophisticated constructions. For example, when more than k players participate in the reconstruction phase, we can incorporate Reed-Solomon error correction into our CISS scheme in order to reduce the success probability of cheaters. This will be a direction for our future work.

Acknowledgments. R.X. is supported by The China Scholarship Council, No. 201206340057. K.M. is supported by a *kakenhi* Grant-in-Aid for Young Scientists (B) 24700013 from Japan Society for the Promotion of Science.

The authors would like to thank the anonymous reviewers of IWSEC 2014 for their helpful comments.

References

1. Blarkley, G.R.: Safeguarding cryptographic keys. In: Proceedings of AFIPS 1979 National Computer Conference, vol. 48, pp. 313–317 (1979)
2. Choudhury, A.: Brief announcement: optimal amortized secret sharing with cheater identification. In: Kowalski, D., Panconesi, A. (eds.) Proceedings of the 2012 ACM Symposium on Principles of Distributed Computing (PODC 2012), pp. 101–102. ACM, New York (2012)

3. Simmons, G.J.: A survey of information authentication. Proceedings of the IEEE 76(5), 603–620 (1988)
4. Desmedt, Y., Frankel, Y., Yung, M.: Multi-receiver/multi-sender network security: efficient authenticated multicast/feedback. In: Eleventh Annual Joint Conference of the IEEE Computer and Communications Societies, INFOCOM 1992, pp. 2045–2054. IEEE (1992)
5. Canetti, R.: Security and composition of multiparty cryptographic protocols. Journal of Cryptology 13(1), 143–202 (2000)
6. Kurosawa, K., Obana, S., Ogata, W.: t-cheater identifiable (k, n) threshold secret sharing schemes. In: Coppersmith, D. (ed.) CRYPTO 1995. LNCS, vol. 963, pp. 410–423. Springer, Heidelberg (1995)
7. Martin, K.M.: Challenging the adversary model in secret sharing schemes. In: Coding and Cryptography II. Proceedings of the Royal Flemish Academy of Belgium for Science and the Arts, pp. 45–63 (2008)
8. McEliece, R.J., Sarwate, D.V.: On sharing secrets and Reed-Solomon codes. Commun. ACM 24(9), 583–584 (1981)
9. Obana, S.: Almost optimum t-Cheater Identifiable secret sharing schemes. In: Paterson, K.G. (ed.) EUROCRYPT 2011. LNCS, vol. 6632, pp. 284–302. Springer, Heidelberg (2011)
10. Rabin, T., Ben-Or, M.: Verifiable secret sharing and multiparty protocols with honest majority. In: Johnson, D.S. (ed.) Proceedings of the Twenty-first Annual ACM Symposium on Theory of Computing (STOC 1989), pp. 73–85. ACM, New York (1989)
11. Reed, I.S., Solomon, G.: Polynomial codes over certain finite fields. J. Soc. Ind. Appl. Math. 8(2), 300–304 (1960)
12. Safavi-Naini, R., Wang, H.: New results on multi-receiver authentication codes. In: Nyberg, K. (ed.) EUROCRYPT 1998. LNCS, vol. 1403, pp. 527–541. Springer, Heidelberg (1998)
13. Shamir, A.: How to Share a Secret. Commun. ACM 22(11), 612–613 (1979)
14. Tompa, M., Woll, H.: How to share a secret with cheaters. In: Odlyzko, A.M. (ed.) CRYPTO 1986. LNCS, vol. 263, pp. 261–265. Springer, Heidelberg (1987), Journal version in: J. Cryptol. 1(2), 133–138 (1988)
15. Xu, R., Morozov, K., Takagi, T.: On cheater identifiable secret sharing schemes secure against rushing adversary. In: Sakiyama, K., Terada, M. (eds.) IWSEC 2013. LNCS, vol. 8231, pp. 258–271. Springer, Heidelberg (2013)

Cheating Detectable Secret Sharing Schemes Supporting an Arbitrary Finite Field*

Satoshi Obana and Kazuya Tsuchida

Hosei University, Japan
obana@hosei.ac.jp

Abstract. In this paper, we present k-out-of-n threshold secret sharing scheme which can detect share forgery by at most $k-1$ cheaters. Though, efficient schemes with such a property are presented so far, some schemes cannot be applied when a secret is an element of $\mathbb{F}_{2^N}$ and some schemes require a secret to be an element of a multiplicative group. The schemes proposed in the paper possess such a merit that a secret can be an element of arbitrary finite field. Let $|\mathcal{S}|$ and ϵ be the size of secret and successful cheating probability of cheaters, respectively. Then the sizes of share $|\mathcal{V}_i|$ of two proposed schemes respectively satisfy $|\mathcal{V}_i| = (2 \cdot |\mathcal{S}|)/\epsilon$ and $|\mathcal{V}_i| = (4 \cdot |\mathcal{S}|)/\epsilon$ which are only 2 and 3 bits longer than the existing lower bound.

Keywords: Secret Sharing, Cheating Detection, Arbitrary Finite Field.

1 Introduction

Secret sharing scheme is a fundamental primitive in designing various cryptographic protocols in distributed environment. It enables us to securely manage a secret in a way that only a qualified set of users can recover the secret and no information about the secret is revealed to non-qualified set of users. Because of its importance, secret sharing have been studied actively so far since the seminal paper by Shamir [23] and Blakley [4].

Tompa and Woll have pointed out that in Shamir's k-out-of-n threshold secret sharing scheme is vulnerable to share forgery [24]. More precisely, they pointed out that even a single user can cheat other users with probability 1 by submitting forged shares in Shamir's threshold scheme. They also presented a scheme which can detect the fact of cheating when invalid shares are submitted. Since the paper by Tompa and Wall, cheating prevention has been one of the hottest issues in the study of secret sharing scheme, and various models (e.g., cheating detection [1–3, 5, 7, 8, 12, 16, 18, 19, 24], cheater identification [10, 11, 13–15, 20, 21, 25], robust secret sharing [9, 22], etc.) have been presented so far.

In this paper, we study secret sharing schemes capable of detecting cheating. More precisely, we study k-out-of-n threshold secret sharing scheme which can detect share forgery by at most $k-1$ cheaters. There are two different models for

---

* This work was supported by JSPS KAKENHI Grant Number 24800064.

M. Yoshida and K. Mouri (Eds.): IWSEC 2014, LNCS 8639, pp. 88–97, 2014.

secret sharing schemes capable of detecting such cheating. Carpentieri, De Santis and Vaccaro [7] first considered a model in which cheaters who *know* the secret try to make another user reconstruct an invalid secret. We call this model the *"CDV model."* In [19], Ogata, Kurosawa and Stinson introduced another model assuming weaker cheaters who *do not* know the secret in forging their shares. We call this model the *"OKS model."* As noted in [16], the merit of schemes secure in CDV model is that schemes are guaranteed to be secure regardless of the probability distribution of a secret to be shared. On the other hand, schemes secure in OKS model cannot guarantee security when the probability distribution of a secret is very much biased. However, once we can assume the probability distribution of a secret is not so much biased, schemes secure in OKS model possess a particular merit in that the size of share can be made smaller than schemes secure in CDV model. In fact, it is shown in [19] that when a secret is uniformly distributed, the lower bound of the size of share $|\mathcal{V}_i|$ is $(|\mathcal{S}| - 1)/\epsilon^2 + 1$ in CDV model, whereas the lower bounds of the size of share in the OKS model is $(|\mathcal{S}| - 1)/\epsilon + 1$ where $|\mathcal{S}|$ and ϵ denote the size of the secret to be shared and the successful cheating probability of cheaters. Therefore, when we want to share a small size of secret, and we require a security level of $\epsilon \approx 1/|\mathcal{S}|$ (which is often the case when sharing a small size of secret), the lower bound of bit length of share in OKS model is about 33% shorter than the bound in CDV model.

The contribution of the paper is to present cheating detectable k-out-of-n threshold secret sharing schemes which are suitable for sharing a small size of secret (i.e., $\epsilon \approx 1/|\mathcal{S}|$) and are proven to be secure against $k - 1$ cheaters in OKS model. The proposed schemes possess an extra merit in that they support an arbitrary finite field, that is, the proposed schemes guarantee security no matter what finite field a secret belongs to. We note that the proposed schemes are the first schemes which possesses such a property. Though efficient schemes suitable for sharing a small size of secret are presented so far [3, 8, 17, 19], some schemes cannot be applied when a secret is an element of $\mathbb{F}_{2^N}$ and some schemes require a secret to be an element of a multiplicative group or an element of a special type of a finite field or an additive group. Therefore, to show the existence of schemes supporting an arbitrary finite field is interesting from a theoretical point of view. Furthermore, when we employ secret sharing scheme as a building block of cryptographic protocols, supporting an arbitrary finite field will become a highly desired property. For example, consider a case in which we want to execute computation over an elliptic curve over $\mathbb{F}_{3^N}$ in a distributed manner using secure multi-party computation (MPC for short). In such the case, we must employ a secret sharing scheme supporting $\mathbb{F}_{3^N}$ since the algebraic structure must be preserved to enable MPC. Since today's cryptographic protocol often uses multiple algebraic structures (e.g., $\mathbb{F}_{2^N}, \mathbb{F}_{3^N}$, and $\mathbb{F}_p$) in a single protocol, a secret sharing scheme employed as a building block of such a protocol is desired to support as many mathematical structures as possible for easy implementation of the protocol, which motivate us to consider a cheating detectable secret sharing schemes supporting an arbitrary finite field.

The proposed schemes are not only capable of supporting an arbitrary finite field but also efficient with respect to sizes of shares. Let $|\mathcal{S}|$ and ϵ be the size of secret and successful cheating probability of cheaters, respectively. Then the sizes of share $|V_i|$ of two proposed schemes respectively satisfy $|\mathcal{V}_i| = (2 \cdot |\mathcal{S}|)/\epsilon$ and $|\mathcal{V}_i| = (4 \cdot |\mathcal{S}|)/\epsilon$ which are only 2 and 3 bits longer than the lower bound.

It should be noted that here we focus on the problem of detecting cheating by cheaters with unlimited computational power, and therefore, schemes based on computational assumptions (e.g., [20]) are not within the scope of this paper.

2 Preliminaries

2.1 Secret Sharing Schemes

In secret sharing schemes, there are n users $\mathcal{P} = \{P_1, \ldots, P_n\}$ and a dealer D. The set of users who are allowed to reconstruct the secret is characterized by an *access structure* $\Gamma \subseteq 2^{\mathcal{P}}$; that is, users $P_{i_1}, \ldots, P_{i_k}$ are allowed to reconstruct the secret if and only if $\{P_{i_1}, \ldots, P_{i_k}\} \in \Gamma$ (for instance, the access structure of a k-out-of-n threshold secret sharing scheme is defined by $\Gamma = \{\mathcal{A} \mid \mathcal{A} \in 2^{\mathcal{P}}, |\mathcal{A}| \geq k\}$.) A model consists of two algorithms: ShareGen and Reconst. Share generation algorithm ShareGen takes a secret $s \in \mathcal{S}$ as input and outputs a list $(v_1, v_2, \ldots, v_n)$. Each $v_i \in \mathcal{V}_i$ is called a *share* and is given to a user P_i. In a usual setting, ShareGen is invoked by the dealer. Secret reconstruction algorithm Reconst takes a list of shares and outputs a secret $s \in \mathcal{S}$.

A secret sharing scheme is called *perfect* if the following two conditions are satisfied for the output $(v_1, \ldots, v_n)$ of ShareGen($\hat{s}$) where the probabilities are taken over the random tape of ShareGen.

1. if $\{P_{i_1}, \ldots, P_{i_k}\} \in \Gamma$ then $\Pr[\text{Reconst}(v_{i_1}, \ldots, v_{i_k}) = \hat{s}] = 1$,
2. if $\{P_{i_1}, \ldots, P_{i_k}\} \notin \Gamma$ then $\Pr[\mathcal{S} = s \mid \mathcal{V}_{i_1} = v_{i_1}, \ldots, \mathcal{V}_{i_k} = v_{i_k}] = \Pr[\mathcal{S} = s]$ for any $s \in \mathcal{S}$.

2.2 Secret Sharing Schemes Secure against Cheating

A secret sharing schemes capable of detecting cheating was first presented by Tompa and Woll [24]. They considered the scenario in which cheaters who do not belong to the access structure submit forged shares in the secret reconstruction phase. Such cheaters will succeed if another users in the reconstruction accepts an incorrect secret.

As in ordinary secret sharing schemes, this model consists of two algorithms. A share generation algorithm ShareGen is the same as that in the ordinary secret sharing schemes. A secret reconstruction algorithm Reconst is slightly changed: it takes a list of shares as input and outputs either a secret or the special symbol $\perp$ ($\perp \notin \mathcal{S}$.) Reconst outputs $\perp$ if and only if cheating has been detected. To formalize the models, we define the following simple game for any (k, n) threshold secret sharing scheme $\mathbf{SS} = (\text{ShareGen}, \text{Reconst})$ and for any (not necessarily polynomially bounded) Turing machine $\mathcal{A} = (\mathcal{A}_1, \mathcal{A}_2)$, where $\mathcal{A}$ represents cheaters

$P_{i_1}, \ldots, P_{i_{k-1}}$ who try to cheat P_{i_k}. Please note that we will focus on the (k, n) threshold type access structure throughout the paper.

Game($\mathbf{SS}, \mathcal{A}$)
$\qquad s \leftarrow \mathcal{S}; \quad$ // according to the probability distribution over $\mathcal{S}$.
$\qquad (v_1, \ldots, v_n) \leftarrow \mathsf{ShareGen}(s);$
$\qquad (i_1, \ldots, i_{k-1}) \leftarrow \mathcal{A}_1(X);$
$\qquad$ // set $X = s$ for the CDV model, $X = \emptyset$ for the OKS model.
$\qquad (v'_{i_1}, \ldots, v'_{i_{k-1}}, i_k) \leftarrow \mathcal{A}_2(v_{i_1}, \ldots, v_{i_{k-1}}, X);$

The advantage of cheaters is expressed as $Adv(\mathbf{SS}, \mathcal{A}) = \Pr[s' \in \mathcal{S} \wedge s' \neq s]$, where $s' = \mathsf{Reconst}(v'_{i_1}, v'_{i_2}, \ldots, v'_{i_{k-1}}, v_{i_k})$ and the probability is taken over the distribution of $\mathcal{S}$, and over the random tapes of $\mathsf{ShareGen}$ and $\mathcal{A}$.

Definition 1. *A (k, n) threshold secret sharing scheme $\mathbf{SS}$ is called a (k, n, ϵ)-secure secret sharing scheme if $Adv(\mathbf{SS}, \mathcal{A}) \leq \epsilon$ for any cheater $\mathcal{A}$.*

2.3 Previous Work

In this subsection, we briefly review the known bounds and constructions of (k, n, ϵ)-secure secret sharing schemes. A lower bound for the size of shares in the CDV model is described as follows:

Proposition 1. *[7] In the CDV model, the size of shares for $(k, n, \epsilon_{\mathsf{CDV}})$-secure secret sharing schemes is lower bounded by $|\mathcal{V}_i| \geq \frac{|\mathcal{S}|}{\epsilon_{\mathsf{CDV}}}$.*

Ogata et al. improved this bound when the secret is uniformly distributed:

Proposition 2. *[19] In the CDV model, if the secret is uniformly distributed, then the size of shares $|\mathcal{V}_i|$ for $(k, n, \epsilon_{\mathsf{CDV}})$-secure secret sharing schemes is lower bounded by $|\mathcal{V}_i| \geq \frac{|\mathcal{S}|-1}{\epsilon_{\mathsf{CDV}}^2} + 1$.*

Ogata et al. also presented the lower bound for the size of shares for $(k, n, \epsilon_{\mathsf{OKS}})$-secure secret sharing scheme in the OKS model as follows.

Proposition 3. *[19] In the OKS model, the size of shares for $(k, n, \epsilon_{\mathsf{OKS}})$-secure secret sharing schemes is lower bounded by $|\mathcal{V}_i| \geq \frac{|\mathcal{S}|-1}{\epsilon_{\mathsf{OKS}}} + 1$.*

Ogata et al. presented an optimum $(k, n, \epsilon_{\mathsf{OKS}})$-secure secret sharing schemes that satisfies the bound of Proposition 3 with equality [19].

Proposition 4. *[19] There exists a $(k, n, \epsilon_{\mathsf{OKS}})$-secure secret sharing scheme in the OKS model such that $|\mathcal{V}_i| = \frac{|\mathcal{S}|-1}{\epsilon_{\mathsf{OKS}}} + 1$. The scheme is $(k, n, \epsilon_{\mathsf{OKS}})$-secure if the secret is uniformly distributed.*

Though the scheme is optimum with respect to size of share, the scheme possesses such a drawback that the parameter of the size of secret is very much limited. Namely, if we require $\epsilon \approx 1/|\mathcal{S}|$ the size of the secret $|\mathcal{S}|$ must satisfy $|\mathcal{S}| = q + 1$ where $q^2 + q + 1$ is a prime power.

Cabello, Padró and Sáez presented nearly optimum $(k, n, \epsilon_{\mathsf{OKS}})$-secure secret sharing scheme in the OKS model [8].

Proposition 5. *[8] There exists a $(k, n, \epsilon_{\mathsf{OKS}})$-secure secret sharing scheme in the OKS model such that $|\mathcal{S}| = p, |\mathcal{V}_i| = |\mathcal{S}|/\epsilon_{\mathsf{OKS}}$ and $\epsilon_{\mathsf{OKS}} = 1/p$.*

In the scheme presented in [8], a secret can be almost an arbitrary element of finite field. Though, unfortunately, the scheme does not guarantee security when a secret is an element of $\mathbb{F}_{2^N}$. More precisely, $\epsilon_{\mathsf{OKS}} = 1$ holds when we apply the scheme to a secret s such that $s \in \mathbb{F}_{2^N}$.

Araki and Ogata presented a $(k, n, \epsilon_{\mathsf{OKS}})$ schemes in the OKS model which are also nearly optimum with respect to the size of secret [3].

Proposition 6. *[3] There exists a $(k, n, \epsilon_{\mathsf{OKS}})$-secure secret sharing scheme in the OKS model such that $|\mathcal{S}| = (p-1)^N, |\mathcal{V}_i| \approx |\mathcal{S}|/\epsilon_{\mathsf{OKS}}$ and $\epsilon_{\mathsf{OKS}} = 1/(p-1)$.*

Though the scheme possesses many desired properties, a secret s must be an element of $\mathbb{Z}_p^*$ and, therefore, does not support $\mathbb{F}_{2^N}$ which is suited for dealing with digital data in current computers.

Araki and Ogata also presented a $(k, n, \epsilon_{\mathsf{OKS}})$ scheme in which a secret can be an element of an arbitrary finite field.

Proposition 7. *[3] There exists a $(k, n, \epsilon_{\mathsf{OKS}})$-secure secret sharing scheme in the OKS model such that $|\mathcal{S}| = p^N, |\mathcal{V}_i| = p^{N+2}$ and $\epsilon_{\mathsf{OKS}} = (N+1)/p$.*

Though the scheme supports an arbitrary finite field, the successful cheating probability ϵ_{OKS} must satisfy $\epsilon \geq 1/\sqrt{|\mathcal{S}|}$, which is suitable for sharing a large secret, but not necessarily suitable for sharing a small size of secret.

To summarize the previous work on secret sharing schemes capable of detecting cheating, we realize that there is no existing scheme which satisfy all the following requirements:

- The secret can be an element of an arbitrary finite field, that is, the scheme is secure no matter what finite field the secret belongs to.
- The scheme provide adequate level of security even if the size of secret is relatively small. More precisely, the scheme supports ϵ such that $\epsilon \approx 1/|\mathcal{S}|$.
- The size of share is small. It is desired that $|\mathcal{V}_i| \approx |\mathcal{S}|/\epsilon$ (i.e., nearly optimum with respect to the bound presented in Proposition 3.)

3   Proposed Schemes

In this section, we propose two efficient $(k, n, \epsilon_{\mathsf{OKS}})$-secure secret sharing schemes in the OKS model which are proven to be secure when a secret is uniformly distributed. The proposed schemes possess such a merit that a secret to be shared can be an element of an arbitrary finite field, which is not the case in most existing schemes.

The basic idea behind both constructions is to share a secret s and its check digit $A(s)$ using Shamir's k-out-of-n secret sharing scheme where both s and $A(s)$ are elements of the same finite field $\mathbb{F}$. In the proposed schemes, verification functions $A : \mathbb{F} \to \mathbb{F}$ are carefully chosen so that the successful cheating probability is small for any finite field $\mathbb{F}$. The sizes of share $|\mathcal{V}_i|$ in the proposed schemes satisfy $|\mathcal{V}_i| = (2 \cdot |\mathcal{S}|)/\epsilon_{\mathsf{OKS}}$ and $|\mathcal{V}_i| = (4 \cdot |\mathcal{S}|)/\epsilon_{\mathsf{OKS}}$, which are only two and three bits longer than the lower bound given in Proposition 3, respectively.

3.1   Scheme with a Check Digit Based on Polynomial

In the first scheme, the verification function $A : \mathbb{F} \to \mathbb{F}$ is defined by $A(s) = s^2 + s^3$. We should note that a verification function $A'(s) = s^2$ used in [8] does not guarantee security when a secret is an element of $\mathbb{F}_{2^N}$, and a verification function $A''(s) = s^3$ does not guarantee security when a secret is an element of $\mathbb{F}_{3^N}$. Nevertheless, when we use $A(s) = A'(s) + A''(s)$ as a verification function, the security of the scheme is proven for any finite field $\mathbb{F}$. The share generation algorithm ShareGen and the share reconstruction algorithm Reconst of the first scheme is described as follows where p is an arbitrary prime power.

Share Generation: On input a secret $s \in \mathbb{F}_p$, the share generation algorithm ShareGen outputs a list of shares $(v_1, \ldots, v_n)$ as follows:

1. Generate a random polynomials $f_s(x) \in \mathbb{F}_p[X]$ and $f_a(x) \in \mathbb{F}_p[X]$ of degree at most $k - 1$ such that $f_s(0) = s$ and $f_a(0) = s^2 + s^3$.
2. Compute $v_i = (f_s(i), f_a(i))$ and output $(v_1, \ldots, v_n)$.

Secret Reconstruction and Validity Check: On input a list of m shares $(v_{i_1}, \ldots, v_{i_m})$ (where $m \geq k$), the secret reconstruction algorithm Reconst outputs a secret s or $\perp$ as follows:

1. Reconstruct $\hat{f}_s(x)$ and $\hat{f}_a(x)$ from $v_{i_1}, \ldots, v_{i_m}$ using Lagrange interpolation.
2. If $\deg(\hat{f}_s) > k - 1$ or $\deg(\hat{f}_a) > k - 1$ holds, output $\perp$.
3. Compute $\hat{s} = \hat{f}_s(0)$ and $\hat{a} = \hat{f}_a(0)$.
4. Output $\hat{s}$ if $\hat{a} = \hat{s}^2 + \hat{s}^3$ holds. Otherwise Reconst outputs $\perp$.

The properties of the first scheme is summarized by the following theorem.

Theorem 1. *The above scheme is (k, n, ϵ)-secure secret sharing schemes in the OKS model with parameters $|\mathcal{S}| = p$ and $|\mathcal{V}_i| = p^2 (= (2 \cdot |\mathcal{S}|)/\epsilon)$. When the secret is uniformly distributed over $\mathbb{F}_p$, the successful cheating probability $\epsilon = \mathrm{Adv}(\mathrm{SS}, \mathcal{A})$ of any cheater $\mathcal{A}$ satisfies $\epsilon = 1/p$ if $p = 3^N$, or $\epsilon = 2/p$ otherwise.*

The size of shares in the first scheme is only two bits longer than the lower bound of Proposition 3 since $\frac{2|\mathcal{S}|}{\epsilon} < 4(\frac{|\mathcal{S}|-1}{\epsilon} + 1)$ holds when $|\mathcal{S}| > 2$.

Proof. We consider the worst case where just k users take part in secret reconstruction. This case is the worst since $\deg(\hat{f}_s) < k$ and $\deg(\hat{f}_a) < k$ hold with probability 1 in this case. Without loss of generality, we can assume users $P_1, \ldots, P_{k-1}$ are cheaters who try to cheat user P_k. Now, consider such a situation that cheater P_i $(1 \leq i \leq k - 1)$ submits a (possibly forged) share $v'_i = (v_{s,i} + \delta_{s,i}, v_{a,i} + \delta_{a,i})$ and P_1 submits a unforged share $v_k = (v_{s,k}, v_{a,k})$ to Reconst. Since $\hat{s}$ and $\hat{a}$ is computed using Lagrange interpolation, the value of $\hat{s}$ is described as follows where s is an original secret:

$$\hat{s} = \left(\sum_{i=1}^{k-1} \prod_{j=1, j \neq i}^{k} \frac{-j}{i-j} (v_{s,i} + \delta_{s,i}) \right) + \prod_{j=1}^{k-1} \frac{-j}{k-j} v_{s,k}$$

$$= \left(\sum_{i=1}^{k} \prod_{j=1, j \neq i}^{k} \frac{-j}{i-j} v_{s,i} \right) + \left(\sum_{i=1}^{k-1} \prod_{j=1, j \neq i}^{k} \frac{-j}{i-j} \delta_{s,i} \right) = s + \delta_s$$

Here, $\delta_s = \sum_{i=1}^{k-1}(\prod_{j=1,j\neq i}^{k}\frac{-j}{i-j}\delta_{s,i})$ is not only known to cheaters but also arbitrarily controlled by cheaters by choosing $\delta_{s,i}$ $(1 \leq i \leq k-1)$ appropriately. With the same discussion, $\hat{a}$ is also denoted as $\hat{a} = s^2 + s^3 + \delta_a$ where δ_a is known to and arbitrarily controlled by cheaters. Now we will evaluate the successful cheating probability ϵ of cheaters $P_1, \ldots, P_{k-1}$. From the definition of Reconst, it is clear that cheaters succeed in cheating if $\hat{a} = \hat{s}^2 + \hat{s}^3$ holds. Since $\hat{s} = s + \delta_s$ and $\hat{a} = s^2 + s^3 + \delta_a$ hold, this equation is equivalent to the following equation where $\delta_s \neq 0$:

$$3\delta_s s^2 + (3\delta_s^2 + 2\delta_s)s + \delta_s^2 + \delta_s^3 - \delta_a = 0. \tag{1}$$

Therefore, cheaters succeeds in cheating if the original secret s is a root of eq. (1). Since $\delta_s \neq 0$, it is easy to see that the coefficient of s^2 of eq. (1) (i.e., $3\delta_s$) cannot be zero if the order p of the finite field satisfy $p \neq 3^N$. Therefore, there are at most two roots for eq. (1) and the successful cheating probability ϵ satisfies $\epsilon = 2/p$ when the secret is uniformly distributed over $\mathbb{F}_p$. Now we consider the case where $p = 3^N$ holds. In this case, eq. (1) is equivalent to $2\delta_s s + \delta_s^2 + \delta_s^3 - \delta_a = 0$ since $3 = 0$ holds in $\mathbb{F}_{3^N}$. It is obvious that the number of roots of the above equation becomes one. Therefore $\epsilon = 1/p$ holds when $p = 3^N$.   □

3.2   A Scheme with a Check Digit Based on Multiplicative Inverse

The first scheme can be viewed as a patch to the scheme presented in [8] so that the resulting scheme can be secure even when the secret is an element of $\mathbb{F}_{2^N}$. In this subsection, we show how to construct a scheme supporting an arbitrary finite field in more direct manner. Namely, in the second scheme, we use multiplicative inverse as a verification function. We choose $A(s) = s^{-1}$ as a verification function because a verification function A must be a non-linear function, and multiplicative inverse is one of the most fundamental non-linear functions in finite field. Moreover, unlike s^2 and s^3, s^{-1} does not reflects a characteristics of underlying finite field when s is manipulated to $s+\delta_s$. However, multiplicative inverse s^{-1} cannot be directly used as a check digit for $s \in \mathbb{F}$ since multiplicative inverse cannot be defined when $s = 0$ holds. Therefore, we define $A(0) = 1$ (multiplicative identity of $\mathbb{F}$) as an exception so that $A : \mathbb{F} \to \mathbb{F}$ is defined for any finite field $\mathbb{F}$ and for any input $s \in \mathbb{F}$. The complete description of the second scheme is described as follows where p is an arbitrary prime power.

Share Generation: On input a secret $s \in \mathbb{F}_p$, the share generation algorithm ShareGen outputs a list of shares $(v_1, \ldots, v_n)$ as follows:

1. Generate a random polynomials $f_s(x) \in \mathbb{F}_p[X]$ and $f_a(x) \in \mathbb{F}_p[X]$ of degree at most $k-1$ such that $f_s(0) = s$ $f_a(0) = A(s)$ where $A(s)$ is defined as follows:

$$A(s) = \begin{cases} s^{-1} & (\text{if } s \neq 0) \\ 1 & (\text{if } s = 0) \end{cases}$$

2. Compute $v_i = (f_s(i), f_a(i))$ and output $(v_1, \ldots, v_n)$.

Secret Reconstruction and Validity Check: On input a list of m shares $(v_{i_1}, \ldots, v_{i_m})$, the secret reconstruction algorithm Reconst outputs a secret s or $\perp$ as follows:

1. Reconstruct $\hat{f}_s(x)$ and $\hat{f}_a(x)$ from $v_{i_1}, \ldots, v_{i_m}$ using Lagrange interpolation.
2. If $\deg(\hat{f}_s) > k - 1$ or $\deg(\hat{f}_a) > k - 1$ holds, output $\perp$.
3. Output $\hat{s}$ if $\hat{a} = A(\hat{s})$ holds, or Reconst outputs $\perp$ otherwise.

The properties of the first scheme is summarized by the following theorem.

Theorem 2. *The above scheme is (k, n, ϵ)-secure secret sharing schemes in the OKS model with parameters $|\mathcal{S}| = p$ and $|\mathcal{V}_i| = p^2 (= (4 \cdot |\mathcal{S}|)/\epsilon)$. When the secret is uniformly distributed over $\mathbb{F}_p$, the successful cheating probability $\epsilon = \text{Adv}(\mathbf{SS}, \mathcal{A})$ of any cheater $\mathcal{A}$ satisfies $\epsilon = 4/p$ if $p = 2^N$, or $\epsilon = 3/p$ otherwise.*

The size of shares in the second scheme is only three bits longer than the lower bound of Proposition 3 since $\frac{4|\mathcal{S}|}{\epsilon} < 8(\frac{|\mathcal{S}|-1}{\epsilon} + 1)$ holds when $|\mathcal{S}| > 2$.

Proof. As in the proof of Theorem 1, we consider the worst case where just k users take part in secret reconstruction and assume users $P_1, \ldots, P_{k-1}$ are cheaters who try to cheat user P_k. Now, consider such a situation that cheater P_i $(1 \leq i \leq k-1)$ submits a (possibly forged) share $v'_i = (v_{s,i} + \delta_{s,i}, v_{a,i} + \delta_{a,i})$ and P_1 submits a unforged share $v_k = (v_{s,k}, v_{a,k})$ to Reconst. As the same discussion done in proving Theorem 1, $\hat{s}$ and $\hat{a}$ reconstructed from submitted shares can be written by $\hat{s} = s + \delta_s$ and $\hat{a} = A(s) + \delta_a$, respectively, where s is an original secret, and $\delta_s \neq 0$ and δ_a are known to and arbitrarily controlled by cheaters.

Now we will evaluate the successful cheating probability ϵ of cheaters $P_1, \ldots, P_{k-1}$. From the definition of Reconst, it is clear that cheaters succeed in cheating if $A(s) + \delta_a = A(s + \delta_s)$ holds. There are the following three cases to consider, and we will clarify a condition on s, δ_s and δ_a such that cheaters succeed in cheating cheating if the condition is satisfied for each case.

Case 1 ($s = 0$ and $s + \delta_s \neq 0$): In this case, $A(s) = 1$, $\hat{s} = \delta_s$ and $\hat{a} = A(s) + \delta_a = 1 + \delta_a$ hold. Therefore, cheaters succeeds in cheating if $1 + \delta_a = \delta_s^{-1}$ (or equivalently, $\delta_a = \delta_s^{-1} - 1$) holds.
Case 2 ($s \neq 0$ and $s + \delta_s = 0$): In this case, $A(s) = s^{-1}$, $\hat{s} = s + \delta_s = 0$ and $\hat{a} = A(s) + \delta_a = s^{-1} + \delta_a$ hold. Therefore, cheaters succeeds in cheating if $s^{-1} + \delta_a = 1$ (or equivalently, $\delta_a = \delta_s^{-1} + 1$) holds.
Case 3 ($s \neq 0$ and $s + \delta_s \neq 0$): In this case, $A(s) = s^{-1}$, $\hat{s} = s + \delta_s$ and $\hat{a} = A(s) + \delta_a = s^{-1} + \delta_a$ hold. Therefore, cheaters succeeds in cheating if $s^{-1} + \delta_a = (s + \delta_s)^{-1}$ (or equivalently, $(s^{-1} + \delta_a)(s + \delta_s) = 1$) holds.

Therefore, the best strategy for cheaters is to choose δ_s and δ_a such that $\delta_a = \delta_s^{-1} - 1$ or $\delta_a = \delta_s^{-1} + 1$ holds. We will evaluate the successful cheating probability ϵ in such cases. Now suppose $p \neq 2^N$, and cheaters control $\hat{s} = s + \delta_s$ and $\hat{a} = A(s) + \delta_a$ so that they satisfy $\delta_a = \delta_s^{-1} + 1$. In this case, cheaters succeed in cheating if $s = 0$ holds or the secret s is a root of equation $(s^{-1} + \delta_a)(s + \delta_s) = 1$, which is equivalent to the following equation:

$$\delta_a s^2 + \delta_a \delta_s s + \delta_s = 0 \tag{2}$$

It is obvious that there are at most two roots which satisfy above equation. Therefore, the successful cheating probability ϵ satisfies $\epsilon = 3/p$ since there are at most three values of s with which cheaters succeeds in cheating. It is easy to see that $\epsilon = 3/p$ holds when cheaters control $\hat{s} = s + \delta_s$ and $\hat{a} = A(s) + \delta_a$ so that they satisfy $\delta_a = \delta_s^{-1} - 1$.

Now suppose $p = 2^N$. In this case $\delta_s^{-1} + 1 = \delta_s^{-1} - 1$ holds since $1 = -1$ holds in $\mathbb{F}_{2^N}$. Therefore, cheaters who control $\hat{s} = s + \delta_s$ and $\hat{a} = A(s) + \delta_a$ so that they satisfy $\delta_a = \delta_s^{-1} + 1$ succeeds in cheating with probability $4/p$ since cheater succeeds in cheating if $s = 0$ or $s + \delta_s = 0$ holds or s is a root of eq. (2).   □

4 Concluding Remarks

In this paper, we present k-out-of-n threshold secret sharing schemes which can detect share forgery by at most $k-1$ cheaters. The schemes proposed in the paper possess such a merit that a secret can be an element of arbitrary finite field. Let $|\mathcal{S}|$ and ϵ be the size of secret and successful cheating probability of cheaters, respectively. Then the sizes of share $|V_i|$ of two proposed schemes respectively satisfy $|\mathcal{V}_i| = (2 \cdot |\mathcal{S}|)/\epsilon$ and $|\mathcal{V}_i| = (4 \cdot |\mathcal{S}|)/\epsilon$ which are only 2 and 3 bits longer than the lower bound. It is easy to see that the verification function used in the proposed schemes can be apply to any linear secret sharing schemes to make them secure against share forgery by non-qualified set of users.

To construct a scheme supporting an arbitrary finite field and the size of share is smaller than the proposed schemes is our future challenge.

References

1. Araki, T.: Efficient (k,n) Threshold Secret Sharing Schemes Secure Against Cheating from $n - 1$ Cheaters. In: Pieprzyk, J., Ghodosi, H., Dawson, E. (eds.) ACISP 2007. LNCS, vol. 4586, pp. 133–142. Springer, Heidelberg (2007)
2. Araki, T., Obana, S.: Flaws in Some Secret Sharing Schemes Against Cheating. In: Pieprzyk, J., Ghodosi, H., Dawson, E. (eds.) ACISP 2007. LNCS, vol. 4586, pp. 122–132. Springer, Heidelberg (2007)
3. Araki, T., Ogata, W.: A Simple and Efficient Secret Sharing Scheme Secure against Cheating. IEICE Trans. Fundamentals E94-A(6), 1338–1345 (2011)
4. Blakley, G.R.: Safeguarding cryptographic keys. In: Proc. AFIPS 1979, National Computer Conference, vol. 48, pp. 313–317 (1979)
5. Brickell, E.F., Stinson, D.R.: The Detection of Cheaters in Threshold Schemes. SIAM Journal on Discrete Mathematics 4(4), 502–510 (1991)
6. Carpentieri, M.: A Perfect Threshold Secret Sharing Scheme to Identify Cheaters. Designs, Codes and Cryptography 5(3), 183–187 (1995)
7. Carpentieri, M., De Santis, A., Vaccaro, U.: Size of Shares and Probability of Cheating in Threshold Schemes. In: Helleseth, T. (ed.) EUROCRYPT 1993. LNCS, vol. 765, pp. 118–125. Springer, Heidelberg (1994)
8. Cabello, S., Padró, C., Sáez, G.: Secret Sharing Schemes with Detection of Cheaters for a General Access Structure. Designs, Codes and Cryptography 25(2), 175–188 (2002)

9. Cevallos, A., Fehr, S., Ostrovsky, R., Rabani, Y.: Unconditionally-secure Robust Secret Sharing with Compact Shares. In: Pointcheval, D., Johansson, T. (eds.) EUROCRYPT 2012. LNCS, vol. 7237, pp. 195–208. Springer, Heidelberg (2012)
10. Choudhury, A.: Brief announcement: Optimal Amortized Secret Sharing with Cheater Identification. In: Proc. PODC 2012, p. 101. ACM (2012)
11. Cramer, R., Damgård, I.B., Fehr, S.: On the Cost of Reconstructing a Secret, or VSS with Optimal Reconstruction Phase. In: Kilian, J. (ed.) CRYPTO 2001. LNCS, vol. 2139, pp. 503–523. Springer, Heidelberg (2001)
12. Cramer, R., Dodis, Y., Fehr, S., Padró, C., Wichs, D.: Detection of Algebraic Manipulation with Applications to Robust Secret Sharing and Fuzzy Extractors. In: Smart, N.P. (ed.) EUROCRYPT 2008. LNCS, vol. 4965, pp. 471–488. Springer, Heidelberg (2008)
13. Kurosawa, K., Obana, S., Ogata, W.: t-Cheater Identifiable (k, n) Threshold Secret Sharing Schemes. In: Coppersmith, D. (ed.) CRYPTO 1995. LNCS, vol. 963, pp. 410–423. Springer, Heidelberg (1995)
14. McEliece, R.J., Sarwate, D.V.: On Sharing Secrets and Reed-Solomon Codes. Communications of the ACM 24(9), 583–584 (1981)
15. Obana, S.: Almost Optimum t-Cheater Identifiable Secret Sharing Schemes. In: Paterson, K.G. (ed.) EUROCRYPT 2011. LNCS, vol. 6632, pp. 284–302. Springer, Heidelberg (2011)
16. Obana, S., Araki, T.: Almost Optimum Secret Sharing Schemes Secure Against Cheating for Arbitrary Secret Distribution. In: Lai, X., Chen, K. (eds.) ASIACRYPT 2006. LNCS, vol. 4284, pp. 364–379. Springer, Heidelberg (2006)
17. Ogata, W., Araki, T.: Cheating Detectable Secret Sharing Schemes for Random Bit String. IEICE Trans. Fundamentals E96-A(11), 2230–2234 (2013)
18. Ogata, W., Eguchi, H.: Cheating Detectable Threshold Scheme against Most Powerful Cheaters for Long Secrets. Designs, Codes and Cryptography (published online, October 2012)
19. Ogata, W., Kurosawa, K., Stinson, D.R.: Optimum Secret Sharing Scheme Secure against Cheating. SIAM Journal on Discrete Mathematics 20(1), 79–95 (2006)
20. Pedersen, T.P.: Non-interactive and Information-Theoretic Secure Verifiable Secret Sharing. In: Feigenbaum, J. (ed.) CRYPTO 1991. LNCS, vol. 576, pp. 129–140. Springer, Heidelberg (1992)
21. Rabin, T., Ben-Or, M.: Verifiable Secret Sharing and Multiparty Protocols with Honest Majority. In: Proc. STOC 1989, pp. 73–85 (1989)
22. Rabin, T.: Robust Sharing of Secrets When the Dealer is Honest or Cheating. Journal of the ACM 41(6), 1089–1109 (1994)
23. Shamir, A.: How to Share a Secret. Communications of the ACM 22(11), 612–613 (1979)
24. Tompa, M., Woll, H.: How to Share a Secret with Cheaters. Journal of Cryptology 1(3), 133–138 (1989)
25. Xu, R., Morozov, K., Takagi, T.: On Cheater Identifiable Secret Sharing Schemes Secure against Rushing Adversary. In: Sakiyama, K., Terada, M. (eds.) IWSEC 2013. LNCS, vol. 8231, pp. 258–271. Springer, Heidelberg (2013)

Secure Multi-Party Computation for Elliptic Curves

Koutarou Suzuki and Kazuki Yoneyama

NTT Secure Platform Laboratories
3-9-11 Midori-cho Musashino-shi Tokyo 180-8585, Japan
{suzuki.koutarou,yoneyama.kazuki}@lab.ntt.co.jp

Abstract. In this paper, we propose the first multi-party computation protocols for scalar multiplication and other basic operations on elliptic curves, which achieve constant round complexity and linear communication complexity. The key idea is adopting point addition formula without conditional branch, i.e., Edwards curve.

Keywords: multi-party computation, elliptic curve, scalar multiplication, Edwards curve.

1 Introduction

Multi-party computation (MPC) for general circuits is fundamental for cryptographic protocol researches [22,23,7,3,12]. On the other hand, another research direction is constructing efficient protocol for specific functions, i.e., integer arithmetic (addition and multiplication), comparison of values, testing equality, modulo reduction and integer division. The seminal work in this direction is done by Damgård et al. [10], which provided the first efficient constant round protocol for bit-decomposition (BD), which was firstly considered in [1]. After that, some succession works [19,17,20,15,16,18] improve communication complexity of protocols for these functions.

Our Contribution. Although all previous studies on efficient MPC protocols deal with computations in finite fields, we focus on computations on *elliptic curves*. We propose the first MPC protocols for *scalar multiplication* and other basic operations on elliptic curves, with *constant round complexity* and *linear communication complexity*.

From the theoretical point of view, we first realize a new class of algebraic operations, i.e, point addition and scalar multiplication on elliptic curve, by MPC protocols, while MPC protocols for operations on the finite fields, the Boolean algebra, and finite rings [9] have been studied well.

From the practical point of view, our MPC protocol for EC scalar multiplication can provide wider class of applications for EC-based cryptosystems than ordinary threshold EC decryption techniques. For example, the conversion between AES encrypted message and EC encrypted message without revealing the message, and the generation of EC signature on AES encrypted message without revealing the message, are possible, though these are not realizable using threshold EC decryption technique.

Problems and Our Technique. Although our construction mainly follows after the construction of exponentiation in finite fields [16], there are two difficulties in the case of EC scalar multiplication as follows.

M. Yoshida and K. Mouri (Eds.): IWSEC 2014, LNCS 8639, pp. 98–108, 2014.

First, on ordinary Weierstrass form EC, if two points to be added are same, the *point addition operation* does not work and the *doubling operation* is necessary. However, we cannot change the operation according to added values in MPC, because information about equality of input values is leaked to an adversary. Thus, we must avoid the special doubling operation. Notice that if we adopt dummy execution, we need equality checking in finite field, however this requires a large amount of communication complexity.

Second, on ordinary Weierstrass form EC, the unit element with respect to point addition in affine coordinates is in a special form, i.e., *the point at infinity*. If the unit element appears in an input of point addition, we cannot deal with it by the point addition operation, and a special procedure according to the point at infinity is necessary. However, we cannot change the operation according to added values in MPC. Hence, we must avoid the special procedure for the point at infinity. Notice that if we adopt projective coordinate, point does not have unique representation, thus privacy of point addition MPC protocol hard to be proven.

We resolve the above problems by an idea inspired by techniques against *side channel attacks* [8,13,14,6,4]. In the research field of the implementation security, side channel attacks (e.g., simple power analysis) against EC cryptosystems and the counter-measures have been actively studied. There are roughly two kinds of countermeasures: one is to add redundant computations to basic operations, and the other is to use special types of curves. In this paper, we adopt the latter approach to construct MPC protocols on EC. Specifically, we adopt Edwards form EC [11], where the addition formula can be used also for doubling, and the unit element can be represented as a point on a curve in affine coordinate as in section 2.2. Thus, the same addition formula can be applicable for all cases, and we can solve both of the above problems with Edwards form EC.

2   Preliminaries

2.1   Known MPC Techniques

Let $\mathcal{P}_1, ..., \mathcal{P}_n$ be n parties. Let p be a prime of bit length $l = \lceil \log_2 p \rceil$. We use a linear secret sharing scheme (LSSS) on $\mathbb{Z}_p$ and secure MPC protocols for addition and multiplication. We denote by $[a]_p$ that $a \in \mathbb{Z}_p$ is shared among n parties $\mathcal{P}_1, ..., \mathcal{P}_n$ by the LSSS. We also denote by $[a]_B = ([a_1]_p, ..., [a_l]_p)$ that bit representation $a_i \in \{0, 1\} \subset \mathbb{Z}_p$ of $a = \sum_{i=1}^{l} a_i 2^{i-1} \in \mathbb{Z}_p$ is shared among n parties $\mathcal{P}_1, ..., \mathcal{P}_n$ by the LSSS.

The *addition protocol* Add takes shared values $[a]_p, [b]_p$ $(a, b \in \mathbb{Z}_p)$ as input and outputs shared addition $[a+b \mod p]_p$, denoted as $[a+b \mod p]_p \leftarrow$ Add($[a]_p, [b]_p$) (denoted as $[a+b]_p$ for simplicity). The *public multiplication protocol* PubMul takes public value $k \in \mathbb{Z}_p$ and shared value $[a]_p$ $(a \in \mathbb{Z}_p)$ as input and outputs shared multiplication $[ka \mod p]_p$, denoted as $[ka \mod p]_p \leftarrow$ PubMul($k, [a]_p$) (denoted as $[ka]_p$ for simplicity). We assume both Add and PubMul can be executed without communication.

The *multiplication protocol* Mul takes shared values $[a]_p, [b]_p$ $(a, b \in \mathbb{Z}_p)$ as input and outputs shared multiplication $[ab \mod p]_p$, denoted as $[ab \mod p]_p \leftarrow$ Mul($[a]_p, [b]_p$) (denoted as $[a \cdot b]_p$ for simplicity). We assume Mul has constant round complexity with respect to l.

The *reveal protocol* Reveal takes a shared value $[a]_p$ $(a \in \mathbb{Z}_p)$ as input and outputs the value $a \in \mathbb{Z}_p$, denoted as $a \leftarrow$ Reveal($[a]_p$). Notice that we measure the round complexity of a protocol by that of Mul as unit, and the communication complexity by that of Mul as unit. We assume Reveal has 1 round complexity and $1/n$ communication complexity (in terms of the number of executions of multiplication protocol Mul).

Our protocol uses following known protocols [10,19,17,20,15,16]: The *secure inversion protocol* Inv takes a shared value $[a]_p$ ($a \in \mathbb{Z}_p$) as input and outputs shared inversion $[a^{-1} \mod p]_p$, and requires 2 round complexity and 2 communication complexity [2,10,17], denoted as $[a^{-1} \mod p]_p \leftarrow \text{Inv}([a]_p)$.

The *shared random value generation protocol* Rand takes no input and outputs shared random value $[r]_p$ ($r \in \mathbb{Z}_p$), requires 1 round complexity and 1 communication complexity [10], denoted as $[r]_p \leftarrow \text{Rand}()$.

The *conditional selection protocol* Cond takes a shared bit $[b]_p$ and shared values $[a_1]_p, [a_0]_p$ ($a_1, a_0 \in \mathbb{Z}_p$) as input and outputs shared value $[a_b]_p$, and requires 1 round complexity and 1 communication complexity [19], denoted as $[a_b]_p \leftarrow \text{Cond}([b]_p, [a_1]_p, [a_0]_p)$.

The *bitwise less-than protocol* BitLessThan takes bit-wise shared values $[a]_B, [b]_B$, ($a, b \in \mathbb{Z}_p$) as input and outputs shared bit $[a \overset{?}{<} b]_p$, requires 6 round complexity and $14l$ communication complexity [20,15], denoted as $[a \overset{?}{<} b]_p \leftarrow \text{BitLessThan}([a]_B, [b]_B)$.

The *bitwise shared random value generation protocol* SolvedBits takes no input and outputs bit-wise shared random value $[r]_B = ([r_1]_p, ..., [r_l]_p)$ ($r_i \in_U \{0, 1\} \subset \mathbb{Z}_p$) and shared random value $[r]_p$ ($r = \sum_{i=1}^{l} r_i 2^{i-1} \in \mathbb{Z}_p$), requires 7 round complexity and $56l$ communication complexity [20], denoted as $([r]_B, [r]_p) \leftarrow \text{SolvedBits}()$.

2.2 Edwards Form Elliptic Curves

We briefly introduce Edwards curve and its addition formula. For details, please refer to [11,4,5]. Let $p > 3$ be a prime and $\mathbb{Z}_p = \mathbb{F}_p$ be the prime field of order p. Let $E : x^2 + y^2 = c^2(1 + dx^2y^2)$ be a Edwards form elliptic curve defined over $\mathbb{F}_p$, where c and d are constant ($c, d \in \mathbb{F}_p$), and $cd(1 - c^4d) \neq 0$.

We describe rational point P on E by using $P = (x_P, y_P) \in \mathbb{F}_p^2$. If d is a quadratic nonresidue, the elliptic curve addition formula is given as follows. For $P = (x_P, y_P)$, $Q = (x_Q, y_Q)$ s.t. $P, Q \in E(\mathbb{F}_p)$, addition $P + Q = R = (x_R, y_R)$ of P and Q is defined by

$$x_R = \frac{x_P y_Q + y_P x_Q}{c(1 + dx_P x_Q y_P y_Q)}, \text{ and } y_R = \frac{y_P y_Q - x_P x_Q}{c(1 - dx_P x_Q y_P y_Q)}.$$

The unit element is $O = (0, c)$ (i.e., the point at infinity is not needed), and the opposite of $P = (x_P, y_P)$ is $-P = (-x_P, y_P)$, w.r.t. the elliptic curve addition defined above. Since the above addition formula works in the case that $P = Q$, the doubling formula is the same as the addition formula.

Let $G = \langle P_0 \rangle \subset E(\mathbb{F}_p)$ be cyclic group generated by point P_0 of prime order m. We can assume $m < p$ by selecting parameters appropriately.

3   Proposed MPC Protocols for Elliptic Curve Scalar Multiplication

In this section, we propose unconditionally secure multi-party computation (MPC) protocol EC-Exp-Pri (Fig.8), that securely compute elliptic curve scalar multiplication with

Table 1. Efficiency of the proposed protocols, where $l = \lceil \log_2 m \rceil$ is the bit length of m, n is the number of parties, and k is the number of inputs

Protocol	Round Complexity	Communication Complexity
$[P + Q]_p \leftarrow$ EC-Add$([P]_p, [Q]_p)$	5	11
$[P]_p$ or $[Q]_p \leftarrow$ EC-Cond$([b]_p, [P]_p, [Q]_p)$	1	2
$[R]_p \leftarrow$ EC-Rand$()$	$5\lceil \log n \rceil + 1$	$11(n-1) + 2$
$([R]_p, [aR]_p) \leftarrow$ EC-Rand-Pair(a)	$5\lceil \log n \rceil + 1$	$22(n-1) + 4$
$[\sum_{i=1}^{k} P_i]_p \leftarrow$ EC-Add-UF$([P_1]_p, ..., [P_k]_p)$	$5\lceil \log n \rceil + 18$	$11kn + 13k + 4$
$[eP]_p \leftarrow$ EC-Exp-Pub$([P]_p, e)$	$5\lceil \log n \rceil + 13$	$22n + 8$
$[eP]_p \leftarrow$ EC-Exp-Bit$([P]_p, [e]_B)$	$10\lceil \log n \rceil + 32$	$33nl + 23l + 4$
$[eP]_p \leftarrow$ EC-Exp-Pri$([P]_p, [e]_p)$	$15\lceil \log n \rceil + 71$	$33nl + 94l + 44n + 46$

private base point and private exponent, with constant round and linear communication complexity with respect to the bit length $l = \lceil \log_2 m \rceil$ of exponent m (we regard the number n of parties as constant as in previous works [10,19,17,20,15,16]). We also prepare MPC protocols for basic operations on elliptic curve, and these protocols are summarized in Table.1.

Notice that we measure the round complexity of a protocol by that of Mul as unit, and the communication complexity by that of Mul as unit. For each step of protocols shown in Figures, we describe the number of rounds R and the communication complexity C (in terms of the number of executions of multiplication protocol Mul) as the form /* R, C. */ for readability.

If underlying secret sharing scheme and multiplication protocol are perfectly secure against passive adversary, the proposed protocols are also perfectly secure against passive adversary. If underlying secret sharing scheme and multiplication protocol are perfectly or unconditionally secure against active adversary, the proposed protocols are unconditionally secure against active adversary, since we use "cut-and-choose" in protocol EC-Rand-Pair and that has negligible error.

We denote sharing of point as $[P]_p = ([x_P]_p, [y_P]_p)$. Cyclic group $G = \langle P_0 \rangle \subset E(\mathbb{Z}_p)$ of order m and generator P_0 are given to protocols as public parameter.

3.1 Elliptic Curve Addition in Edwards Form

We construct MPC protocol EC-Add (Fig.1) for elliptic curve addition.

The protocol EC-Add takes two points $[P]_p, [Q]_p$ as input and outputs the point $[P+Q]_p$. The protocol requires 5 rounds and 11 multiplications. In the protocol EC-Add, elliptic curve addition formula described in section.2.2 is computed in parallel.

The point is that point on elliptic curve has unique representation since we adopt affine coordinate, thus two inputs and output are one-to-one corresponding and this guarantees perfect privacy of the point addition MPC protocol.

Notice that, no communication is necessary to compute the opposite $[-P]_p = ([-x_P]_p, [y_P]_p)$ from $[P]_p = ([x_P]_p, [y_P]_p)$.

Protocol: $[R]_p \leftarrow$ EC-Add($[P]_p, [Q]_p$).
Inputs: $[P]_p = ([x_P]_p, [y_P]_p), [Q]_p = ([x_Q]_p, [y_Q]_p)$ s.t. $P, Q \in G$.
Outputs: $[R = P + Q]_p = ([x_R]_p, [y_R]_p)$.

1. Compute $[u = x_P \cdot y_Q]_p, [v = y_P \cdot x_Q]_p, [s = y_P \cdot y_Q]_p$, and $[t = x_P \cdot x_Q]_p$.
   /* 1, 4. */
2. Compute $[w = u \cdot v]_p$.
   /* 1, 1. */
3. Compute $[g]_p \leftarrow$ Inv($[c(1 + dw)]_p$), and $[h]_p \leftarrow$ Inv($[c(1 - dw)]_p$).
   /* 2, 4. */
4. Compute $[x_R = (u + v) \cdot g]_p$, and $[y_R = (s - t) \cdot h]_p$.
   /* 1, 2. */
5. Output $[R]_p = ([x_R]_p, [y_R]_p)$.

Fig. 1. Description of EC-Add that requires 5 rounds and 11 multiplications

---

Protocol: $[R]_p \leftarrow$ EC-Cond($[b]_p, [P]_p, [Q]_p$).
Inputs: $[b]_p$ s.t. $b \in \{0, 1\} \subset \mathbb{Z}_p, [P]_p = ([x_P]_p, [y_P]_p), [Q]_p = ([x_Q]_p, [y_Q]_p)$ s.t. $P, Q \in G$.
Outputs: $[R = P]_p$ if $b = 1$, or $[R = Q]_p$ if $b = 0$.

1. Compute $[x_R = b \cdot (x_P - x_Q) + x_Q]_p$, and $[y_R = b \cdot (y_P - y_Q) + y_Q]_p$.
   /* 1, 2. */
2. Output $[R]_p = ([x_R]_p, [y_R]_p)$.

Fig. 2. Description of EC-Cond that requires 1 rounds and 2 multiplications

3.2 Conditional Point Selection

We construct MPC protocol **EC-Cond** (Fig.2) for conditional selection of elliptic curve point.

The protocol **EC-Cond** takes a bit $[b]_p$ and two points $[P]_p, [Q]_p$ as input and outputs the point $[P]_p$ if $b = 1$ and the point $[Q]_p$ if $b = 0$. The protocol requires 1 rounds and 2 multiplications.

3.3 Random Point Generation

We construct MPC protocols **EC-Rand** (Fig.3) and **EC-Rand-Pair** (Fig.4) for random elliptic curve point generation by extending the construction of [10].

The protocol **EC-Rand** takes no input and outputs random point $[R]_p$. The protocol requires $5\lceil \log n \rceil + 1$ rounds and $11(n - 1) + 2$ multiplications.

In the protocol **EC-Rand**, each party $\mathcal{P}_i$ selects random $r_i \in_U \mathbb{Z}_m$ and computes point $R_i = r_i P_0 \in G$ using generator $P_0 \in G$, and shares it, then all party compute sum $[R = \sum_{i=1}^{n} R_i]_p$ of these using **EC-Add**. We can take the sum in $\lceil \log n \rceil$ rounds and $n - 1$ times invocations of **EC-Add** by Wallence Tree method [21], e.g., for the case of $n = 4$ we compute $P_{12} = P_1 + P_2, P_{34} = P_3 + P_4$ and then compute $P_{12} + P_{34}$.

Protocol: $[R]_p \leftarrow$ EC-Rand().

Inputs: No input.

Outputs: $[R]_p = ([x_R]_p, [y_R]_p)$ s.t. $R \in_U G$.

1. Each party $\mathcal{P}_i$ generates random point $R_i \in G$ and shares $[R_i]_p$ $(i = 1, ..., n)$.
   /* 1, 2. */
2. Compute $[R = \sum_{i=1}^n R_i]_p$ using EC-Add.
   /* $5\lceil \log n \rceil$, $11(n-1)$. */
3. Output $[R]_p$.

Fig. 3. Description of EC-Rand that requires $5\lceil \log n \rceil + 1$ rounds and $11(n-1)+2$ multiplications

---

Protocol: $([R]_p, [aR]_p) \leftarrow$ EC-Rand-Pair(a).

Inputs: $a \in \mathbb{Z}_p$

Outputs: $[R]_p = ([x_R]_p, [y_R]_p)$ s.t. $R \in_U G$ and $[aR]_p$.

1. Each party $\mathcal{P}_i$ generates random point $R_i \in G$ and computes $aR_i \in G$ and shares $[R_i]_p$ and $[aR_i]_p$ $(i = 1, ..., n)$.
   /* 1, 4. */
2. Compute $[R = \sum_{i=1}^n R_i]_p$ and $[aR = \sum_{i=1}^n aR_i]_p$ using EC-Add.
   /* $5\lceil \log n \rceil$, $22(n-1)$. */
3. Output $([R]_p, [aR]_p)$.

Fig. 4. Description of EC-Rand-Pair that requires $5\lceil \log n \rceil + 1$ rounds and $22(n-1) + 4$ multiplications

The protocol EC-Rand-Pair takes $a \in \mathbb{Z}_p$ and outputs random points $([R]_p, [aR]_p)$. The protocol requires $5\lceil \log n \rceil + 1$ rounds and $22(n-1) + 4$ multiplications.

In the protocol EC-Rand-Pair, each party $\mathcal{P}_i$ generates random point $R_i \in_U G$ and aR_i and shares them, then all party compute sums $[R = \sum_{i=1}^n R_i]_p$ and $[aR = \sum_{i=1}^n aR_i]_p$ of these using EC-Add. We can take the sums in $\lceil \log n \rceil$ rounds and $2(n-1)$ times invocations of EC-Add.

When the adversary is active, we need to ensure that (R_i, aR_i) are correctly formed with respect to constant a. To guarantee this, we can use cut-and-choose method as mentioned in [10,16]. To perform cut-and-choose checking, party $\mathcal{P}_i$ generates random $([S_k]_p, [aS_k]_p)$, computes $([S_k + R_i]_p, [aS_k + aR_i]_p)$, jointly generates a random bit, and opens and checks one of them according to the random bit. All n parties perform this procedure for $k = 1, ..., w$ in parallel. The cut-and-choose checking requires $O(1)$ rounds and $O(wn)$ multiplications.

3.4 Unbounded Fan-in Elliptic Curve Addition

We construct MPC protocols EC-Add-UF (Fig.5) for unbounded fan-in elliptic curve addition by extending the construction of [2,10].

The protocol EC-Add-UF takes k points $[P_1]_p, ..., [P_k]_p$ as input and outputs point $[\sum_{i=1}^k P_i]_p$. The protocol requires $5\lceil \log n \rceil + 17$ rounds and $11kn + 13k + 2$ multiplications.

Protocol: $[R]_p \leftarrow$ EC-Add-UF$([P_1]_p, ..., [P_k]_p)$.
Inputs: $[P_1]_p, ..., [P_k]_p$ s.t. $P_1, ..., P_k \in G$.
Outputs: $[R = \sum_{i=1}^{k} P_i]_p = ([x_R]_p, [y_R]_p)$.

1. Generate $[S_i]_p \leftarrow$ EC-Rand$()$ $(i = 1, ..., k)$.
   /* $5\lceil \log n \rceil + 1, (11(n-1) + 2)k$. */
2. Compute $[T_i]_p \leftarrow$ EC-Add$([-S_{i-1}]_p, [P_i]_p)$ $(i = 2, ..., k)$ and set $[T_1]_p = [P_1]_p$.
   /* 5, $11(k-1)$. */
3. Compute $[U_i]_p \leftarrow$ EC-Add$([T_i]_p, [S_i]_p)$ $(i = 1, ..., k)$.
   /* 5, $11k$. */
4. Reveal $U_i = (x_{U_i}, y_{U_i}) \leftarrow$ Reveal$(([x_{U_i}]_p, [y_{U_i}]_p))$ $(i = 1, ..., k)$.
   /* 1, 2. */
5. Compute $U = (x, y) = \sum_{i=1}^{k} U_i$ and share $[U]_p = ([x]_p, [y]_p)$.
   /* 1, 2. */
6. Compute $[R]_p \leftarrow$ EC-Add$([U]_p, [-S_k]_p)$.
   /* 5, 11. */
7. Output $[R]_p$.

Fig. 5. Description of EC-Add-UF that requires $5\lceil \log n \rceil + 18$ rounds and $11kn + 13k + 4$ multiplications

In the protocol EC-Add-UF, all parties jointly generate k random points $[S_1]_p, ..., [S_k]_p$, compute $[U_1 = P_1 + S_1]_p, [U_2 = -S_1 + P_2 + S_2]_p..., [U_k = -S_{k-1} + P_k + S_k]_p$, reveal $U_1, ..., U_k$ and compute $U = \sum_{i=1}^{k} U_i = (\sum_{i=1}^{k} P_i) + S_k$, and finally compute $[U - S_k = \sum_{i=1}^{k} P_i]_p$.

The protocol is unconditionally secure.

Lemma 1. *Protocol EC-Add-UF is unconditionally secure.*

Proof. In the protocol, only $U_i = (x_{U_i}, y_{U_i}) \in G$ $(i = 1, ..., k)$ is revealed. For revealed $U_i = -S_{i-1} + P_i + S_i \in G$ $(i = 1, ..., k)$, where we denote $S_0 = O$, and for all $P_i' \in G$ $(i = 1, ..., k)$, there exists unique $S_i' \in G$ $(i = 1, ..., k)$ s.t. $U_i = -S_{i-1} + P_i + S_i = -S_{i-1}' + P_i' + S_i' \in G$ $(i = 1, ..., k)$ holds, where we denote $S_0' = O$. Therefore, no information about P_i is revealed. □

3.5 Elliptic Curve Scalar Multiplication

We construct MPC protocols EC-Exp-Pub (Fig.6), EC-Exp-Bit (Fig.7), and EC-Exp-Pri (Fig.8), to securely compute elliptic curve scalar multiplication by extending the construction of [10].

The protocol EC-Exp-Pub takes shared point $[P]_p$ and public exponent e as input and outputs shared point $[eP]_p$. The protocol requires $5\lceil \log n \rceil + 13$ rounds and $22n + 8$ multiplications. The technique to construct the protocol is corresponding to the public exponentiation protocol in [10]; but, we optimize the protocol for elliptic curve scalar multiplication.

In the protocol EC-Exp-Pub, all parties jointly generate random points $[S]_p$ and $[eS]_p$, compute $[T = P + S]_p$, reveal T and compute $U = eT$, and finally compute $[R = U - eS = e(P + S) - eS = eP]_p$.

Protocol: $[R]_p \leftarrow$ EC-Exp-Pub$([P]_p, e)$.
Inputs: $[P]_p = ([x_P]_p, [y_P]_p)$ s.t. $P \in G, e \in \mathbb{Z}_p$.
Outputs: $[R = eP]_p = ([x_R]_p, [y_R]_p)$.
    1. Generate $([S]_p, [eS]_p) \leftarrow$ EC-Rand-Pair(e).
       /* $5\lceil \log n \rceil + 1, 22(n - 1) + 4$. */
    2. Compute $[T]_p \leftarrow$ EC-Add$([P]_p, [S]_p)$.
       /* $5, 11$. */
    3. Reveal $T = (x_T, y_T) \leftarrow$ Reveal$([x_T]_p, [y_T]_p)$.
       /* $1, 2$. */
    4. Compute $U = (x, y) = eT$ and share $[U]_p = ([x]_p, [y]_p)$.
       /* $1, 2$. */
    5. Compute $[R]_p \leftarrow$ EC-Add$([U]_p, [-eS]_p)$.
       /* $5, 11$. */
    6. Output $[R]_p$.

Fig. 6. Description of EC-Exp-Pub that requires $5\lceil \log n \rceil + 13$ rounds and $22n + 8$ multiplications

Protocol: $[R]_p \leftarrow$ EC-Exp-Bit$([P]_p, [e]_B)$.
Inputs: $[P]_p = ([x_P]_p, [y_P]_p)$ s.t. $P \in G, [e]_B = ([e_1]_p, ..., [e_l]_p)$ s.t. $e_i \in \{0, 1\} \subset \mathbb{Z}_p$.
Outputs: $[R = eP]_p = ([x_R]_p, [y_R]_p)$ s.t. $e = \sum_{i=1}^{l} e_i 2^{i-1}$.
    1. Compute $[A_i]_p \leftarrow$ EC-Exp-Pub$([P]_p, 2^{i-1})$ $(i = 1, ..., l)$.
       /* $5\lceil \log n \rceil + 13, 22nl + 8l$. */
    2. Compute $[B_i]_p \leftarrow$ EC-Cond$([e_i]_p, [A_i]_p, [O]_p)$ $(i = 1, ..., l)$.
       /* $1, 2l$. */
    3. Compute $[R]_p \leftarrow$ EC-Add-UF$([B_1]_p, ..., [B_l]_p)$.
       /* $5\lceil \log n \rceil + 18, 11nl + 13l + 4$. */
    4. Output $[R]_p$.

Fig. 7. Description of EC-Exp-Bit that requires $10\lceil \log n \rceil + 32$ rounds and $33nl + 23l + 4$ multiplications

The protocol is unconditionally secure.

Lemma 2. *Protocol* EC-Exp-Pub *is unconditionally secure.*

Proof. In the protocol, only $T = (x_T, y_T) \in G$ is revealed. For revealed $T = P + S \in G$, and for all $P' \in G$, there exists unique $S' \in G$ s.t. $T = P + S = P' + S' \in G$ holds. Therefore, no information about P is revealed. □

The protocol EC-Exp-Bit takes shared point $[P]_p$ and bit-wise shared exponent $[e]_B$ as input and outputs shared point $[eP]_p$. The protocol requires $10\lceil \log n \rceil + 32$ rounds and $33nl + 23l + 4$ multiplications. The technique to construct the protocol is corresponding to the private exponentiation protocol for bit-wise shared exponents in [10]; but, we optimize the protocol for elliptic curve scalar multiplication.

In the protocol EC-Exp-Bit, all parties compute $[A_i = 2^{i-1}P]_p$, compute $[B_i = e_i A_i = e_i 2^{i-1}P]_p$, and finally compute $[(\sum_{i=1}^{l} e_i 2^{i-1})P = eP]_p$.

Protocol: $[R]_p \leftarrow$ EC-Exp-Pri($[P]_p, [e]_p$).
Inputs: $[P]_p = ([x_P]_p, [y_P]_p)$ s.t. $P \in G$, $[e]_p$ s.t. $e \in \mathbb{Z}_p$.
Outputs: $[R = eP]_p = ([x_R]_p, [y_R]_p)$.

1. Compute $([s]_B = ([s_1]_p, ..., [s_l]_p), [s]_p) \leftarrow$ SolvedBits().
   /* 7, 56l. */
2. Compute $[t]_p = [e]_p + [s]_p$ and $t \leftarrow$ Reveal($[t]_p$), where $t = (t_0 ... t_l)$.
   /* 1, 1. */
3. Share $[t]_B = ([t_1]_p, ..., [t_l]_p)$.
   /* 1, l. */
4. Compute $[f]_p \leftarrow$ BitLessThan($[t]_B, [s]_B$).
   /* 6, 14l. */
5. Compute $[T]_p \leftarrow$ EC-Exp-Pub($[P]_p, t$), $[U]_p \leftarrow$ EC-Exp-Pub($[P]_p, p$).
   /* $5\lceil \log n \rceil + 13$, $44n + 16$. */
6. Compute $[V]_p \leftarrow$ EC-Add($[T]_p, [U]_p$).
   /* 5, 11. */
7. Compute $[W]_p \leftarrow$ EC-Cond($[f]_p, [V]_p, [T]_p$).
   /* 1, 3. */
8. Compute $[S]_p \leftarrow$ EC-Exp-Bit($[P]_p, ([s_1]_p, ..., [s_l]_p)$).
   /* $10\lceil \log n \rceil + 32$, $33nl + 23l + 4$. */
9. Compute $[R]_p \leftarrow$ EC-Add($[W]_p, [-S]_p$).
   /* 5, 11. */
10. Output $[R]_p$.

Fig. 8. Description of EC-Exp-Pri that requires $15\lceil \log n \rceil + 71$ rounds and $33nl + 94l + 44n + 46$ multiplications

The protocol EC-Exp-Pri takes shared point $[P]_p$ and shared exponent $[e]_p$ as input and outputs shared point $[eP]_p$. The protocol requires $15\lceil \log n \rceil + 71$ rounds and $33nl + 94l + 44n + 46$ multiplications. The technique to construct the protocol is corresponding to the private exponentiation protocol in [16]; but, we optimize the protocol for elliptic curve scalar multiplication.

In the protocol EC-Exp-Pri, all parties jointly generate random $[s]_p$, compute $[t = e + s \mod p]_p$, compute $W = (t + p)P$ if $t < s$ or $W = tP$ if $t \geq s$, and finally compute $[R = W - sP = (e + s)P - sP = eP]_p$. Here, we take care of the fact that $e + s$ may exceed by the modulus p in the computation of $t = e + s \mod p$. If $e + s \geq p$, $t + p = e + s$ holds as integer and $t < s$ holds by $e < p$. If $e + s < p$, $t = e + s$ holds as integer and $t \geq s$ holds by $e \geq 0$. Thus, we compute $(t + p)P = (e + s \mod m)P$ if $t < s$ or $tP = (e + s \mod m)P$ if $t \geq s$, where m is the order of cyclic group $G = \langle P \rangle$.

The protocol is unconditionally secure.

Lemma 3. *Protocol* EC-Exp-Pri *is unconditionally secure.*

Proof. In the protocol, only $t \in \mathbb{Z}_p$ is revealed. For revealed $t = e + s \in \mathbb{Z}_p$, and for all $e' \in \mathbb{Z}_p$, there exists unique $s' \in \mathbb{Z}_p$ s.t. $t = e + s = e' + s' \in \mathbb{Z}_p$ holds. Therefore, no information about e is revealed.   □

Acknowledgments. The authors would like to thank the anonymous reviewers for their valuable comments.

References

1. Algesheimer, J., Camenisch, J.L., Shoup, V.: Efficient Computation Modulo a Shared Secret with Application to the Generation of Shared Safe-Prime Products. In: Yung, M. (ed.) CRYPTO 2002. LNCS, vol. 2442, pp. 417–432. Springer, Heidelberg (2002)
2. Bar-Ilan, J., Beaver, D.: Non-Cryptographic Fault-Tolerant Computing in Constant Number of Rounds of Interaction. In: PODC 1989, pp. 201–209 (1989)
3. Ben-Or, M., Goldwasser, S., Wigderson, A.: Completeness Theorems for Non-Cryptographic Fault-Tolerant Distributed Computation. In: STOC 1988, pp. 1–10 (1988)
4. Bernstein, D.J., Lange, T.: Faster Addition and Doubling on Elliptic Curves. In: Kurosawa, K. (ed.) ASIACRYPT 2007. LNCS, vol. 4833, pp. 29–50. Springer, Heidelberg (2007)
5. Bernstein, D.J., Lange, T.: Inverted Edwards Coordinates. In: Boztaş, S., Lu, H.-F. (eds.) AAECC 2007. LNCS, vol. 4851, pp. 20–27. Springer, Heidelberg (2007)
6. Brier, E., Joye, M.: Weierstraß Elliptic Curves and Side-Channel Attacks. In: Naccache, D., Paillier, P. (eds.) PKC 2002. LNCS, vol. 2274, pp. 335–345. Springer, Heidelberg (2002)
7. Chaum, D., Crépeau, C., Damgård, I.: Multiparty Unconditionally Secure Protocols (Extended Abstract). In: STOC 1988, pp. 11–19 (1988)
8. Clavier, C., Joye, M.: Universal Exponentiation Algorithm. In: Koç, Ç.K., Naccache, D., Paar, C. (eds.) CHES 2001. LNCS, vol. 2162, pp. 300–308. Springer, Heidelberg (2001)
9. Cramer, R., Fehr, S., Ishai, Y., Kushilevitz, E.: Efficient multi-party computation over rings. In: Biham, E. (ed.) EUROCRYPT 2003. LNCS, vol. 2656, pp. 596–613. Springer, Heidelberg (2003)
10. Damgård, I., Fitzi, M., Kiltz, E., Nielsen, J.B., Toft, T.: Unconditionally Secure Constant-Rounds Multi-party Computation for Equality, Comparison, Bits and Exponentiation. In: Halevi, S., Rabin, T. (eds.) TCC 2006. LNCS, vol. 3876, pp. 285–304. Springer, Heidelberg (2006)
11. Edwards, H.M.: A Normal Form for Elliptic Curves. Bulletin of the American Mathematical Society 44, 393–422 (2007)
12. Goldreich, O., Micali, S., Wigderson, A.: How to Play any Mental Game or A Completeness Theorem for Protocols with Honest Majority. In: STOC 1987, pp. 218–229 (1987)
13. Joye, M., Quisquater, J.-J.: Hessian Elliptic Curves and Side-Channel Attacks. In: Koç, Ç.K., Naccache, D., Paar, C. (eds.) CHES 2001. LNCS, vol. 2162, pp. 402–410. Springer, Heidelberg (2001)
14. Liardet, P.-Y., Smart, N.P.: Preventing SPA/DPA in ECC Systems Using the Jacobi Form. In: Koç, Ç.K., Naccache, D., Paar, C. (eds.) CHES 2001. LNCS, vol. 2162, pp. 391–401. Springer, Heidelberg (2001)
15. Ning, C., Xu, Q.: Multiparty Computation for Modulo Reduction without Bit-Decomposition and a Generalization to Bit-Decomposition. In: Abe, M. (ed.) ASIACRYPT 2010. LNCS, vol. 6477, pp. 483–500. Springer, Heidelberg (2010)
16. Ning, C., Xu, Q.: Constant-Rounds, Linear Multi-party Computation for Exponentiation and Modulo Reduction with Perfect Security. In: Lee, D.H., Wang, X. (eds.) ASIACRYPT 2011. LNCS, vol. 7073, pp. 572–589. Springer, Heidelberg (2011)
17. Nishide, T., Ohta, K.: Multiparty Computation for Interval, Equality, and Comparison Without Bit-Decomposition Protocol. In: Okamoto, T., Wang, X. (eds.) PKC 2007. LNCS, vol. 4450, pp. 343–360. Springer, Heidelberg (2007)
18. Ohara, K., Ohta, K., Suzuki, K., Yoneyama, K.: Constant Rounds Almost Linear Complexity Multi-party Computation for Prefix Sum. In: Pointcheval, D., Vergnaud, D. (eds.) AFRICACRYPT. LNCS, vol. 8469, pp. 285–299. Springer, Heidelberg (2014)

19. Toft, T.: Primitives and Applications for Multi-party Computation. Ph.D. thesis, University of Aarhus (2007)
20. Toft, T.: Constant-Rounds, Almost-Linear Bit-Decomposition of Secret Shared Values. In: Fischlin, M. (ed.) CT-RSA 2009. LNCS, vol. 5473, pp. 357–371. Springer, Heidelberg (2009)
21. Wallace, C.S.: A Suggestion for a Fast Multipliers. IEEE Trans. on Electronic Comp. EC-13(1), 14–17 (1964)
22. Yao, A.C.C.: Protocols for Secure Computations (Extended Abstract). In: FOCS 1982, pp. 160–164 (1982)
23. Yao, A.C.C.: How to Generate and Exchange Secrets (Extended Abstract). In: FOCS 1986, pp. 162–167 (1986)

More Constructions of Re-splittable Threshold Public Key Encryption

Satsuya Ohata[1,2], Takahiro Matsuda[2],
Goichiro Hanaoka[2], and Kanta Matsuura[1]

[1] The University of Tokyo, Tokyo, Japan
{satsuya,kanta}@iis.u-tokyo.ac.jp
[2] National Institute of Advanced Industrial Science and Technology, Ibaraki, Japan
{t-matsuda,hanaoka-goichiro}@aist.go.jp

Abstract. The concept of threshold public key encryption (TPKE) with the special property called key re-splittability (re-splittable TPKE, for short) was introduced by Hanaoka et al. (CT-RSA 2012), and used as one of the building blocks for constructing their proxy re-encryption scheme. In a re-splittable TPKE scheme, a secret key can be split into a set of secret key shares not only once, but also multiple times, and the security of the TPKE scheme is guaranteed as long as the number of corrupted secret key shares under the same splitting is smaller than the threshold. In this paper, we show several new constructions of re-splittable TPKE scheme by extending the previous (ordinary) TPKE schemes.

Keywords: Threshold Public Key Encryption, Key Re-splittability.

1 Introduction

Threshold public key encryption (TPKE) is a kind of public key encryption where a secret key is distributed among n decryption servers so that partial decryption shares from at least t servers are needed for decryption. In TPKE, an entity called *combiner* has a ciphertext c that it wishes to decrypt. The combiner sends c to the decryption servers and receives partial decryption shares from at least t out of n decryption servers. Then, the combiner combines these t partial decryption shares into a complete decryption of c. No information about the plaintext is leaked, even if the number of the corrupted users is up to $t - 1$. Ideally, there is no other interaction in the system, namely the servers need not talk to each other during the decryption. Such threshold encryption systems are called non-interactive. We usually require that TPKE scheme has *robustness*. That is, if decryption of a valid ciphertext fails, the combiner can identify the decryption servers that supplied invalid partial decryption shares.

Not only the functionality of TPKE is useful in the real world, but TPKE is used as a building block in the generic construction of another cryptosystem. Hanaoka et al. [8] showed a generic construction of proxy re-encryption (PRE) using TPKE as one of the building blocks. To achieve the functionality and prove the security of the PRE scheme in [8], the underlying TPKE scheme should have

M. Yoshida and K. Mouri (Eds.): IWSEC 2014, LNCS 8639, pp. 109–118, 2014.
© Springer International Publishing Switzerland 2014

a special (but natural) property called *key re-splittability*. In TPKE with key re-splittability (re-splittable TPKE, for short), a secret key can be split into a set of secret key shares not only once, but also multiple times, and the security of the TPKE scheme is guaranteed as long as the number of corrupted secret key shares under the same splitting is smaller than the threshold. We can understand that re-splittable TPKE is a cryptosystem in which the mechanism of a proactive secret sharing [7] is applied to its secret key. That is, we can re-distribute the secret key shares without changing the original public/secret keys. We also study key re-splittability for TPKE in this paper.

Hanaoka et al. gave a formal security definition of re-splittable TPKE, and proposed a concrete construction by extending the ordinary TPKE scheme by Arita and Tsurudome [2]. In [8], however, only one construction was given. The main motivation of this paper is to show more constructions of re-splittable TPKE schemes.

1.1   Our Contribution

In this paper, we propose several new constructions of re-splittable TPKE by extending the existing (ordinary) TPKE schemes. The efficiency of our schemes is not degraded at all from the corresponding underlying TPKE schemes. Concretely, we present the following constructions:

1. **Re-splittable TPKE scheme based on the *decisional linear (DLIN) assumption*:** We construct the first re-splittable TPKE scheme based on the DLIN assumption by extending Arita and Tsurudome's TPKE scheme [2]. Compared with the construction of [8] based on the decisional bilinear Diffie-Hellman (DBDH) assumption, we do not need pairing computations in the combining algorithm (assuming the input decryption shares are known to be valid). On the other hand, the other algorithms (encrypt, share decrypt, and share verify) are somewhat slower.

2. **Re-splittable TPKE scheme based on the DBDH assumption *without signature*:** We construct a re-splittable TPKE scheme based on the DBDH assumption by extending Lai et al's TPKE scheme [10]. The scheme based on [8] is also based on the DBDH assumption, and needs a one-time strongly unforgeable signature in the construction. Our construction, however, does not need a signature scheme.

3. **Re-splittable TPKE scheme based on the *hashed Diffie-Hellman (HDH) assumption*:** We construct a re-splittable TPKE scheme based on the HDH assumption by extending Gan et al's TPKE scheme [6]. This scheme also does not need a signature scheme in the construction. Though the assumption on which the security is based is different from our second construction, all of the algorithms of this scheme is more efficient than it.

1.2   Related Work

Desmedt and Frankel [4] introduced the concept of TPKE. Their scheme needs an interaction among decryption servers to decrypt a ciphertext. The first non-interactive and CCA secure TPKE scheme was proposed by Shoup and Gennaro [13]. They proposed two constructions, one is based on the computational Diffie-Hellman (CDH) assumption and the other is based on the decisional Diffie-Hellman (DDH) assumption. To prove the security of these schemes, we need a random oracle. Later, Boneh, Boyen, and Halevi [3] proposed the TPKE scheme based on the DBDH assumption in the standard model. Subsequently, Arita and Tsurudome [2] proposed two more efficient TPKE schemes than [3]. One of their schemes is based on the DBDH assumption and the other is based on the DLIN assumption. Later, Lai et al. [10] proposed a new technique to construct an efficient public key encryption scheme and applied it to construct a TPKE scheme. Though [3] and [2] use a signature scheme in the constructions, the scheme in [10] does not use it. Subsequently, Gan et al. [6] proposed a TPKE scheme based on the HDH assumption. Libert and Yung [11] proposed an adaptively secure TPKE scheme by using composite order groups. The same authors [12] also proposed a framework for the construction of adaptively secure TPKE based on the so-called all-but-one perfectly sound threshold hash proof systems, from which we can obtain concrete instantiations based on the DLIN, the external Diffie-Hellman (XDH) assumptions in prime order bilinear groups, and one based on some assumption in composite order bilinear groups.

There are some schemes based on non-discrete logarithm type assumptions. Wee [14] showed a CCA secure TPKE scheme based on the factoring assumption in the random oracle model. Dodis and Katz [5] proposed a generic construction of TPKE from any chosen ciphertext secure PKE. However, the model of TPKE is different from [3], (arguably) currently a more popular model of TPKE on which the security model of re-splittable TPKE is based.

In summary, to the best of our knowledge, none of the previous works other than [8] considered the key re-splittability of TPKE.

2   Preliminaries

In this section, we review the basic notation, and the definitions of bilinear groups, related number theoretic assumptions, and the cryptographic primitives.

Notation. $\mathbb{N}$ denotes the set of all natural numbers, and for $n \in \mathbb{N}$, we let $[n] := \{1, \ldots, n\}$. "$x \leftarrow y$" denotes that x is chosen uniformly at random from y if y is a finite set, x is output from y if y is a function or an algorithm, or y is assigned to x otherwise. "$x\|y$" denotes a concatenation of x and y. "$|x|$" denotes the size of the set if x is a finite set or bit length of x if x is a string. "PPT" stands for *probabilistic polynomial-time*. If $\mathcal{A}$ is a probabilistic algorithm then $y \leftarrow \mathcal{A}(x)$ denotes that $\mathcal{A}$ computes y as output by taking x as input. $x := y$ denotes that x is defined as y. Without loss of generality, we consider that a secret key contains the information of the corresponding public key. k denotes the security parameter.

2.1 Bilinear Map and Assumptions

Bilinear Map. Groups $(\mathbb{G}, \mathbb{G}_T)$ of prime order p are called *bilinear groups* if there is a mapping $e : \mathbb{G} \times \mathbb{G} \to \mathbb{G}_T$ with the following properties. (1)Bilinearity: $e(g^a, g^b) = e(g, g)^{ab}$ for any $g \in \mathbb{G}$ and $a, b \in \mathbb{Z}$. (2)Efficient computability: given $g, h \in \mathbb{G}$, $e(g, h) \in \mathbb{G}_T$ is efficiently computable. (3)Non-degeneracy: $e(g, g) \neq 1_{\mathbb{G}_T}$ whenever $g \neq 1_{\mathbb{G}}$.

For convenience, we introduce a bilinear group generator BG that takes 1^k as input and outputs a description $(p, \mathbb{G}, \mathbb{G}_T, e)$ of bilinear groups where p is a k-bit prime. This process is written as $(p, \mathbb{G}, \mathbb{G}_T, e) \leftarrow \mathsf{BG}(1^k)$.

Decisional Bilinear Diffie-Hellman (DBDH) Assumption: We define the advantage of an adversary $\mathcal{A}$ in solving the decisional bilinear Diffie-Hellman (DBDH) problem as $\mathsf{Adv}_{\mathcal{A}}^{\mathrm{DBDH}}(k) = |\Pr[\mathcal{A}(g, g^a, g^b, g^c, e(g, g)^{abc}) = 1] - \Pr[\mathcal{A}(g, g^a, g^b, g^c, e(g, g)^z) = 1]|$, where $(p, \mathbb{G}, \mathbb{G}_T, e) \leftarrow \mathsf{BG}(1^k)$, $g \leftarrow \mathbb{G}$, and $a, b, c, z \leftarrow \mathbb{Z}_p$. We say that the DBDH assumption holds when the advantage $\mathsf{Adv}_{\mathcal{A}}^{\mathrm{DBDH}}(k)$ is negligible for any PPT adversary $\mathcal{A}$.

Decisional Linear (DLIN) Assumption: We define the advantage of an adversary $\mathcal{A}$ in solving the decisional linear (DLIN) problem as $\mathsf{Adv}_{\mathcal{A}}^{\mathrm{DLIN}}(k) = |\Pr[\mathcal{A}(g_1, g_2, g_3, g_1^a, g_2^b, g_3^{a+b}) = 1] - \Pr[\mathcal{A}(g_1, g_2, g_3, g_1^a, g_2^b, g_3^z) = 1]|$, where $(p, \mathbb{G}, \mathbb{G}_T, e) \leftarrow \mathsf{BG}(1^k)$, $g_1, g_2, g_3 \leftarrow \mathbb{G}$, and $a, b, z \leftarrow \mathbb{Z}_p$. We say that the DLIN assumption holds when the advantage $\mathsf{Adv}_{\mathcal{A}}^{\mathrm{DLIN}}(k)$ is negligible for any PPT adversary $\mathcal{A}$.

Hashed Diffie-Hellman (HDH) Assumption: Here, H is a hash function that takes an element in $\mathbb{G}$ as input, and outputs a string in $\{0, 1\}^l$.

We define the advantage of an adversary $\mathcal{A}$ in solving the hashed Diffie-Hellman (HDH) problem as $\mathsf{Adv}_{\mathcal{A}}^{\mathrm{HDH}}(k) = |\Pr[\mathcal{A}(g, g^a, g^b, H(g^{ab})) = 1] - \Pr[\mathcal{A}(g, g^a, g^b, R) = 1]|$, where $(p, \mathbb{G}, \mathbb{G}_T, e) \leftarrow \mathsf{BG}(1^k)$, $g \leftarrow \mathbb{G}$, $a, b \leftarrow \mathbb{Z}_p$, and $R \leftarrow \{0, 1\}^l$. We say that the HDH assumption holds when the advantage $\mathsf{Adv}_{\mathcal{A}}^{\mathrm{HDH}}(k)$ is negligible for any PPT adversary $\mathcal{A}$.

2.2 Other Building Blocks

Signature. A signature scheme consists of the following three PPT algorithms (SKG, Sign, SVer): The key generation algorithm SKG that takes 1^k as input, and outputs a verification key svk and a signing key ssk. The signing algorithm Sign that takes ssk and a message m as input, and outputs a signature σ. The verification algorithm SVer that takes svk, m, and σ as input, and outputs $\top$ (meaning "accept") or $\bot$ (meaning "reject"). We require the standard correctness for a signature scheme, namely, for any $(ssk, svk) \leftarrow \mathsf{SKG}(1^k)$ and any message m, we have $\mathsf{SVer}(svk, m, \mathsf{Sign}(ssk, m)) = \top$.

We will use one-time strong unforgeability [1]. Since this is a standard security notion, we omit the formal definition in this proceeding version.

Collision Resistant Hash Function. We define the advantage of an adversary $\mathcal{A}$ in finding the collision of a hash function H as $\mathsf{Adv}_{\mathcal{A}}^{\mathrm{CRHF}}(k) = \Pr[(m_0, m_1) \leftarrow \mathcal{A}(H) : H(m_0) = H(m_1) \wedge m_0 \neq m_1]$, where H is picked randomly. We say H is a collision resistant hash function if for any PPT adversary $\mathcal{A}$, $\mathsf{Adv}_{\mathcal{A}}^{\mathrm{CRHF}}(k)$ is negligible.

3   Re-splittable Threshold Public Key Encryption

In this section, we review the model and the security definitions of re-splittable TPKE. The concept of re-splittable threshold public key encryption (TPKE) was introduced in [8]. It is a special class of TPKE in which a secret key can be split multiple times, and security of the scheme is maintained as long as the number of corrupted secret key shares *under the same splitting* is less than the threshold.

Syntax. A re-splittable TPKE scheme consists of the following six PPT algorithms:

TKG This is the key generation algorithm that takes 1^k, n, and t such that $0 < t \leq n$ as input, and outputs a public key tpk and a secret key tsk.

TEnc This is the encryption algorithm that takes tpk and a plaintext m as input, and outputs a ciphertext c.

TSplit This is the key-splitting algorithm that takes tsk as input, and outputs n secret key shares $tsk_1, \cdots, tsk_n$ and a verification key tvk.

TShDec This is the share-decryption algorithm that takes tpk, a secret key share tsk_i (where $i \in [n]$) output by TSplit, and c as input, and outputs a decryption share μ_i (which could be the special symbol $\perp$ meaning that c is invalid).

TShVer This is the share-verification algorithm that takes tpk, tvk, c, an index $i \in [n]$, and a decryption share μ as input, and outputs $\top$ or $\perp$. When the output is $\top$, we say that μ is a valid decryption share of the ciphertext c.

TCom This is the combining algorithm that takes tpk, tvk, c, and t decryption shares (generated under distinct secret key shares) as input, and outputs a decryption result m (which could be the special symbol $\perp$).

For any $k \in \mathbb{N}$, any polynomials t, n such that $0 < t \leq n$, any $(tpk, tsk) \leftarrow$ TKG$(1^k, n, t)$ and any $(tsk_1, \cdots, tsk_n, tvk) \leftarrow$ TSplit(tsk), we require the following two correctness properties: (1) For any ciphertext c, if $\mu =$ TShDec(tpk, tsk_i, c), then we have TShVer$(tpk, tvk, c, i, \mu) = \top$. (2) For any m, if c is output from TEnc(tpk, m) and $S = \{\mu_{s_1}, \cdots, \mu_{s_t}\}$ is a set of decryption shares (i.e. $\mu_{s_i} =$ TShDec(tpk, tsk_{s_i}, c) for all $i \in [t]$), then we have TCom$(tpk, tvk, c, S) = m$.

Chosen Ciphertext Security. CCA security of a re-splittable TPKE scheme is defined using the following game between a challenger and an adversary $\mathcal{A}$: The challenger first runs $(tpk, tsk) \leftarrow$ TKG$(1^k, n, t)$ and gives tpk to $\mathcal{A}$. Then $\mathcal{A}$ can adaptively make the following types of queries.

Split&corruption query: On input a set of indices $S = \{s_1, \cdots, s_{t-1}\}$, the challenger runs $(tsk_1, \cdots, tsk_n, tvk) \leftarrow \mathsf{TSplit}(tsk)$ and returns $(tsk_{s_1}, \cdots, tsk_{s_{t-1}}, tvk)$ to $\mathcal{A}$. The challenger also stores $\{tsk_i\}_{i\in[n]}$ and tvk for later share decryption queries from $\mathcal{A}$.

Share decryption query: On input (tvk, i, c), where tvk is required to be one of the answers to previously asked split&corruption queries, $i \in [n]$, and $c \neq c^*$, the challenger finds tsk_i that is previously generated together with tvk, and returns a decryption share $\mu_i \leftarrow \mathsf{TShDec}(tpk, tsk_i, c)$ to $\mathcal{A}$.

Challenge query: This query is asked only once. On input (m_0, m_1), the challenger randomly picks $b \in \{0, 1\}$ and returns $c^* \leftarrow \mathsf{TEnc}(tpk, m_b)$ to $\mathcal{A}$.

Finally, $\mathcal{A}$ outputs its guess b' for b, and wins the game if $b = b'$. We define the advantage of $\mathcal{A}$ by $\mathsf{Adv}^{\mathsf{CCA\text{-}RS\text{-}TPKE}}_{(\mathcal{A},n,t)}(k) = |\Pr[b = b'] - 1/2|$.

We say that a re-splittable TPKE scheme is *CCA secure*, if for any PPT adversary $\mathcal{A}$ and for any polynomials t and n with $0 < t \leq n$, $\mathsf{Adv}^{\mathsf{CCA\text{-}RS\text{-}TPKE}}_{(\mathcal{A},n,t)}(k)$ is negligible.

Decryption Consistency. Decryption consistency is defined using the game which is defined in the same way as the CCA game, except that the challenge query is not considered.

$\mathcal{A}$ finally outputs a ciphertext c, a verification key tvk, and two sets of decryption shares $S = \{\mu_{s_1}, \ldots, \mu_{s_t}\}$ and $S' = \{\mu'_{s'_1}, \ldots, \mu'_{s'_t}\}$. $\mathcal{A}$ wins the game if the following four conditions are simultaneously satisfied: (1) tvk is one of verification keys returned as a response to one of $\mathcal{A}$'s split&corruption queries. (2) All shares in S and S' are valid for a ciphertext c under tvk. That is, $\forall \mathsf{TShVer}(tpk, tvk, c, i, \{\mu_i\}_{i\in[t]}) = \top$. (3) S and S' are sets that are distinct regardless of re-ordering the elements. (4) $\mathsf{TCom}(tpk, tvk, c, S) \neq \mathsf{TCom}(tpk, tvk, c, S')$. We let $\mathsf{Adv}^{\mathsf{DC\text{-}RS\text{-}TPKE}}_{(\mathcal{A},n,t)}(k)$ denote the probability of $\mathcal{A}$ winning in this game.

We say that a re-splittable TPKE scheme has *decryption consistency*, if for any PPT adversary $\mathcal{A}$ and for any polynomials t and n such that $0 < t \leq n$, $\mathsf{Adv}^{\mathsf{DC\text{-}RS\text{-}TPKE}}_{(\mathcal{A},n,t)}(k)$ is negligible.

4   Proposed Re-splittable TPKE Schemes

In this section, we propose several concrete re-splittable TPKE schemes, and prove their security. Each of our schemes is an extension of the existing ordinary TPKE schemes, and we show how to implement the TSplit algorithm for each of them. For each scheme, the assumption on which the security is based is exactly the same as one on which the original scheme is based. Furthermore, the efficiency (ciphertext size and the computational costs) of each scheme is also essentially the same as the corresponding underlying scheme.

Due to the lack of space, we omit the formal security proofs. The proofs follow closely to those of the underlying TPKE schemes. Roughly speaking, secret key shares of these TPKE schemes consist of secret sharings of one "*master*" secret key tsk, where Shamir's secret sharing using polynomials is used. A reduction

$\mathsf{TKG}(1^k, n, t)$:
$(p, \mathbb{G}, \mathbb{G}_T, e) \leftarrow \mathsf{BG}(1^k)$; Select a collision resistant hash function H
$g_1 \leftarrow \mathbb{G}$; $x_1, x_2, y_1, y_2 \leftarrow \mathbb{Z}_p$; $g_3 := g_1^{x_1}$; $g_2 := g_3^{\frac{1}{x_2}}$; $u_1 := g_1^{y_1}$; $u_2 := g_2^{y_2}$
$tpk := (p, \mathbb{G}, \mathbb{G}_T, e, H, g_1, g_2, g_3, u_1, u_2)$, $tsk := (x_1, x_2)$;
return (tpk, tsk).

$\mathsf{TEnc}(tpk, m)$:
$(p, \mathbb{G}, \mathbb{G}_T, e, H, g_1, g_2, g_3, u_1, u_2) \leftarrow tpk$; $(svk, ssk) \leftarrow \mathsf{SKG}(1^k)$; $r_1, r_2 \leftarrow \mathbb{Z}_p$
$C_1 := g_1^{r_1}$; $C_2 := g_2^{r_2}$; $D_1 := (g_3^{H(svk)} u_1)^{r_1}$; $D_2 := (g_3^{H(svk)} u_2)^{r_2}$; $E := m \cdot g_3^{r_1 + r_2}$
$\sigma \leftarrow \mathsf{Sign}(ssk, C_1 \| C_2 \| D_1 \| D_2 \| E)$
return $c := (C_1, C_2, D_1, D_2, E, \sigma, svk)$.

$\mathsf{TSplit}(tsk)$:
$(x_1, x_2) \leftarrow tsk$
$f_1, f_2 \leftarrow \mathbb{Z}_p[X]$ satisfying $\deg(f_1) = \deg(f_2) = t - 1$, $f_1(0) = x_1$ and $f_2(0) = x_2$
For all $i \in [n]$, $tsk_i := (f_1(i), f_2(i))$; $tvk := \{g_1^{f_1(i)}, g_2^{f_2(i)}\}_{i \in [n]}$
return $(\{tsk_i\}_{i \in [n]}, tvk)$.

$\mathsf{TShDec}(tpk, tsk_i, c)$:
$(p, \mathbb{G}, \mathbb{G}_T, e, H, g_1, g_2, g_3, u_1, u_2) \leftarrow tpk$; $(f_1(i), f_2(i)) \leftarrow tsk_i$
$(C_1, C_2, D_1, D_2, \sigma, svk) \leftarrow c$
if $\mathsf{SVer}(svk, C_1 \| C_2 \| D_1 \| D_2 \| E, \sigma) = \bot$, then return $\mu_i := \bot$
if $e(C_1, g_3^{H(svk)} u_1) \neq e(D_1, g_1)$ or $e(C_2, g_3^{H(svk)} u_2) \neq e(D_2, g_2)$, then return $\mu_i := \bot$
return $\mu_i = (\mu_{1.i}, \mu_{2.i}) := (C_1^{f_1(i)}, C_2^{f_2(i)})$.

$\mathsf{TShVer}(tpk, tvk, c, i, \mu_i)$:
$(p, \mathbb{G}, \mathbb{G}_T, e, H, g_1, g_2, g_3, u_1, u_2) \leftarrow tpk$; $\{g_1^{f_1(i)}, g_2^{f_2(i)}\}_{i \in [n]} \leftarrow tvk$
$(C_1, C_2, D_1, D_2, E, \sigma, svk) \leftarrow c$; $(\mu_{1.i}, \mu_{2.i}) \leftarrow \mu_i$
if $\mathsf{SVer}(svk, \sigma, C_1 \| C_2 \| D_1 \| D_2 \| E) = \bot$ or
$e(C_1, g_3^{H(svk)} u_1) \neq e(D_1, g_1)$ or $e(C_2, g_3^{H(svk)} u_2) \neq e(D_2, g_2)$, then
      if $\mu_i = \bot$, then return $\top$; else return $\bot$
else if $e(\mu_{1.i}, g_1) \neq e(C_1, g_1^{f_1(i)})$ or $e(\mu_{2.i}, g_2) \neq e(C_2, g_2^{f_2(i)})$, then return $\bot$
else return $\top$.

$\mathsf{TCom}(tpk, tvk, c, \{\mu_i\}_{i \in [t]})$:
$(p, \mathbb{G}, \mathbb{G}_T, e, H, g_1, g_2, g_3, u_1, u_2) \leftarrow tpk$; $\{g_1^{f_1(i)}, g_2^{f_2(i)}\}_{i \in [n]} \leftarrow tvk$
$(C_1, C_2, D_1, D_2, E, \sigma, svk) \leftarrow c$; $\{\mu_{1.i}, \mu_{2.i}\}_{i \in [t]} \leftarrow \{\mu_i\}_{i \in [t]}$
if $\exists i \in [t] : \mathsf{TShVer}(tpk, tvk, c, i, \mu_i) = \bot$, then return $\bot$
return $m = E / \{(\prod_{i=1}^{t} \mu_{1.i}^{\lambda_{1.i}}) \cdot (\prod_{i=1}^{t} \mu_{2.i}^{\lambda_{2.i}})\}$
using Lagrange coefficients $\{\lambda_i\}_{i \in [t]}$ satisfying $f_j(0) = \Sigma_{i=1}^{t} \lambda_{j.i} f_j(i)$.

Fig. 1. The re-splittable TPKE scheme eAT

algorithm in the security proofs can answer Split&Corruption queries of an adversary multiple times, by choosing a new polynomial f such that $f(0) = tsk$ for each query to realize secret sharing of tsk.

4.1 Construction Based on Arita and Tsurudome's Scheme

We show the construction of a re-splittable TPKE scheme based on the Arita and Tsurudome scheme [2] as in Fig.1. Here, we call it eAT. Compared with the construction of [8] based on the DBDH assumption, this scheme does not need pairing computations in the combining algorithm (assuming the input decryption shares are known to be valid). On the other hand, the other algorithms (TEnc, TShDec, and TShVer) are somewhat slower.

$\mathsf{TKG}(1^k, n, t):$ $(p, \mathbb{G}, \mathbb{G}_T, e) \leftarrow \mathsf{BG}(1^k);$ select a collision resistant hash function H $g, h, u, v, d \leftarrow \mathbb{G} \quad x \leftarrow \mathbb{Z}_p$ $tpk := (p, \mathbb{G}, \mathbb{G}_T, e, H, g, h, Z = e(g,h)^x, u, v, d),\ tsk := x;$ return $(tpk, tsk).$
$\mathsf{TEnc}(tpk, m):$ $(p, \mathbb{G}, \mathbb{G}_T, e, H, g, h, Z, u, v, d) \leftarrow tpk$ $r, s \leftarrow \mathbb{Z}_p;\ C_0 := m \cdot Z^s;\ C_1 := g^s;\ \omega := H(C_0, C_1);\ C_2 := (u^\omega v^r d)^s$ return $c := (C_0, C_1, C_2, r).$
$\mathsf{TSplit}(tsk):$ $x \leftarrow tsk;\ f \leftarrow \mathbb{Z}_p[X]$ satisfying $\deg(f) = t - 1$ and $f(0) = x$ For all $i \in [n],\ tsk_i := h^{f(i)};\ tvk := \{g^{f(i)}\}_{i \in [n]}$ return $(\{tsk_i\}_{i \in [n]}, tvk).$
$\mathsf{TShDec}(tpk, tsk_i, c):$ $(p, \mathbb{G}, \mathbb{G}_T, e, H, g, h, Z, u, v, d) \leftarrow tpk;\ h^{f(i)} \leftarrow tsk_i$ $(C_0, C_1, C_2) \leftarrow c;\ \omega := H(C_0, C_1)$ if $e(C_1, u^\omega v^r d) \neq e(g, C_2),$ then return $\mu_i := \perp;$ else $\gamma \leftarrow \mathbb{Z}_p$ return $\mu_i := (\mu_{1.i}, \mu_{2.i}) = (tsk_i \cdot (u^\omega v^r d)^\gamma, g^\gamma).$
$\mathsf{TShVer}(tpk, tvk, c, i, \mu_i):$ $(p, \mathbb{G}, \mathbb{G}_T, e, H, g, h, Z, u, v, d) \leftarrow tpk;\ \{g^{f(i)}\}_{i \in [n]} \leftarrow tvk$ $(C_0, C_1, C_2) \leftarrow c;\ (\mu_{1.i}, \mu_{2.i}) \leftarrow \mu_i;\ \omega := H(C_0, C_1)$ if $e(C_1, u^\omega v^r d) \neq e(g, C_2),$ $\quad$ if $\mu_i = \perp,$ then return $\top;$ else return $\perp$ if $e(g, \mu_{1.i}) \neq e(g^{f(i)}, h) \cdot e(u^\omega v^r d, \mu_{2.i}),$ then return $\perp$ else return $\top.$
$\mathsf{TCom}(tpk, tvk, c, \{\mu_i\}_{i \in [t]}):$ $(p, \mathbb{G}, \mathbb{G}_T, e, H, g, h, Z, u, v, d) \leftarrow tpk;\ \{g^{f(i)}\}_{i \in [n]} \leftarrow tvk$ $(C_0, C_1, C_2) \leftarrow c;\ \{tsk_i \cdot (u^\omega v^r d)^\gamma, g^\gamma\}_{i \in [t]} \leftarrow \{\mu_i\}_{i \in [t]}$ if $\exists i \in [t],\ \mathsf{TShVer}(tpk, tvk, c, i, \mu_i) = \perp,$ then return $\perp$ else return $m = C_0 \cdot e(C_2, \prod_{i=1}^t \mu_{2.i}^{\lambda_i})/e(C_1, \prod_{i=1}^t \mu_{1.i}^{\lambda_i})$ using Lagrange coefficients $\{\lambda_i\}_{i \in [t]}$ satisfying $f(0) = \Sigma_{i=1}^t \lambda_i f(i).$

Fig. 2. The re-splittable TPKE scheme eLDLK

Theorem 1. *If the DLIN assumption on* $(\mathbb{G}, \mathbb{G}_T)$ *holds, the signature scheme is one-time strongly unforgeable, and* H *is a collision resistant hash function, then the re-splittable TPKE scheme* eAT *is CCA secure.*

Theorem 2. *The re-splittable TPKE scheme* eAT *has decryption consistency unconditionally.*

4.2 Construction Based on Lai et al's Scheme

Here, we show the construction of a re-splittable TPKE scheme based on the Lai et al. scheme [10] as in Fig.2. Here, we call it eLDLK. The scheme based on [8] is also based on the DBDH assumption, and needs a one-time strongly unforgeable signature in the construction. Our construction, however, does not need a signature scheme.

$\mathsf{TKG}(1^k, n, t)$:
$(p, \mathbb{G}, \mathbb{G}_T, e) \leftarrow \mathsf{BG}(1^k)$
select a hash function $H_2 : \mathbb{G} \to \{0,1\}^{|m|}$
select a collision resistant hash function H_1
$g, u, v, d \leftarrow \mathbb{G};\ x \leftarrow \mathbb{Z}_p;\ g_1 := g^x$
$tpk := (p, \mathbb{G}, \mathbb{G}_T, e, H_1, H_2, g, g_1, u, v, d);\ tsk := x;$
return (tpk, tsk).

$\mathsf{TEnc}(tpk, m)$:
$(p, \mathbb{G}, \mathbb{G}_T, e, H_1, H_2, g, g_1, u, v, d) \leftarrow tpk$
$r, s \leftarrow \mathbb{Z}_p;\ C_0 := m \oplus H_2(g_1^s);\ C_1 := g^s;\ \omega := H_1(C_0, C_1);\ C_2 := (u^\omega v^r d)^s$
return $c := (C_0, C_1, C_2, r)$.

$\mathsf{TSplit}(tsk)$:
$x \leftarrow tsk;\ f \leftarrow \mathbb{Z}_p[X]$ satisfying $\deg(f) = t - 1$ and $f(0) = x$
$tsk_i := f(i);\ tvk := \{g^{f(i)}\}_{i \in [n]}$
return $(\{tsk_i\}_{i \in [n]}, tvk)$

$\mathsf{TShDec}(tpk, tsk_i, c)$:
$(p, \mathbb{G}, \mathbb{G}_T, e, H_1, H_2, g, g_1, u, v, d) \leftarrow tpk;\ f(i) \leftarrow tsk_i$
$(C_0, C_1, C_2, r) \leftarrow c\ \ \omega := H_1(C_0, C_1)$
if $e(C_1, u^\omega v^r d) \neq e(g, C_2)$, then return $\perp$
return $\mu_i := C_1^{f(i)}$.

$\mathsf{TShVer}(tpk, tvk, c, i, \mu_i)$:
$(p, \mathbb{G}, \mathbb{G}_T, e, H_1, H_2, g, g_1, u, v, d) \leftarrow tpk;\ \{g^{f(i)}\}_{i \in [n]} \leftarrow tvk$
$(C_0, C_1, C_2, r) \leftarrow c;\ C_1^{f(i)} \leftarrow \mu_i;\ \omega := H_1(C_0, C_1)$
if $e(C_1, u^\omega v^r d) \neq e(g, C_2)$,
   if $\mu_i = \perp$, then return $\perp$; else return $\top$
if $e(\mu_i, g) \neq e(C_1, g^{f(i)})$, then return $\perp$
return $\top$.

$\mathsf{TCom}(tpk, tvk, c, \{\mu_i\}_{i \in [t]})$:
$(p, \mathbb{G}, \mathbb{G}_T, e, H_1, H_2, g, g_1, u, v, d) \leftarrow tpk;\ \{g^{f(i)}\}_{i \in [n]} \leftarrow tvk$
$(C_0, C_1, C_2, r) \leftarrow c;\ \{C_1^{f(i)}\}_{i \in [t]} \leftarrow \{\mu_i\}_{i \in [t]}$
if $\exists i \in [t]$, $\mathsf{TShVer}(tpk, tvk, c, i, \mu_i) = \perp$, then return $\perp$
else return $m = C_0 \oplus H_2(\prod_{i=1}^{t} \mu_i^{\lambda_i})$
using Lagrange coefficients $\{\lambda_i\}_{i \in [t]}$ satisfying $f(0) = \Sigma_{i=1}^{t} \lambda_i f(i)$.

Fig. 3. The re-splittable TPKE scheme eGWW+

Theorem 3. *If the DBDH assumption holds in* $(\mathbb{G}, \mathbb{G}_T)$ *and H is a collision resistant hash function, then the re-splittable TPKE scheme* eLDLK *is CCA secure.*

Theorem 4. *The re-splittable TPKE scheme* eLDLK *has decryption consistency unconditionally.*

4.3 Construction Based on Gan et al's Scheme

Here, we show the construction of a re-splittable TPKE scheme based on the Gan et al. scheme [6] as in Fig.3. Here, we call it eGWW+. As with the eLDLK scheme, this scheme also does not need a signature scheme in the construction. Though the assumption on which the security is based is different from eLDLK scheme, each algorithm of this scheme is more efficient than the corresponding algorithm of eLDLK.

Theorem 5. *If the HDH assumption on* $(\mathbb{G}, \mathbb{G}_T, H_2)$ *holds and* H_1 *is a collision resistant hash function, then the re-splittable TPKE scheme* eGWW+ *is CCA secure.*

Theorem 6. *The re-splittable TPKE scheme* eGWW+ *has decryption consistency unconditionally.*

References

1. An, J.H., Dodis, Y., Rabin, T.: On the Security of Joint Signature and Encryption. In: Knudsen, L.R. (ed.) EUROCRYPT 2002. LNCS, vol. 2332, pp. 83–107. Springer, Heidelberg (2002)
2. Arita, S., Tsurudome, K.: Construction of Threshold Public-Key Encryptions through Tag-Based Encryptions. In: Abdalla, M., Pointcheval, D., Fouque, P.-A., Vergnaud, D. (eds.) ACNS 2009. LNCS, vol. 5536, pp. 186–200. Springer, Heidelberg (2009)
3. Boneh, D., Boyen, X., Halevi, S.: Chosen Ciphertext Secure Public Key Threshold Encryption Without Random Oracles. In: Pointcheval, D. (ed.) CT-RSA 2006. LNCS, vol. 3860, pp. 226–243. Springer, Heidelberg (2006)
4. Desmedt, Y., Frankel, Y.: Threshold cryptosystems. In: Brassard, G. (ed.) CRYPTO 1989. LNCS, vol. 435, pp. 307–315. Springer, Heidelberg (1990)
5. Dodis, Y., Katz, J.: Chosen-Ciphertext Security of Multiple Encryption. In: Kilian, J. (ed.) TCC 2005. LNCS, vol. 3378, pp. 188–209. Springer, Heidelberg (2005)
6. Gan, Y., Wang, L., Wang, L., Pan, P., Yang, Y.: Efficient Construction of CCA-Secure Threshold PKE Based on Hashed Diffie-Hellman Assumption. Comput. J. 56(10), 1249–1257 (2013)
7. Herzberg, A., Jarecki, S., Krawczyk, H., Yung, M.: Proactive Secret Sharing Or: How to Cope with Perpetual Leakage. In: Coppersmith, D. (ed.) CRYPTO 1995. LNCS, vol. 963, pp. 339–352. Springer, Heidelberg (1995)
8. Hanaoka, G., Kawai, Y., Kunihiro, N., Matsuda, T., Weng, J., Zhang, R., Zhao, Y.: Generic Construction of Chosen Ciphertext Secure Proxy Re-Encryption. In: Dunkelman, O. (ed.) CT-RSA 2012. LNCS, vol. 7178, pp. 349–364. Springer, Heidelberg (2012)
9. Kiltz, E.: Chosen-Ciphertext Security from Tag-Based Encryption. In: Halevi, S., Rabin, T. (eds.) TCC 2006. LNCS, vol. 3876, pp. 581–600. Springer, Heidelberg (2006)
10. Lai, J., Deng, R.H., Liu, S., Kou, W.: Efficient CCA-Secure PKE from Identity-Based Techniques. In: Pieprzyk, J. (ed.) CT-RSA 2010. LNCS, vol. 5985, pp. 132–147. Springer, Heidelberg (2010)
11. Libert, B., Yung, M.: Adaptively Secure Non-interactive Threshold Cryptosystems. In: Aceto, L., Henzinger, M., Sgall, J. (eds.) ICALP 2011, Part II. LNCS, vol. 6756, pp. 588–600. Springer, Heidelberg (2011)
12. Libert, B., Yung, M.: Non-interactive CCA-Secure Threshold Cryptosystems with Adaptive Security: New Framework and Constructions. In: Cramer, R. (ed.) TCC 2012. LNCS, vol. 7194, pp. 75–93. Springer, Heidelberg (2012)
13. Shoup, V., Gennaro, R.: Securing Threshold Cryptosystems against Chosen Ciphertext Attack. In: Nyberg, K. (ed.) EUROCRYPT 1998. LNCS, vol. 1403, pp. 1–16. Springer, Heidelberg (1998)
14. Wee, H.: Threshold and Revocation Cryptosystems via Extractable Hash Proofs. In: Paterson, K.G. (ed.) EUROCRYPT 2011. LNCS, vol. 6632, pp. 589–609. Springer, Heidelberg (2011)

How to Effectively Decrease the Resource Requirement in Template Attack?

Hailong Zhang[1,2]

[1] State Key Laboratory of Information Security,
Institute of Information Engineering, Chinese Academy of Sciences
Minzhuang Road 89-A, Beijing, 100093, P.R. China
[2] University of Chinese Academy of Sciences
zhanghailong@iie.ac.cn

Abstract. Under the assumption that one has a reference device identical to the target device and thus be well capable of characterizing the power leakages of the target device, Template Attack (TA) is widely accepted to be the strongest power analysis attack. However, a disadvantage of TA is that, its resource requirement is usually large, i.e. in order to accurately characterize the power leakages of the target device, one usually needs to use a large number of power traces in profiling. In practice, the large resource requirement of TA hinders its application. Therefore, it is utmost important to effectively decrease the resource requirement of TA, and make it applicable in practice. In light of this, we propose Bivariate Template Attack (BTA) in this paper. The central idea of BTA is to consider the joint leakages of all interesting points in a pairwise manner. We note that, when the same interesting points are used, BTA and TA can characterize and exploit the same amount of power leakages. However, compared with TA, the resource requirement of BTA is usually small. In fact, both simulated and real experiments will verify that, compared with TA, BTA requires less power traces in profiling to reach the same key-recovery efficiency.

Keywords: Side Channel Attacks, Power Analysis Attacks, Template Attack, Resource Requirement, Key-Recovery Efficiency.

1 Introduction

There exist side channel leakages when a cryptographic device is in operation. One can use the side channel leakages of a cryptographic device to recover the key used by the cryptographic device, and that is the idea of side channel attacks. In practice, side channel attacks pose serious threat to the physical security of different cryptographic devices.

The first successful side channel attack was reported by Kocher [12], in which the timing information of a cryptographic device was used to recover the correct key. Since then, different forms of side channel attacks, such as power analysis attacks [13] and electromagnetic analysis [11] were proposed. Among these attacks, power analysis attacks have received the most attention. The reasons are

M. Yoshida and K. Mouri (Eds.): IWSEC 2014, LNCS 8639, pp. 119–133, 2014.

that power analysis attacks are very powerful and they can be easily conducted in practice [15].

In [13], Kocher et al. first proposed Differential Power Analysis (DPA). Since then, different forms of power analysis attacks were proposed consecutively, such as Template Attack (TA) [6], Correlation Power Analysis (CPA) [3], Stochastic Model based Power Analysis (SMPA) [19], Partitioning Power Analysis (PPA) [14], Mutual Information Analysis (MIA) [9], and Differential Cluster Analysis (DCA) [5], etc. Among different forms of attacks, TA is widely accepted to be the strongest form of power analysis attack. The reasons are two folds: firstly, in profiling, one can use a reference device identical to the target device to accurately characterize the power leakages of the target device; secondly, in key-recovery, the probability based distinguisher, i.e. the maximum likelihood principle is used to efficiently recover the key used by the target device.

1.1   Related Work

Although TA is widely accepted to be the strongest power analysis attack, in practice, some technical problems exist in TA, and they strongly influence the key-recovery efficiency of TA. Therefore, one needs to carefully address these problems to increase the key-recovery efficiency of TA.

Firstly, in order to fully use of the power leakages of the target device, the power leakages at different interesting points are used. Therefore, one needs to use certain technique to efficiently choose the interesting points. In light of this, different techniques were proposed, and they can be divided into two groups. Techniques in the first group are heuristic, in that one assumes the interesting points are those that induce the largest variability. For example, in [17], Rechberger and Oswald suggested using the sum of difference technique to choose the interesting points; in [2], Agrawal et al. suggested using DPA to choose the interesting points; in [10], Gierlichs et al. proposed using T-Test to choose the interesting points, and the effectiveness of T-Test was verified by Batina et al. in [5]. Also, Bär et al. proposed using the modified T-Test to choose the interesting points [4]. Techniques in the second group are Principal Component Analysis (PCA) [1,7] and Fisher Linear Discriminant Analysis (FLDA) [18]. As the authors said, using techniques in the second group, the interesting points can be chosen in principled way and automatically. In summary, many works have faced with the problem of how to efficiently choose the interesting points to increase the key-recovery efficiency of TA, and different techniques were proposed to answer this question.

Secondly, in TA, one usually needs to use a large number of power traces in profiling to accurately characterize the power leakages of the target device. In practice, when the number of power traces used in profiling is limited, the key-recovery efficiency of TA is strongly influenced. It is usually assumed that the decrease of the key-recovery efficiency of TA is posed by the problems related to the covariance matrices of different templates [22]. When a small number of power traces is used in profiling, the covariance matrices are not accurately characterized, which will severely influence the key-recovery efficiency of TA. In order to accurately characterize the covariance matrices, one usually needs to use a large number of power traces in profiling. In practice, the large resource requirement of TA hinders its practical application. However, how to effectively decrease the resource requirement of TA while not decrease the amount of power leakages it uses is still an open question. In light of this, we try to propose a method to effectively decrease the resource requirement of TA, and make it applicable in practice.

1.2   Contribution

We propose Bivariate Template Attack (BTA) in this paper. The central idea of BTA is to consider the joint leakages of all interesting points in a pairwise manner. We argue that, when the same interesting points are used, BTA and TA can characterize and exploit the same amount of power leakages. However, in BTA, the problems related to the covariance matrices of different templates are effectively alleviated. Therefore, compared with TA, BTA needs less power traces in profiling to accurately characterize the power leakages of the target device.

   We evaluate the resource requirement of BTA and TA in both simulated and real attacking scenarios. Experimental results verify that, compared with TA, BTA requires less power traces in profiling to reach the same key-recovery efficiency. Therefore, we note that, BTA is suitable to be used in practical attacking scenarios.

1.3   Organization

This paper is organized as follows. The principle of TA is given in section 2. In section 3, we show the principle of BTA. Then, in section 4, we evaluate the resource requirement of BTA and TA in different attacking scenarios. Finally, conclusions are given in section 5.

2   Template Attack

There exist two phases in TA, i.e. profiling and key-recovery. In profiling, one can accurately characterize the power leakages of the target device with the help of the reference device. In key-recovery, the characterized information about the power leakages of the target device can be used to recover the key used by the target device.

2.1   Profiling

Firstly, in order to accurately characterize the power leakages of the target device, one needs to use a large number of power traces in profiling. One can operate the reference device n times for the randomly chosen plaintexts $p_1, p_2, ..., p_n$.

Using the measurement setup, one can measure and obtain n power traces: $I_1, I_2, ..., I_n$.

Then, one needs to choose t interesting points. For example, as Agrawal et al. suggested [2], one can use DPA to choose the interesting points. Because the key used by the reference device is usually assumed to be known, one can actually compute and obtain only one DPA differential trace. The interesting points are those points that induce significant DPA peaks in the differential trace.

In TA, the power leakages at different interesting points are assumed to follow the *multivariate normal distribution*. Therefore, one needs to use the mean vectors and the covariance matrices to respectively characterize the signals and the noises at different interesting points. Before characterizing the power leakages at different interesting points, one firstly needs to divide the power traces into different groups. Usually, the power traces corresponding to the same value of the target intermediate value v are divided into the same group. If we denote the power traces in the ith group as $I_1, I_2, ..., I_{n_i}$; then,

$$\mathbf{m}^i = \frac{1}{n_i} \sum_{j=1}^{n_i} \mathbf{x}^j, \quad \mathbf{C}^i = \frac{1}{n_i} \sum_{j=1}^{n_i} (\mathbf{x}^j - \mathbf{m}^i)^T (\mathbf{x}^j - \mathbf{m}^i), \tag{1}$$

where $\mathbf{x}^j$ denotes the power leakages of power trace I_j at t interesting points. Here, we call $(\mathbf{m}^i, \mathbf{C}^i)$ a *template*.

2.2 Key-Recovery

Firstly, one needs to obtain a small number of power traces $I_1, ..., I_a$ measured from the target device. Then, for each power trace $I_j, j \in [1, a]$, one computes the match probability $P_{i,j}$ between the power leakages $\mathbf{x}^j$ contained in power trace I_j and the template $(\mathbf{m}^i, \mathbf{C}^i)$:

$$P_{i,j}(\mathbf{x}^j; (\mathbf{m}^i, \mathbf{C}^i)) = \frac{\exp(-\frac{1}{2}(\mathbf{x}^j - \mathbf{m}^i)^T (\mathbf{C}^i)^{-1} (\mathbf{x}^j - \mathbf{m}^i))}{\sqrt{(2\pi)^t \cdot \det(\mathbf{C}^i)}}. \tag{2}$$

Finally, one multiplies the match probabilities $P_{i,1}, ..., P_{i,a}$ together:

$$P_i(\mathbf{x}^1, ..., \mathbf{x}^a; (\mathbf{m}^i, \mathbf{C}^i)) = \prod_{j=1}^{a} P_{i,j}(\mathbf{x}^j; (\mathbf{m}^i, \mathbf{C}^i)). \tag{3}$$

If a key hypothesis k is correct, then the match probability P_i between the power leakages $\mathbf{x}^1, ..., \mathbf{x}^a$ and the template $(\mathbf{m}^i, \mathbf{C}^i)$ will be high. Otherwise, the match probability P_i between the power leakages $\mathbf{x}^1, ..., \mathbf{x}^a$ and the template $(\mathbf{m}^i, \mathbf{C}^i)$ will be low.

According to the maximum likelihood principle, among different match probabilities, the largest match probability P_{max} indicates the key k^* used by the target device. Therefore, by comparing the match probabilities computed under different key hypotheses, one can recover the key used by the target device.

3   Bivariate Template Attack

The assumption made in BTA is the same as that made in TA, i.e. the power leakages at different interesting points are assumed to follow the *multivariate normal distribution*. If we denote the power leakages at interesting points $1, 2, ..., t$ as the random variables $X_1, X_2, ..., X_t$; then, the random vector $\mathbf{X} = [X_1, X_2, ..., X_t]$ follows the *multivariate normal distribution*. According to [8], we have Theorem 1:

Theorem 1. *If the random vector* $\mathbf{X} = [X_1, X_2, ..., X_t]$ *follows the multivariate normal distribution, and* $Y_p, p \in [1, l]$ *is the linear combination of* $X_1, X_2, ..., X_t$, *i.e.* $Y_p = \sum_{q=1}^{t} a_q X_q$, *then the vector* $\mathbf{Y} = [Y_1, Y_2, ..., Y_l]$ *follows the multivariate normal distribution.*

Theorem 1 shows that, if $X_p, X_q, p, q \epsilon [1, t]$ are two random variables of the random vector $\mathbf{X}$, then the random vector $\mathbf{X}_{p,q} = [X_p, X_q]$ follows the *bivariate normal distribution*. In fact, when t interesting points are chosen, one can actually combine and obtain $\frac{t(t-1)}{2}$ random vectors, and each of them follows the *bivariate normal distribution*.

In profiling, one can use the power traces measured from the reference device to accurately characterize the templates corresponding to each combined vector $\mathbf{X}_{p,q}, p, q \in [1, t]$. In key-recovery, one can use the maximum likelihood principle to efficiently recover the correct key k^*.

3.1   Profiling

In order to accurately characterize the power leakages of the target device, one needs to operate the reference device n times for the randomly chosen plaintexts $p_1, p_2, ..., p_n$. Using the measurement setup, one can measure and obtain n power traces $I_1, I_2, ..., I_n$. Before characterizing the power leakages of the target device, one needs to use certain technique to choose t interesting points. For example, like in TA, in BTA, one can also use DPA to choose the interesting points. Because each combined vector $\mathbf{X}_{p,q}, p, q \in [1, t]$ follows the bivariate normal distribution, one can use the mean vectors and the covariance matrices to respectively characterize the signals and the noises at interesting points p and q.

Before characterizing the templates corresponding to each combined vector $\mathbf{X}_{p,q}, p, q \in [1, t]$, one needs to first divide the power traces into different groups according to the value of the target intermediate value v. Then, using the power traces in the same group, one can characterize the templates corresponding to the random vector $\mathbf{X}_{p,q}, p, q \in [1, t]$. If we denote the power traces in the ith group as $I_1, I_2, ..., I_{n_i}$; then,

$$\mathbf{m}_{p,q}^i = \frac{1}{n_i} \sum_{j=1}^{n_i} \mathbf{x}_{p,q}^j, \quad \mathbf{C}_{p,q}^i = \frac{1}{n_i} \sum_{j=1}^{n_i} (\mathbf{x}_{p,q}^j - \mathbf{m}_{p,q}^i)^T (\mathbf{x}_{p,q}^j - \mathbf{m}_{p,q}^i), \qquad (4)$$

where $\mathbf{x}_{p,q}^j$ denotes the power leakages of power trace I_j at interesting points p and q. Obviously, $(\mathbf{m}_{p,q}^i, \mathbf{C}_{p,q}^i)$ is a template for random vector $\mathbf{X}_{p,q}$. If we denote the number of possible values of v as $|V|$, then one can characterize and obtain $|V|$ templates for the random vector $\mathbf{X}_{p,q}$.

In fact, if the same interesting points are chosen, then one can obtain the templates of BTA from the templates of TA, and vice versa. For example, if we denote $\mathbf{m}^i$ as:

$$\mathbf{m}^i = (m_1^i, m_2^i, ..., m_t^i), \tag{5}$$

then

$$\mathbf{m}_{p,q}^i = (m_p^i, m_q^i), \quad p, q \in [1, t]. \tag{6}$$

Also, if we denote $\mathbf{C}^i$ as:

$$\mathbf{C}^i = [cov(X_1, X_1), ..., cov(X_1, X_t); ...; cov(X_t, X_1), ..., cov(X_t, X_t)], \tag{7}$$

where $cov(X_p, X_q), p, q \in [1, t]$ denotes the covariance between the random variables X_p and X_q, then

$$\mathbf{C}_{p,q}^i = [cov(X_p, X_p), cov(X_p, X_q); cov(X_q, X_p), cov(X_q, X_q)]. \tag{8}$$

Therefore, we note that, if the same interesting points are chosen, BTA and TA can characterize and exploit the same amount of power leakages.

3.2 Key-Recovery

Like in TA, in BTA, one also uses the maximum likelihood principle to recover the correct key. However, unlike in TA, in BTA, the power leakages at different interesting points are considered in a pairwise manner.

In order to recover the key used by the target device, one needs to obtain a small number of power traces $I_1, I_2, ..., I_a$ measured from the target device. For each power trace $I_j, j \in [1, a]$, one needs to compute the match probability $P_{i,j}$ between the power leakages $\mathbf{x}_{p,q}^j$ contained in power trace I_j and the template $(\mathbf{m}_{p,q}^i, \mathbf{C}_{p,q}^i)$:

$$P_{i,j}(\mathbf{x}_{p,q}^j; (\mathbf{m}_{p,q}^i, \mathbf{C}_{p,q}^i)) = \frac{\exp(-\frac{1}{2}(\mathbf{x}_{p,q}^j - \mathbf{m}_{p,q}^i)^T (\mathbf{C}_{p,q}^i)^{-1}(\mathbf{x}_{p,q}^j - \mathbf{m}_{p,q}^i))}{\sqrt{(2\pi)^2 \cdot \det(\mathbf{C}_{p,q}^i)}}. \tag{9}$$

Then, one multiplies the match probabilities $P_{i,1}, ..., P_{i,a}$ together:

$$P_{p,q}^i(\mathbf{x}_{p,q}^1, ..., \mathbf{x}_{p,q}^a; (\mathbf{m}_{p,q}^i, \mathbf{C}_{p,q}^i)) = \prod_{j=1}^{a} P_{i,j}(\mathbf{x}_{p,q}^j; (\mathbf{m}_{p,q}^i, \mathbf{C}_{p,q}^i)). \tag{10}$$

Finally, one multiplies the match probabilities $P_{1,2}^i, ..., P_{t-1,t}^i$ together:

$$P_{overall} = \prod_{p=1}^{t-1} \prod_{q=p+1}^{t} P_{p,q}^i(\mathbf{x}_{p,q}^1, ..., \mathbf{x}_{p,q}^a; (\mathbf{m}_{p,q}^i, \mathbf{C}_{p,q}^i)). \tag{11}$$

If a key hypothesis k is correct; then, the match probability $P_{overall}$ will be high. Otherwise, the match probability $P_{overall}$ will be low. According to the maximum likelihood principle, among all match probabilities, the highest match probability P_{max} indicates the correct key k^*. Therefore, by comparing the match probabilities computed under different key hypotheses, one can recover the key k^* used by the target device.

It needs to be noted that, the bivariate combination style rather than other combination styles is considered in this paper. The reason is that, the size of the covariance matrix in a bivariate template is small. Because of the small size of the covariance matrix in a bivariate template, the problems related to the covariance matrices of different templates are not serious, and the key-recovery efficiency of BTA is not significantly influenced. Also, we note that, in this paper, multiplication is empirically adopted as the combination style in BTA to combine the match probabilities. The reason is that this combination style works well in our experiments. However, whether or not there exist other combination styles which can help further increase the key-recovery efficiency of BTA is not clear, which will be left as an open problem.

3.3   Comparison between BTA and TA

It can be seen from the working principle of BTA that, when the same interesting points are used, BTA and TA can actually characterize and exploit the same amount of power leakages, except that they use the power leakages at different interesting points in a different manner.

In BTA, the power leakages at different interesting points are considered in a pairwise manner. Therefore, no matter how many interesting points are used, the size of the covariance matrices of different templates is always $2*2$, i.e. each row and each column of the covariance matrices all have 2 elements. However, in TA, the power leakages at different interesting points are jointly considered. Therefore, when t interesting points are used, the size of the covariance matrices of different templates is $t*t$, i.e. each row and each column of the covariance matrices all have t elements. Of course, when two interesting points are used, BTA and TA exploit the power leakages at different interesting points in the same manner, and they are actually the same.

Ye and Eisenbarth showed in [22] that, when a small number of power traces is used in profiling, the computation of the covariance matrices will be remarkably impacted by noises. Especially, when the covariance matrices are badly-conditioned, numerical problems may exist during the matrix inversion. In practice, these problems strongly influence the key-recovery efficiency of TA. In fact, experimental results will show that, when the number of power traces used in profiling is limited, the more interesting points are used, i.e. the larger the size of the covariance matrices is, the more serious the problems related to the covariance matrices will be, and the lower the key-recovery efficiency of TA will be. Therefore, in order to eliminate the problems related to the covariance matrices, one needs to use a large number of power traces in profiling.

However, in BTA, no matter how many interesting points are used, the size of the covariance matrices of different templates is always small. Because of the small size of the covariance matrices, the impact of noises on the computation of the covariance matrices will be relatively small, and numerical problems related to the covariance matrices of different templates will rarely occur. In this case, compared with TA, BTA needs less power traces in profiling to eliminate the problems related to the covariance matrices of different templates. Therefore, BTA can effectively decrease the number of power traces needed in profiling while not decrease the amount of power leakages it uses. Overall, compared with TA, BTA is more applicable in practice, which poses serious threat on the practical security of a cryptographic device.

4   Experimental Results

We will evaluate and compare the resource requirement of BTA and TA in both simulated and real attacking scenarios. Success Rate (SR) proposed in [20] will be used as the evaluation metric. SR is defined as the probability that one can successfully recover the correct key, and it is widely used in side channel attacks to evaluate the key-recovery efficiency of an attacking method.

It needs to be noted that, because of the variety of the values of the parameters, it is impossible to evaluate and compare the resource requirement of BTA and TA in all attacking scenarios. Therefore, we only evaluate the resource requirement of BTA and TA in some typical attacking scenarios. Specifically, in the simulated experiments, we will compare the resource requirement of BTA and TA in different noise level attacking scenarios. In the real experiments, the evaluation platform is an unprotected software implementation of the AES on a microcontroller. However, we note that, BTA as an attacking method should perform well in a wide spectrum of attacking scenarios.

4.1   Simulated Experiments

In the simulated attacking scenarios, the signals at a single interesting point are assumed to follow the Bit Weight (BW) power model, i.e. the power leakage of each bit of the target intermediate value is different, and each bit of the target intermediate value leaks independently. The power leakage of each bit of the target intermediate value is randomly chosen from the interval [1, 10]. It needs to be noted that this simulation method is similar to that used in [21]. Correlation coefficient is used to measure the cross correlation between noises at different interesting points, and the correlation coefficient between noises at different interesting points is set to 0.4. It needs to be noted that, this value is set empirically. In the real attacking scenarios, the correlation coefficient between noises at different interesting points is usually around 0.4. The SNR is defined as: $SNR = \frac{Var(S_p)}{Var(N_p)}$, where $Var(S_p)$ and $Var(N_p)$ respectively denote the variance of the signals and the variance of the noises at interesting point p. Finally, noises at different interesting points are assumed to follow the multivariate normal distribution.

Firstly, we will evaluate the resource requirement of BTA and TA in the *low level noise* attacking scenario. The SNR is set to 0.2. We will vary the number of profiling traces and key-recovery traces. In each case, we will do 500 tests to estimate the SR of BTA and TA.

Figure 1 (a)-(b) show that, when 50 power traces are used in key-recovery, BTA requires less power traces in profiling than TA to reach the same key-recovery efficiency. Especially, when a small number of power traces (for example, less than 10,000 power traces) is used in profiling, more interesting points will further decrease the key-recovery efficiency of TA. Figure 1 (c)-(d) show that, when 6 interesting points, the key-recovery efficiency of BTA is higher than that of TA either 8,000 or 16,000 power traces are used in profiling. However, the key-recovery efficiency of TA increases when more power traces are used in profiling.

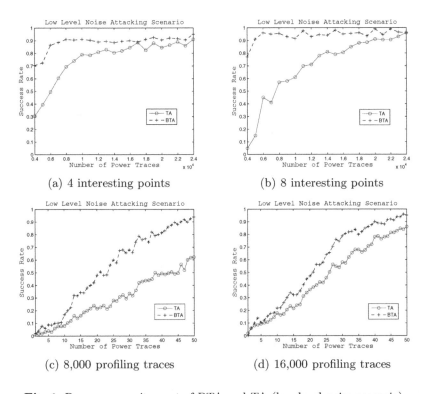

(a) 4 interesting points

(b) 8 interesting points

(c) 8,000 profiling traces

(d) 16,000 profiling traces

Fig. 1. Resource requirement of BTA and TA (low level noise scenario)

The reason is that, no matter how many interesting points are used, the size of the covariance matrices of BTA is always small, and the influence of noises on the computation of the covariance matrices of BTA will not be serious. Therefore, a small number of power traces is needed in profiling to eliminate the problems related to the covariance matrices. Comparatively, because of the large size of the covariance matrices of TA, it usually needs a large number of power traces in profiling to eliminate the problems related to the covariance matrices. Especially, when more interesting points are used, the size of the covariance matrices of TA becomes larger, and more power traces are needed in profiling. Overall, in the low level noise attacking scenario, the resource requirement of BTA is small compared with that of TA.

Then, we will evaluate the resource requirement of BTA and TA in the *medium level noise* attacking scenario. The SNR is set to 0.1. We will vary the number of profiling traces and key-recovery traces. In each case, we will do 500 tests to estimate the SR of BTA and TA.

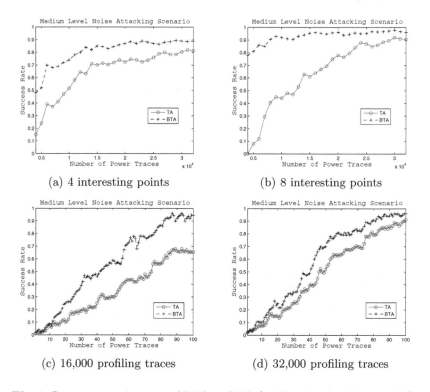

(a) 4 interesting points

(b) 8 interesting points

(c) 16,000 profiling traces

(d) 32,000 profiling traces

Fig. 2. Resource requirement of BTA and TA (medium level noise scenario)

Figure 2 (a)-(b) show that, when 90 power traces are used in key-recovery, the resource requirement gap between BTA and TA becomes larger when more interesting points are used. Figure 2 (c)-(d) show that, when 6 interesting points are used, the key-recovery efficiency of TA increases as the number of power traces used in profiling increases. Overall, in the medium level noise attacking scenario, the resource requirement of BTA is smaller than the resource requirement of TA.

Finally, we will evaluate the resource requirement of BTA and TA in the *high level noise* attacking scenario. The SNR is set to 0.05. In Figure 3 (a)-(b), 180 power traces are used in key-recovery. In Figure 3 (c)-(d), 6 interesting points are used. In each case, we will do 500 tests to estimate the SR of BTA and TA.

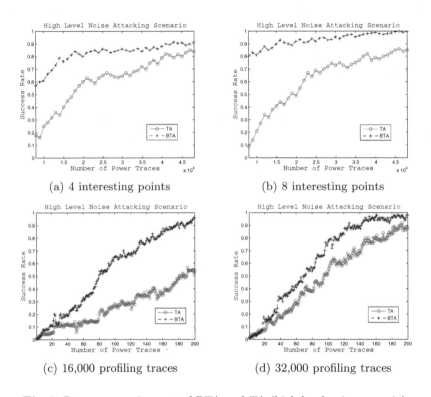

(a) 4 interesting points

(b) 8 interesting points

(c) 16,000 profiling traces

(d) 32,000 profiling traces

Fig. 3. Resource requirement of BTA and TA (high level noise scenario)

Figure 3 shows that, in the high level noise attacking scenario, the resource requirement of BTA and TA both increases. This is because noises will pose serious threat on the computation of the covariance matrices of different templates. Also, as the noise level increases, the resource requirement gap between BTA and TA becomes larger.

The reason is that, because of the larger size of the covariance matrices of TA, noises will pose more serious threat on the computation of the covariance matrices of TA. Comparatively, because of the smaller size of the covariance matrices of BTA, the influence of noises on the computation of the covariance matrices of BTA is less serious. Overall, BTA is particularly suitable to be used in the *high level noise* attacking scenario.

4.2   Real Experiments

Our experimental platform is an unprotected software implementation of the
AES running on an 8-bit STC89C58 microcontroller. The clock frequency of the
microcontroller is set to 22.1184 MHz. The power traces are sampled with an
Agilent DSA90404A digital oscilloscope and a differential probe by measurement
over a 20Ω resistor in the ground line of the microcontroller. The sampling
rate is set to 100MS/s. The plaintexts are randomly chosen from an uniform
distribution to simulate a known plaintext attacking scenario [5]. The 1st and
the 2nd S-Box outputs of the 1st round AES encryption are chosen as the target
intermediate values. The interesting points are determined by using the DPA
attack [2], and the points resulting in significant DPA peaks are chosen as the
interesting points. We note that using DPA to choose the interesting points is a
common technique in this area. In order to decrease the noise level, the average of
10 power traces corresponding to the same plaintext is computed. 20,000 power
traces are collected to accomplish the experiments.

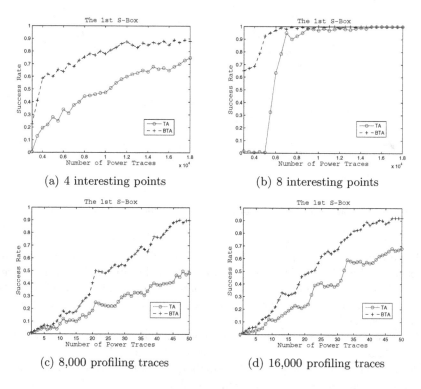

(a) 4 interesting points   (b) 8 interesting points

(c) 8,000 profiling traces   (d) 16,000 profiling traces

Fig. 4. Resource Requirement of BTA and TA (S-Box-1)

Firstly, the 1st S-Box output of the 1st round AES encryption is chosen as
the target intermediate value. We will vary the number of profiling traces and

key-recovery traces. In Figure 4 (a)-(b), 50 power traces are used in key-recovery. In Figure 4 (c)-(d), 6 interesting points are used. In each case, we will do 500 tests to estimate the SR of BTA and TA.

Figure 4 (a)-(b) show that, in the low level noise scenario, both BTA and TA need a small number of profiling traces to accurately characterize the power leakages of the target device. Comparatively, BTA needs less power traces in profiling than TA to reach the same key-recovery efficiency. Also, the number of profiling traces needed decreases as the number of interesting points increases. This is because more interesting points will bring more power leakages, which helps improve the key-recovery efficiency of BTA and TA. Figure 4 (c)-(d) show that, as the number of power traces used in profiling increases, the templates of TA are characterized more and more accurately. In this case, the key-recovery efficiency of TA increases. However, even if $16,000$ profiling traces are used, the key-recovery efficiency of BTA is still higher than that of TA.

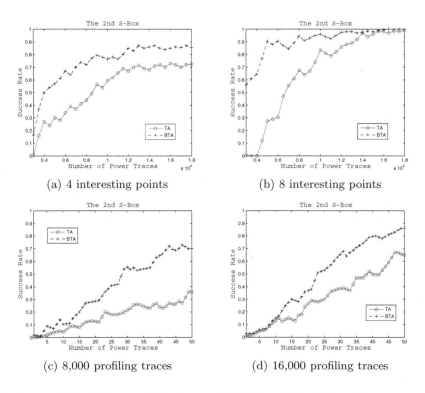

(a) 4 interesting points

(b) 8 interesting points

(c) 8,000 profiling traces

(d) 16,000 profiling traces

Fig. 5. Resource Requirement of BTA and TA (S-Box-2)

Secondly, the 2nd S-Box output of the 1st round AES encryption is chosen as the target intermediate value. We will vary the number of profiling traces and key-recovery traces. In Figure 5 (a)-(b), 50 power traces are used in key-recovery.

In Figure 5 (c)-(d), 6 interesting points are used. In each case, we will do 500 tests to estimate the SR of BTA and TA.

Figure 5 shows that, in each case, the key-recovery efficiency of BTA is higher than that of TA. Firstly, more interesting points bring more power leakages, which helps improve the key-recovery efficiency of BTA and TA. Secondly, more profiling traces help increase the accuracy of the templates, which helps improve the key-recovery efficiency of BTA and TA. Overall, the real experiments verify that, compared with TA, BTA can effectively decrease the number of power traces needed in profiling.

5   Conclusions

We propose BTA to effectively decrease the resource requirement in TA. We note that, when the same interesting points are chosen, BTA and TA can characterize and exploit the same amount of power leakages. However, because of the relatively smaller size of the covariance matrices of BTA, it usually needs less power traces than TA in profiling to eliminate the problems related to the covariance matrices. We experimentally evaluate the resource requirement of BTA and TA in both simulated and real scenarios. Evaluation results show that, compared with TA, BTA usually needs less power traces in profiling to reach the same key-recovery efficiency. Therefore, we note that, BTA is suitable to be used in practice to evaluate the physical security of different cryptographic devices.

Acknowledgements. This work is supported in part by the National Natural Science Foundation of China (Nos. 61272478, 61100225 and 61170282), the Strategic Priority Research Program of the Chinese Academy of Sciences (No. XDA06010701), the one Hundred Talents Project of the Chinese Academy of Sciences, and the SKLOIS Research Funding (No. 2014-ZD-03). I would like to thank Professor Yongbin Zhou and Professor Dengguo Feng for their insightful comments. Their comments help me improve this paper.

References

1. Archambeau, C., Peeters, E., Standaert, F.-X., Quisquater, J.-J.: Template Attacks in Principal Subspaces. In: Goubin, L., Matsui, M. (eds.) CHES 2006. LNCS, vol. 4249, pp. 1–14. Springer, Heidelberg (2006)
2. Agrawal, D., Rao, J.R., Rohatgi, P., Schramm, K.: Templates as Master Keys. In: Rao, J.R., Sunar, B. (eds.) CHES 2005. LNCS, vol. 3659, pp. 15–29. Springer, Heidelberg (2005)
3. Brier, E., Clavier, C., Olivier, F.: Correlation Power Analysis with a Leakage Model. In: Joye, M., Quisquater, J.-J. (eds.) CHES 2004. LNCS, vol. 3156, pp. 16–29. Springer, Heidelberg (2004)
4. Bär, M., Drexler, H., Pulkus, J.: Improved Template Attacks. In: COSADE 2010 (2010)

5. Batina, L., Gierlichs, B., Lemke-Rust, K.: Differential Cluster Analysis. In: Clavier, C., Gaj, K. (eds.) CHES 2009. LNCS, vol. 5747, pp. 112–127. Springer, Heidelberg (2009)
6. Chari, S., Rao, J.R., Rohatgi, P.: Template Attacks. In: Kaliski Jr., B.S., Koç, Ç.K., Paar, C. (eds.) CHES 2002. LNCS, vol. 2523, pp. 13–28. Springer, Heidelberg (2003)
7. Elaabid, M.A., Guilley, S.: Practical Improvements of Profiled Side-Channel Attacks on a Hardware Crypto-Accelerator. In: Bernstein, D.J., Lange, T. (eds.) AFRICACRYPT 2010. LNCS, vol. 6055, pp. 243–260. Springer, Heidelberg (2010)
8. Fukunaga, K.: Introduction to Statistical Pattern Recognition. Elsevier, New York (1990)
9. Gierlichs, B., Batina, L., Tuyls, P., Preneel, B.: Mutual Information Analysis. In: Oswald, E., Rohatgi, P. (eds.) CHES 2008. LNCS, vol. 5154, pp. 426–442. Springer, Heidelberg (2008)
10. Gierlichs, B., Lemke-Rust, K., Paar, C.: Template vs. Stochastic Methods - A Performance Analysis for Side Chennel Cryptanalysis. In: Goubin, L., Matsui, M. (eds.) CHES 2006. LNCS, vol. 4249, pp. 15–29. Springer, Heidelberg (2006)
11. Gandolfi, K., Mourtel, C., Olivier, F.: Electromagnetic Analysis: Concrete Results. In: Koç, Ç.K., Naccache, D., Paar, C. (eds.) CHES 2001. LNCS, vol. 2162, pp. 251–261. Springer, Heidelberg (2001)
12. Kocher, P.C.: Timing Attacks on Implementations of Diffie-Hellman, RSA, DSS, and Other Systems. In: Koblitz, N. (ed.) CRYPTO 1996. LNCS, vol. 1109, pp. 104–113. Springer, Heidelberg (1996)
13. Kocher, P.C., Jaffe, J., Jun, B.: Differential Power Analysis. In: Wiener, M. (ed.) CRYPTO 1999. LNCS, vol. 1666, pp. 388–397. Springer, Heidelberg (1999)
14. Le, T.-H., Clédière, J., Canovas, C., Robisson, B., Servière, C., Lacoume, J.-L.: A Proposition for Correlation Power Analysis Enhancement. In: Goubin, L., Matsui, M. (eds.) CHES 2006. LNCS, vol. 4249, pp. 174–186. Springer, Heidelberg (2006)
15. Mangard, S., Oswald, E., Popp, T.: Power Analysis Attacks. Springer, Heidelberg (2007)
16. Oswald, E., Mangard, S.: Template Attacks on Masking—Resistance Is Futile. In: Abe, M. (ed.) CT-RSA 2007. LNCS, vol. 4377, pp. 243–256. Springer, Heidelberg (2006)
17. Rechberger, C., Oswald, E.: Practical Template Attacks. In: Lim, C.H., Yung, M. (eds.) WISA 2004. LNCS, vol. 3325, pp. 440–456. Springer, Heidelberg (2005)
18. Standaert, F.-X., Archambeau, C.: Using Subspace-Based Template Attacks to Compare and Combine Power and Electromagnetic Information Leakages. In: Oswald, E., Rohatgi, P. (eds.) CHES 2008. LNCS, vol. 5154, pp. 411–425. Springer, Heidelberg (2008)
19. Schindler, W., Lemke, K., Paar, C.: A Stochastic Model for Differential Side Channel Cryptanalysis. In: Rao, J.R., Sunar, B. (eds.) CHES 2005. LNCS, vol. 3659, pp. 30–46. Springer, Heidelberg (2005)
20. Standaert, F.-X., Malkin, T.G., Yung, M.: A Unified Framework for the Analysis of Side-Channel Key Recovery Attacks. In: Joux, A. (ed.) EUROCRYPT 2009. LNCS, vol. 5479, pp. 443–461. Springer, Heidelberg (2009)
21. Whitnall, C., Oswald, E., Mather, L.: An Exploration of the Kolmogorov-Smirnov Test as a Competitor to Mutual Information Analysis. In: Prouff, E. (ed.) CARDIS 2011. LNCS, vol. 7079, pp. 234–251. Springer, Heidelberg (2011)
22. Ye, X., Eisenbarth, T.: Wide Collisions in Practice. In: Bao, F., Samarati, P., Zhou, J. (eds.) ACNS 2012. LNCS, vol. 7341, pp. 329–343. Springer, Heidelberg (2012)

Deterministic Hard Fault Attack on Trivium

Avijit Dutta[1] and Goutam Paul[2]

[1] Dept. of Computer Science & Engineering,
Jadavpur University, Kolkata 700 032, India
avijit2dutta@gmail.com
[2] Cryptology and Security Research Unit (CSRU),
R. C. Bose Centre for Cryptology & Security,
Indian Statistical Institute, Kolkata 700 108, India
goutam.paul@isical.ac.in

Abstract. So far, the major work in fault attack on Trivium has been confined to the soft fault attacks where the attacker injects some faults at random position and at random time in the cipher state and analyze a simplified version of the cipher. Besides this, there is also some result on hard fault attack [Hu et al., 2009] on Trivium where the attacker sets the value 0 at any random position of 288 bit state of the cipher permanently. In this approach the key of the cipher is determined with success probability not less than 0.2291. In this paper, we introduce another type of hard fault attack, called a *deterministic hard fault attack* on Trivium, by setting the value 1 at three particular positions of 288 bit state permanently. We call it *deterministic* because the internal state is revealed deterministically. More specifically, we show that if we observe 117 original keystream and 236 faulty keystream, we can retrieve the original state of the cipher in $2^{23.85}$ time with success probability 1.

Keywords: Deterministic hard fault attack, eSTREAM, Fault attack, Hard fault attack, Stream cipher, Trivium.

1 Introduction

Trivium is one of the hardware oriented synchronous stream ciphers and eSTREAM finalist [3]. It was designed by De Cannière and Preneel in 2005. It has an internal state $S = (s_0, \ldots s_{287})$ of length 288 bits consisting of three NFSRs A, B and C of length 93, 84 and 111 bits respectively.

The cipher takes an 80-bit secret key $K = (K_0, \ldots, K_{79})$ and an 80-bit IV $= (IV_0, \ldots, IV_{79})$. Key bits are loaded into register A, where the remaining bits of register A are set to 0. IV bits are loaded into register B, where the remaining bits of register B are set to 0 and all the bits of register C are set to 0 except the last three bits which are set to 1. Then it is iterated for $4 \cdot 288 = 1152$ rounds to update the state bits of the cipher without generating the keystream. This is known as *Key Scheduling Algorithm* (KSA). After key scheduling, keystream generation begins, where after each round, one bit of keystream z is generated and each of the 288 state bits are updated, out of which few state bits are updated

M. Yoshida and K. Mouri (Eds.): IWSEC 2014, LNCS 8639, pp. 134–145, 2014.

$$
\begin{array}{ll}
\textbf{Input: } \text{288 bit state } (s_0, s_1, \ldots, s_{287}) \\
\textbf{Output: } \text{Keystream } z = (z_1, z_2, \ldots) \\
\textbf{for } r = 1 \textit{ to } \text{as many bits required } \textbf{do} \\
\quad 1 \quad t_1 \leftarrow s_{65} + s_{92}; \\
\quad 2 \quad t_2 \leftarrow s_{161} + s_{176}; \\
\quad 3 \quad t_3 \leftarrow s_{242} + s_{287}; \\
\quad 4 \quad z_r \leftarrow t_1 + t_2 + t_3; \\
\quad 5 \quad t_1 \leftarrow t_1 + s_{90} \cdot s_{91} + s_{170}; \\
\quad 6 \quad t_2 \leftarrow t_2 + s_{174} \cdot s_{175} + s_{263}; \\
\quad 7 \quad t_3 \leftarrow t_3 + s_{285} \cdot s_{286} + s_{68}; \\
\quad 8 \quad (s_0, s_1, s_2, \ldots, s_{92}) \leftarrow (t_3, s_0, \ldots, s_{91}); \\
\quad 9 \quad (s_{93}, s_{94}, s_{95}, \ldots, s_{176}) \leftarrow (t_1, s_{93}, \ldots, s_{175}); \\
\quad 10 \quad (s_{177}, s_{178}, s_{181}, \ldots, s_{287}) \leftarrow (t_2, s_{177}, \ldots, s_{286}); \\
\textbf{end}
\end{array}
$$

Algorithm 1. Pseudo-Random Generation Algorithm (PRGA) of Trivium

nonlinearly. This is called *Pseudo-Random Generation Algorithm* (PRGA). In this context, it is to be noted that the generated keystream bit at each round t (i.e. z_t) is a linear combination of two specific state bits values from each of the three registers A,B,C at round $t - 1$ and thus this stream cipher is called *Trivium* ("Tri" means three). We summarize the PRGA in Algorithm 1.

1.1 Existing Works

There are some cryptanalytic attempts on Trivium [2, 8, 10, 11, 13–17] that do not consider the fault model. However, we limit our discussion to only the relevant fault attacks.

The first fault attack on stream cipher was proposed by Hoch and Shamir [6]. In literature, basically two types of fault attacks are there. One is *soft fault attack* and another is *hard fault attack*. In soft fault attack, an attacker is assumed to have the power to inject the fault at any random locations of the state. Therefore, when the attacker injects fault for multiple times then it is also assumed that the attacker can reset the system each time to get back the original state.

Hojsik and Rudolf [4] applied a kind of soft fault attack called *differential fault attack* on Trivium, where the attacker can inject an one bit fault into any of the random locations of 288 bits state of Trivium and consequently obtains difference of the keystream bit which is XOR of the original keystream bit and the faulty keystream bit and then recovers the whole state of the cipher with only 43 random fault injections.

As an improvement to this attack, Hojsik and Rudolf [5] adopted a different technique of differential fault attack called *floating fault attack*, where shifting of the state in time is similar to floating of the state. They showed that using this approach, the number of fault injections have significantly reduced from 43 faults to 3.2 faults on average of 10000 experiments with observation of 800 bit keystream. In floating fault attack model, the number of variables are significantly extended by denoting every new state bit as a new variable while not forgetting the connection given by the Trivium state evolution.

The authors in [12] reduced the number of fault injections to just 2 with only 420 bit keystream observations. They improved the attack using the SAT solver and improving the equation preprocessing phase and finally they were successful to recover the entire state of the cipher. From their experimental result, it has been reported that using 420 bit keystream the entire state can be recovered in almost 138.653 seconds.

As opposed to soft fault attack, Yupu Hu et al. showed [7] that Trivium is weak under soft fault analysis and analyzed hard fault attack model on Trivium. Unlike the soft fault attack, in hard fault attack, an attacker injects fault at a random location of the states permanently. Authors reported that if an attacker sets the value of some random location of 288 bit states permanently to 0, then depending on the position of the injected fault, attacker can recover the key with success probability not less than 0.2291.

1.2   Summary of the Attack

In this paper, we consider *deterministic hard fault attack* model where the three particular state bits are stuck at value 1 forever from time $t = 0$. Similar model has been considered in [9] studying the behavior of RC4 when the index j is stuck at a certain value not known to the attacker. The seminal work on differential fault analysis [1] also considers similar hard fault for DES. In the first phase, by observing 236 faulty keystream bits, we develop 236 linear equations from the observed faulty keystream bits and solving them we find the solution of $s_j^{(0)}$, $0 \leq j \leq 68$, $91 \leq j \leq 170$, $175 \leq j \leq 263$, $286 \leq j \leq 287$. At this stage, specific 48 variables remain unused and we show that we can recover the internal state with a complexity of 2^{52}. However, we introduce a second phase to reduce the overall attack complexity. In this phase, we observe 117 original keystream bits which are generated from the same cipher state at time $t = 0$ (but this time without injecting the fault) and develop 73 polynomial equations of degree ≤ 2 out of which total 44 linear and nonlinear equations have been used. Our *back and forth* strategy (described in Section 3) recovers the complete internal state in approximately $2^{23.85}$ complexity, with a success probability of 1.

Notations. We use $S^{(t)}$ to denote the entire state of the cipher at time t. We have also considered $s_j^{(t)}$ to denote the value of state bit s_j at time t. Therefore $S^{(t)} = \left\{ s_j^{(t)} | 0 \leq j \leq 287 \right\}$. Note that we have considered the index (j) of the state bit starting from 0 instead of 1. We use z_{t+1} to denote the non-faulty keystream bit at time $t + 1$ and z'_{t+1} to denote the faulty keystream bit at time $t + 1$. We set $t = 0$ at the instant when the *hard fault* is introduced. We want to recover the state $S^{(0)}$, i.e., the state just before the fault is introduced during the PRGA.

2   Partial State Recovery from Faulty Keystream

This is the first phase of our attack model where the state bits s_{90}^0, s_{174}^0, s_{285}^0 are stuck at 1. According to Step 4 of Algorithm 1, keystream generation function at time t is a linear combination of the state bits at time $t-1$. That means,

$$z_t' = s_{65}^{(t-1)} + s_{92}^{(t-1)} + s_{161}^{(t-1)} + s_{176}^{(t-1)} + s_{242}^{(t-1)} + s_{287}^{(t-1)}, \qquad t \geq 1. \tag{1}$$

According to Steps 8, 9, 10 of Algorithm 1, we have

$$s_r^{(t+1)} \leftarrow s_{r-1}^{(t)}, \qquad 1 \leq r \leq 92, \ \ 94 \leq r \leq 176, \ \ 178 \leq r \leq 287.$$

We can write Equation (1) at time $t+1$ as a linear combination of the state bits at time $t = 0$ in the following way.

$$z_{t+1}' = s_{65-t}^{(0)} + s_{92-t}^{(0)} + s_{161-t}^{(0)} + s_{176-t}^{(0)} + s_{242-t}^{(0)} + s_{287-t}^{(0)}, \qquad 0 \leq t \leq 65. \tag{2}$$

Note that the structure of this equation will remain intact up to $t = 65$. When $t = 66$, then $s_0^{(1)}$ and $s_{177}^{(1)}$ will appear in Equation (2) and make the equation nonlinear, because according to Algorithm 1, $s_0^{(t)}$ and $s_{177}^{(t)}$ are nonlinear functions of the state bits at time $t-1$. Now, $s_{90}^{(0)}$, $s_{174}^{(0)}$ and $s_{285}^{(0)}$ appear in quadratic term of the nonlinear state update equations.

$$s_0^{(t+1)} \leftarrow s_{242}^{(t)} + s_{287}^{(t)} + s_{285}^{(t)} \cdot s_{286}^{(t)} + s_{68}^{(t)}, \tag{3}$$

$$s_{93}^{(t+1)} \leftarrow s_{65}^{(t)} + s_{92}^{(t)} + s_{90}^{(t)} \cdot s_{91}^{(t)} + s_{170}^{(t)}, \tag{4}$$

$$s_{177}^{(t+1)} \leftarrow s_{161}^{(t)} + s_{176}^{(t)} + s_{174}^{(t)} \cdot s_{175}^{(t)} + s_{263}^{(t)}. \tag{5}$$

Therefore, if their values are stuck at 1 forever, all these nonlinear state update equations will become linear equations and as a result of that, keystream generation equation will become linear forever, since no nonlinearity is introduced into the system of keystream equations.

The assumption of our model, i.e., $(s_{90}^{(0)} = s_{174}^{(0)} = s_{285}^{(0)} = 1)$, makes the state bit variables $\left\{ s_{69}^{(0)}, s_{70}^{(0)}, \ldots, s_{90}^{(0)} \right\}$, $\left\{ s_{171}^{(0)}, s_{172}^{(0)}, \ldots, s_{174}^{(0)} \right\}$ and $\left\{ s_{264}^{(0)}, s_{265}^{(0)}, \ldots, s_{285}^{(0)} \right\}$ unused.

Theorem 1. *Let U_r be the set of used variables amongst $s_0^{(0)}, s_1^{(0)}, \ldots, s_{287}^{(0)}$ up to round r. $|U_r|$ monotonically increases from 0 to 240 as r increases from 0 to 86 and U_r remains fixed for $r \geq 86$.*

Proof. Let A_u, B_u and C_u denote the used variables of register A, B and C respectively. Now from Equation (2), and according to the assumption of our model, the first 66 equations will include the following variables in A_u, B_u and C_u respectively.

$$A_u \leftarrow \left\{ s_0^0, \ldots, s_{65}^0 \right\} \cup \left\{ s_{91}^0, s_{92}^0 \right\}, \qquad B_u \leftarrow \left\{ s_{96}^0, \ldots, s_{161}^0 \right\} \cup \left\{ s_{175}^0, s_{176}^0 \right\},$$

$$C_u \leftarrow \left\{ s^0_{177}, ..., s^0_{242} \right\} \cup \left\{ s^0_{286}, s^0_{287} \right\}.$$

According to the assumption of our model, nonlinear state update equations become linear and we can write the state update equations Equation (3), (4), (5) in terms of the state bit variables $s^{(0)}_j$ in the following way:

$$s^{t+1}_0 = s^{(0)}_{242-t} + s^{(0)}_{287-t} + s^{(0)}_{286-t} + s^{(0)}_{68-t}, \qquad 0 \leq t \leq 65. \tag{6}$$

$$s^{t+1}_{93} = s^{(0)}_{65-t} + s^{(0)}_{92-t} + s^{(0)}_{91-t} + s^{(0)}_{170-t}, \qquad 0 \leq t \leq 65. \tag{7}$$

$$s^{t+1}_{177} = s^{(0)}_{161-t} + s^{(0)}_{176-t} + s^{(0)}_{175-t} + s^{(0)}_{263-t}, \qquad 0 \leq t \leq 68. \tag{8}$$

By considering Equation (2) and Equations (6) to (8), three new variables will be added in each of the set A_u, B_u and C_u from round $r = 67$ to round $r = 69$. That means A_u, B_u and C_u will be updated to

$$A_u \leftarrow \left\{ s^0_0, ..., s^0_{68} \right\} \cup \left\{ s^0_{91}, s^0_{92} \right\}, \qquad B_u \leftarrow \left\{ s^0_{93}, ..., s^0_{161} \right\} \cup \left\{ s^0_{175}, s^0_{176} \right\},$$

$$C_u \leftarrow \left\{ s^0_{177}, ..., s^0_{242} \right\} \cup \left\{ s^0_{261}, s^0_{262}, s^0_{263} \right\} \cup \left\{ s^0_{286}, s^0_{287} \right\}.$$

By observing Equation (2), Equations (6) to (8) and according to the assumption of our model, the highest indexed state bit variable that can be included into the set $A_u \setminus \left\{ s^0_{91}, s^0_{92} \right\}$ is $s^{(0)}_{68}$. Similarly, the highest indexed state bit variable that can be included into the set $B_u \setminus \left\{ s^0_{175}, s^0_{176} \right\}$ is $s^{(0)}_{170}$. Likewise, the highest indexed state bit variable that can be included into the set $C_u \setminus \left\{ s^0_{286}, s^0_{287} \right\}$ is $s^{(0)}_{263}$. Note that, up to round $r = 69$, the highest indexed state bit variables of set A_u and C_u have already been included into the corresponding set.

Now, note that the highest indexed state bit variable of set A_u up to round $r = 66$ is $s^{(0)}_{65}$ and the highest indexed state bit variable that can be included into set A_u is $s^{(0)}_{68}$. Thus, the gap of the variables is filled up at round $r = 69$. Therefore, from round $r = 70$ onward, no variables will be added into set A_u. Variables will be added only into set B_u and C_u. In round $r = 70$, B_u will include $s^{(0)}_{170}$ and C_u will include $s^{(0)}_{260}$ as new variables. Now, note that there is a gap of variables to be included in set B_u and C_u, which is between $s^{(0)}_{161}$ to $s^{(0)}_{170}$ for set B_u and between $s^{(0)}_{242}$ to $s^{(0)}_{260}$ for set C_u. Therefore, the distance of this gap for set B_u is $(169 - 162) = 7$ and for set C_u is $(259 - 243) = 16$. Therefore we need to iterate for max $\{16, 7\} = 16$ more rounds to have the usability of each of the remaining variables at least once, since each round contributes at least one new variable in the set B_u and C_u from round 70. Therefore at round $r = 86$, $|U_r|$ becomes 240 and the set U_r becomes

$$U_r \leftarrow \left\{ s^{(0)}_0, s^{(0)}_1 \ldots s^{(0)}_{68} \right\} \cup \left\{ s^{(0)}_{91}, s^{(0)}_{92} \right\} \cup \left\{ s^{(0)}_{93}, s^{(0)}_{94} \ldots s^{(0)}_{170} \right\} \cup \left\{ s^{(0)}_{175}, s^{(0)}_{176} \right\} \cup$$

$$\left\{ s^{(0)}_{177}, s^{(0)}_{178} \ldots s^{(0)}_{263} \right\} \cup \left\{ s^{(0)}_{286}, s^{(0)}_{287} \right\}.$$

Now, from round $r \geq 87$, if we express the equation of keystream bit in terms of the initial state bits $s^{(0)}_j$, one can find all the state bits appear in equation at round $r \geq 87$ are included in set U_{86}. Therefore, no new variables will be added into set U_{86} for round $r \geq 87$ and therefore, $|U_r|$ remains fixed at 240 for $r \geq 86$.   □

Since beyond round 86, no new state variable is used, we could have stopped the equation construction process and solved the resulting system of 86 linear equations in 240 variables. But the rank of the system is 86 and so we had to guess $(240 - 86) = 154$ variables.

Towards a more efficient method, we continue the equation construction process and the rank of the system of equations monotonically increases up to $r = 236$. From round 237 onwards, the rank remains the same. So we have 236 independent equations in 240 variables.

We solve it using Gaussian elimination method and found the unique solution of 228 variables and total of 8 independent linear equations of 12 unknowns state bit variables which are written as follows:

$$s_{67}^{(0)} = s_{286}^{(0)} + c_1,$$
$$s_{68}^{(0)} = s_{286}^{(0)} + s_{287}^{(0)} + c_2,$$
$$s_{91}^{(0)} = s_{262}^{(0)} + s_{286}^{(0)} + c_3,$$
$$s_{92}^{(0)} = s_{262}^{(0)} + s_{263}^{(0)} + s_{287}^{(0)} + c_4,$$
$$s_{169}^{(0)} = s_{262}^{(0)} + s_{286}^{(0)} + c_5,$$
$$s_{170}^{(0)} = s_{263}^{(0)} + s_{286}^{(0)} + s_{287}^{(0)} + c_6,$$
$$s_{175}^{(0)} = s_{262}^{(0)} + c_7,$$
$$s_{176}^{(0)} = s_{262}^{(0)} + s_{263}^{(0)} + c_8,$$

where $c_i \in \{0, 1\}$ for $1 \leq i \leq 8$. From the above set of equations we found that the occurrence of four particular variables $s_{262}^{(0)}, s_{263}^{(0)}, s_{286}^{(0)}, s_{287}^{(0)}$ is maximum. So we guess the value of state bit variables $s_{262}^{(0)}, s_{263}^{(0)}, s_{286}^{(0)}, s_{287}^{(0)}$ which solves the remaining $(12-4) = 8$ unknown variables which are $s_{67}^{(0)}, s_{68}^{(0)}, s_{91}^{(0)}, s_{92}^{(0)}, s_{169}^{(0)}, s_{170}^{(0)}, s_{175}^{(0)}, s_{176}^{(0)}$.

3   Recovery of Remaining State Bits from Non-faulty Keystream

In the first phase, $288 - 240 = 48$ state bits never appeared in any equation and hence remain undetermined. Guessing 48 unused variables along with 4 variables from Section 2 yields the time complexity of key recovery as 2^{52}. Towards improving this time complexity, we choose to solve for 48 undetermined variables. To solve them, we choose the non-faulty keystream path, generated from the same state $S^{(0)}$ but without injection of the fault. We solve the resulting system of polynomial equations of degree d, $1 \leq d \leq 2$, in a back and forth way. This phase consists of two subphases. In the first subphase, we express each of the non-faulty keystream bit as a linear combination of the state bit variables $s_j^{(0)}$ and in the next subphase, we express each of the non-faulty keystream bit as a nonlinear combination of the state bit variables $s_j^{(0)}$. Only a subset of these linear and nonlinear equations have been considered in our approach. After a certain time, when we find an equation of a specific structure in the second subphase, then we stop the equation generation process and start to solve the equations in back and forth way with the linear equations developed in the first subphase.

3.1 Non-faulty Linear Phase

We can express the non-faulty keystream bit at round $t+1$ in terms of the state bit variables $s_j^{(0)}$ from the equation at Step 4 of Algorithm 1 as follows:

$$z_{t+1} = s_{65-t}^{(0)} + s_{92-t}^{(0)} + s_{161-t}^{(0)} + s_{176-t}^{(0)} + s_{242-t}^{(0)} + s_{287-t}^{(0)}, \quad 0 \leq t \leq 65. \quad (9)$$

Up to $t = 65$, the keystream generation equation is linear. At $t = 66$, state bit variables $s_0^{(1)}$ and $s_{177}^{(1)}$ appear in the keystream equation and since the original state update equation is nonlinear, the keystream equation becomes nonlinear at $t = 66$.

Since we have already solved 240 variables in the first phase of our attack, it is evident that many equations developed in the second phase will contain all known state bit variables and hence we discard them. For example, the first two equations at round $r = 1$ and round $r = 2$ contain all known state bit variables and they have not been considered. From round $3 \leq r \leq 24$, the equations contain at least one unused state bit variable and as a result they have been considered into our set of equations. Again from round $r = 25$ to round $r = 66$, the equations contain all known state bit variables and hence they have not been considered into our set of equations. Therefore, together 22 out of 66 linear equations have been considered which contain at least one of the remaining unused 48 state bit variables.

Interestingly, these 22 linear equations cover all the 48 unused state bit variables. So, we could have used these linear equations and solved them by using Gaussian elimination, but all these 22 linear equations are linearly independent and hence the rank of these 22 linear equations is 22. Since we have 48 unknown state bit variables and rank becomes 22, we had to guess (48-22)=26 variables. Thus, the total number of guessed variables from phase 1 and phase 2 altogether would have become $4 + 26 = 30$ and the complexity of the attack would become 2^{30}. In order to reduce this complexity, we consider some nonlinear equations developed in subphase 2 and we show that it leads to fewer number of variables to be guessed.

3.2 Non-faulty Nonlinear Phase

As we have mentioned in Section 3.1, the first 66 rounds of PRGA are linear and the non-linearity is introduced into the keystream generation Equation (9) afterwards. In these nonlinear equations, whenever known terms (state bit variables which have already been solved) appear in the equation, we substitute their value in the corresponding equation and generate many polynomial equations of degree d, $1 \leq d \leq 2$. So, basically equations are formed by the substitution of the values of the solved state bit variables. In this case also, since we have already solved 240 state bit variables in Section 2, many of the nonlinear equations contain no unknown state bit variables and hence we remove those equations from the set E of our considered equations.

Since nonlinear terms are introduced into the PRGA from round $r = 67$, we obtain nonlinear equations from this round. We continue the equation generation process until we find an equation of the form "$a + b = c$", where a and b are unknown state bit variables and c is a known term so that if one guesses any one of a or b, the other variable can be assigned a definite value. We find such type of equation in round $r = 117$ for the first time. In particular, the equation is

$$
\begin{aligned}
s_{264}^{(0)} + s_{171}^{(0)} = {} & z_{116} + s_{192}^{(0)} + s_{123}^{(0)} + s_{33}^{(0)} + s_{138}^{(0)} + s_{111}^{(0)} + s_{213}^{(0)} + s_{219}^{(0)} \\
& + s_{156}^{(0)} + s_{258}^{(0)} + s_{124}^{(0)} \cdot s_{125}^{(0)} + s_{126}^{(0)} + s_{235}^{(0)} \cdot s_{236}^{(0)} + s_{237}^{(0)} \\
& + s_{43}^{(0)} \cdot s_{44}^{(0)} + s_{58}^{(0)} \cdot s_{59}^{(0)} + s_{60}^{(0)} + s_{169}^{(0)} \cdot s_{170}^{(0)} + s_{262}^{(0)} \cdot s_{263}^{(0)} \quad (10)
\end{aligned}
$$

which is derived from the equation at Step 4 of Algorithm 1 by expressing the keystream generation equation in terms of the state bits $s_j^{(0)}$. Now, in Equation (10), we guess the value of $s_{171}^{(0)}$ and solve the state bit variable $s_{264}^{(0)}$. The state bit variable $s_{264}^{(0)}$ also appears in the equation at round $r = 116$, and so using the value of $s_{264}^{(0)}$ and guessing the value of another state bit variable $s_{172}^{(0)}$, we solve the state bit variable $s_{265}^{(0)}$. In this way, starting from equation at round $r = 117$, we go back up to 8 consecutive equations and with guessing of 4 particular state bit variables $s_{171}^{(0)}, s_{172}^{(0)}, s_{173}^{(0)}, s_{174}^{(0)}$, we solve the state bit variables $s_{264}^{0}, s_{265}^{(0)}, \dots, s_{272}^{(0)}$. Let us denote the set of solved state bit variables in subphase 2 as V. Now, if we would go back to one more equation, that means equation at round $r = 108$ for solving the state bit variable $s_{273}^{(0)}$, a new unknown state bit variable $s_{69}^{(0)}$ appears. In particular, the equation is

$$
\begin{aligned}
s_{69}^{(0)} + s_{271}^{(0)} \cdot s_{272}^{(0)} + s_{273}^{(0)} = {} & z_{107} + s_{201}^{(0)} + s_{132}^{(0)} + s_{44}^{(0)} + s_{147}^{(0)} + s_{120}^{(0)} + s_{222}^{(0)} + s_{228}^{(0)} \\
& + s_{180}^{(0)} + s_{133}^{(0)} \cdot s_{134}^{(0)} + s_{135}^{(0)} + s_{244}^{(0)} \cdot s_{245}^{(0)} + s_{246}^{(0)} \\
& + s_{52}^{(0)} \cdot s_{53}^{(0)} + s_{67}^{(0)} \cdot s_{68}^{(0)} \quad (11)
\end{aligned}
$$

which is derived from the equation at Step 4 of Algorithm 1 by expressing the keystream generation equation in terms of the state bits $s_j^{(0)}$.

Note that in Equation (11), all of the state bit variables are known except $s_{273}^{(0)}$ and $s_{69}^{(0)}$. To solve for $s_{273}^{(0)}$, we have to guess $s_{69}^{(0)}$. But that would lead to over estimation of the number of state bit variables to be guessed and hence we stop. We call it a *stop-point*. Note that the stop-point is a point in our considered set of equations, where we go for solving an equation of the form: "$a+b = c$", where $a, b \notin V$.

To remove this stop-point, we go back to subphase 1 in Section 3.1, where using the solution of the solved variables from the set V, we try to solve as many equations as possible until we reach again to the stop-point in subphase 1. Each time we solve an equation in any of the two subphases, we add the solution to the set of solved variables V. Now, once we reach to stop-point in subphase 1, we again come back to subphase 2 and using the solved variables of set V, we again try to solve as many equations as possible until we again reach to the stop-point in subphase 2.

Once we reach to the stop-point again, we go back to subphase 1. In this way until all of the 48 variables are solved, this *"back and forth"* method of solving the equations continues. This process will eventually terminate, since the number of unknown state bit variables are finite and once we solve a specific state bit variable, we do not consider that again.

Since we solve 48 unknown state bit variables out of which only 4 specific variables have been guessed, we solve 22 variables $s_{264}^{(0)}, s_{265}^{(0)}, \ldots, s_{285}^{(0)}$ in subphase 2 using the back and forth strategy, and using the same technique in subphase 1, we solve 22 variables which are state bit variables $s_{69}^{(0)}, s_{70}^{(0)}, \ldots, s_{90}^{(0)}$.

Thus, in subphase 2, starting from equation at round $r = 117$, we solve for the variables $s_{264}^{(0)}, s_{265}^{(0)}, \ldots, s_{285}^{(0)}$ by considering 22 consecutive previous rounds equations, coupled with the last 11 linear equations from subphase 1. So the round number, where we encounter the last nonlinear equation in subphase 2 is $(117 - 22) = 95$. As has been mentioned already, the nonlinear equations start to generate from round 67 and hence $(95 - 67) + 1 = 29$ nonlinear equations in subphase 2 are redundant for our use.

We summarize both the phases of our state recovery method in Algorithm 2.

4   Performance Analysis

We present the time complexity of our state recovery algorithm in the following result.

Theorem 2. *The total time complexity of Algorithm 2 is approximately $2^{23.85}$.*

Proof. Step 1 of the algorithm takes input an augmented matrix of dimension 236×241 and produces the unique solution of 228 state bit variables and a system of 8 linear independent equations. Total time complexity of Gaussian elimination method in this step is $241 \times 241 \times 236 \approx 2^{23.70}$.

Step 3 of the algorithm solves 8 linear equations for all possible combinations of free variables and in each of the equation contains at most 4 terms which are linearly combined as shown in Section 2. Therefore, the total time complexity to solve 8 linear equations for obtaining the value of 8 variables excluding the guessed variables is 8×3. Since Step 2 will be iterated for 16 times, so the overall time complexity of Step 2 and Step 3 of the algorithm is $16 \times 8 \times 3 \approx 2^{8.58}$

Step 5 of the algorithm solves total 44 linear and nonlinear equations in cyclic way of solving the equations in subphase 1 and subphase 2 as described in Section 3.2. Each of the equations contains at most 29 terms, therefore at most 28 operations are to be performed. So the time complexity of solving remaining 44 variables excluding the guessed 4 variables is 28×44. Since Step 4 of the algorithm is executed for $16 \times 16 = 256$ times, therefore the total time complexity of Step 4 and Step 5 of the algorithm is $16 \times 16 \times 28 \times 44 \approx 2^{18.226}$.

Input: 236×241 dimension linear augmented matrix augmented with 236
faulty keystream z'_t, set of considered 44 polynomial equations E of
degree at most 2, and 117 original keystream z_t.

Output: S^0.

1 Feed the augmented matrix of dimension 236×241 to Gaussian elimination method;

2 **for** *each of the possible combinations of free variables* $s^0_{262}, s^0_{263}, s^0_{286}, s^0_{287}$ **do**

3   Solve the dependent variables $s^0_{67}, s^0_{68}, s^0_{91}, s^0_{92}, s^0_{169}, s^0_{170}, s^0_{175}, s^0_{176}$ from 8 linear equations as mentioned in Section 2;

4   **for** *each of the possible combination of free variables* $s^0_{171}, s^0_{172}, s^0_{173}, s^0_{174}$ **do**

5   Solve all of the remaining 48 unused variables from set of equations E and 117 original keystream bits z_t by back and forth solving technique that has been described in 3.2;

6   **for** $t = 1$ *to* 288 **do**

7   generate keystream z''_t from the current solution state;

8   **if** $z_t \neq z''_t$ **then**

9   discard the current solution state and go for next solution state;

         end

      end

10   **if** *the keystream z and z' matches in all the 288 rounds* **then**

11   output the recovered state as the correct solution;

      end

   end

end

Algorithm 2. State Recovery Algorithm

Step 6 to Step 9 of the algorithm check the solution whether it should be considered or discarded. Keystream is generated for round $r = 288$ and in each round there is a linear combination of six variables and state update equation. There is at most 17 operations to be performed in each round. Since this step is executed for $16 \times 16 \times 288$ times, therefore the total time complexity of Step 6 to Step 9 of the algorithm is $16 \times 16 \times 288 \times 17 \approx 2^{20.25}$.

So, the overall time complexity of the algorithm is $2^{23.70} + 2^{8.58} + 2^{18.226} + 2^{20.25} \approx 2^{23.85}$.   □

Table 1 shows how our attack compares with other existing attacks. An unoptimized simple C implementation of our algorithm took 2 seconds on average (over 1000 experiments) to recover the entire state $S^{(0)}$ with probability 1 on a Intel(R) Core^{TM} 2 Duo CPU, each CPU running at 2.8 GHz.

Table 1. Comparison with existing attacks

Attack	Nature of faults	#Faults	#Keystream bits		Complexity
			Faulty	Non-faulty	
[4, Section 5.4]	Soft	200	180	180	$2^{44.2}$
[4, Section 5.5]	Soft	43 (approx)	280	280	Couple of seconds.
[5, Section 5.5]	Soft	3.2 (average)	800	800	$2^{37.7}$
[12, Section 6]	Soft	2 (average)	420	420	138.653 seconds
[7]	Hard	6378.89	9048	0	−
Ours	Hard	708	236	117	$2^{23.85}$

5 Future Work and Conclusion

We introduce a deterministic hard fault attack on Trivium. It recovers the state of the cipher in almost $2^{23.85}$ simple operations, with the observation of total 236 faulty and 117 non faulty keystream bits. We also show that our attack model is better than the existing fault attack models in terms of the time taken to recover the state of the cipher. As a future work, we plan to improve our attack to recover the state of the cipher of Trivium by reducing our assumptions without significant decrease in the efficiency of the attack. For example, one can introduce hard fault into any one or two of the three state bit locations which are involved in quadratic terms of state update equation (see Step 5 to 7 of Algorithm 1) instead of all three. We also plan to analyze similar attacks on other hardware stream ciphers that have non-linear state update and/or keystream generation equations.

References

1. Biham, E., Shamir, A.: Differential fault analysis of secret key cryptosystems. In: Kaliski Jr., B.S. (ed.) CRYPTO 1997. LNCS, vol. 1294, pp. 513–525. Springer, Heidelberg (1997)
2. Borghoff, J.: Mixed-integer Linear Programming in the Analysis of Trivium and Ktantan. Cryptology ePrint Archive, Report 2012/676
3. De Cannière, C., Preneel, B.: Trivium: A Stream Cipher Construction Inspired by Block Cipher Design Principles. eSTREAM, ECRYPT Stream Cipher Project, Report 2005/30 (2005), http://www.ecrypt.eu.org/stream
4. Hojsík, M., Rudolf, B.: Differential fault analysis of Trivium. In: Nyberg, K. (ed.) FSE 2008. LNCS, vol. 5086, pp. 158–172. Springer, Heidelberg (2008)
5. Hojsík, M., Rudolf, B.: Floating fault analysis of Trivium. In: Chowdhury, D.R., Rijmen, V., Das, A. (eds.) INDOCRYPT 2008. LNCS, vol. 5365, pp. 239–250. Springer, Heidelberg (2008)
6. Hoch, J.J., Shamir, A.: Fault Analysis of Stream Ciphers. In: Joye, M., Quisquater, J.-J. (eds.) CHES 2004. LNCS, vol. 3156, pp. 240–253. Springer, Heidelberg (2004)
7. Hu, Y., Zhang, F., Zhang, Y.: Hard Fault Analysis of Trivium. Cryptology ePrint Archive, Report 2009/333
8. Khazaei, S., Hasanzadeh, M.M., Kiaei, M.S.: Linear Sequential Circuit Approximation of Grain and Trivium Stream Ciphers. Cryptology ePrint Archive, Report 2006/141

9. Maitra, S., Paul, G.: Recovering RC4 Permutation from 2048 Keystream Bytes if j Is Stuck. In: Mu, Y., Susilo, W., Seberry, J. (eds.) ACISP 2008. LNCS, vol. 5107, pp. 306–320. Springer, Heidelberg (2008)
10. Maximov, A., Biryukov, A.: Two Trivial Attacks on Trivium. Cryptology ePrint Archive, Report 2007/021
11. McDonald, C., Charnes, C., Pieprzyk, J.: An Algebraic Analysis of Trivium Ciphers based on the Boolean Satisfiability Problem. Cryptology ePrint Archive, Report 2007/129
12. Mohamed, M.S.E., Bulygin, S., Buchmann, J.: Improved Differential Fault Analysis of Trivium. In: Proceedings of the COSADE 2011-Second International Workshop on Constructuve Side-Channel Analysis and Secure Design (2011)
13. Mroczkowski, P., Szmidt, J.: Corrigendum to: The Cube Attack on Stream Cipher Trivium and Quadraticity Tests. Cryptology ePrint Archive, Report 2010/032
14. Priemuth-Schmid, D., Biryukov, A.: Slid Pairs in Salsa20 and Trivium. Cryptology ePrint Archive, Report 2008/405
15. Raddum, H.: Cryptanalytic results on Trivium. Technical Report 2006/039, The eSTREAM Project (March 27, 2006), http://ecrypt.eu.org/stream/papersdir/2006/039.ps
16. Teo, S., Wong, K.K., Bartlett, H., Simpson, L., Dawson, E.: Algebraic analysis of Trivium-like ciphers. Cryptology ePrint Archive, Report 2013/240
17. Wong, K.K., Bard, G.V.: Improved Algebraic Cryptanalysis of QUAD, Bivium and Trivium via Graph Partitioning on Equation Systems. Cryptology ePrint Archive, Report 2010/349

DPA Resilience of Rotation-Symmetric S-boxes

Muhammet Ali Evci[1] and Selçuk Kavut[2]

[1] Cyber Security Institute, Informatic and Information Security Research Center,
TÜBİTAK, 41400, Kocaeli, Turkey
mali.evci@tubitak.gov.tr
[2] Department of Electronics Engineering, Gebze Institute of Technology – GYTE,
41400, Kocaeli, Turkey
skavut@gyte.edu.tr

Abstract. We regenerate the S-boxes that achieve the best possible trade-off between nonlinearity and differential uniformity in the class of 6×6 rotation-symmetric S-boxes (RSSBs) that are bijective, and then classify them in terms of transparency order. We find that although the transparency order ≥ 5.638 for the inverse function over $\mathbb{F}_{2^6}$, which can also be considered as rotation-symmetric, there exist RSSBs with the same nonlinearity and differential uniformity as those of the inverse function, having transparency order as low as 5.238. Motivated by this, we perform a steepest-descent-like iterative search algorithm in the class of 8×8 RSSBs and attain S-boxes with nonlinearity 104, differential uniformity 6, and transparency orders noticeably better than that of the AES S-box. Finally, replacing the AES S-box with those found by the search algorithm, we implement differential power analysis (DPA) attacks on SASEBO-GII and give a comparison of the results.

1 Introduction

In most of the block cipher cryptosystems, the S-boxes (substitution boxes) are the only nonlinear components, and hence the strength of these cryptosystems depends heavily on the cryptographic properties of the S-boxes. On one hand, most of these properties such as nonlinearity, differential uniformity, and algebraic degree protects the cyptosystem against linear [12], differential [1], and higher order differential [10] cryptanalyses respectively, which are independent from the hardware design of the S-boxes. On the other hand, the side channel analysis (SCA) relies on the hardware's leakages such as the timing of operations [8], power consumption [9], and electromagnetic radiation [19], and therefore the cryptographic primitives used in a cryptosystem should also be resistant against SCA. In this direction, the resistance of an S-box to side channel attacks is quantified in [18] which introduces the notion of transparency order of an S-box. Then, it was shown [3] that some highly nonlinear S-boxes (including the AES S-box) constructed using power maps over $\mathbb{F}_{2^n}$ have bad transparency orders. However, there are still no construction methods of the S-boxes with low transparency order, which achieve high nonlinearity, low differential uniformity, and high algebraic degree. Recently, a constrained random search is

M. Yoshida and K. Mouri (Eds.): IWSEC 2014, LNCS 8639, pp. 146–157, 2014.

performed [13] yielding 8×8 S-boxes with lower transparency orders than that of the AES S-box. Subsequently, a search in the class of rotation-symmetric S-boxes (RSSBs) is carried out in [14], which improves both transparency order and nonlinearity results in [13]. Then, in [17], using genetic algorithms the transparency order obtained in [14] is noticeably improved at the price of weaker nonlinearity and differential uniformity. In this paper, we improve the traditional cryptographic properties such as nonlinearity, differential uniformity, and absolute indicator along with the transparency order when compared with those in the literature.

Let $s : \mathbb{F}_{2^n} \to \mathbb{F}_{2^n}$ be an S-box. Then, in a normal basis over $\mathbb{F}_{2^n}$, the S-boxes for which $(s(\alpha))^2 = s(\alpha^2)$, $\forall \ \alpha \in \mathbb{F}_{2^n}$, can be considered as rotation-symmetric [20]. It was shown [20] that the S-boxes described as a sum of power maps and exponentiations over finite fields are linearly equivalent to RSSBs. Hence, most of the S-box constructions, including the inverse function [16] (used as S-box in the AES), can be regarded as RSSBs, which demonstrates the fact that the class of RSSBs contains cryptographically desirable nonlinear S-boxes.

In [7], the bijective RSSBs of size 6×6 achieving the best possible trade-off between nonlinearity and differential uniformity in the class, i.e., with nonlinearity 24 and differential uniformity 4, are classified in terms of absolute indicator and algebraic degree. We regenerate those S-boxes and compute their transparency orders, which shows the existence of the S-boxes with significantly low transparency orders among them. Motivated by this, we perform a search in the class of 8×8 RSSBs that are bijective utilizing a steepest-descent-like iterative search algorithm [6], and find S-boxes with transparency order better than that of the AES S-box, attaining the other cryptographic properties comparable to those of the AES S-box. Further, using SASEBO-GII (Side-channel Attack Standard Evaluation Board-GII), we implement differential power analysis (DPA) [9] attacks on AES containing these S-boxes and compare their DPA resistance using the success rate [22] as our SCA security metric.

The remainder of this paper is organized as follows. In the following section, we survey the basic definitions and cryptographic criteria of S-boxes. In Section 3, we find the affine transformations under which the transparency order is invariant, and present the transparency orders of 6×6 RSSBs in [7] with nonlinearity 24 and differential uniformity 4. In Section 4, the cryptographic properties of the 8×8 RSSBs generated by the steepest-descent-like iterative search algotihm are given and compared with those of the S-boxes in the literature. Section 5 presents the implementation results of the DPA attacks on SASEBO-GII. Finally, we conclude the paper in Section 6.

2   Preliminaries

2.1   Cryptographic Properties

An $n \times m$ S-box F is defined as a mapping $F : \mathbb{F}_2^n \to \mathbb{F}_2^m$, which is called n-variable Boolean function if $m = 1$. Most of the block cipher cryptosystems use the S-boxes with $n = m$. The S-box F can be considered as a combination of n-variable Boolean functions, i.e., $F(x) = (f_0(x), f_1(x), \ldots, f_{m-1}(x))$, where $x \in \mathbb{F}_2^n$. The functions f_i of S are called coordinate functions and the non-zero linear combinations $v \cdot F$ for all $v \in \mathbb{F}_2^{m*}$ are called component functions.

The Walsh-Hadamard transform of an $n \times m$ S-box F is an even integer-valued function $W_F : \mathbb{F}_2^n \times \mathbb{F}_2^m \to [-2^n, 2^n]$ defined as

$$W_F(\omega, v) = \sum_{x \in \mathbb{F}_2^n} (-1)^{\omega \cdot x \oplus v \cdot F(x)} \quad, \tag{1}$$

where the inner product is over $\mathbb{F}_2$ and $\omega \in \mathbb{F}_2^n$. Nonlinearity of F is given by the minimum nonlinearity of all $2^m - 1$ component functions, which can be expressed in terms of the Walsh-Hadamard transformation, that is,

$$\begin{aligned} NL_F &= \min_{v \in \mathbb{F}_2^{m*}} \{NL_{v \cdot F}\} \quad, \\ &= \min_{v \in \mathbb{F}_2^{m*}} \left\{ 2^{n-1} - \frac{1}{2} \max_{\omega \in \mathbb{F}_2^n} |W_F(\omega, v)| \right\} \quad, \\ &= 2^{n-1} - \frac{1}{2} \max_{\substack{\omega \in \mathbb{F}_2^n, \\ v \in \mathbb{F}_2^{m*}}} |W_F(\omega, v)| \quad, \end{aligned} \tag{2}$$

where $NL_{v \cdot F}$ is the nonlinearity of the component function $v \cdot F$. NL_F is equivalently defined as the minimum Hamming distance of all component functions from all n-variable affine functions. Highly nonlinear S-boxes are required in a cryptosystem to resist against linear cryptanalysis and to achieve good confusion properties.

The autocorrelation function of F is defined as

$$r_F(a, v) = \sum_{x \in \mathbb{F}_2^n} (-1)^{v \cdot (F(x) \oplus F(x \oplus a))} \quad, \tag{3}$$

where $a \in \mathbb{F}_2^n$. There are two important cryptographic criteria called global avalance characteristics (GAC) [24] related to the autocorrelation spectrum, which are used to have good diffusion properties. The maximum absolute value in the autocorrelation spectrum, except the origin $(a, v) = ((0, 0, \ldots, 0), (0, 0, \ldots, 0))$, is referred to as the absolute indicator, denoted as

$$\Delta_F = \max_{\substack{a \in \mathbb{F}_2^{n*}, \\ v \in \mathbb{F}_2^{m*}}} |r_F(a, v)| \quad, \tag{4}$$

and the other one is known as the sum-of-squares indicator, given by

$$\sigma_F = \sum_{a \in \mathbb{F}_2^m} \sum_{v \in \mathbb{F}_2^{n*}} r_F^2(a, v) \quad. \tag{5}$$

The differential uniformity δ_F [16] of an $n \times m$ S-box F is defined as the maximum number of solutions of the equation $F(x) \oplus F(x \oplus \gamma) = \beta$, where $\gamma \neq (0, 0, \ldots, 0)$, i.e.,

$$\delta_F = \max_{\substack{\gamma \in \mathbb{F}_2^{n*}, \\ \beta \in \mathbb{F}_2^m}} |\{x \in \mathbb{F}_2^n | F(x) \oplus F(x \oplus \gamma) = \beta\}| , \qquad (6)$$

Accordingly, F is called differentially-δ_F uniform. A cryptographically desirable S-box is required to have low differential uniformity, which makes the probability of occurence of a particular pair of input and output differences (γ, β) low, and hence provides resistance against differential cryptanalysis.

The S-box F can be uniquely represented as a multivariate polynomial over $\mathbb{F}_2^m$, called its algebraic normal form:

$$F(x_0, x_1, \ldots, x_{n-1}) = \sum_{u \in \mathbb{F}_2^n} G(u) \prod_{i=0}^{n-1} x_i^{u_i} , \qquad (7)$$

where the coordinate functions of $G : \mathbb{F}_2^n \to \mathbb{F}_2^m$ are the Möbius transforms of those of F. The maximum Hamming weight of u such that $G(u) \neq (0, 0, \ldots, 0)$ is called the algebraic degree of F and denoted by $d^\circ(F)$.

In [15], the DPA signal-to-noise ratio (SNR) is modeled and utilized to improve the side channel signals. After that, in [5], the DPA SNR of an S-box is formulated in terms of its Walsh spectrum as follows by modeling the so-called ghost peaks as noise.

$$SNR(F) = m2^n \left(\sum_{w \in \mathbb{F}_2^n} \left(\sum_{\substack{v \in \mathbb{F}_2^m, \\ wt(v)=1}} W_F(w, v) \right)^4 \right)^{-\frac{1}{2}} . \qquad (8)$$

Then, extending the study of DPA SNR in [5] from the single-bit DPA to the multi-bit DPA, the transparency order is proposed in [18] to quantify the resistance of an S-box to DPA attacks. For an $n \times m$ S-box F, it is defined as[1]

$$\tau_F = \max_{\beta \in \mathbb{F}_2^m} \left(|m - 2wt(\beta)| - \frac{1}{2^{2n} - 2^n} \sum_{a \in \mathbb{F}_2^{n*}} \left| \sum_{\substack{v \in \mathbb{F}_2^m, \\ wt(v)=1}} (-1)^{v \cdot \beta} r_F(a, v) \right| \right) , \qquad (9)$$

where $wt(v)$ is the Hamming weight of v.

---

[1] While preparing this paper, Chakraborty et al. [4] have very recently proven that the maximization over all $\beta \in \mathbb{F}_2^m$ is redundant in the definition. They also redefine the transparency order by taking the cross-correlation terms between the coordinate functions of F into account. Unfortunately, we did not have time to include this definition in our comparison.

2.2   RSSBs

Rotation-symmetric S-boxes were defined in [20]. Let

$$\rho^k(x_0, x_1, \ldots, x_{n-1}) = (x_{0+k \ (\mathrm{mod} \ n)}, x_{1+k \ (\mathrm{mod} \ n)}, \ldots, x_{n-1+k \ (\mathrm{mod} \ n)}) \quad (10)$$

be the k-cyclic shift operator. An S-box F is called rotation-symmetric if

$$\rho^k(F(x)) = F(\rho^k(x)) \ \forall \ x = (x_0, x_1, \ldots, x_{n-1}) \in \mathbb{F}_2^n \text{ and } 1 \le k \le n. \quad (11)$$

Let F be generated from $s : \mathbb{F}_{2^n} \to \mathbb{F}_{2^n}$ using a normal basis for $\mathbb{F}_{2^n}$. Then, as indicated in [20], the S-boxes satisfying $(s(\alpha))^2 = s(\alpha^2)$, $\forall \ \alpha \in \mathbb{F}_{2^n}$, can be regarded as rotation-symmetric.

The orbit of $x \in \mathbb{F}_2^n$ under the cyclic rotation is given by the set $G(x) = \{\rho^k(x) \mid 1 \le k \le n\}$. Let g_n be the number of distinct orbits. Using Burnside's lemma, it can be shown [21] that $g_n = \frac{1}{n} \sum_{t|n} \phi(t) 2^{\frac{n}{t}} (\approx \frac{2^n}{n})$, where $\phi(t)$ is the Euler's *phi*-function. The lexicographically first element within the ith orbit is called the orbit representative and denoted by Λ_i, where $1 \le i \le g_n$.

3   Transparency Orders of 6×6 RSSBs

In the class of 6×6 bijective RSSBs, the S-boxes achieving the the highest non-linearity and the lowest differential uniformity, i.e., with nonlinearity 24 and differential uniformity 4, are classified [7] in terms of absolute indicator and algebraic degree. Here, through regenerating those S-boxes, we compute their transparency orders and present the results in Table 1. The lower bound in [3] gives that the transparency order ≥ 5.638 for the inverse function over $\mathbb{F}_{2^6}$, which can be regarded as rotation-symmetric [20]. However, as it is seen from the table there exist RSSBs which, while achieving the nonlinearity, differential uniformity, and algebraic degree of the inverse function, have transparency order < 5.638. On the other hand, as can be noticed from the last row of the table, the transparency order can be reduced to 5.238 without sacrificing the nonlinearity and differential uniformity properties of the inverse function.

From Theorem 10 in [7], we know that the number of affine equivalent RSSBs of size 6×6 is equal to 64×12. We have computed that the transparency order of the RSSBs that are affine equivalent to the inverse function over $\mathbb{F}_{2^6}$ ranges between 5.714 and 5.762. In fact, this result stems from the fact that the transparency order is not invariant under some affine transformations. The following proposition gives the affine transformations under which the transparency order of an S-box is invariant.

Proposition 1. *Let $S(x)$ be an $n \times n$ S-box and τ_S be its transparency order. Then, the transparency order τ_T of $T(x) = S(xA \oplus d) \oplus e$ is equal to τ_S, where A is a nonsigular binary matrix and $d, e \in \{0, 1\}^n$.*

Table 1. The classification of 6×6 RSSBs having nonlinearity 24 and differential uniformity 4 with respect to their absolute indicator, algebraic degree, and transparency order

Absolute Indicator	Degree	Transparency order	Number of S-boxes
16	**5**	$\geq \mathbf{5.714}, \leq \mathbf{5.810}$	$\mathbf{128 \times 12}$
24	4	$\geq 5.452, \leq 5.905$	11776×12
32	3	$\geq 5.333, \leq 5.810$	640×12
32	4	$\geq 5.333, \leq 5.905$	411648×12
40	4	$\geq 5.380, \leq 5.905$	1140800×12
40	**5**	$\geq \mathbf{5.619}, \leq \mathbf{5.762}$	$\mathbf{128 \times 12}$
48	4	$\geq 5.380, \leq 5.905$	233216×12
64	2	$\geq 5.714, \leq 5.905$	192×12
64	3	$\geq 5.380, \leq 5.905$	10432×12
64	**4**	$\geq \mathbf{5.238}, \leq \mathbf{5.905}$	$\mathbf{523328 \times 12}$

Proof. Let $T(x) = S(xA \oplus d)B \oplus e$, i.e., $T(x)$ is any S-box that is affine equivalent to $S(x)$, where B is a nonsingular binary matrix. For simlicity, let

$$\tau_T = \max_{\beta \in \mathbb{F}_2^n} \left(|n - 2wt(\beta)| - \frac{D_T}{2^{2n} - 2^n} \right), \quad (12)$$

where $D_T = \sum_{a \in \mathbb{F}_2^{n*}} \left| \sum_{\substack{v \in \mathbb{F}_2^n, \\ wt(v)=1}} (-1)^{v \cdot \beta} \sum_{x \in \mathbb{F}_2^n} (-1)^{v \cdot \{T(x) \oplus T(x \oplus a)\}} \right|$. Then, it follows that,

$$D_T = \sum_{a \in \mathbb{F}_2^{n*}} \left| \sum_{\substack{v \in \mathbb{F}_2^n, \\ wt(v)=1}} (-1)^{v \cdot \beta} \sum_{x \in \mathbb{F}_2^n} (-1)^{v \cdot \{S(xA \oplus d)B \oplus S((x \oplus a)A \oplus d)B\}} \right|$$

$$= \sum_{a \in \mathbb{F}_2^{n*}} \left| \sum_{\substack{v \in \mathbb{F}_2^n, \\ wt(v)=1}} (-1)^{v \cdot \beta} \sum_{y \in \mathbb{F}_2^n} (-1)^{v \cdot \{(S(y) \oplus S(y \oplus aA))B\}} \right|$$

$$= \sum_{u \in \mathbb{F}_2^{n*}} \left| \sum_{\substack{v \in \mathbb{F}_2^n, \\ wt(v)=1}} (-1)^{v \cdot \beta} \sum_{y \in \mathbb{F}_2^n} (-1)^{v \cdot \{(S(y) \oplus S(y \oplus u))B\}} \right|. \quad (13)$$

which gives $\tau_T = \tau_S$, if B is the identity matrix. □

Hence, it suffices to compute the transparency orders of $S(x)B$ for all nonsingular binary matrices B, whose total number is $\prod_{i=0}^{n-1}(2^n - 2^i)$ [11], to find those of the S-boxes that are affine equivalent to $S(x)$.

Let $S(x)$ be rotation-symmetric and $C^r(u)$, $u \in \mathbb{F}_2^n$, be a circulant matrix that is formed by taking u as its first row and cyclically rotating each other row by r positions to the left relative to the preceding row. Then, from [7], the RSSBs affine equivalent to $S(x)$ are in the form of $S(xC^q(a)\oplus d)C^p(b)\oplus e$, where $a, b \in \mathbb{F}_2^n$, $d, e \in \{(0,0,\ldots,0),(1,1,\ldots,1)\}$, $C^q(a), C^p(b)$ are nonsingular circulant matrices over $\mathbb{F}_2$, and p, q are prime to n such that $pq \equiv 1 \pmod{n}$. While Prop. 1 suggests that it is sufficient to compute the transparency orders of $S(x)C^p(b)$ to find the RSSB with minimum transparency order among those that are affine equivalent to $S(x)$, the following proposition reduces the number of the matrices $C^p(b)$ by a factor of $\frac{1}{n}$.

Lemma 2. *Let p be relatively prime to n and $C^p(b)$ be an $n \times n$ nonsingular circulant matrix, where $b \in \mathbb{F}_2^n$. Then, $xC^p(\rho^k(b)) = \rho^{n-kr}(x)C^p(b)$ for all $1 \leq k \leq n$, where $x \in \mathbb{F}_2^n$ and $rp \equiv 1 \pmod{n}$ for some $0 < r < n$.*

Proof. Let $B = C^p(b)$ and B_k be the kth column of B. Then, the proof follows from the fact given by [7] that $B_k = \rho^{(k-1)r}(B_1)$ as follows:

$$
\begin{aligned}
xC^p(\rho^k(b)) &= (xB_{k+1}, xB_{k+2}, \ldots, xB_n, \ldots, xB_k) \\
&= (x\rho^{kr}(B_1), x\rho^{(k+1)r}(B_1), \ldots, x\rho^{(n-1)r}(B_1), \ldots, x\rho^{(k-1)r}(B_1)) \\
&= (\rho^{n-kr}(x)B_1, \rho^{n-kr}(x)B_2, \ldots, \rho^{n-kr}(x)B_{n-k}, \ldots, \rho^{n-kr}(x)B_n) \\
&= \rho^{n-kr}(x)C^p(b) \ .
\end{aligned}
\tag{14}
$$

$\square$

Proposition 3. *Let $S(x)$ be an $n \times n$ RSSB. Then, the transparency order of $S(x)C^p(b)$ is equal to that of $S(x)C^p(\rho^k(b))$ for all $1 \leq k \leq n$.*

Proof. Let τ_k be the transparency order of $S(x)C^p(\rho^k(b))$. Then, it follows from Lemma 2 that

$$
\begin{aligned}
D_k &= \sum_{a \in \mathbb{F}_2^{n*}} \left| \sum_{\substack{v \in \mathbb{F}_2^n, \\ wt(v)=1}} (-1)^{v \cdot \beta} \sum_{x \in \mathbb{F}_2^n} (-1)^{v \cdot \{S(x)C^p(\rho^k(b)) \oplus S(x \oplus a)C^p(\rho^k(b))\}} \right| \\
&= \sum_{a \in \mathbb{F}_2^{n*}} \left| \sum_{\substack{v \in \mathbb{F}_2^n, \\ wt(v)=1}} (-1)^{v \cdot \beta} \sum_{x \in \mathbb{F}_2^n} (-1)^{v \cdot \{S(\rho^{n-kr}(x))C^p(b) \oplus S(\rho^{n-kr}(x \oplus a))C^p(b)\}} \right| \\
&= \sum_{u \in \mathbb{F}_2^{n*}} \left| \sum_{\substack{v \in \mathbb{F}_2^n, \\ wt(v)=1}} (-1)^{v \cdot \beta} \sum_{y \in \mathbb{F}_2^n} (-1)^{v \cdot \{(S(y) \oplus S(y \oplus u))C^p(b)\}} \right| \ ,
\end{aligned}
\tag{15}
$$

where $rp \equiv 1 \pmod{n}$ for some $0 < r < n$, and hence $\tau_k = \tau_n$ for all $1 \leq k \leq n$.

$\square$

Therefore, in order to obtain different transparency orders of the affine equivalent RSSBs in the form of $S(xC^q(a) \oplus d)C^p(b) \oplus e$, we only need to find those of $S(x)C^p(b)$ where $b \in \mathbb{F}_2^n$ are different up to rotation. Note that while the number of affine equivalent RSSBs to $S(x)$ is given [7] as $4N^2 n\varphi(n)$, our result shows that there can be at most $N\varphi(n)$ different transparency orders among them, where $\varphi(n)$ is Euler's totient function and N is the number of $n \times n$ nonsingular circulant matrices over $\mathbb{F}_2^n$ that are different up to permutations of rows.

We have then computed the transparency orders of the RSSBs affine equivalent to the inverse function over $\mathbb{F}_{2^8}$ for which the lower bound in [3] gives the transparency order ≥ 7.812. It is found that the transparency orders take values between 7.849 and 7.873. As a consequence, it seems the transparency order slightly changes among the affine equivalent RSSBs.

4   Search for 8×8 RSSBs

Motivated by the existence of 6×6 RSSBs with high nonlinearity and low transparency order, we attempt to search for 8×8 RSSBs with such desirable cryptographic properties, utilizing the steepest-descent-like iterative search algorithm [6]. In each iteration, the search algorithm tries to minimize the following cost function:

$$Cost(S) = \frac{A}{(g_n-1)(2^{4n}-2^{3n})} \sum_{i=2}^{g_n} \sum_{\omega \in \mathbb{F}_2^n} \left(W_S^2(\omega, \Lambda_i) - 2^n\right)^2 + \frac{1}{n}\tau_S , \qquad (16)$$

where $\Lambda_i \in \mathbb{F}_2^n$ is a non-zero orbit representative, $W_S(\omega, \Lambda_i)$ is the Walsh-Hadamard transform of the component function $\Lambda_i S(x)$, and A is the tuning parameter which is used to balance between nonlinearity and transparency order and takes values between 40 and 120 in our experiments.

The inner summation in the right-hand side of the equation is called sum of squared errors [23] which is a measure of the squared distance to bent functions both in terms of Walsh-Hadamard and autocorrelation spectra, since

$$\sum_{a \neq (0,\dots,0)} r_S^2(a, \Lambda_i) = 2^{-n} \sum_{\omega} \left(W_S^2(\omega, \Lambda_i) - 2^n\right)^2 . \qquad (17)$$

Clearly, then, the sum of squared errors takes it maximum value $2^{4n} - 2^{3n}$ if the Boolean function f is an affine function. Further, recall from [7] that the component function $\Lambda_i S(x)$ is linearly equivalent to $\rho^k(\Lambda_i)S(x)$ for any $1 \leq k \leq n$, and hence the sum of squared errors is invariant under the cyclic rotation of Λ_i. Therefore, we take only the component functions $\Lambda_i S(x)$ corresponding to the nonzero orbit representatives $\Lambda_i \in \mathbb{F}_2^n$ into account (supposing $\Lambda_1 = (0, \dots, 0)$, the outer summation is indexed from $i = 2$ to g_n). Keeping in mind from [18] that the transparency order takes it maximum value n if all the component functions are bent, notice that the coefficients $\frac{1}{(g_n-1)(2^{4n}-2^{3n})}$ and $\frac{1}{n}$ normalize the double summation and τ_S to unity respectively. Consequently, while the first term of the cost function maximizes the nonlinearity the second term minimizes the transparency order in such a way that the tuning parameter A governs the trade-off between nonlinearity and transparency order, both of which conflict with each other.

Since the best nonlinearity that we achieve in the class of RSSBs of size 8×8 by the steepest-descent-like iterative search algorithm is 104, we mainly consider the RSSBs with nonlinearity 104. In the following table we compare the cryptographic properties of our best attained results with those of the AES S-box and the S-boxes known in the literature. From Table 2, it is seen that the nonlinearity 104 and the transparency order 7.31 are better than those given in [13,14,17]. Further, the SNR of RSSB # 1 is the lowest one among all the S-boxes while its differential uniformity is the closest one to that of the AES S-box. Notice that RSSB #4 has the worst SNR value in the table, although it has the lowest transparency order.

Table 2. Comparison of the transparency orders of our best achieved RSSBs along with those of the AES S-box and the S-boxes in the literature

	NL_S	δ_S	Δ_S	$d°(S)$	τ_S	$SNR(S)$
AES S-box	112	4	32	7	7.86	9.599
S-boxes in [13]	98	-	≥ 88	7	≥ 7.782	≥ 8.54
S-boxes in [17]	98	12	104	7	7.358	5.825
	100	12	104	7	7.53	5.44
RSSBs in [14]	102	8, 10, 12	80, 88, 96	7	≥ 7.76	-
RSSB # 1	104	6	80	7	7.627	4.675
RSSB # 2	104	8	88	7	7.555	7.044
RSSB # 3	104	8	72	7	7.476	9.155
RSSB # 4	102	8	88	7	7.31	11.78

5   Implementation Results on SASEBO-GII

A cryptographic algorithm implemented on FPGAs provides a side channel such as power consumption, timing behaviour, or electromagnetic emanations that leaks data sensitive information. DPA attacks measure the power consumption of a cryptographic device, which contains information related to the device's internal data. An attacker uses power models like Hamming Weight or Hamming Distance to statistically correlate the measurements with the power estimates. In correlation power analysis (CPA) [2], which can be considered as an efficient multi-bit DPA, the relationship between the power consumption and the data that is processed by the cryptographic device is assumed to be linear. Hence, the correlation between the power model and the power consumption becomes maximum if the hypothetical key is the actual key. In both analyses, an attacker does not need a detailed knowledge about the cryptographic device.

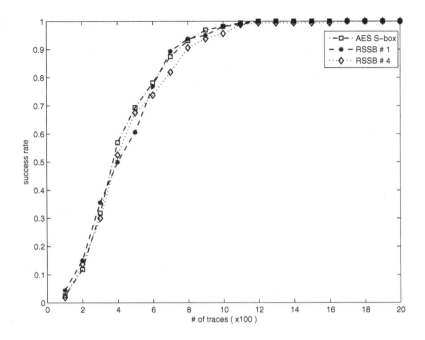

Fig. 1. The global success rates for the AES S-box, RSSB #1, and RSSB #4

We perform CPA using Pearson's correlation, which reflects the degree of linear relationship between two variables, in conjunction with Hamming distance model. The correlation coefficient $\mathcal{R}(P, H)$ between the hypothetical power consumption H and the power consumption P of the device is given by

$$\mathcal{R}(P, H) = \frac{N \sum_{i=1}^{N} P_i H_i - \sum_{i=1}^{N} P_i \sum_{i=1}^{N} H_i}{\sqrt{N \sum_{i=1}^{N} P_i^2 - \left(\sum_{i=1}^{N} P_i\right)^2} \sqrt{N \sum_{i=1}^{N} H_i^2 - \left(\sum_{i=1}^{N} H_i\right)^2}} , \quad (18)$$

where N is the number of measurements.

The evaluation of our S-boxes in Table 1 is realized on SASEBO-GII. The board contains two FPGAs: Xilinx Virtex-5 and Spartan-3A. The former one (called cryptographic FPGA) is used to run the actual cryptographic algorithm, while the latter one (control FPGA) communicates with the cryptographic FPGA using a local bus interface in an efficient manner. The measurements for the evaluation are taken from a PC-based oscilloscope with 1 GS/s sampling rate.

In order to evaluate the DPA resistance of the FPGA implementations, we have exploited lookup tables (LUTs) in such a way that the S-box used in AES-128 is replaced with one of the four RSSBs in Table 1 using 16 LUTs. In Fig. 1, we compare the S-boxes RSSB #1 and RSSB #4 with the AES S-box by means of the success rate as defined in [22]. More specifically, we first compute the success rate, i.e, the probability of the guessed key byte being correct for a given number of power traces, for each byte of the last round key. Then, we take the average over all 16 key bytes to obtain the global success rate (GSR) for each of the four RSSBs and the AES S-box. We find that the number of traces required to achieve 100 % GSR is the same (1200) for all the RSSBs # 1-3 and the AES S-box; however, RSSB # 4 requires 1700 traces to guess all the key bytes correctly. Hence, as there is no noticeable difference among the first three RSSBs, the GSRs for RSSB #2 and RSSB #3 are not shown in Fig. 1. We observe that the GSR for RSSB # 4 is very close to 100 % ($\geq 99, 38\%$) after 1200 traces.

6   Conclusions

Noting that the transparency order is not invariant under some affine transformations, we find that there exist 6×6 bijective RSSBs with the highest nonlinearity and the lowest differential unifomity in the class of RSSBs, which achieve transparency order as low as 5.238, while the inverse function over $\mathbb{F}_{2^6}$ has the transparency order ≥ 5.638. Then, we search for 8×8 RSSBs with high nonlinearity and low transparency order and find S-boxes with nonlinearity 104, differential uniformity 6, and transparency orders noticeably lower than that of the AES S-box. These cryptographic properties improve the results in [14,13,17]. However, on one hand, our implementation results on SASEBO-GII show that even a relatively high decrease (around 5% when we compare the AES S-box with RSSB #3) in the transparency order of an S-box may not improve its DPA resistance. On the other hand, an improvement of the transparency order can increase the SNR, and hence both of these metrics should be considered together to construct S-boxes that are resistant against DPA attacks. Finally, we should mention that our results do not indicate the RSSBs in Table 2 are superior to the AES S-box, rather they give some ideas to strengthen the DPA resistivity and should be interpreted as an independent confirmation of analogous results.

References

1. Biham, E., Shamir, A.: Differential Cryptanalysis of DES-like Cryptosystems. Journal of Cryptology 4(1), 3–72 (1991)
2. Brier, E., Clavier, C., Olivier, F.: Correlation Power Analysis with a Leakage Model. In: Joye, M., Quisquater, J.-J. (eds.) CHES 2004. LNCS, vol. 3156, pp. 16–29. Springer, Heidelberg (2004)
3. Carlet, C.: On Highly Nonlinear S-Boxes and Their Inability to Thwart DPA Attacks. In: Maitra, S., Madhavan, C.E.V., Venkatesan, R. (eds.) INDOCRYPT 2005. LNCS, vol. 3797, pp. 49–62. Springer, Heidelberg (2005)
4. Chakraborty, K., Maitra, S., Sarkar, S., Mazumdar, B., Mukhopadhyay, D.: Redefining the Transparency Order (2014), http://eprint.iacr.org/2014/367.pdf
5. Guilley, S., Hoogvorst, P., Pacalet, R.: Differential Power Analysis Model and Some Results. In: Quisquater, J.-J., Paradinas, P., Deswarte, Y., Kalam, A.A.E. (eds.) CARDIS 2004. IFIP, vol. 153, pp. 127–142. Springer, Boston (2004)
6. Kavut, S., Yücel, M.D.: A New Algorithm for the Design of Strong Boolean Functions (in Turkish). In: First National Cryptology Symposium, METU, Ankara, Türkiye, pp. 95–105 (2005)

7. Kavut, S.: Results on Rotation-Symmetric S-boxes. Information Sciences 201, 93–113 (2012)
8. Kocher, P.C.: Timing Attacks on Implementations of Diffie-Hellman, RSA, DSS, and Other Systems. In: Koblitz, N. (ed.) CRYPTO 1996. LNCS, vol. 1109, pp. 104–113. Springer, Heidelberg (1996)
9. Kocher, P.C., Jaffe, J., Jun, B.: Differential Power Analysis. In: Wiener, M. (ed.) CRYPTO 1999. LNCS, vol. 1666, pp. 388–397. Springer, Heidelberg (1999)
10. Lai, X.: Higher Order Derivatives and Differential Cryptanalysis. In: Blahut, R.E., Costello Jr., D., Maurer, U., Mittelholzer, T. (eds.) Communications and Cryptography. The Springer International Series in Engineering and Computer Science, vol. 276, pp. 227–233. Springer, US (1994)
11. Lewis, T.G., Payne, W.H.: Generalized Feedback Shift Register Pseudorandom Number Algorithm. Journal of the ACM (JACM) 20(3), 456–468 (1973)
12. Matsui, M.: Linear Cryptanalysis Method for DES Cipher. In: Helleseth, T. (ed.) EUROCRYPT 1993. LNCS, vol. 765, pp. 386–397. Springer, Heidelberg (1994)
13. Mazumdar, B., Mukhopadhyay, D., Sengupta, I.: Constrained Search for a Class of Good Bijective S-boxes with Improved DPA Resistivity. IEEE Transactions on Information Forensics and Security 8(12), 2154–2163 (2013)
14. Mazumdar, B., Mukhopadhyay, D., Sengupta, I.: Design and Implementation of Rotation Symmetric S-boxes with High Nonlinearity and High DPA Resiliency. In: IEEE International Symposium on Hardware-Oriented Security and Trust (HOST), pp. 87–92 (2013)
15. Messerges, T.S., Dabbish, E.A., Sloan, R.H.: Investigations of Power Analysis Attacks on Smartcards. In: USENIX Workshop on Smartcard Technology, pp. 151–161 (1999)
16. Nyberg, K.: Differentially Uniform Mappings for Cryptography. In: Helleseth, T. (ed.) EUROCRYPT 1993. LNCS, vol. 765, pp. 55–64. Springer, Heidelberg (1994)
17. Picek, S., Ege, B., Batina, L., Jakobovic, D., Chmielewski, L., Golub, M.: On Using Genetic Algorithms for Intrinsic Side-channel Resistance: The Case of AES S-box. In: The First Workshop on Cryptography and Security in Computing Systems, CS2 2014, pp. 13–18. ACM, New York (2014)
18. Prouff, E.: DPA Attacks and S-Boxes. In: Gilbert, H., Handschuh, H. (eds.) FSE 2005. LNCS, vol. 3557, pp. 424–441. Springer, Heidelberg (2005)
19. Quisquater, J.-J., Samyde, D.: ElectroMagnetic Analysis (EMA): Measures and Countermeasures for Smart Cards. In: Attali, S., Jensen, T. (eds.) E-smart 2001. LNCS, vol. 2140, pp. 200–210. Springer, Heidelberg (2001)
20. Rijmen, V., Barreto, P.S.L.M., Filho, D.L.G.: Rotation Symmetry in Algebraically Generated Cryptographic Substitution Tables. Inf. Process. Lett. 106(6), 246–250 (2008)
21. Stănică, P., Maitra, S.: Rotation Symmetric Boolean Functions - Count and Cryptographic Properties. Discrete Applied Mathematics 156(10), 1567–1580 (2008)
22. Standaert, F.-X., Malkin, T.G., Yung, M.: A Unified Framework for the Analysis of Side-Channel Key Recovery Attacks. In: Joux, A. (ed.) EUROCRYPT 2009. LNCS, vol. 5479, pp. 443–461. Springer, Heidelberg (2009)
23. Yücel, M.D.: Alternative Nonlinearity Criteria for Boolean Functions. Electrical and Electronics Engineering Department, Middle East Technical University, Memorandum No. 2001-1, Ankara, Turkey (2001)
24. Zhang, X.-M., Zheng, Y.: GAC - the Criterion for Global Avalanche Characteristics of Cryptographic Functions. Journal of Universal Computer Science 1(5), 320–337 (1996)

A Technique Using PUFs for Protecting Circuit Layout Designs against Reverse Engineering[*]

Dai Yamamoto[1,2], Masahiko Takenaka[1], Kazuo Sakiyama[2], and Naoya Torii[1]

[1] FUJITSU Laboratories Ltd., Kanagawa, Japan
{yamamoto.dai,ma,torii.naoya}@jp.fujitsu.com
[2] The University of Electro-Communications, Tokyo, Japan
{yamamoto.dai,sakiyama}@uec.ac.jp

Abstract. Recently, considerable interests have been focused on Physically Unclonable Functions (PUFs) as an anti-counterfeiting technology for Integrated Circuits (ICs). PUFs are used for more secure authentication mechanisms than conventional ones, and enable us to distinguish genuine from counterfeit ICs. However, sophisticated reverse-engineering approaches, which diminish intellectual property (IP), have still been a big problem for IC designs except PUFs. The IC designs include various circuits such as audio-video-processing circuit, communication circuit, etc., which are based on their manufactures' trade secrets. Hence the counterfeit production and information leakage through the reverse engineering of such valuable circuits are major threats to IC manufactures. In this paper, we use PUFs not for authentication but for protection of IP of IC designs. We propose a new method of the IP protection, by using HCI-SA (Hot Carrier Injection-Sense Amplifier) PUFs proposed in 2013. The HCI-SA PUF, one of the memory-based PUFs, has two great properties: one is that its response has a perfect reliability, and another is that the value of response can be fully controlled by manufactures. We design various logic gates (e.g. NAND, XOR) by using the HCI-SA PUFs, which is completely identical and impossible to be distinguished from the IC layout information. These PUF-based logic gates make ICs more resistant to a reverse-engineering attack.

Keywords: Physically Unclonable Function, Sense Amplifier, Hot Carrier Injection, Reverse Engineering, Intellectual Property Protection.

1 Introduction

Secure authentication using smart cards such as banking, transportation, and public ID cards, have spread recently. The difficulty of counterfeiting smart cards had been considered based on cryptographic hardware that stores a secret key on its internal IC memory with making it invisible to the outside. The secret key, however, could be revealed by reverse engineering such as de-packaging and

---

[*] The preliminary version of this paper was presented in a Japanese domestic symposium without peer review [20].

M. Yoshida and K. Mouri (Eds.): IWSEC 2014, LNCS 8639, pp. 158–173, 2014.
© Springer International Publishing Switzerland 2014

analyzing the IC design [16]. To defend against this threat, Physically Unclonable Functions (PUFs) have emerged as a solution [11]. Generally, each IC chip has different physical characteristics such as gate drive capability or wire delay. Conventional ICs for mass production work identically by minimizing the difference of the physical characteristics. In contrast, PUFs on IC chips maximize the physical characteristics [6] [7]. PUFs generate the unique output values (responses) to the same input value (challenge) for each individual IC chip. In spite of the unique responses, PUFs have a completely identical circuit structure, which makes it quite difficult for attackers to identify the value of response by using PUF layout information (e.g. mask pattern). PUFs are expected to be a breakthrough technology for anti-counterfeiting devices, making cloning impossible even when the design is revealed.

Circuits implemented on an IC chip are roughly classified into two types: circuit used for authentication and circuit for other general purposes. Conventional PUFs are embedded as a part of the former circuits, and are utilized for authenticating whether the circuits are genuine. Concretely, PUFs are assumed to be used for secret key generation or challenge-and-response authentication. The former type of circuits, therefore, keeps high tolerance to the reverse engineering since it is quite difficult to make counterfeit PUFs and reveal their responses from their mask pattern information. The latter type of circuits includes, for example, audio-video-processing circuit, communication circuit and cryptographic circuit for message encryption, etc. These circuits are based on a lot of trade secrets (i.e. IP) of their manufactures. For example, the trade secrets consist of circuit design itself, various setting parameters and original algorithms, etc. Of course, there have been some countermeasures for threats of extracting the IP and counterfeiting the latter circuits (e.g. layout-level gate camouflaging). These countermeasures, however, have not lead to a fundamental solution for the threats. The revealed trade secrets enable an attacker to improve her own IC designs or illegally sell themselves.

Our Contributions. In this paper, we apply PUFs to the latter type of circuits. Consequently, we use PUFs not for authentication but for protecting circuit designs against reverse engineering. We propose a new method of designing circuit structure by using HCI-SA (Hot Carrier Injection-Sense Amplifier) PUFs which were proposed in 2013. The HCI-SA PUF is one of the memory-based PUFs (e.g. SRAM PUFs). HCI-SA PUF is similar to SRAM PUF in that each HCI-SA cell outputs 1-bit response like an SRAM cell. In contrast, the HCI-SA PUF (consisting of HCI-SA cells) has the following advantages:

Error-Free Response: The reliability of response is 100% (i.e. the responses are stable for repeated measurements).
Controllable Response: The value of response (0 or 1) is fully controllable by manufactures.

Note that the second advantage is based on our original idea. The HCI-SA cell whose responses are controlled should no longer be called PUF but "Physically

Unclonable Circuit (PUC)". PUCs can be regarded as circuits with a secure memory, whose stored value cannot be identified by its layout information. This property is quite similar to other PUFs.

In this paper, we configure general-purpose circuits with the HCI-SA cells, outputting 1-bit constant value. We propose a method of designing various logic gates (e.g. NAND, XOR) themselves based on the combinations of the HCI-SA cells. Each logic gate consisting of HCI-SA cells is identical, so impossible to be reverse-engineered. This is a significant advantage of HCI-SA cells over non-volatile memory cells. Our method can be applied to any circuit, which increases its tolerance to reverse engineering dramatically.

Organization of the Paper. The rest of the paper is organized as follows. Section 2 gives an outline of the SA PUFs, the HCI-SA PUFs and the reverse engineering. Section 3 explains the motivation of this research: the applications of PUFs. Section 4 proposes our methods of protecting circuit design and discusses how to choose the appropriate gates to which our proposed method is applied. Section 5 applies our methods to the S-box circuit of KASUMI cipher as a case study. Finally, in Sect. 6 we summarize our work and comment on future directions.

2   Background Art

2.1   Sense Amplifier PUF

Sense amplifier (SA) is a circuit that amplifies the voltage difference between two signals. The SA is mainly used to sense and refresh one bit of data stored in a memory cell. Figure 1 shows the circuit structure of an SA cell, which is regarded as the circuit comparing two signals: (IN1,IN2). When the voltage level of IN1 is higher than that of IN2, the output signals (OUT1, OUT2) are (1, 0), and vice versa. Each SA cell has the unique value of the offset voltage: positive or negative polarity (i.e. bias). This uniqueness is provided by process variation in the SA cell occurring in the manufacturing process of each IC chip.

The SA PUF, composed of SA cells, utilizes the difference of each biased offset voltage. When the voltage level of IN1 is very close to that of IN2, the output signal OUT1 (i.e. response) is strongly affected by the biased offset voltage. Consequently, the responses can be extracted from this unique bias. The SA PUF is similar to SRAM PUF in that each SA cell outputs 1-bit response like an SRAM cell. SA cells with a large bias generate the highly reliable responses (i.e. stable responses for repeated measurements). However, some SA cells have an extremely small bias, which leads to unreliable responses. This is a serious problem for SA PUFs as with other PUFs.

2.2   Hot-Carrier-Injection SA PUF

To solve this problem, the HCI-SA PUF was proposed by M. Bhargava et.al in CHES 2013 [3]. The bias of the offset voltage in the SA cell can be increased

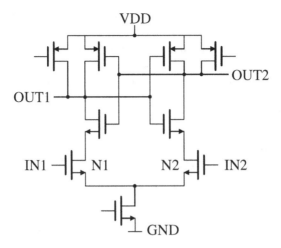

Fig. 1. Sense amplifier circuit (StrongARM) [3]

by increasing the difference of threshold voltages V_{TH}'s between devices N1 and N2. As a result, this increased bias realizes 100% reliable response. In order to increase the difference of V_{TH}'s, the V_{TH}'s are forcibly shifted by the HCI aging stress. The response OUT1 become 1 absolutely when V_{TH} of N1 is much larger (approximately > 40mV) than that of N2 [3]. This increase in V_{TH} is achieved in one-time HCI stress duration of 125 seconds [3]. The construction of HCI-SA PUFs is composed of the following two steps.

Step 1: Measuring and memorizing the offset polarity
Step 2: Increasing the difference of V_{TH} by the HCI stress

In Step1, the value of response (OUT1) in an SA cell is measured and stored into a 1-bit external memory cell. This step enables us to check which polarity of the offset voltage (i.e. positive or negative) the SA cell has. In Step2 using HCI stress, the offset after HCI stress becomes the same sign as the offset before HCI stress and a higher magnitude. This HCI stress realizes 100% reliable responses of HCI-SA PUFs.

2.3   Reverse Engineering of ICs

We define the reverse engineering of ICs, which is a big threat to their manufactures, causing infringement of IP and their counterfeits. We assume that the reverse engineering approaches are classified into two categories: static analysis and dynamic analysis.

In the static analysis, the ICs are in power-off state. The structure and functionality of the IC (i.e. gate-level netlist) is revealed by using its mask pattern images. An attacker obtains the mask pattern images through de-packaging the IC and de-layering individual IC layers by using corrosive chemicals. By contrast,

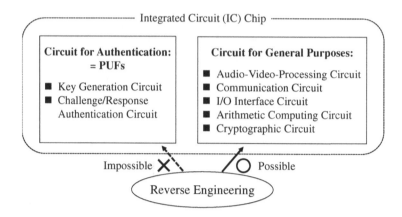

Fig. 2. Structure of an IC chip, which consist of circuit for authentication and circuit for other general purposes

in the dynamic analysis, the ICs are in power-on state. An attacker performs non-invasive attacks (e.g. photonic emission analysis), or even invasive attacks (e.g. reading signal pluses on wires with microprobes). In this paper, we propose a countermeasure against the static analysis; the dynamic analysis is out of scope. This reason is discussed in Sect. 4.4.

3   Motivation: Applications of PUFs

IC chips are implemented on embedded systems such as smart cards and mobile phones, etc. Circuits on an IC chip are roughly classified into two types: circuit for authentication and circuit for other general purposes, as shown in Fig. 2.

Conventional PUFs are embedded as a part of the former circuits, and are utilized for authenticating whether the circuits are genuine (original). Concretely, PUFs are used for secret key generation and challenge-and-response authentication. An original PUF circuit cannot be counterfeited by reverse engineering because it is impossible for an attacker to reveal the responses of the PUF even when obtaining mask pattern images of the PUF. Furthermore, we consider that the attacker extracts the gate-level netlist of the PUF from its mask pattern, and implements the PUF on her own IC chip. Even in this case, the responses of her PUF are completely different from that of the original PUF due to the different physical characteristics between her and original PUFs. This enables us to distinguish original PUFs from counterfeit ones. Therefore, PUFs are assumed to be effective authentication devices for anti-counterfeiting ICs.

On the other hand, main features of ICs are provided by general circuits such as audio-video-processing circuit, communication circuit, I/O interface circuit, arithmetic computing circuit and cryptographic circuit for message encryption. In FPGA (Field-Programmable Gate Array), circuit information, called *bitstream*, is stored in an external memory (e.g. Programmable ROM or flash ROM), and is downloaded into an FPGA when power is on. All of the circuit information is protected by being encrypted using a secret key extracted as PUF responses [8]. In contrast, general circuits are directly implemented on IC chips, hence are easily accessible for an attacker through the reverse engineering [16]. Nevertheless, no discussion on the use of PUFs for protecting general circuits has been reported yet, as far as we know. The general circuits include the IP of their manufactures. Therefore, it is important to use PUFs not only for authentication circuits but for protecting circuit design against reverse engineering. The next section proposes a new method of designing the structure of general circuits by using HCI-SA PUFs.

4   Proposed Methods

Section 4.1 discusses HCI-SA PUFs whose responses are controllable by their manufactures. Sections 4.2 and 4.3 propose new methods of making a structure of any logic gate using the HCI-SA PUFs, which prevent the extraction of gate-level netlist from mask pattern images.

4.1   Physically Unclonable Circuit: Response-Controllable PUF

The main purpose of the HCI-SA PUF proposed in [3] is to improve the reliability of responses in SA PUFs. Therefore, the *naive* response (i.e. offset polarity before HCI stress) is measured and memorized in Step1, as explained in Sect. 2.2. In this paper, we consider that manufactures of HCI-SA PUFs can skip Step1 and can freely determine the polarity sign of the offset voltage after HCI stress, regardless of that before HCI stress (i.e. naive polarity sign). This means that the manufactures are capable of setting the value of responses after HCI stress as they want. We predict that the amount of HCI stress becomes larger (more than 125 seconds [3]) because the polarity sign set by manufacturers is sometimes opposite to the naive polarity sign. If the amount of HCI stress is not sufficient, there is a high possibility that the responses do not achieve 100% of reliability. We believe that controlling responses is feasible for manufactures. The proof of concept, however, should be performed based on real IC chips, which includes in future work.

We assume that the polarity signs to HCI-SA PUFs are provided from outside of IC chips. This is because, if an on-chip instrument is implemented to store the polarity signs, the logic function consisting HCI-SA cells can be reverse-engineered readily. The developers of HCI-SA PUFs have proposed a serial and externally controlled reinforcement of the polarity signs in order to reduce the size of HCI-SA cells [3]. This is why we consider that our assumption is reasonable.

We define the HCI-SA PUFs whose responses are controlled by their manufactures as HCI-SA **PUC** (Physically Unclonable Circuit). The reason why we distinguish PUCs from PUFs is that responses of PUFs are determined only by physical characteristics of ICs (i.e. uncontrollable), while that of PUCs are controllable. We, therefore, consider that HCI-SA PUCs should not be categorized into PUFs. HCI-SA PUCs have the following three characteristics:

Error-Free Response: The responses have 100% of reliability.

Controllable Response: The value of response is fully controllable by manufactures.

Tolerance to Reverse Engineering: The value of response cannot be identified using their mask pattern images.

We suggest that there is almost no difference of responses between HCI-SA PUCs and other types of PUFs (e.g. SRAM PUF and original HCI-SA PUFs) in terms of the tolerance to reverse engineering since the both responses are not identified even when their mask pattern is revealed. Furthermore, we consider that HCI-SA PUCs can be used even for PUFs, embedded as authentication circuits. The responses of each HCI-SA PUC have high entropy if they are determined based on cryptographic random number generators. In this case, the HCI-SA PUCs have extremely high uniqueness, one of the most important metrics of PUFs. Some readers might consider that non-volatile memory such as embedded flash memory and electrical fuse can be substituted for HCI-SA PUCs in terms of storing and outputting the constant value. The non-volatile memory, however, does not satisfy the third condition: tolerance to reverse engineering, the most important characteristic for PUFs. The HCI-SA PUCs can be regarded as secure memory whose stored value cannot be identified by its mask pattern.

In the following, we discuss security requirements for HCI-SA PUCs in detail.

One-Time Programmability. In this paper, we assume that HCI-SA PUCs have one-time programmability. This one-time programmability is a reasonable assumption under the static analysis, as mentioned in Sect. 2.3. However, if an attacker can perform the dynamic analysis, she may possibly overwrite the HCI effect and may obtain the information about responses of HCI-SA cells. In order to prevent the reprogramming, we assume that the HCI writing interfaces should be unavailable once manufacturing IC chips are complete, or a mechanism to detect the reprograming (e.g. hardware duplication against fault injection attacks) should be implemented. We consider that the feasibility of the one-time programmability should be experimentally clarified in future work.

Undetectability of Hot Carriers. An existence of hot carriers in HCI-SA cells directly corresponds to secret information: responses of HCI-SA PUCs. Therefore, the hot carriers must be undetectable for the security of HCI-SA PUCs. In principle, the hot carriers are measurable by using an emission probe etc. since they physically exist in HCI-SA cells. However, we believe that it is practically difficult to detect the hot carriers. This reason is that, once an attacker performs reverse engineering such as de-packaging and de-layering of IC chips, the hot carriers will flow out and change from original state. At the moment, this undetectability is based on an assumption rather than a fact.

We consider that the undetectability of hot carriers should be experimentally clarified in future work.

4.2   Proposed Method (1)

In the proposed method (1), we design the N-input logic gates in general circuits (e.g. AND, OR, XOR, NAND, NOR, XNOR gates) based on the HCI-SA PUCs. For example, we replace various 2-input conventional logic gates with the proposed gates using HCI-SA PUCs, as shown in Fig. 3. Let A and B be input signals to a logic gate, and X be an output signal from the gate. The output X of each proposed gate is obtained as the output from a 4-to-1 multiplexer whose inputs are 4-bit responses from HCI-SA PUCs. In the manufacturing process of ICs, each value of the response is controlled by the HCI stress according to a truth table for a logic gate. Signals A and B correspond to selection inputs for a multiplexer. It is impossible for an attacker to identify the value of X in a proposed gate from its mask pattern images. This is because each mask pattern of the proposed gate with HCI-SA PUCs is completely identical.

Gate Size of an HCI-SA PUC (HCI-SA Cell). We evaluate the gate size of a one-bit HCI-SA cell. In following discussion, one gate is equivalent to a 2-input NAND gate. The gate size of a 1-bit SRAM cell is a half of the 2-input NAND gate (i.e. 0.5 gates) according to our logic synthesis on a 0.18-μm ASIC process [5]. In [3], the HCI-SA cell is equivalent to 10 times of SRAM cell area. The gate size of the HCI-SA cell is, therefore, estimated to be 5 gates. Note that the HCI-SA cell does not include the memory cell for storing the offset polarity in Step1, as mentioned in Sect. 2.2, because the Step1 is not necessary for manufacturing our proposed gates.

The proposed gate in Fig. 3 consists of four HCI-SA cells and a 1-bit 4-to-1 multiplexer. The gate size of the multiplexer is 5 gates [1], so the gate size of the proposed gate is 25 gates.

How Many Proposed Gates are Applied to General Circuits? In order to implement general circuits with high tolerance to reverse engineering, IC manufactures should replace as many conventional logic gates with proposed gates as possible. Note that the more proposed gates in a general circuit are, the larger the gate size of the circuit is. Therefore, the manufactures should take into account the trade-off between the tolerance to reverse engineering and the gate size.

An attacker has six candidates of a proposed gate, i.e. AND, OR, XOR, NAND, NOR, XNOR. If a general circuit includes M proposed gates, the total pattern of proposed gates is $6^M (\approx 2^{2.58 \cdot M})$. According to the RC5-72 challenge [4], the problem requiring 2^{72} operations has not been solved by brute force until now. Therefore, at least 28 (obtained by solving $2^{2.58 \cdot M} > 2^{72}$) proposed gates should be applied to the general circuit for preventing brute force guessing. In practice, more than 28 proposed gates are desirable to be implemented because a

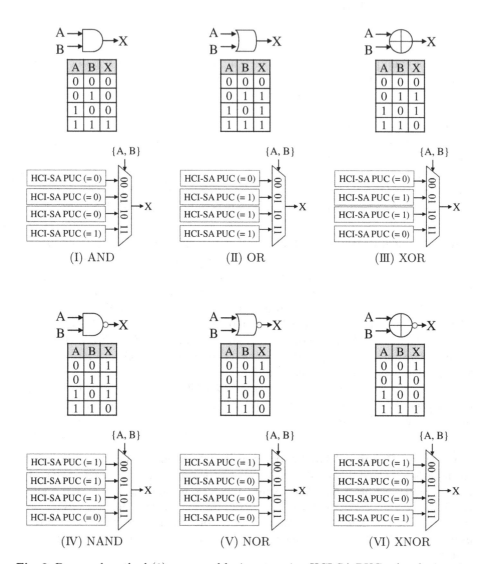

Fig. 3. Proposed method (1): proposed logic gate using HCI-SA PUCs. Any logic gate can be replaced with the proposed gates for the tolerance to reverse engineering.

lot of information may be learned from the overall circuit structure. In that sense, the number of 28 proposed gates can be considered to a minimum requirement.

Which Logic Gates are Replaced with the Proposed Gates? It is important for IC manufactures to choose the appropriate gates to which our proposed method is applied. This is because, if some logic gates are randomly replaced with the proposed gates, many of them are isolated, therefore an attacker can easily identify the functionality of proposed gates [13]. To solve this, researchers have introduced the methods of selecting the appropriate gates in order to maximize the cost of reverse engineering. The introduced methods can realize that:

– the functionality of the proposed gates can only be resolved by brute force and
– the extracted gate-level netlist produces outputs which are different from those of the genuine netlist, 50% output bits differ for every input pattern.

In [13], *camouflaged* gates were assumed to be used as the countermeasure against the reverse engineering of ICs, instead of our proposed gates based on HCI-SA PUCs. These camouflaged gates are similar to our proposed gates, in that the mask pattern images are identical[1] regardless of the functionality of gates. The technique to choose the camouflaged gates, introduced in [13], is also applied to our proposed gates.

New Threat: Reduction of Gate Candidates Considering Circuit Redundancy. We discuss the new threat which has not been considered in [13]. In general, the structure of general circuits is optimized to reduce its redundancy by using logic synthesis tools (e.g. Synopsys Design Compiler). By excluding the candidates which cause the circuit redundancy, an attacker might be able easily to identify the functionality of proposed gates. This is explained by a very simple circuit as shown in Fig. 4. P1 is implemented by the proposed gate based on HCI-SA PUCs, whose functionality is unclear for an attacker. The attacker can, however, guess that P1 is not an XOR gate. This is because, if P1 is an XOR gate, the functionality of this circuit is equivalent to an XNOR gate. It is not natural that the functionality of the XNOR gate is implemented using XOR and NOT gates since these are redundant. Consequently, by taking into consideration the circuit redundancy, an attacker can reduce the number of candidates of P1 from six to four (AND, OR, NAND, NOR). The above-mentioned example is based on a very simple circuit, while general circuits consisting of many logic gates are also exposed to the same threat. This enables an attacker to resolve the functionality of the proposed gates more efficiently than a brute-force approach.

To prevent the aforementioned threat, we propose the idea that designers of ICs make a part of a general circuit redundant before being replaced with the proposed gates. For example in Fig, 4, some XOR gates in a general circuit are

---

[1] Strictly speaking, the camouflaged gates are not completely identical, especially at side view of them. In contrast, our proposed gates are identical even at side view.

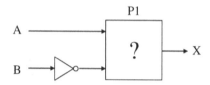

Fig. 4. P1 is implemented by the proposed gate. An attacker cannot identify its functionality using its mask pattern images.

implemented using XNOR and NOT gates. Similarly, some XNOR gates are implemented using XOR and NOT gates. After making these gates redundant, these XOR and XNOR gates are implemented by the proposed gates based on HCI-SA PUCs. This idea maintains the number of candidates of P1 at six, which forces an attacker to use a brute-force approach.

4.3   Proposed Method (2)

The proposed method (1) can increase the tolerance to reverse engineering of any logic gate, while the gate size of the proposed gate becomes larger than that of a standard logic gate. To suppress the increase of the gate size, a simple wire is made redundant and implemented by HCI-SA PUCs in the proposed method (2).

We focus on the N-input logic gates whose part of input values are constant bits. For example, we design two types of 2-input XOR gates by using HCI-SA PUCs, as shown in Fig. 5. One type of XOR gate has an input 1, and the other type has an input 0 (equivalent to simple wire). The input values 1(0) are generated from HCI-SA PUCs which outputs 1(0), respectively. Note that the latter type of XOR gates can be inserted as many as manufactures want because there are wires all over the circuit. This increases the tolerance to reverse engineering of general circuits dramatically because an attacker has to distinguish all of the HCI-SA PUCs outputting 0 or 1. Similarly, NOT gates and simple wires are also implemented by HCI-SA PUFs, as shown in Fig. 6.

The proposed gates in Figs. 5 and 6, consist of an HCI-SA cell and an XOR gate. The gate size of the XOR gate is 2.5 gates [1], so the gate size of the proposed gate is 7.5 gates.

In conclusion, high tolerance to reverse engineering of general circuits can be realized by combining the proposed method (1), as applied to any logic gate, with the proposed method (2), as applied to any wire with a small gate size.

4.4   Discussion: Targeting on Static Analysis

We discuss the reason why the attack range is limited to static analysis in this paper. We consider that our proposed methods mentioned in Sect. 4.2 and 4.3 have high usability even assuming only static analysis. The reason is as follows.

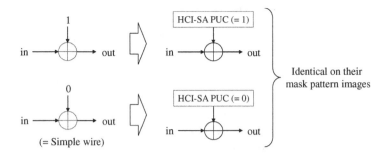

Fig. 5. Proposed method (2) for 2-input XOR gates

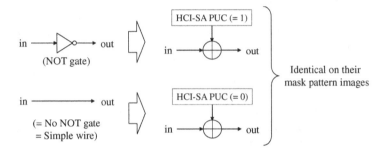

Fig. 6. Proposed method (2) for NOT gate and wire

Recently, fabless manufacturers have been widely spread, and they commonly provide outside fabrication companies with mask pattern information. In this situation, there is a risk that the mask pattern information (i.e. manufacture's IP) can be leaked not only to the outside fabrication companies but also to malicious parties. In contrast, when the proposed methods are used, IC chips can be manufactured by split companies: outside fabrication company and trusted company. The fabrication company manufacturers IC chips according to the mask pattern information, and then the trusted company performs the reinforcement process to provide HCI-SA PUCs with HCI stress. This split fabrication prevents the outside fabrication company from identifying the functionality of circuits masked by HCI-SA PUCs. Countermeasures against IP leakage are considered an important issue. In fact, some papers about the split fabrication have been presented in HOST 2014 [17] [9] [18].

As far as we know, there is no method of completely preventing any dynamic analysis. For example, if an attacker can perform the dynamic analysis, the hot carriers may possibly be able to be caught through side channel attacks (e.g. simple photonic emission analysis [14]). To prohibit such optical emission attacks, we need other countermeasure techniques such as an active shield or mesh on the backside of IC chips [14]. The security of HCI-SA PUCs against the dynamic analysis should be experimentally discussed in future work.

5   Case Study - Applying Proposed Methods to KASUMI

In this section, we present a case study of applying the proposed methods to an S-Box circuit of KASUMI block cipher [15]. Note that the S-Box circuit of KASUMI, properly speaking, does not need to be protected from reverse engineering because the specification of KASUMI block cipher is public information. In this case study, we assume that the S-Box circuit of KASUMI block cipher is manufacture's IP and explain how to use the proposed methods.

Let the 7-bit variable x and y be the input and output of the KASUMI 7-bit S-box S_7, respectively. Figure 7(I) shows the structure of circuit for making the 2nd output bit ($y[2]$) of the S_7. The proposed methods are applied to five spots labeled by (a), (b), (c), (d) and (e) in Fig. 7(I). Figure 7(II) shows the structure of circuit S_7 after applying the proposed methods. In spot (a), an AND gate is configured by the proposed method (1) shown in Fig. 3. In spot (b), 1-bit constant value applied to an OR gate is generated by an HCI-SA PUC, this being the proposed method (2) shown in Fig. 5. In spots (c) and (d), each NOT gate is replaced with an XOR gate whose one of input value (=1) is generated by an HCI-SA PUC. In spot (e), the simple wire is implemented by an XOR gate whose one of input value (=0) is generated by an HCI-SA PUC.

The circuit, as shown in Fig. 7(II), is 50 gates larger than the circuit, as shown in Fig. 7(I). Here, we use the equivalencies 1 AND/OR = 1.5 NAND gate and 1 NOT = 0.5 NAND gate, introduced in [1]. The tolerant to reverse engineering can be increased if the proposed methods are applied to more spots in the S-Box circuit. According to the discussion in Sect. 4.2, the gate size of a proposed gate, as depicted in Fig. 3, is estimated to be 25 gates. Further, at least 28 proposed gates are needed to prevent brute force guessing. The increase of the gate size is, therefore, estimated to be around 700 (= 25 gates · 28) gates. To our knowledge, the smallest KASUMI circuit to date is 2,990 gates [19]. Therefore, the KASUMI circuit including these proposed gates is small enough for embedded systems such as smart cards and mobile phones.

Meanings of Applying the Proposed Methods to S-Box Circuit. We discuss on the meaning of applying the proposed methods to the circuit of the S-Box whose specification is modified from its original. In general, it is recommended that cryptographic algorithms be open to the public because the security of the algorithms is always being evaluated by many specialists. On the other hand, the algorithm of an S-Box is sometimes modified in order for the reduction of area size or power consumption of the S-Box circuit [12], keeping its cryptographic security. This modified algorithm is very important as manufacture's IP, therefore the reverse engineering of the S-Box circuit is a big threat to its designer. Our proposed methods are very useful for protecting the modified S-Box circuit. The modified S-Box circuit is used not only in the general circuit for message encryption, but even in the authentication circuit based on cryptographic algorithms. Furthermore, even if IC manufactures use a public cryptographic algorithm in their ICs, but do not want anyone except themselves to know about the algorithm, they can use our proposed methods.

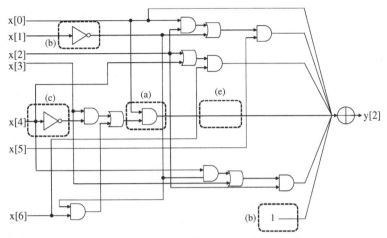

(I) Before applying the proposed methods.

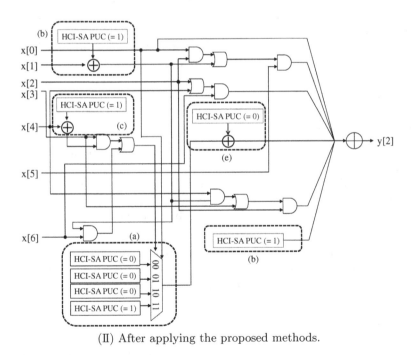

(II) After applying the proposed methods.

Fig. 7. Circuit structure for making the 2nd output bit ($y[2]$) of the KASUMI 7-bit S-box S_7

6   Conclusion

In this paper, we utilized HCI-SA PUFs, properly speaking, HCI-SA PUCs for making the circuit designs secret. The output from each HCI-SA PUC (HCI-SA cell) is controllable by its manufacture, therefore we distinguished PUCs from PUFs. We designed the proposed gates whose functionalities are equivalent to those of any logic gate (e.g. NAND, XOR) by using HCI-SA PUCs. The proposed gates were completely identical and impossible to be distinguished by using its mask pattern images. It is important which logic gates are replaced with the proposed gates. If the selected gates are not optimized, an attacker can get a hint of the circuit redundancy. As a result, an attacker may be able to resolve the functionality of them more efficiently than a brute-force approach. We, therefore, proposed another method for implementing a simple wire by HCI-SA PUCs and realizing high tolerant to reverse engineering with a small increase of gates. We showed a case study of applying the proposed methods to an S-Box circuit of KASUMI block cipher, assuming that the circuit is manufacture's IP.

PUCs will not be necessarily implemented by HCI-SA PUCs in the future. In [2], the reliability of SRAM PUFs can be improved by the accelerated aging of the SRAM cells (e.g. high temperature of supply voltage). All memory-based PUFs have a possibility of using for PUCs.

The proposed gates are also used for protecting the intellectual property of FPGAs, i.e. a bitstream. The bitstream is stored in a programmable ROM and encrypted by a secret key on an FPGA. The secret key, however, could be revealed through side-channel attacks [10]. The bitstream can be configured by the proposed gates instead of the programmable ROM. It is reasonable to apply the proposed gates to a part of circuit which is especially valuable and changeless.

Future work will include:

- The proof of the concept for HCI-SA PUCs through experiments based on real IC chips.
- Experimental verification of the security requirements for HCI-SA PUCs: one-time programmability and undetectability of hot carriers.
- The tolerance of HCI-SA PUCs against dynamic analysis.

Acknowledgements. The authors are very much thankful to the anonymous reviewers for useful comments in the review process. In particular, we thank our shepherd for valuable suggestions to improve this paper.

References

1. Batina, L., Lano, J., Mentens, N., Örs, S.B., Preneel, B., Verbauwhede, I.: Energy, Performance, Area Versus Security Trade-offs for Stream Ciphers. In: The State of the Art of Stream Ciphers (ECRYPT 2004), pp. 302–310 (2004)
2. Bhargava, M., Cakir, C., Mai, K.: Reliability Enhancement of Bi-Stable PUFs in 65nm Bulk CMOS. In: Hardware-Oriented Security and Trust (HOST 2012), pp. 25–30 (2012)

3. Bhargava, M., Mai, K.: A High Reliability PUF Using Hot Carrier Injection Based Response Reinforcement. In: Bertoni, G., Coron, J.-S. (eds.) CHES 2013. LNCS, vol. 8086, pp. 90–106. Springer, Heidelberg (2013)
4. Distributed.net. Project RC5-72, http://www.distributed.net/RC5
5. Fujitsu Semiconductor Ltd. CS86 technology, http://www.fujitsu.com/downloads/MICRO/fma/pdf/e620209_CS86_ASIC.pdf
6. Gassend, B., Clarke, D., Lim, D., van Dijk, M., Devadas, S.: Identification and Authentication of Integrated Circuits. In: Concurrency and Computation: Practice and Experiences, pp. 1077–1098 (2004)
7. Gassend, B., Clarke, D., van Dijk, M., Devadas, S.: Silicon Physical Random Functions. In: The 9th ACM Conference on Computer and Communications Security (CCS 2002), pp. 148–160 (2002)
8. Guajardo, J., Kumar, S.S., Schrijen, G.-J., Tuyls, P.: FPGA Intrinsic PUFs and Their Use for IP Protection. In: Paillier, P., Verbauwhede, I. (eds.) CHES 2007. LNCS, vol. 4727, pp. 63–80. Springer, Heidelberg (2007)
9. Jagasivamani, M., Gadfort, P., Sika, M., Bajura, M., Fritze, M.: Split Fabrication Obfuscation: Metrics and Techniques. In: Hardware-Oriented Security and Trust, HOST 2014 (2014)
10. Moradi, A., Barenghi, A., Kasper, T., Paar, C.: On the Vulnerability of FPGA Bitstream Encryption Against Power Analysis Attacks: Extracting Keys from Xilinx Virtex-II FPGAs. In: The 18th ACM Conference on Computer and Communications Security (CCS 2011), pp. 111–124 (2011)
11. Pappu, R.S.: Physical One-Way Functions. PhD thesis, Massachusetts Institute of Technology (2001)
12. Rahimunnisa, K., Zach, M.P., Kumar, S.S., Jayakumar, J.: Efficient Techniques for the Implementation of AES SubByte and MixColumn Transformations. In: Meghanathan, N., Nagamalai, D., Chaki, N. (eds.) Advances in Computing & Inform. Technology. AISC, vol. 176, pp. 497–506. Springer, Heidelberg (2012)
13. Rajendran, J., Sam, M., Sinanoglu, O., Karri, R.: Security Analysis of Integrated Circuit Camouflaging. In: The 20th ACM Conference on Computer and Communications Security (CCS 2013), pp. 709–720 (2013)
14. Schlösser, A., Nedospasov, D., Krämer, J., Orlic, S., Seifert, J.-P.: Simple Photonic Emission Analysis of AES. In: Prouff, E., Schaumont, P. (eds.) CHES 2012. LNCS, vol. 7428, pp. 41–57. Springer, Heidelberg (2012)
15. Third Generation Partnership Project. 3GPP TS 35.202 v7.0.0 Document 2: KASUMI Specification (2007)
16. Torrance, R., James, D.: The State-of-the-Art in IC Reverse Engineering. In: Clavier, C., Gaj, K. (eds.) CHES 2009. LNCS, vol. 5747, pp. 363–381. Springer, Heidelberg (2009)
17. Vaidyanathan, K., Das, B.P., Sumbul, E., Liu, R., Pileggi, L.: Building Trusted ICs using Split Fabrication. In: Hardware-Oriented Security and Trust, HOST 2014 (2014)
18. Vaidyanathan, K., Liu, R., Sumbul, E., Zhu, Q., Franchetti, F., Pileggi, L.: Efficient and Secure Intellectual Property (IP) Design for Split Fabrication. In: Hardware-Oriented Security and Trust (HOST 2014) (2014)
19. Yamamoto, D., Itoh, K., Yajima, J.: Compact Architecture for ASIC and FPGA Implementation of the KASUMI Block Cipher. IEICE Transactions on Fundamentals of Electronics, Communications and Computer Sciences 94-A(12), 2628–2638 (2011)
20. Yamamoto, D., Takenaka, M., Torii, N.: A Novel Technique using PUFs against Copying Circuit Designs (in Japanese). In: The 31st Symposium on Cryptography and Information Security (SCIS 2014) (2014)

Hydra: An Energy-Efficient Programmable Cryptographic Coprocessor Supporting Elliptic-Curve Pairings over Fields of Large Characteristics

Yun-An Chang[1], Wei-Chih Hong[2], Ming-Chun Hsiao[1],
Bo-Yin Yang[2], An-Yeu Wu[1], and Chen-Mou Cheng[1]

[1] National Taiwan University, Taipei, 10617, Taiwan
ghfjdksl@gmail.com,
mingchun@access.ee.ntu.edu.tw,
andywu@ntu.edu.tw,
ccheng@cc.ee.ntu.edu.tw
[2] Academia Sinica, Taipei, 11529, Taiwan
wchong@iis.sinica.edu.tw, by@crypto.tw

Abstract. Bilinear pairings on elliptic curves have many applications in cryptography and cryptanalysis. Pairing computation is more complicated compared to that of other popular public-key cryptosystems. Efficient implementation of cryptographic pairing, both software- and hardware-based approaches, has thus received increasing interest. In this paper, we focus on hardware implementation and present the design of Hydra, an energy-efficient programmable cryptographic coprocessor that supports various pairings over fields of large characteristics. We also present several implementations of Hydra, among which the smallest only uses 116 K gates when synthesized in TSMC 90 nm standard cell library. Despite the extra programmability, our design is competitive compared even with specialized implementations in terms of time-area-cycle product, a common figure of merit that provides a good measure of energy efficiency. For example, it only takes 3.04 ms to compute an optimal ate pairing over Barreto-Naehrig curves when the chip operates at 200 MHz. This is certainly a very small time-area-cycle product among all hardware implementations of cryptographic pairing in the current literature.

1 Introduction

Bilinear pairings on elliptic curves were introduced in the middle of 1990's for cryptanalytic purposes, e.g., to break cryptographic protocols whose security is based on the hardness of the elliptic-curve discrete-logarithm problem [14,9]. In 2000, Joux showed that they can also be used for tripartite key agreement [12]. Since then, many constructive pairing-based schemes were proposed, such as identity-based encryption [2], identity-based signatures [4], as well as short signatures [3].

Pairing computation is much more complicated compared to that of other popular public-key cryptosystems. Efficient implementation of cryptographic pairing has thus received increasing interest, both software- and hardware-based approaches, pursuing

M. Yoshida and K. Mouri (Eds.): IWSEC 2014, LNCS 8639, pp. 174–186, 2014.

higher speed or, in the cases of hardware implementation, smaller time-area-cycle product (ATC product), a common figure of merit that provides a good measure of energy efficiency.

For example, Kammler et al. reported a hardware implementation of a cryptographic coprocessor for various pairings of 128-bit security [13]. Although this is not the first programmable architecture, it is the first one that supports 128-bit security level. Fan, Vercauteren, and Verbauwhede improved the multiplication algorithm for Barreto-Naehrig (BN) curves with special parameters to achieve a higher speed [8]. However, as they took advantage of the chosen parameters, the result is only applicable to BN curves.

For field-programmable gate arrays (FPGAs), Ghosh, Mukhopadhyay, and Roychowdhury exploited the special arithmetic units in some FPGAs and gave the first FPGA pairing implementation with 128-bit security level [10]. In their proposed architecture, multiple homogeneous arithmetic units are used in parallel to exploit the inherent parallelism in pairing computation. Recently, Cheung et al. experimented with Montgomery multiplication in residue number systems [5], and Ghosh, Roychowdhury, and Das explored η_T pairing over binary curves [11]. Both implementations achieved good results with respect to speed.

In this paper, we will present the design and implementation of Hydra, an energy-efficient programmable cryptographic coprocessor that supports various pairings at 128-bit security level. Unlike the general architecture of, e.g., Kammler et al. [13], our design is optimized for carrying out pairing computation over fields of large characteristics. As a result, our design stays competitive in terms of ATC product even compared with specialized implementations such as that of Fan, Vercauteren, and Verbauwhede [8]. For example, our smallest implementation of Hydra only uses 116 K gates when synthesized in TSMC 90 nm standard cell library and has a latency of 3.04 ms when running at 200 MHz. This is certainly a very small time-area-cycle product among all hardware implementations of cryptographic pairing in the current literature.

The organization of the rest of this paper is as follows. In Section 2, we will first give a brief introduction to cryptographic pairings for the subsequent exposition. We will present the main ideas behind Hydra's architectural design in Section 3. We will then go through the detailed design of datapath in Section 4 and control in Section 5. To conclude, we will compare our implementation results with the state of the arts in Section 6.

2 Background

2.1 Bilinear Pairings

Let G_1, G_2, and G_T be abelian groups. A bilinear pairing is a map $\alpha : G_1 \times G_2 \to G_T$ with the following properties.

1. Bilinearity: $\alpha(mP, Q) = \alpha(P, mQ) = \alpha(P, Q)^m$ for $m \in \mathbb{Z}$.
2. Non-degeneracy: For all nonzero $P \in G_1$, there exists $Q \in G_2$ such that $\alpha(P, Q) \neq 1$, and vice versa.
3. Computability: $\alpha(P, Q)$ can be efficiently computed.

Most cryptographic pairings work on elliptic curves. There are many choices for the map α as well as the curves. In this work, we use Barreto-Naehrig (BN) curves [1] and optimal ate pairing [19] as an example, but other pairings can also be accelerated by our Hydra coprocessor.

2.2 Barreto-Naehrig Curves

Barreto-Naehrig curves are pairing-friendly elliptic curves over prime field $\mathbb{F}_p$ with embedding degree $k = 12$ [1]. They are defined by the equation $E : y^2 = x^3 + b, b \neq 0$. Let n denote the group order of $E(\mathbb{F}_p)$. Then p and r can be parameterized as

$$p(u) = 36x^4 - 36x^3 + 24x^2 - 6x + 1 \text{ and}$$
$$n(u) = 36x^4 - 36x^3 + 18x^2 - 6x + 1,$$

where $u \in \mathbb{Z}$ is an integer such that p and n are both prime numbers. We follow the work of Kammler *et al.* [13] and choose $b = 24$ and $u =$ 0x6000000000001F2D. This yields a key security parameter p of 256 bits.

2.3 Computing Optimal Ate Pairing

Algorithm 1 shows how to compute an optimal ate pairing. We base our design on Schwabe's high-quality software implementation [18] with further optimization on register usage.

Algorithm 1. Optimal ate pairing over Barreto-Naehrig curves

Require: $P \in G_1, Q \in G_2, s = 6t + 2 = \sum_{i=0}^{L-1} s_i 2^i, s_i \in \{0, 1\}$
Ensure: $\alpha_{opt}(P, Q)$
1: $T \leftarrow Q; f \leftarrow 1;$
2: **for** $i = L - 2$ **to** 0 **do**
3:     $f \leftarrow f^2 \cdot l_{T,T}(P); T \leftarrow 2T;$
4:     **if** $s_i == 1$ **then**
5:         $f \leftarrow f \cdot l_{T,Q}; T \leftarrow T + Q$
6:     **end if**
7: **end for**
8: $Q_1 \leftarrow \pi_p(Q); Q_2 \leftarrow \pi_{p^2}(Q);$
9: $f \leftarrow f \cdot l_{T,Q_1}(P); T \leftarrow T + Q_1$
10: $f \leftarrow f \cdot l_{T,-Q_2}(P); T \leftarrow T - Q_2$
11: $f \leftarrow f^{\frac{(p^{12}-1)}{r}};$
12: **return** f

The first part of Algorithm 1 is the Miller loop, first proposed by Miller [15] and later enhanced by others. It is a standard double-and-add loop performing the elliptic-curve arithmetic, including line addition and line doubling. After each line function, an $\mathbb{F}_{p^{12}}$ multiplication is performed.

The second part is the final exponentiation, which takes the output of the Miller loop $f \in \mathbb{F}_{p^{12}}$ and computes $f^{\frac{(p^{12}-1)}{l}}$. Here we use the method of Devegili, Scott, and Dahab [7] and split $\frac{p^{12}-1}{l}$ to $(p^6-1)(p^2+1)(\frac{p^4-p^2+1}{l})$ to speed up the computation.

Overall, the main computations are those of the line functions and $\mathbb{F}_{p^{12}}$ operations. We construct $\mathbb{F}_{p^{12}}$ as a series of tower fields as follows.

$$\mathbb{F}_{p^{12}} = \mathbb{F}_{p^6}[Z]/(Z^2 - \tau) \text{ with } \tau = Y$$
$$\uparrow$$
$$\mathbb{F}_{p^6} = \mathbb{F}_{p^2}[Y]/(Y^3 - \xi) \text{ with } \xi = (X+1)$$
$$\uparrow$$
$$\mathbb{F}_{p^2} = \mathbb{F}_p[X]/(X^2 - \sigma) \text{ with } \sigma = -2$$
$$\uparrow$$
$$\mathbb{F}_p$$

In this case, an $\mathbb{F}_{p^{12}}$ operation can be implemented by a series of $\mathbb{F}_p$ operations. Furthermore, the elliptic curve $E(\mathbb{F}_p)$ itself lives in $\mathbb{F}_p$. As a result, all computations can be decomposed into a set of $\mathbb{F}_p$ multiplications and additions. As we will see subsequently, we exploit this fact to get a better speed at a moderate price in terms of control logic.

3   High-Level Architectural Design

Fig. 1 shows the the five major blocks of the Hydra architecture, namely, Axpy Engine, Data Cache, Decoder, Instruction Cache, and Top Control. The main design philosophy behind Hydra's architecture is the separation of data and control, a key enabler for both programmability and high-throughput data processing. As shown in Fig. 1, data flows from Data Cache to Axpy Engine, the main computational unit of Hydra, and gets written back to Data Cache via Decoder and Top Control after being processed, as some of the results may be used by the latter two blocks for control purposes. On the other hand, control information is mainly passed from Decoder to Data Cache via Top Control after instructions are fetched from Instruction Cache and decoded at Decoder. Moreover, Top Control also handles the input and output of the entire coprocessor, interfacing with the host processor via the AMBA (Advanced Microcontroller Bus Architecture) High-performance Bus (AHB), so Hydra can easily work with any host processor that speaks this protocol such as ARM microprocessors. As a result, a typical workflow might look as follows.

1. The host processor checks the status of the coprocessor until it is in the idle state.
2. The host processor sets the environment registers of the coprocessor via Slave Port (shown as the "S" at the bottom of Top Control in Fig. 1), including the entry point of the program, as well as the addresses of the source and target data.

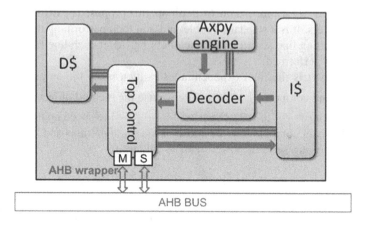

Fig. 1. High-level architectural design of Hydra

3. The host processor activates the coprocessor by sending a signal to the related control register.
4. Through Master Port (shown as the "M" at the bottom of Top Control in Fig. 1), the coprocessor loads the instructions to Instruction Cache from external memory.
5. The coprocessor runs the program accordingly and loads the input data from external memory via Master Port.
6. After the computation finishes, the coprocessor notifies the host processor using an interrupt mechanism.

In synthesizing a cryptographic coprocessor for pairing, most of the silicon area is for implementing the arithmetic unit (AU) that computes finite-field multiplications and additions inside Hydra's Axpy Engine. Furthermore, multipliers like the one in Fig. 2 typically takes up the most area because multiplication tends to be much more expensive than addition.

Further analysis shows that to compute an optimal ate pairing, we need about 18500 $\mathbb{F}_p$ multiplications and 85000 additions/subtractions. Typically, a multiplication operation takes about 5 times or more cycles than an addition/subtraction operation. This means that the time spent on multiplication is roughly the same as that on addition/subtraction, which is quite different from the typical multiplication-bound algorithms.

In this case, it is advantageous to use *heterogeneous* AUs, some of which have complete functionality (called full AU, or FAU), while others are only capable of computing addition and subtraction (called add-only AU, or AAU). Since an AAU is much smaller than an FAU, we expect a higher resource utilization if there is enough parallelism to be extracted by our scheduler.

Optimal resource allocation and scheduling on a set of heterogeneous computational units is in general a hard problem and has been intensely studied in the past. Here we are dealing with the most general cases because we are working with application-specific integrated circuits (ASIC). As we have seen earlier in this section, our architecture is similar to a general-purpose processor. For example, we use a *register file* to connect

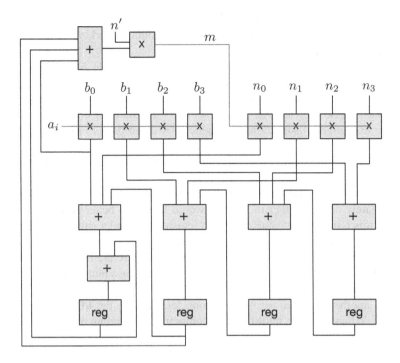

Fig. 2. A four-limb Montgomery multiplier

all AUs, which is actually implemented as part of Data Cache in Hydra. This greatly simplifies inter-AU communication, as all communication will need to go through the register file as the central hub. Also, as long as the register file is large enough, we can completely eliminate load/store operations from/to external memory. Furthermore, our compiler generates straight-line code, so there is no branch and loop, which further simplifies the analysis.

Now that we have a better understanding of our problem, we turn to the literature to seek solutions. We have tried without success several traditional methods, such as using critical path as the main heuristic for scheduling, as the memory required is unacceptably large. So far, most works in the literature focus on achieving the best speed performance. Although some of these works also take communication into account, none of them have considered memory constraints. The closest work to ours is perhaps that of Cordes, Marwedel, and Mallik [6], in which various constraints including a limit on the number of parallel tasks on the target system-on-chip (SoC) are taken into account, but the memory constraint was not considered.

In this paper, we experiment with one of the simplest methods, namely, the greedy method, to see if it can accelerate our pairing computations. That is, we use a simple in-order architecture in which an instruction is issued if all its dependencies have been resolved, and there is available AU to execute the instruction. This makes the hardware design relatively simple and shifts some work to compiler, which will need to come up with a plan of resource allocation and schedule. It bases its decision on information including the sequence of instructions to be executed and the resource constraints such as the composition of the heterogeneous AUs and the amount of working memory available to hold the intermediary results.

We briefly describe our design here. In each cycle each idle AU will sequentially search for a subsequent instruction whose input data is ready and can be done by this AU. If such an instruction exists and there is enough space in the working memory, it will be issued to the AU. The AU will be set in a busy state for however many cycles required to execute the instruction, after which it will go back to idle state and try to grab more work to do.

In searching for instructions, an AU only looks for the type of instructions that it can execute and skip the other types. Naturally, there is a trade-off in computation vs. memory because each additional AU will require additional working memory, so it is not immediately clear whether more AUs would lead to a better ATC product. Here we resolve this issue by imposing a limit on register use, under which AAUs will only fire when there is still a reasonable amount of memory available. In other words, FAUs have higher priorities in instruction issuing whenever there are ready multiplications. However, if there is not enough memory space for executing a multiplication, FAUs can also be used for additions/subtractions.

There is another resource we need to consider, namely, the I/O bandwidth of the register file. When there are multiple AUs competing for reading respective input data from the register file, the bandwidth limitation introduces extra delay, which in turns imposes an upper bound for the amount of parallelism we can achieve.

Putting all these together, our compiler will generate a schedule for each of the AUs, dictating what instruction and when each of the AUs should execute, as well as a resource allocation plan, dictating which register should hold what intermediary result. Our compiler automatically searches through the solution space of all feasible schedules and resource allocations.

4   Datapath Design

4.1   Full Arithmetic Unit

As we need to deal with general moduli, we use the well-known Montgomery method for computing modular multiplication $A \times B \mod N$ [16]. The basic idea is to compute $\bar{A} = AR$ and $\bar{B} = BR$ first, and then compute $(\bar{A} \times \bar{B})R^{-1} \mod N$ using the Montgomery reduction algorithm. With a good choice of R (usually a power of two), the operation could be computed efficiently.

Our implementation is a direct realization of Montgomery's algorithm. Fig. 2 shows an example of a four-limb multiplier, and in our actual implementation there are 17 limbs. We use 256-bit operands in the arithmetic units. Also, we use 272 bits to represent a single $\mathbb{F}_p$ element to allow further optimization such as lazy reduction.

Operands A, B, and N are divided into 17 limbs: a_i's, b_j's, and n_k's. It takes 17 cycles to compute the partial products and 3 more cycles, the carries. In the i-th cycle ($0 \leq i < 17$), the partial products of $a_i \times B$ and $m \times N$ are computed using 34 16-bit multipliers and then added with the shifted intermediate results from the previous cycle to produce the intermediate results r_j's. The value of m is obtained by summing the most significant part of r_0 and the least significant part of r_1 from the previous cycle, as well as the product $a_i \times b_0$, then multiplied by n'.

Carries are not propagated among the adders in Fig. 2 within the 17 multiply-and-add cycles. As a result, the r_j's could be at most $16 \times 2 + \lceil \log_2 17 \rceil = 37$ bits wide, which decides the width of the adders as well as that of the registers. After the 17 multiply-and-add cycles, 6 adders are reused to add up the carries in 3 cycles. For the sake of clarity, the wires and MUXs required for reusing the adders are omitted in Fig. 2. The critical path, as illustrated in Fig. 2, consists of 3 multipliers and 3 adders.

4.2   Add-Only Arithmetic Unit

An AAU consists of an array of 17 adders and can calculate $A + B$ in a single cycle, as well as its carry in another cycle. Since we only add two 16-bit numbers per adder, the intermediate result will be at most 17-bit wide. Unlike the carry computation in FAU, AAU only need to carry 1 bit, so both the register size and the number of cycles can be significantly reduced. Using a design similar to carry-select adders, the carry computation in AAU is very fast compared with that in FAU.

The critical path of AAU is not important, as it is dominated by FAU. Synthesis results show that the area of an AAU is only about 1/10 of that of an FAU. This is largely due to lack of multipliers, use of narrow adders (17 vs. 37), and possibly a shorter critical path.

5   Control Design

There are three essential parameters in Hydra's design: the numbers of FAUs and AAUs, as well as the register-file size. Through simulation, we found that the combination of one FAU and two AAUs delivers the best performance, which we will describe in more detail in Section 6. Fig. 3 illustrates conceptually all the relevant components, including datapath and control, for supporting heterogeneous AUs. The counter serves as the synchronization unit by providing the cycle number. An operation code consists of the addresses of the input and output data, as well as the cycle number that it should be issued. The decoder decides what operation need to be done in this cycle according to the operation code and the counter value.

Each AU has its own decoder and a separate list of operation codes. These decoders are independent of each other, i.e., there is no communication among them. Therefore, the compiler takes full responsibility of making sure there is no conflict among the operations of all the components.

In each cycle, the decoder (implemented inside Decoder) decides on one of the following operations according to the code that matches current counter value.

1. Idle.
2. Send the address for reading data from the register file.
3. Retrieve data and forward it to the AU. This could be done concurrently with operation 2 in the same cycle.
4. Start the computation of the corresponding AU. This could be done concurrently with operation 3 in the same cycle.

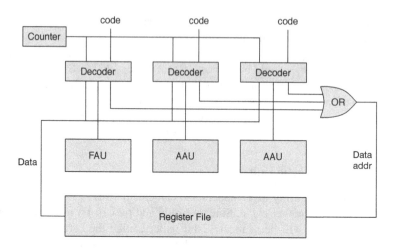

Fig. 3. Conceptual design of heterogeneous datapath and its control

5. Retrieve data from an AU, send the address and the data to be stored to register file. This cannot happen concurrently with operations 2 and 3, as there is only one address port in each register file.

Below we describe in more detail Hydra's instruction and data scheduling mechanisms, which is responsible for instruction loading and data management for Axpy Engine. It will prepare the corresponding instruction fetch and data loading of corresponding operation for Axpy Engine. Typically, the scheduling unit would load and decode the instruction from Instruction Cache and send the corresponding addresses to Data Cache for data loading. Furthermore, the scheduling unit will handle instructions like jump and data rescheduling. This way Axpy Engine can concentrate on data processing and avoid unnecessary idle states.

Hydra uses a data prefetch mechanism. To deal with data loading, a general-purpose processor usually uses either extra cycle or specific instruction to maintain. In both cases, the datapath will be in idle state, waiting for data loading. Hydra uses three instruction buffers. The first instruction buffer, the preloading buffer, stores the instruction after the next instruction. The second instruction buffer stores the next instruction itself, and we call the instruction stored in this buffer the "preparing instruction." The last instruction buffer is current buffer, which stores the instruction being executed in Axpy Engine. In general, we can decode the addresses from the instruction in the preloading buffer and send them to Data Cache for data prefetching, so after the current instruction finishes execution, the data will be ready at Data Cache. While the preparing instruction is about finish, the input register of Axpy Engine can be loaded with the corresponding data from Data Cache. This way the preloading instruction can be executed with the corresponding data already ready in input registers. In the case with single-cycle instructions followed by a multi-cycle instruction, the preparing instruction buffer serves as the temporal preloading instruction buffer, as the current instruction cannot finish in one cycle. With such scheduling mechanisms, we can overlap data loading with data processing in one instruction. Moreover, the prefetch technique avoids the conflict between data loading and processing. We use similar mechanisms for prefetching from and writing back to external memory.

6   Performance Evaluation and Concluding Remarks

As mentioned in Section 5, there are three essential parameters in the proposed coprocessor design. In this section, we first investigate the settings with best performance via architectural exploration and then compare our results against the state of the arts.

All our designs are synthesized using Synopsys Design Compiler. In addition, SRAM blocks such as Data Cache and the register file in it are generated by Artisan's memory compiler. For architectural exploration, we use Bluespec System Verilog [17]. These designs are then synthesized using TSMC standard cell libraries for their 90 nm and 130 nm technologies. However, Bluespec's synthesis results are typically 2–3 times less efficient in terms of ATC product than hand-coded designs using low-level hardware description languages such Verilog or VHDL. Therefore, after finding out the best set of parameters, we hand-code a design using Verilog and synthesize it using TSMC 90 nm technology.

Table 1 shows the performance of Bluespec's synthesis results using different numbers of FAUs and AAUs while keeping register-file size fixed. Using more AAUs should

Table 1. The performance achieved by a single-bank, 96-entry register file

Number of FAU	1	1	1	2	2	2	2
Number of AAU	1	2	3	1	2	3	4
Area (k gates)	144	157	168	246	256	268	280
Total time (ms)	4.34	3.60	3.62	3.23	2.72	2.57	2.55
ATC product	626.20	565.42	608.24	793.47	696.93	687.93	714.42

result in better timing results, but the marginal improvement diminishes as the following start to surface.

1. Multiplication-related operations become the bottleneck of the design, so adding extra AAUs can no longer shift any load from the FAU.
2. The bandwidth of the register file becomes fully occupied.
3. Last but not least, the register file itself becomes fully occupied.

From then on, the increase in area cannot bring in proportional improvement in speed, making it disadvantageous to add more AAUs. As seen in Table 1, with only one FAU, the bound is two AAUs.

Deploying more FAUs will increase this bound of adding more AAUs. However, we hit the limitation imposed by register-file bandwidth, and the extra FAU will compete for the bandwidth with other AUs. In this case, the bound becomes three AAUs, and the resultant ATC products are all worse than using only one FAU.

Table 2. The performance achieved by one FAU and two AAUs

Register-file size	80	88	96	128	160
Total time (ms)	5.14	4.67	4.60	4.58	4.57

Table 2 shows the performance of Bluespec's synthesis results using different sizes of register files in the setting of one FAU plus two AAUs. Increasing the number of registers means that there will be more spare registers for the extra AAUs to fetch next operations and thus improves the speed performance. This phenomenon becomes more noticeable when there are more AAUs. However, this comes at a price of a larger register file, so in general it does not improve the ATC product at all.

In Table 3, we compare the performance of our designs against that of two best works from the literature. We stress that it is in general very difficult to compare the perfor-

Table 3. Performance comparisons

	Technology	Total area	Cycle time	Total time	ATC product
This work (hand-coded Verilog)	90 nm	116 k gates	5 ns	3.04 ms	353.6
This work (Bluespec)	90 nm	157 k gates	5.92 ns	3.6 ms	565.2
This work (Bluespec)	130 nm	166 k gates	9.73 ns	5.88 ms	976.2
Kammler et al. [13]	130 nm	164 k gates	2.96 ns	15.8 ms	2591.2
Fan, Vercauteren, and Verbauwhede [8]	130 nm	183 k gates	4.9 ns	2.91 ms	532.5

mance of designs using different fabrication technologies. Furthermore, architectural differences also make fair comparison even more difficult, so here we can only try our best to compare apple to apple.

When compared against the design by Kammler et al. [13], it is clear that our designs achieve better ATC products. This is mainly because they have a scalar design in which a significant portion of the transistors are allocated to non-datapath components such as control/decoding logic and SRAM. Furthermore, a significant portion of the energy is typically consumed by the circuitry that supports execution of software programs in a processor architecture. A scalar design means that the density of the program code tends to be quite low, resulting in a much less efficient design in terms of energy consumption. In return, the benefit of such an approach is a processor that is capable of executing a wide variety of programs not limited to cryptographic pairing. In contrast, our design is a coprocessor and would require the help from a microcontroller in a complete system.

Lastly, it is even more challenging to compare our result with that of Fan, Vercauteren, and Verbauwhede [8]. First, although our synthesis result at 90 nm seems better than theirs at 130 nm in terms of ATC product, it is difficult to tell whether this is merely due to advancement of fabrication technologies. There are several ways we can do a back-of-envelope estimation, and the best we can say is that these two designs are roughly on par with 10–15% of error. On the one hand, our design provides full connectivity with industry standard AMBA AHB as well as a high degree of programmability that would allow the support of, e.g., elliptic curve cryptography on curves over large characteristics. In order to achieve this flexibility, our design needs to load programs from external memories, while on the other hand, their design does not require interfacing with external memories because they are specialized for Barreto-Naehrig curves. At the end, the only conclusion we can draw from this apple-orange comparison is that the two designs are roughly on par with different directions of optimization.

Acknowledgments. This work was also supported by National Science Council, National Taiwan University and Intel Corporation under Grants NSC102-2911-I-002-001 and NTU103R7501.

References

1. Barreto, P.S.L.M., Naehrig, M.: Pairing-friendly elliptic curves of prime order. In: Preneel, B., Tavares, S. (eds.) SAC 2005. LNCS, vol. 3897, pp. 319–331. Springer, Heidelberg (2006)
2. Boneh, D., Franklin, M.: Identity-based encryption from the weil pairing. In: Kilian, J. (ed.) CRYPTO 2001. LNCS, vol. 2139, pp. 213–229. Springer, Heidelberg (2001)
3. Boneh, D., Lynn, B., Shacham, H.: Short signatures from the Weil pairing. Journal of Cryptology 17(4), 297–319 (2004)
4. Cha, J.C., Cheon, J.H.: An identity-based signature from gap Diffie-Hellman groups. In: Desmedt, Y.G. (ed.) PKC 2003. LNCS, vol. 2567, pp. 18–30. Springer, Heidelberg (2003)
5. Cheung, R.C.C., Duquesne, S., Fan, J., Guillermin, N., Verbauwhede, I., Yao, G.X.: FPGA implementation of pairings using residue number system and lazy reduction. In: Preneel, B., Takagi, T. (eds.) CHES 2011. LNCS, vol. 6917, pp. 421–441. Springer, Heidelberg (2011)
6. Cordes, D., Marwedel, P., Mallik, A.: Automatic parallelization of embedded software using hierarchical task graphs and integer linear programming. In: CODES+ISSS, Montreal, QC, Canada, pp. 267–276 (2010)
7. Devegili, A.J., Scott, M., Dahab, R.: Implementing cryptographic pairings over Barreto-Naehrig curves. In: Takagi, T., Okamoto, T., Okamoto, E., Okamoto, T. (eds.) Pairing 2007. LNCS, vol. 4575, pp. 197–207. Springer, Heidelberg (2007)
8. Fan, J., Vercauteren, F., Verbauwhede, I.: Faster $\mathbb{F}_p$-arithmetic for cryptographic pairings on Barreto-Naehrig curves. In: Clavier, C., Gaj, K. (eds.) CHES 2009. LNCS, vol. 5747, pp. 240–253. Springer, Heidelberg (2009)
9. Frey, G., Rück, H.-G.: A remark concerning m-divisibility and the discrete logarithm in the divisor class group of curves. Mathematics of Computation 62, 865–874 (1994)
10. Ghosh, S., Mukhopadhyay, D., Roychowdhury, D.: High speed flexible pairing cryptoprocessor on FPGA platform. In: Joye, M., Miyaji, A., Otsuka, A. (eds.) Pairing 2010. LNCS, vol. 6487, pp. 450–466. Springer, Heidelberg (2010)
11. Ghosh, S., Roychowdhury, D., Das, A.: High speed cryptoprocessor for η_T pairing on 128-bit secure supersingular elliptic curves over characteristic two fields. In: Preneel, B., Takagi, T. (eds.) CHES 2011. LNCS, vol. 6917, pp. 442–458. Springer, Heidelberg (2011)
12. Joux, A.: A one round protocol for tripartite Diffie-Hellman. In: Bosma, W. (ed.) ANTS-IV. LNCS, vol. 1838, pp. 385–394. Springer, Heidelberg (2000)
13. Kammler, D., Zhang, D., Schwabe, P., Scharwaechter, H., Langenberg, M., Auras, D., Ascheid, G., Mathar, R.: Designing an ASIP for cryptographic pairings over Barreto-Naehrig curves. In: Clavier, C., Gaj, K. (eds.) CHES 2009. LNCS, vol. 5747, pp. 254–271. Springer, Heidelberg (2009)

14. Menezes, A.J., Okamoto, T., Vanstone, S.A.: Reducing elliptic curve logarithms to logarithms in a finite field. IEEE Transactions on Information Theory 39(5), 1639–1646 (1993)
15. Miller, V.S.: The Weil pairing, and its efficient calculation. Journal of Cryptology 17(4), 235–261 (2004)
16. Montgomery, P.L.: Modular multiplication without trial division. Mathematics of Computation 44, 519–521 (1985)
17. Nikhil, R.: Bluespec System Verilog: efficient, correct RTL from high level specifications. In: MEMOCODE 2004, San Diego, CA, USA, pp. 69–70 (2004)
18. Schwabe, P.: Pairing computation on BN curves,
    http://cryptojedi.org/crypto/#bnpairings
19. Vercauteren, F.: Optimal pairings. IEEE Transactions on Information Theory 56(1), 455–461 (2010)

On the Security Proof of an Authentication Protocol from Eurocrypt 2011

Kosei Endo* and Noboru Kunihiro

The University of Tokyo, Japan
kunihiro@k.u-tokyo.ac.jp

Abstract. This paper discusses the security of one of authentication protocols proposed by Kiltz et al. at Eurocrypt 2011. Kiltz et al. claimed that the protocol is secure against active attacks. However, they did not give rigorous security proof and just mentioned that the scheme would be secure. In this paper, we introduce a new problem that is as hard as the learning parity with noise problem and prove the active security of the protocol under the assumption that the problem is hard. By combining our result with that of Rizomiliotis and Gritzalis, we obtain complete proof of the Man-in-the-Middle (MIM) security of the protocol.

Keywords: RFID, Authentication Protocol, LPN Problem, HB-Family.

1 Introduction

Radio Frequency Identification (RFID) technology is one of the most important research topics. RFID has good features such as data rewritability, stain resistance, water resistance, permeability, low cost. For these usefulness, many applications which use RFID system to the transportation and managements are developed. On the other hand, it is a challenging task since RFID-tag is low-resource device which only allows low-cost protocol, e.g., it is difficult to load the public key encryption system such as RSA on the RFID-tag. Thus, constructing lightweight protocol which can be loaded on that low-resources device such as RFID is very important.

1.1 Previous Works

At Asiacrypt 2001, Hopper and Blum [10] proposed a lightweight two-pass authentication protocol called the HB protocol. The HB protocol requires only basic AND and XOR operations and it has been proved to be secure against passive attacks [10, 12, 13] via reduction to the learning parity with noise (LPN) problem which is well-known NP-complete problem [1]. However, it is insecure against a stronger adversary, active adversary, who has ability to impersonate a reader and interact with legitimate tags [10–13]. At Crypto 2005, Juels and Weis [11] proposed a modified HB protocol called the HB$^+$ protocol . The

---

* Currently, he is working at Iwaki Sogo High School.

M. Yoshida and K. Mouri (Eds.): IWSEC 2014, LNCS 8639, pp. 187–203, 2014.
© Springer International Publishing Switzerland 2014

HB^+ protocol has been proved to be secure against active attacks [11–13]. In the same year, Gilbert et al. [9] showed that the HB^+ protocol was insecure against a Man-in-the-Middle (MIM) attack. Specifically, they described a linear time MIM attack against the HB^+ protocol that is called the GRS MIM attack. Many variants of the HB^+ protocol [3–5, 16] were proposed to prevent the GRS attack, but all of them were shown to be insecure later [6, 7]. At Eurocrypt 2008, Gilbert et al. [8] extended the HB^+ protocol and proposed a new protocol called the $HB^\#$ that only requires three-pass communication and secure against GRS MIM attacks. While two vectors are shared by the tag and the reader as the secret keys in the HB^+ protocol, two matrices are shared by the tag and the reader as the secret keys in the $HB^\#$ protocol. Owning to the increasing the size of secret keys, the $HB^\#$ protocol achieves stronger security and reduces the communication complexity. However, at Asiacrypt 2008, Ouafi et al. [17] described a MIM attack against the $HB^\#$ protocol. After that, several three-pass protocols [2, 15, 19] that resist MIM attacks were proposed. Three-pass authentication protocols which have stronger security had been well studied. From a practical aspect, however, two-pass authentication protocol is more desirable than three-pass authentication protocol. Construction of a two-pass authentication scheme with even the active security had been open problem for a long time. At Eurocrypt 2011, Kiltz et al. [14] proposed a two-pass authentication protocol called the AUTH protocol. The AUTH protocol is the first two-pass protocol which achieves the active security and yields a large improvement in term of round complexity. In [14], Kiltz et al. also suggested two variants of the AUTH protocol, which we call the $AUTH^+$ protocol and the $AUTH^\#$ protocol. In the $AUTH^+$ protocol, the computational complexity decreases in exchange for increasing the number of secret keys. In the $AUTH^\#$ protocol, the communication complexity decreases in exchange for the increasing the size of secret keys like the $HB^\#$ protocol. At WiSec 2013, Rizomiliotis and Gritzalis [20] later claimed that the $AUTH^\#$ protocol has stronger security than what was predicted.

1.2   Our Contributions

Kiltz et al. claimed that the active security of the $AUTH^\#$ protocol is proved under the $SLPN^*$ assumption which is known to be probabilistic polynomial time equivalent to the LPN assumption [18]. However, they did not give rigorous security proof and it seems to be difficult to construct reduction from the $SLPN^*$ assumption to the active security of the $AUTH^\#$ protocol. Whereas Rizomiliotis and Gritzalis [20] proved the MIM security of the $AUTH^\#$ protocol under the assumption that the $AUTH^\#$ protocol is secure against the active adversaries, there is a gap of the security proof since the active security of the $AUTH^\#$ has not been proved.

In this paper, we prove the active security of the $AUTH^\#$ protocol. We take a modular approach for proving it, which simplifies the proof. For this proof, we introduce a new computational assumption, which we call the $MSLPN^*$ assumption. This assumption is based on the $SLPN^*$ assumption. We show that the

MSLPN* assumption is probabilistic polynomial time equivalent to the SLPN* assumption.

After that, we prove that the AUTH# protocol is secure against active adversaries under the MSLPN* assumption. Combining our result and that of Rizomiliotis and Gritzalis, we complete the security proof of the AUTH# protocol against the General MIM attack.

1.3   Organizations

This paper is organized as follows. In Section 2, we describe the necessary background on the authentication protocol and the AUTH# protocol which we focus on. In Section 3, we introduce the MSLPN* assumption and prove that the MSLPN* assumption is probabilistic polynomial time equivalent to the SLPN* assumption. In Section 4, we prove that the AUTH# protocol is secure against active attacks under the MSLPN* assumption. In Section 5, we draw our conclusions.

2   Preliminaries

2.1   Notation

We denote the set of integers modulo 2 by $\mathbb{Z}_2$. We use normal, bold and capital bold letters such as x, $\mathbf{x}$ and $\mathbf{X}$ to denote single elements, vectors and matrices over $\mathbb{Z}_2$, respectively. For a vector $\mathbf{x}$, $\mathbf{x}[i]$ denotes the i-th element of $\mathbf{x}$, and for a matrix $\mathbf{X}$, $\mathbf{X}_{i,j}$ denotes the (i,j)-th element of $\mathbf{X}$. We denote the sampling of a value x with uniform distribution over a finite set X by $x \xleftarrow{\$} X$. For a distribution Y, we write $y \leftarrow Y$ to denote y is chosen according to the distribution Y. For $\mathbf{a} \in \mathbb{Z}_2^n$, $\mathrm{wt}(\mathbf{a})$ denotes the Hamming weight of the vector $\mathbf{a}$. We use $|\mathbf{a}|$ to denote the length of $\mathbf{a}$. The inverse of $\mathbf{b} \in \mathbb{Z}_2^n$ is written as $\overline{\mathbf{b}}$; i.e., $\overline{\mathbf{b}}[i] = 1 - \mathbf{b}[i]$ for $i = 1, \ldots, n$. The bitwise XOR operation of two vectors $\mathbf{x}$ and $\mathbf{y}$ is represented by $\mathbf{x} \oplus \mathbf{y}$, where $(\mathbf{x} \oplus \mathbf{y})[i] = \mathbf{x}[i] \oplus \mathbf{y}[i]$ for all i. We also use $\mathbf{X} \oplus \mathbf{Y}$ for the bitwise XOR of two binary matrices $\mathbf{X}$ and $\mathbf{Y}$. The bitwise AND operation of two binary vectors $\mathbf{x}$ and $\mathbf{y}$ is written as $\mathbf{x} \wedge \mathbf{y}$; i.e., $(\mathbf{x} \wedge \mathbf{y})[i] = \mathbf{x}[i] \wedge \mathbf{y}[i]$ for all i. For a matrix $\mathbf{X} = (\mathbf{x}_1, \ldots, \mathbf{x}_n) \in \mathbb{Z}_2^{m \times n}$ ($\mathbf{x}_i \in \mathbb{Z}_2^m$) and a vector $\mathbf{y} \in \mathbb{Z}_2^m$, we define by $\mathbf{X} \wedge \mathbf{y} \in \mathbb{Z}_2^{m \times n}$ the matrix such that $\mathbf{X} \wedge \mathbf{y} = (\mathbf{x}_1 \wedge \mathbf{y}, \ldots, \mathbf{x}_n \wedge \mathbf{y})$. We define by $\mathbf{x}_{\downarrow \mathbf{y}}$ the vector obtained by deleting of $\mathbf{x}[i]$ such that $\mathbf{y}[i] = 0$. For example, if $\mathbf{x}^\mathsf{T} = (1,0,1,0,0,1)$ and $\mathbf{y}^\mathsf{T} = (1,1,0,0,1,1)$, then $\mathbf{x}_{\downarrow \mathbf{y}}^\mathsf{T} = (1,0,0,1)$. Note that the length of $\mathbf{x}_{\downarrow \mathbf{y}}$ is $\mathrm{wt}(\mathbf{y})$. For a matrix $\mathbf{X} \in \mathbb{Z}_2^{m \times n}$ and a vector $\mathbf{y} \in \mathbb{Z}_2^m$, $\mathbf{X}_{\downarrow \mathbf{y}}$ denotes the submatrix by deleting of the i-th row of $\mathbf{y}[i]$ such that $\mathbf{y}[i] = 0$. The rank of a matrix $\mathbf{X}$ is denoted by $\mathrm{rank}(\mathbf{X})$. The Bernoulli distribution over $\mathbb{Z}_2$ with bias τ is represented as Ber_τ; i.e., $\Pr[x = 1] = \tau$ if x follows Ber_τ. An algorithm $\mathcal{A}$ is *probabilistic* if $\mathcal{A}$ employs some randomness in the procedure. A probabilistic algorithm $\mathcal{A}$ is *probabilistic polynomial-time* (PPT) if the computation of $\mathcal{A}(\mathbf{x})$ terminates in at most $\mathrm{poly}(|\mathbf{x}|)$ steps for any input $\mathbf{x} \in \mathbb{Z}_2^*$.

2.2   Hard Learning Problems

We define two computational problems, the LPN problem and the SLPN* problem, and provide a proposition that asserts that the difficulties of both problems are probabilistic polynomial time equivalent. Let m and q be positive integers and t, τ and ε be real numbers, where $t > 0$ and $\varepsilon \in (0, 1)$.

LPN Problem. Given a secret $\mathbf{x} \in \mathbb{Z}_2^m$ and $\tau \in (0, 1/2)$, we write $\Lambda_{\tau,m}(\mathbf{x})$ for the distribution over $\mathbb{Z}_2^m \times \mathbb{Z}_2$ whose samples are obtained as $(\mathbf{r}, z)$ where $\mathbf{r} \xleftarrow{\$} \mathbb{Z}_2^m$, $e \leftarrow \mathrm{Ber}_\tau$; $z = \mathbf{r}^\mathsf{T}\mathbf{x} \oplus e$. Let $\Lambda_{\tau,m}(\mathbf{x})$ also denote the oracle that outputs a sample from the distribution $\Lambda_{\tau,m}(\mathbf{x})$. U_{m+1} denotes an oracle that outputs a sample from the uniform distribution over $\mathbb{Z}_2^{m+1}$. The $\mathrm{LPN}_{\tau,m}$ problem is to distinguish oracle access to $\Lambda_{\tau,m}(\mathbf{x})$ from oracle access to U_{m+1}.

Definition 1 (LPN problem). *For a distinguisher $\mathcal{D}$, we defined the $\mathrm{LPN}_{\tau,m}$ advantage of the distinguisher $\mathcal{D}$ as follows:*

$$\mathrm{Adv}_{\tau,m}^{\mathrm{LPN}} = \left| \Pr[\mathcal{D}^{\Lambda_{\tau,m}(\mathbf{x})} \to 1 | \mathbf{x} \xleftarrow{\$} \mathbb{Z}_2^m] - \Pr[\mathcal{D}^{U_{m+1}} \to 1] \right|.$$

The $\mathrm{LPN}_{\tau,m}$ problem is (t, q, ε)-hard if for every distinguisher $\mathcal{D}$, running in time t and making q queries, the $\mathrm{LPN}_{\tau,m}$ advantage of the distinguisher $\mathcal{D}$ is less than ε.

Subset LPN (SLPN*) Problem. Let d be a positive integer where $d \leq l$. We denote by $\Gamma_{\tau,m,d}(\mathbf{x}, \cdot)$ the oracle that upon input $\mathbf{v} \in \mathbb{Z}_2^m$ outputs $\bot$ if $\mathrm{wt}(\mathbf{v}) < d$, and otherwise a sample from the distribution $\Lambda_{\tau,m}(\mathbf{x} \wedge \mathbf{v})$. $U_{m+1}(\cdot)$ is the oracle that upon input $\mathbf{v} \in \mathbb{Z}_2^m$ outputs $\bot$ if $\mathrm{wt}(\mathbf{v}) < d$, and otherwise a sample from the uniform distribution over $\mathbb{Z}_2^{m+1}$. The $\mathrm{SLPN}_{\tau,m,d}^*$ problem is to distinguish oracle access to $\Gamma_{\tau,m,d}(\mathbf{x}, \cdot)$ from oracle access to $U_{m+1}(\cdot)$.

Definition 2 (SLPN* problem). *For a distinguisher $\mathcal{D}$, we defined the $\mathrm{SLPN}_{\tau,m,d}^*$ advantage of the distinguisher $\mathcal{D}$ as follows:*

$$\mathrm{Adv}_{\tau,m,d}^{\mathrm{SLPN}^*} = \left| \Pr[\mathcal{D}^{\Gamma_{\tau,m,d}(\mathbf{x},\cdot)} \to 1 | \mathbf{x} \xleftarrow{\$} \mathbb{Z}_2^m] - \Pr[\mathcal{D}^{U_{m+1}(\cdot)} \to 1] \right|.$$

The $\mathrm{SLPN}_{\tau,m,d}^*$ problem is (t, q, ε)-hard if for every distinguisher $\mathcal{D}$, running in time t and q queries, the $\mathrm{SLPN}_{\tau,m,d}^*$ advantage of the distinguisher $\mathcal{D}$ is less than ε.

For $g \in \mathbb{N}$, the following lemma states that the difficulty of solving the $\mathrm{LPN}_{\tau,m}$ problem and that of solving the $\mathrm{SLPN}_{\tau,l,d+g}^*$ problem are probabilistic polynomial time equivalent. The hardness gap is exponentially small in g [14].

Proposition 1 (Pietrzak [18]). *For $l, d, g \in \mathbb{N}$, where $l \geq d + g$, if the $\mathrm{LPN}_{\tau,d}$ problem is (t, q, ε)-hard, the $\mathrm{SLPN}_{\tau,m,d}^*$ problem is (t', q, ε')-hard, where*

$$t' = t - \mathrm{poly}(l, q) \quad and \quad \varepsilon' = \varepsilon + 2q/2^{g+1}.$$

2.3 Authentication Protocols and Attacks on Them

An authentication protocol is an interactive protocol executed between a tag $\mathcal{T}$ (prover) and a reader $\mathcal{R}$ (verifier), both of which are PPT algorithms. They share a random secret key generated by a key-generation algorithm $KG(1^\lambda)$ for the security parameter λ. After the execution of the authentication protocol, the reader outputs accept if he confirms that the tag is valid and otherwise he outputs reject.

There are three attack models on the authentication protocol, *passive*, *active*, and *Man-in-the-Middle*. All three models proceed in two phases, *the learning phase* and *the forgery phase*. In the learning phase, depending on the model, the attacker is allowed to have some interaction with the tag and reader. In the forgery phase, in all three models, the attacker is only allowed to interact with the reader. The goal of attackers is to cause the reader to output accept in the forgery phase. The differences in the three models depends on the strength of the attackers in the learning phases, which are described as follows.

Passive Attack. In the learning phase, the passive attacker is allowed to observe some interactions between the tag and the reader. In the forgery phase, he loses the access to the tag and attempts to cause the reader to output accept.

Active Attack. In the learning phase, the active attacker is allowed to observe some interactions between the tag and the reader and interact with the tag. In the forgery phase, he executes similarly as the attacker in the passive attack.

Man-in-the-Middle (MIM) Attack. In the learning phase, the MIM attacker is allowed to observe some interactions between the tag and the reader and interact with the tag and the reader. Moreover, he has ability of learning whether the reader outputs accept or reject to the messages sent from the attacker. In the forgery phase, he executes similarly as the attacker in the passive attack.

The active attacker is stronger than the passive attacker since he can send any messages to the tag in the learning phase. The MIM attacker is stronger than the active attacker since he can interact with not only the tag but also the reader in the learning phase[1]. We strictly define the active security and the MIM security of an authentication protocol.

Definition 3. *For an authentication protocol, the protocol is (t, q, ε)-secure against active adversaries if for any active adversary who runs in time t and makes queries q times, he succeeds the attack with probability at most ε. We call the ε the advantage of the active adversary.*

---

[1] In [15], a stronger MIM attack model than the MIM model defined here is introduced. We call it *the strong MIM(sMIM) attack model*. In the sMIM model, there is no phases and the sMIM attacker succeeds attacks if he sends a valid perturbed answer to the reader in polynomial times interactions. We describe the details of the sMIM attack model in Appendix A.

Definition 4. *For an authentication protocol, the protocol is (t, q, ε)-secure against MIM adversaries if for any MIM adversary who runs in time t and makes query q times, he succeds the attack with probability at most ε. We call the ε the advantage of the MIM adversary.*

2.4   The AUTH# Protocol

We describe an authentication protocol proposed by Kiltz et al., which is called the AUTH# protocol. It is described as follows.

- Public parameters
  The authentication protocol has the following public parameters, where l, n depend on the security parameter λ and τ, τ' are constants.
  - $l, n \in \mathbb{N}$: parameters of the secret key $\mathbf{S}$
  - $\tau \in (0, 1/2)$: parameter of the Bernoulli error distribution (Ber_τ)
  - $\tau' = \tau/2 + 1/4$: the acceptance threshold
- Key generation
  Algorithm $\mathrm{KG}(1^\lambda)$ samples $\mathbf{S} \xleftarrow{\$} \mathbb{Z}_2^{2l \times n}$ and returns $\mathbf{S}$ as the secret key to the tag and the reader.
- Authentication protocol
  The AUTH# protocol with the tag $\mathcal{T}_{\tau,n}$ and the reader $\mathcal{R}_{\tau',n}$ is as follows and given in Figure 1. We denote by Ber_τ^n the distribution over $\mathbb{Z}_2^n$ where each vector consists of n independent samples drown from Ber_τ.

  Step1 The reader randomly chooses a bitselector $\mathbf{v} \in \{\mathbf{x} \in \mathbb{Z}_2^{2l} | \mathrm{wt}(\mathbf{x}) = l\}$ and sends it to the tag.

  Step2 The tag receives the bitselector $\mathbf{v}$ and computes the Hamming weight of $\mathbf{v}$.
  - If $\mathrm{wt}(\mathbf{v}) \neq l$, the tag output abort.
  - If $\mathrm{wt}(\mathbf{v}) = l$, the tag chooses a random vector $\mathbf{r} \in \mathbb{Z}_2^l$ and error vector $\mathbf{e}$ which follows Ber_τ^n. He computes $\mathbf{z} := \mathbf{S}_{\downarrow \mathbf{v}}^\top \mathbf{r} \oplus \mathbf{e}$ and sends $(\mathbf{r}, \mathbf{z})$ to the reader.

  Step3-1 The reader receives $(\mathbf{r}, \mathbf{z})$ and checks whether $\mathbf{r}$ is the zero vector or not. If $\mathbf{r} = \mathbf{0}$, he outputs reject.

  Step3-2 The reader computes the Hamming weight of $\mathbf{z} \oplus \mathbf{S}_{\downarrow \mathbf{v}}^\top \mathbf{r}$ and checks whether the Hamming weight gets over the threshold $n\tau'$ or not. If $\mathrm{wt}(\mathbf{z} \oplus \mathbf{S}_{\downarrow \mathbf{v}}^\top \mathbf{r}) \geq n\tau'$, he outputs reject.

  Step3-3 If the reader does not output reject in both **Step3-1** and **Step3-2**, he outputs accept.

In the AUTH# protocol, a valid tag that has the secret key $\mathbf{S}$ successfully authenticates itself to the reader with high enough probability. We call the probability that a valid tag gets reject by mistake the *completeness error* and denote it by $E_c^{\mathrm{AUTH}^\#}$. We evaluate the probability precisely. In **Step 3-1**, the reader checks whether $\mathbf{r}$ is the zero vector or not . The probability of the random vector

Fig. 1. The AUTH$^{\#}$ Protocol

$\mathbf{r} = \mathbf{0}$ is $1/2^l$. In **Step 3-2**, the reader computes the Hamming weight of the vector $\mathbf{z} \oplus \mathbf{S}_{\downarrow\mathbf{v}}^{\mathsf{T}}\mathbf{r}$ and this vector transforms as follows:

$$\mathbf{z} \oplus \mathbf{S}_{\downarrow\mathbf{v}}^{\mathsf{T}}\mathbf{r} = \mathbf{S}_{\downarrow\mathbf{v}}^{\mathsf{T}}\mathbf{r} \oplus \mathbf{e} \oplus \mathbf{S}_{\downarrow\mathbf{v}}^{\mathsf{T}}\mathbf{r} = \mathbf{e}.$$

Note that $\mathbf{e} \leftarrow \mathrm{Ber}_{\tau}^n$ and $\tau' = \tau + (1/4 - \tau/2)$. From the Hoeffding bound, we obtain the following inequality:

$$\Pr[\mathrm{wt}(\mathbf{z} \oplus \mathbf{S}_{\downarrow\mathbf{v}}^{\mathsf{T}}\mathbf{r}) \geq n\tau' | \mathbf{r} \xleftarrow{\$} \mathbb{Z}_2^l, \mathbf{e} \xleftarrow{\$} \mathrm{Ber}_{\tau}^n; \mathbf{z} := \mathbf{S}_{\downarrow\mathbf{v}}^{\mathsf{T}}\mathbf{r} \oplus \mathbf{e}] \leq e^{-2(1/4-\tau/2)^2 n}.$$

From the above, the completeness error of the AUTH$^{\#}$ protocol $E_c^{\mathrm{AUTH}^{\#}}$ is bounded from above as follows;

$$E_c^{\mathrm{AUTH}^{\#}} = \Pr[\mathbf{r} = \mathbf{0} \vee \mathrm{wt}(\mathbf{z} \oplus \mathbf{S}_{\downarrow\mathbf{v}}^{\mathsf{T}}\mathbf{r}) \geq n\tau' | \mathbf{r} \xleftarrow{\$} \mathbb{Z}_2^l, \mathbf{e} \xleftarrow{\$} \mathrm{Ber}_{\tau}^n; \mathbf{z} := \mathbf{S}_{\downarrow\mathbf{v}}^{\mathsf{T}}\mathbf{r} \oplus \mathbf{e}]$$
$$\leq 1/2^l + e^{-2(1/4-\tau/2)^2 n}.$$

Hence, this $E_c^{\mathrm{AUTH}^{\#}}$ is negligible.

In the AUTH$^{\#}$ protocol, an invalid tag that does not have the secret key $\mathbf{s}$ fails authentication with overwhelming probability. We call the probability that an invalid tag sends a response randomly and gets accept by mistake the *soundness error* and denote it by $E_s^{\mathrm{AUTH}^{\#}}$. We evaluate the probability precisely. An invalid tag chooses a random secret key $\mathbf{S}'(\neq \mathbf{S})$. He computes $\mathbf{z}' = \mathbf{S}_{\downarrow\mathbf{v}}'^{\mathsf{T}}\mathbf{r} \oplus \mathbf{e}$, and sends $(\mathbf{r}, \mathbf{z}')$ to the reader. Note that $\mathbf{z}' \oplus \mathbf{S}_{\downarrow\mathbf{v}}^{\mathsf{T}}\mathbf{r} = (\mathbf{S}_{\downarrow\mathbf{v}}' \oplus \mathbf{S}_{\downarrow\mathbf{v}})^{\mathsf{T}}\mathbf{r} \oplus \mathbf{e}$. Since the matrix $\mathbf{S}_{\downarrow\mathbf{v}}'$ is uniformly random over $\mathbb{Z}_2^{l \times n}$, the vector $\mathbf{z}' \oplus \mathbf{S}_{\downarrow\mathbf{v}}^{\mathsf{T}}\mathbf{r}$ is also uniformly random over $\mathbb{Z}_2^n$, i.e., for $i = 1, \ldots n$,

$$\Pr[(\mathbf{z}' \oplus \mathbf{S}_{\downarrow\mathbf{v}}^{\mathsf{T}}\mathbf{r})[i] = 1] = \Pr[(\mathbf{z}' \oplus \mathbf{S}_{\downarrow\mathbf{v}}^{\mathsf{T}}\mathbf{r})[i] = 0] = 1/2.$$

Using the Hoeffding bound again, the soundness error of AUTH$^{\#}$ protocol $E_s^{\mathrm{AUTH}^{\#}}$ is bounded from above as follows:

$$E_s^{\mathrm{AUTH}^{\#}} = \Pr[\mathbf{r} \neq \mathbf{0} \wedge \mathrm{wt}(\mathbf{z}' \oplus \mathbf{S}_{\downarrow\mathbf{v}}^{\mathsf{T}}\mathbf{r}) < n\tau' | \mathbf{R} \xleftarrow{\$} \mathbb{Z}_2^{2l}, \mathbf{e} \xleftarrow{\$} \mathrm{Ber}_{\tau}^n; \mathbf{z}' := \mathbf{S}_{\downarrow\mathbf{v}}^{\mathsf{T}}\mathbf{r} \oplus \mathbf{e}]$$
$$\leq (1 - 1/2^l)e^{-2(1/4-\tau/2)^2 n}.$$

Hence, $E_s^{\mathrm{AUTH}^{\#}}$ is negligible.

We discuss the security of the AUTH$^{\#}$ protocol in Section 4.

3 The MSLPN* Assumption

In this section, we introduce a new computational assumption, which we call the MSLPN* assumption. Then, we prove that the MSLPN* assumption is probabilistic polynomial time equivalent to the LPN assumption with a standard hybrid argument.

3.1 Definition of the MSLPN* Assumption

Matrix SLPN*(MSLPN*) Problem. Given $\mathbf{X} \in \mathbb{Z}_2^{m \times n}$ and $\tau \in (0, 1/2)$, we write $\widetilde{\Lambda}_{\tau,m,n}(\mathbf{X})$ for the distribution whose samples are obtained as $(\mathbf{r}, \mathbf{z})$ where $\mathbf{r} \xleftarrow{\$} \mathbb{Z}_2^m$, $\mathbf{e} \leftarrow \mathrm{Ber}_\tau^n$; $\mathbf{z} := \mathbf{X}^\mathsf{T}\mathbf{r} \oplus \mathbf{e}$. We denote by $\widetilde{\Gamma}_{\tau,m,n,d}(\mathbf{X}, \cdot)$ the oracle the upon input $\mathbf{v} \in \mathbb{Z}_2^m$ outputs $\perp$ if $\mathrm{wt}(\mathbf{v}) < d$, and otherwise a sample from the distribution $\widetilde{\Lambda}_{\tau,m,n}(\mathbf{X} \wedge \mathbf{v})$. $\widetilde{U}_{m+n}(\cdot)$ is the oracle that upon input $\mathbf{v} \in \mathbb{Z}_2^m$ outputs $\perp$ if $\mathrm{wt}(\mathbf{v}) < d$, and otherwise a sample from the uniform distribution over $\mathbb{Z}_2^{m+n}$. The MSLPN$^*_{\tau,m,n,d}$ problem is to distinguish oracle access to $\widetilde{\Gamma}_{\tau,m,n,d}(\mathbf{X}, \cdot)$ and $\widetilde{U}_{m+n}(\cdot)$.

Definition 5. *For a distinguisher $\mathcal{D}$, we define the MSLPN$^*_{\tau,m,n,d}$ advantage of $\mathcal{D}$ as follows:*

$$\mathrm{Adv}^{\mathrm{MSLPN}^*}_{\tau,m,n,d} = \left| \Pr\left[\mathcal{D}^{\widetilde{\Gamma}_{\tau,m,n,d}}(\mathbf{X}, \cdot) \to 1 | \mathbf{X} \xleftarrow{\$} \mathbb{Z}_2^{m \times n} \right] - \Pr\left[\mathcal{D}^{\widetilde{U}_{m+n}(\cdot)} \to 1 \right] \right|.$$

The MSLPN$^*_{\tau,m,n,d}$ problem is (t, q, ε)-hard is for every distinguisher $\mathcal{D}$, which is running time t and q queries, the MSLPN$^*_{\tau,m,n,d}$ advantage of $\mathcal{D}$ is less than ε.

3.2 Equivalence to the SLPN* Assumption

We give a proposition which asserts that the MSLPN* assumption is probabilistic polynomial time equivalent to the SLPN* assumption.

Proposition 2. *If the SLPN$^*_{\tau,m,d}$ problem is (t, q, ε)-hard, the MSLPN$^*_{\tau,m,n,d}$ problem is $(t', q, n\varepsilon)$-hard, where $t' = t - \mathrm{poly}(q, m)$.*

Proof. We assume that the MSLPN$^*_{\tau,m,n,d}$ problem is not $(t', q, n\varepsilon)$-hard, i.e., there is a distinguisher $\mathcal{D}_{\mathrm{MSLPN}}$ whose MSLPN$^*_{\tau,m,n,d}$ advantage is larger than or equal to $n\varepsilon$. Using the distinguisher $\mathcal{D}_{\mathrm{MSLPN}}$ in a black-box way, we can construct a distinguisher $\mathcal{D}_{SLPN}$ whose SLPN$^*_{\tau,m,d}$ advantage is larger than or equal to ε

For $\mathbf{X} = (\mathbf{x}_1, \dots, \mathbf{x}_n) \in \mathbb{Z}_2^{m \times n}$, let $\widetilde{\Gamma}^i_{\tau,m,n,d}(\mathbf{X}, \cdot)$ $(i = 0, \dots, n)$ denote the oracle that upon input $\mathbf{v} \in \mathbb{Z}_2^l$ outputs $\perp$ if $\mathrm{wt}(\mathbf{v}) < d$, otherwise a sample from the distribution $\widetilde{\Lambda}^i_{\tau,m,n}(\mathbf{X} \wedge \mathbf{v})$. The distribution $\widetilde{\Lambda}^i_{\tau,m,n}(\mathbf{X} \wedge \mathbf{v})$ has samples obtained as $(\mathbf{r}, \mathbf{z})$ where $\mathbf{r} \xleftarrow{\$} \mathbb{Z}_2^m$, and for this $\mathbf{r}$, $e_j \leftarrow \mathrm{Ber}_\tau$ $(j = 1, \dots, i)$ and $r_k \xleftarrow{\$} \mathbb{Z}_2$ $(k = i+1, \dots, n)$, $\mathbf{z}$ is computed as follows;

$$\mathbf{z}^\mathsf{T} = ((\mathbf{x}_1 \wedge \mathbf{v})^\mathsf{T}, \dots, (\mathbf{x}_i \wedge \mathbf{v})^\mathsf{T}\mathbf{r} \oplus e_i, r_{i+1}, \dots, r_n).$$

For $i = 0, \ldots, n$, we define

$$p_i = \Pr\left[\mathcal{D}_{\mathrm{MSLPN}}^{\widetilde{\Gamma}^i_{\tau,m,n,d}(\mathbf{X},\cdot)} \to 1 \,\Big|\, \mathbf{X} \xleftarrow{\$} \mathbb{Z}_2^{m \times n}\right].$$

If $i = 0$, since the sample that the distinguisher $\mathcal{D}_{\mathrm{MSLPN}}$ gets from $\widetilde{\Gamma}^i_{\tau,m,n,d}(\mathbf{X},\cdot)$ is same as the sample from the oracle $\widetilde{U}_{m+n}(\cdot)$,

$$p_0 = \Pr\left[\mathcal{D}_{\mathrm{MSLPN}}^{\widetilde{U}_{m+n}(\cdot)} \to 1\right].$$

If $i = n$, since the sample that the distinguisher $\mathcal{D}_{\mathrm{MSLPN}}$ gets from $\widetilde{\Gamma}^i_{\tau,m,n,d}(\mathbf{X},\cdot)$ is same as the sample from the oracle $\widetilde{\Gamma}_{\tau,m,n,d}(\mathbf{X},\cdot)$,

$$p_n = \Pr\left[\mathcal{D}_{\mathrm{MSLPN}}^{\widetilde{\Gamma}_{\tau,m,n,d}(\mathbf{X},\cdot)} \to 1 \,\Big|\, \mathbf{X} \xleftarrow{\$} \mathbb{Z}_2^{m \times n}\right].$$

To run the distinguisher $\mathcal{D}_{MSLPN}$ correctly, the distinguisher $\mathcal{D}_{\mathrm{SLPN}}$ has to simulate oracle in MSLPN* problem for q times oracle accesses by the another distinguisher $\mathcal{D}_{\mathrm{MSLPN}}$. To overcome this simulation challenge, we construct $\mathcal{D}_{\mathrm{SLPN}}$ as follows:

1. Choose $i \in [n]$ randomly, and for $j = 1, \ldots, i-1$, set $\mathbf{x}_j \xleftarrow{\$} \mathbb{Z}_2^m$.
2. Run the distinguisher $\mathcal{D}_{\mathrm{MSLPN}}$. The distinguisher $\mathcal{D}_{\mathrm{SLPN}}$ receives $\mathbf{v}$ as an oracle access from the another distinguisher $\mathcal{D}_{\mathrm{MSLPN}}$, and sends an output sample $(\widetilde{\mathbf{r}}, \widetilde{\mathbf{z}})$ to the another distinguisher $\mathcal{D}_{\mathrm{MSLPN}}$. The output sample $(\widetilde{\mathbf{r}}, \widetilde{\mathbf{z}})$ is constructed as follows:
   - If $\mathrm{wt}(\mathbf{v}) < d$, set $(\widetilde{\mathbf{r}}, \widetilde{\mathbf{z}}) = \perp$.
   - If $\mathrm{wt}(\mathbf{v}) \geq d$, throw the vector $\mathbf{v}$ sent from the distinguisher $\mathcal{D}_{\mathrm{MSLPN}}$ as a query to the oracle in the MSLPN* problem and receive $(\mathbf{r}, z)$ from the oracle. The distinguisher $\mathcal{D}_{\mathrm{SLPN}}$ samples $e_j \leftarrow \mathrm{Ber}_\tau$ and $r_k \xleftarrow{\$} \mathbb{Z}_2$ for $j = 1, \ldots, i-1$ and $k = i+1, \ldots n$. Using these $(\mathbf{r}, z)$, e_j and r_k, the distinguisher $\mathcal{D}_{\mathrm{SLPN}}$ constructs the output sample $(\widetilde{\mathbf{r}}, \widetilde{\mathbf{z}})$ sent to the another distinguisher $\mathcal{D}_{\mathrm{MSLPN}}$. First, set $\widetilde{\mathbf{r}} := \mathbf{r}$. Then, construct $\widetilde{\mathbf{z}}$ as follows. For $j = 1, \ldots, i-1$, compute $(\mathbf{x}_j \wedge \mathbf{v})^{\mathsf{T}}\mathbf{r} \oplus e_j$ and set $\widetilde{\mathbf{z}}[j] := (\mathbf{x}_j \wedge \mathbf{v})^{\mathsf{T}}\mathbf{r} \oplus e_j$. Embed z sent from the oracle in the SLPN* problem at the i-th element of $\widetilde{\mathbf{z}}$. For $k = i+1, \ldots n$, set $\widetilde{\mathbf{z}}[k] := r_k$. From the above, $\widetilde{\mathbf{r}}$ and $\widetilde{\mathbf{z}}$ are written as follows;

$$\widetilde{\mathbf{r}} = \mathbf{r}$$
$$\widetilde{\mathbf{z}}^{\mathsf{T}} = ((\mathbf{x}_1 \wedge \mathbf{v})_1^{\mathsf{T}}\mathbf{r} \oplus e_1, (\mathbf{x}_2 \wedge \mathbf{v})^{\mathsf{T}}\mathbf{r} \oplus e_2, \ldots, (\mathbf{x}_{i-1} \wedge \mathbf{v})^{\mathsf{T}}\mathbf{r} \oplus e_{i-1}, \boxed{z}, r_{i+1}, \ldots, r_n).$$

3. Observe whether the another distinguisher $\mathcal{D}_{\mathrm{MSLPN}}$ outputs 1 or 0. The distinguisher $\mathcal{D}_{\mathrm{SLPN}}$ outputs the bit that $\mathcal{D}_{\mathrm{MSLPN}}$ outputs as is.

From the above construction, we simulate

- $\widetilde{\Gamma}^i(\mathbf{x}, \cdot)$ for an oracle access by the another distinguisher $\mathcal{D}_{\mathrm{MSLPN}}$ if the distinguisher $\mathcal{D}_{\mathrm{SLPN}}$ accesses $\Gamma_{\tau,m,d}(\mathbf{x}, \cdot)$,

- $\widetilde{\varGamma}^{i-1}(\mathbf{x}, \cdot)$ for an oracle access by the another distinguisher $\mathcal{D}_{\mathrm{MSLPN}}$ if the distinguisher $\mathcal{D}_{\mathrm{SLPN}}$ accesses $U_{m+1}(\cdot)$.

Hence, the $\mathrm{SLPN}_{\tau,m,d}$ advantage of the distinguisher $\mathcal{D}_{\mathrm{SLPN}}$ is

$$
\begin{aligned}
\mathrm{Adv}_{\tau,m,d}^{\mathrm{SLPN}^*} &= \left| \Pr\left[\mathcal{D}_{\mathrm{SLPN}}^{\varGamma_{\tau,m,d}(\mathbf{x},\cdot)} \to 1 | \mathbf{x} \xleftarrow{\$} \mathbb{Z}_2^m \right] - \Pr\left[\mathcal{D}_{\mathrm{SLPN}}^{U_{m+1}(\cdot)} \to 1 \right] \right| \\
&= \left| \sum_{i=1}^{n} (\Pr\left[\mathcal{D}_{\mathrm{SLPN}}^{\varGamma_{\tau,m,d}(\mathbf{x},\cdot)} \to 1 | \mathbf{x} \xleftarrow{\$} \mathbb{Z}_2^m; I = i \right] \Pr[I = i] - \Pr\left[\mathcal{D}_{\mathrm{SLPN}}^{U_{m+1}(\cdot)} \to 1 | I = i \right] \Pr[I = i]) \right| \\
&= \frac{1}{n} \left| \sum_{i=1}^{n} \left(\Pr\left[\mathcal{D}_{\mathrm{MSLPN}}^{\widetilde{\varGamma}_{\tau,m,n,d}^{i}(\mathbf{x},\cdot)} \to 1 | \mathbf{X} \xleftarrow{\$} \mathbb{Z}_2^{m \times n} \right] - \Pr\left[\mathcal{D}_{\mathrm{MSLPN}}^{\widetilde{\varGamma}_{\tau,m,n,d}^{i-1}(\mathbf{X},\cdot)} \to 1 | \mathbf{x} \xleftarrow{\$} \mathbb{Z}_2^{m \times n} \right] \right) \right| \\
&= \frac{1}{n} |p_n - p_0| \geq \varepsilon.
\end{aligned}
$$

From the above, the distinguisher $\mathcal{D}_{\mathrm{SLPN}}$ can solve the $\mathrm{SLPN}^*_{\tau,m,d}$ problem with the advantage larger than or equal to ε by using the distinguisher $\mathcal{D}_{\mathrm{MSLPN}}$ who can solve the $\mathrm{MSLPN}^*_{\tau,m,n,d}$ problem. However, this contradicts the hardness assumption of the $\mathrm{SLPN}^*_{\tau,m,d}$ problem.   □

4   Security Proof of the AUTH# Protocol

In this section, we discuss the security of the AUTH# protocol. First, we indicate the incompleteness of the proof by Rizomiliotis and Gritzalis that the AUTH# is secure against MIM attacks. Next, we prove the active security of the AUTH# protocol and fill the gap of the security proof by Rizomiliotis and Gritzalis [20].

4.1   Incompleteness of the Security Proof of AUTH# against MIM Attacks

At WiSec 2013, Rizomiliotis and Gritzalis [20] asserted that the AUTH# protocol is secure against MIM attacks. They adopted the proof technique in the security proof of the HB# protocol against GRS MIM attacks [8]. In detail, they proved the MIM security under the assumption that the AUTH# protocol is secure against active adversaries. However, they did not prove the active security of the AUTH# protocol. Even Kiltz et al. who proposed the AUTH# protocol did not present the proof. Though Kiltz et al. claimed that the security proof of the AUTH# protocol against active adversaries is proved under the SLPN* assumption like that of the AUTH protocol which is original protocol of the AUTH# protocol, it is difficult to construct reduction from the SLPN* assumption to the active security of the AUTH# protocol and we need to introduce a new computational assumption. The new computational assumption is the MSLPN* assumption, which was introduced in previous section. Under the assumption, we prove that the AUTH# protocol is secure against active adversaries. Combining our result and that of Rizomiliotis and Gritzalis, we complete the MIM security proof of the AUTH# protocol.

4.2   Security Proof of the AUTH$^{\#}$ Protocol against Active Attacks

Mainly we adopt the proof of Theorem 1 in [14]. As mentioned above, we reduce the active security of the AUTH$^{\#}$ protocol to the MSLPN* assumption.

Theorem 1. *For any constant $\gamma > 0$, let $d = l/(2+\gamma)$. If the MSLPN$^*_{\tau,2l,n,d}$ problem is (t,q,ε)-hard, the AUTH$^{\#}$ protocol is (t',q,ε')-secure against active adversary, where*

$$t' = t - \mathrm{poly}(q,l), \quad \varepsilon' = \varepsilon + q\alpha' + E_s^{\mathrm{AUTH}^{\#}}$$

for constant $c_\gamma > 0$ that depend only on γ and

$$\alpha' = \frac{\sum_{i=0}^{d-1} \binom{l}{i}\binom{l}{l-i}}{\binom{2l}{l}} \le 2^{-c_\gamma l}.$$

The protocol has the soundness error $E_s^{\mathrm{AUTH}^{\#}}$ which depends only on τ.

Proof. We assume that the AUTH$^{\#}$ protocol is not (t',q,ε')-secure, i.e., there is an active adversary $\mathcal{A}$ who succeeds the active attack with probability at least ε' with running in time at most t and making q queries an honest tag. Using the active adversary $\mathcal{A}$ in a black-box way, we construct a distinguisher $\mathcal{D}_{\mathrm{MSLPN}}$ whose MSLPN$^*_{\tau,2l,n,d}$ advantage is

$$\mathrm{Adv}^{\mathrm{MSLPN}^*}_{\tau,2l,n,d} = \left| \Pr[\mathcal{D}^{\widetilde{\Gamma}_{\tau,2l,n,d}(\mathbf{X},\cdot)}_{\mathrm{MSLPN}} \to 1 | \mathbf{X} \xleftarrow{\$} \mathbb{Z}_2^{2l \times n}] - \Pr[\mathcal{D}^{\widetilde{U}_{2l+n}(\cdot)}_{\mathrm{MSLPN}} \to 1] \right|$$

$$\ge \varepsilon = \varepsilon' - q\alpha' - E_s^{\mathrm{AUTH}^{\#}}.$$

To run the active adversary $\mathcal{A}$ correctly, the distinguisher $\mathcal{D}_{\mathrm{MSLPN}}$ has to simulate an honest tag in the learning phase and an honest reader in the forgery phase. We construct $\mathcal{D}_{\mathrm{MSLPN}}$ as follows:

Setup Initially, the distinguisher $\mathcal{D}_{\mathrm{MSLPN}}$ samples

$$\mathbf{X}^* \xleftarrow{\$} \mathbb{Z}_2^{2l \times n} \quad \text{and} \quad \mathbf{v}^* \xleftarrow{\$} \{\mathbf{x} \in \mathbb{Z}_2^{2l} | \mathrm{wt}(\mathbf{x}) = l\}.$$

Using these $\mathbf{X}^*$ and $\mathbf{v}^*$, the distinguisher $\mathcal{D}_{\mathrm{MSLPN}}$ simulates an honest tag $\mathcal{T}_{\tau,n}(\mathbf{S})$ whose secret key is

$$\mathbf{S} = (\mathbf{X}^* \wedge \mathbf{v}^*) \oplus (\mathbf{X} \wedge \overline{\mathbf{v}^*}), \tag{1}$$

where $\mathbf{X} \in \mathbb{Z}_2^{2l \times n}$ is the secret key that the MSLPN* oracle $\widetilde{\Gamma}_{\tau,2l,n,d}(\mathbf{X},\cdot)$ has.

Learning Phase. In the learning phase of the active attack, the active adversary $\mathcal{A}$ sends a query $\mathbf{v} \in \{\mathbf{x} \in \mathbb{Z}_2^{2l} | \mathrm{wt}(\mathbf{x}) = l\}$ to the distinguisher $\mathcal{D}_{\mathrm{MSLPN}}$. For this query $\mathbf{v}$, the distinguisher $\mathcal{D}_{\mathrm{MSLPN}}$ sets

$$\mathbf{u}^* := \mathbf{v} \wedge \mathbf{v}^* \quad \text{and} \quad \mathbf{u} := \mathbf{v} \wedge \overline{\mathbf{v}^*}.$$

We run the distinguisher $\mathcal{D}_{\mathrm{MSLPN}}$ as follows:

1. Query to the oracle in the MSLPN* problem ($\widetilde{\Gamma}_{\tau,2l,n,d}(\mathbf{X}, \cdot)$ or $\widetilde{U}_{2l+n}(\cdot)$) on the input the vector $\mathbf{u}$. If the oracle's output is $\perp$, output 0 and stop. Otherwise, let $(\hat{\mathbf{r}}_1, \mathbf{z}_1)$ denote the output of the oracle.
2. Sample a vector $\hat{\mathbf{r}}_0 \xleftarrow{\$} \mathbb{Z}_2^{2l}$ and set a vector $\mathbf{z}_0 := (\mathbf{X}^* \wedge \mathbf{u}^*)^\top \mathbf{r}_0$.
3. Set vectors $\mathbf{r} := \hat{\mathbf{r}}_{\downarrow_v} \in \mathbb{Z}_2^l$ and $\mathbf{z} := \mathbf{z}_0 \oplus \mathbf{z}_1 \in \mathbb{Z}_2^n$, where the vector $\hat{\mathbf{r}}$ is uniquely determined such that $\hat{\mathbf{r}}_{\downarrow_{v^*}} = \hat{\mathbf{r}}_{0\downarrow_{v^*}}$ and $\hat{\mathbf{r}}_{\downarrow_{\overline{v^*}}} = \hat{\mathbf{r}}_{1\downarrow_{\overline{v^*}}}$, and send $(\mathbf{r}, \mathbf{z})$ to the active adversary $\mathcal{A}$.

Forgery Phase. In the forgery phase of the active adversary $\mathcal{A}$, we run the distinguisher $\mathcal{D}_{\text{MSLPN}}$ as follows:

1. Send $\mathbf{v}^*$ as a challenge to the active adversary $\mathcal{A}$.
2. Receive an answer $(\mathbf{r}^*, \mathbf{z}^*)$ from the active adversary $\mathcal{A}$.
3. The distinguisher $\mathcal{D}_{\text{MSLPN}}$ outputs 1 if

$$\mathbf{r}^* \neq \mathbf{0} \quad \text{and} \quad \text{wt}(\mathbf{z}^* \oplus \mathbf{S}_{\downarrow_{v^*}} \mathbf{r}^*) \leq n\tau',$$

and 0 otherwise.

The above construction leads following two lemmas. Using these lemmas and triangle inequality, we obtain the following inequality on the MSLPN*$_{\tau,2l,n,d}$ advantage of the distinguisher $\mathcal{D}_{\text{MSLPN}}$ in claim

$$\text{Adv}_{\tau,2l,n,d}^{\text{MSLPN}^*} = \left| \Pr[\mathcal{D}_{\text{MSLPN}}^{\widetilde{\Gamma}_{\tau,2l,n,d}(\mathbf{X},\cdot)} \to 1 | \mathbf{X} \xleftarrow{\$} \mathbb{Z}_2^{2l \times n}] - \Pr[\mathcal{D}_{\text{MSLPN}}^{\widetilde{U}_{2l+n}(\cdot)} \to 1] \right|$$

$$\geq \varepsilon' - q\alpha' - E_s^{\text{AUTH}^\#}.$$

$\square$

From the above construction, following two lemmas are lead.

Lemma 1. *For the above construction, if the distinguisher $\mathcal{D}_{\text{MSLPN}}$ accesses the uniformly random oracle $\widetilde{U}_{2l+n}(\cdot)$, the probability that the active adversary $\mathcal{A}$ answers correct response to the distinguisher $\mathcal{D}_{\text{MSLPN}}$ in the forgery phase is equal to the soundness error of the AUTH$^\#$ protocol, i.e.,*

$$\Pr[\mathcal{D}_{\text{MSLPN}}^{\widetilde{U}_{2l+n}(\cdot)} \to 1] = E_s^{\text{AUTH}^\#}.$$

Proof. If $\mathbf{r}^* = \mathbf{0}$, then $\mathcal{D}_{\text{MSLPN}}$ outputs 0 by definition. Therefore, we consider the case that $\mathbf{r}^* \neq \mathbf{0}$. Since $\mathbf{z}_1$ is uniformly random over $\mathbb{Z}_2^n$ and $\mathbf{r}^* \neq \mathbf{0}$, the answer $(\mathbf{r}, \mathbf{z} = \mathbf{z}_0 \oplus \mathbf{z}_1)$ sent from the distinguisher $\mathcal{D}_{\text{MSLPN}}^{\widetilde{U}_{2l+n}(\cdot)}$ to the active adversary $\mathcal{A}$ are independent of $\mathbf{X}^*$. Thus, for the query $\mathbf{v}^*$ and the answer $(\mathbf{r}^*, \mathbf{z}^*)$ which is computed in 1st step and 2nd step of forgery phase, respectively, the vector $\mathbf{z}^* \oplus \mathbf{S}_{\downarrow_{v^*}}^\top \mathbf{r}^*$ is uniformly random over $\mathbb{Z}_2^n$, and the probability that the second verification in 3rd step of forgery phase does not fail is $\Pr[\text{wt}(\mathbf{z}^* \oplus \mathbf{S}_{\downarrow_{v^*}}^\top \mathbf{r}^*) < n\tau'] = E_s^{\text{AUTH}^\#}$. $\square$

Lemma 2. *For the above construction, if the distinguisher $\mathcal{D}_{\text{MSLPN}}$ accesses the MSLPN* oracle $\widetilde{\Gamma}_{\tau,2l,n,d}(\mathbf{X},\cdot)$, the probability that the active adversary $\mathcal{A}$*

answers correct response to the distinguisher $\mathcal{D}_{\mathrm{MSLPN}}$ *in the forgery phase is larger than or equal to* $\varepsilon - q\alpha'$, *i.e.*,

$$\left| \Pr\left[\mathcal{D}_{\mathrm{MSLPN}}^{\widetilde{\Gamma}_{\tau,2l,n,d}(\mathbf{X},\cdot)} \to 1 | \mathbf{X} \overset{\$}{\leftarrow} \mathbb{Z}_2^{2l\times n} \right] \right| \geq \varepsilon' - q\alpha'.$$

Proof. We separate the proof into two parts. First, we show that the probability that distinguisher $\mathcal{D}_{\mathrm{MSLPN}}$ outputs 1 in the forgery phase is equal to ε' if the distinguisher $\mathcal{D}_{\mathrm{MSLPN}}$ has access to the oracle $\widetilde{\Gamma}_{\tau,2l,n,0}(\mathbf{X},\cdot)$, i.e.,

$$\Pr[\mathcal{D}_{\mathrm{MSLPN}}^{\widetilde{\Gamma}_{\tau,2l,n,0}(\mathbf{X},\cdot)} \to 1 | \mathbf{X} \overset{\$}{\leftarrow} \mathbb{Z}_2^{2l\times n}] \geq \varepsilon'. \tag{2}$$

This inequality means that the distinguisher $\mathcal{D}_{\mathrm{MSLPN}}$ exactly simulates an honest tag $\mathcal{T}_{\tau,n}(\mathbf{S})$ where the simulated secret key $\mathbf{S}$ is defined in Eq. (1) if the distinguisher $\mathcal{D}_{\mathrm{MSLPN}}$ accesses the oracle $\widetilde{\Gamma}_{\tau,2l,n,0}(\mathbf{X},\cdot)$. If the distinguisher $\mathcal{D}_{\mathrm{MSLPN}}$ exactly simulates an honest tag in the learning phase, the active adversary $\mathcal{A}$ sends a valid answer $(\mathbf{r},\mathbf{z})$ in the forgery phase with the probability larger than ε'. Note that the oracle $\widetilde{\Gamma}_{\tau,2l,n,0}(\mathbf{X},\cdot)$ never outputs $\bot$ on arbitrary input $\mathbf{v}$. When the distinguisher $\mathcal{D}_{\mathrm{MSLPN}}$ accesses the oracle $\widetilde{\Gamma}_{\tau,2l,n,0}(\mathbf{X},\cdot)$, he answers $(\mathbf{r},\mathbf{z})$ to the active adversary $\mathcal{A}$ has the same distribution as what the active adversary $\mathcal{A}$ gets when he interacts with an honest tag $\mathcal{T}_{\tau,n}(\mathbf{S})$. To confirm this, we check the learning phase in the above construction.

Learning Phase

1. The distinguisher $\mathcal{D}_{\mathrm{MSLPN}}$ queries to its oracle $\widetilde{\Gamma}_{\tau,2l,n,0}(\mathbf{X},\cdot)$ with $\mathbf{u} :=\mathbf{v} \wedge \overline{\mathbf{v}^*}$ and obtains a sample $(\hat{\mathbf{r}}_1,\mathbf{z}_1)$, where $\hat{\mathbf{r}}_1 \overset{\$}{\leftarrow} \mathbb{Z}_2^{2l}$ and $\mathbf{z}_1 = (\mathbf{X} \wedge \mathbf{u})^{\mathsf{T}}\hat{\mathbf{r}}_1 \oplus \mathbf{e}_1$ for $\mathbf{e}_1 \leftarrow \mathrm{Ber}_\tau^n$. From the construction of the simulated secret key $\mathbf{S}$, the vector $\mathbf{z}_1$ is also expressed as follows:

$$\mathbf{z}_1 = (\mathbf{X} \wedge \mathbf{u})^{\mathsf{T}}\hat{\mathbf{r}}_1 \oplus \mathbf{e}_1 = (\mathbf{S} \wedge \mathbf{u})^{\mathsf{T}}\hat{\mathbf{r}}_1 \oplus \mathbf{e}_1.$$

2. The distinguisher $\mathcal{D}_{\mathrm{MSLPN}}$ samples $\hat{\mathbf{r}}_0 \overset{\$}{\leftarrow} \mathbb{Z}_2^{2l}$ and sets $\mathbf{z}_0 = (\mathbf{X}^* \wedge \mathbf{u}^*)^{\mathsf{T}}\hat{\mathbf{r}}_0$. Since the distinguisher $\mathcal{D}_{\mathrm{MSLPN}}$ knows $\mathbf{X}^*$ and $\mathbf{u}^*$, it has able to calculate $\mathbf{z}_0$. From the construction of the simulated secret key $\mathbf{S}$ again, the vector $\mathbf{z}_0$ is also expressed as follows:

$$\mathbf{z}_0 = (\mathbf{X}^* \wedge \mathbf{u}^*)^{\mathsf{T}}\hat{\mathbf{r}}_0 = (\mathbf{S} \wedge \mathbf{u}^*)^{\mathsf{T}}\hat{\mathbf{r}}_0.$$

3. According to the way of sampling $\hat{\mathbf{r}}_0$ and $\hat{\mathbf{r}}_1$, $\hat{\mathbf{r}}$ is uniformly random over $\mathbb{Z}_2^l$. Using $\mathbf{v} = \mathbf{u} \oplus \mathbf{u}^*$, we obtain

$$\mathbf{z} = \mathbf{z}_0 \oplus \mathbf{z}_1 = (\mathbf{S} \wedge \mathbf{u}^*)^{\mathsf{T}}\hat{\mathbf{r}}_0 \oplus (\mathbf{S} \wedge \mathbf{u})^{\mathsf{T}}\hat{\mathbf{r}}_1 \oplus \mathbf{e}_1$$
$$= (\mathbf{S} \wedge (\mathbf{u} \oplus \mathbf{u}^*))^{\mathsf{T}}\hat{\mathbf{r}} \oplus \mathbf{e}_1 = \mathbf{S}_{\downarrow \mathbf{v}}^{\mathsf{T}}\mathbf{r} \oplus \mathbf{e}.$$

From the above, the answer $(\mathbf{r}, \mathbf{z})$ sent from the distinguisher $\mathcal{D}_{\mathrm{MSLPN}}^{\widetilde{\Gamma}_{\tau,2l,0}(\mathbf{X},\cdot)}$ to the active adversary $\mathcal{A}$ in the learning phase has exactly the same distribution as what the active adversary $\mathcal{A}$ gets when he interacts with an honest tag $\mathcal{T}_{\tau,n}(\mathbf{S})$.

We check whether the distinguisher $\mathcal{D}_{\mathrm{MSLPN}}$ simulates an honest reader in the forgery phase.

Forgery Phase

1. The challenge $\mathbf{v}^*$ sent to the active adversary $\mathcal{A}$ in the forgery phase is in the set $\{\mathbf{x} \in \mathbb{Z}_2^{2l} | \mathrm{wt}(\mathbf{x}) = l\}$, and therefore has the same distribution as a challenge from the valid reader.

2. The distinguisher $\mathcal{D}_{\mathrm{MSLPN}}^{\widetilde{\Gamma}_{\tau,2l,n,0}(\mathbf{X},\cdot)}$ outputs 1 if the answer $(\mathbf{r}^*, \mathbf{z}^*)$ sent from the active adversary $\mathcal{A}$ fulfills that

$$\mathbf{r}^* \neq \mathbf{0} \quad \text{and} \quad \mathrm{wt}(\mathbf{z}^* \oplus \mathbf{S}_{\downarrow_{\mathbf{v}^*}} \mathbf{r}^*) \leq n\tau'$$

for the simulated key $\mathbf{S}$ and the challenge $\mathbf{v}^*$ which is sent from the distinguisher $\mathcal{D}_{\mathrm{MSLPN}}$ in the previous step.

From the assumption, this probability that the distinguisher $\mathcal{D}_{\mathrm{MSLPN}}^{\widetilde{\Gamma}_{\tau,2l,n,0}(\mathbf{X},\cdot)}$ outputs 1 in the forgery phase is at least ε'. Therefore, we have confirmed that the inequality (2) is true.

Then we bound the gap between the probability that $\mathcal{D}_{\mathrm{MSLPN}}$ outputs 1 in the above case and the probability that $\mathcal{D}_{\mathrm{MSLPN}}$ outputs 1 when given access to the oracle $\widetilde{\Gamma}_{\tau,2l,n,d}(\mathbf{S}, \cdot)$ from above, i.e.,

$$\left| \Pr\left[\mathcal{D}_{\mathrm{MSLPN}}^{\widetilde{\Gamma}_{\tau,2l,n,d}(\mathbf{S},\cdot)} \to 1 | \mathbf{S} \xleftarrow{\$} \mathbb{Z}_2^{2l \times n} \right] - \Pr\left[\mathcal{D}_{\mathrm{MSLPN}}^{\widetilde{\Gamma}_{\tau,2l,n,0}(\mathbf{X},\cdot)} \to 1 | \mathbf{S} \xleftarrow{\$} \mathbb{Z}_2^{2l \times n} \right] \right| \leq q\alpha'.$$

Note that the MSLPN* oracle $\widetilde{\Gamma}_{\tau,2l,n,d}(\mathbf{S}, \cdot)$ behaves like the oracle $\widetilde{\Gamma}_{\tau,2l,n,0}(\mathbf{S}, \cdot)$ as long as one never makes a query $\mathbf{v}$ where $\mathrm{wt}(\mathbf{v}) < d$. A_i denotes the event that $\mathrm{wt}(\mathbf{v}_i \wedge \mathbf{v}^*) < d$ for i-th query $\mathbf{v}_i$ chosen by $\mathcal{A}$. Using union bound, we obtain following inequality

$$\left| \Pr[\mathcal{D}_{\mathrm{MSLPN}}^{\widetilde{\Gamma}_{\tau,2l,n,d}(\mathbf{X},\cdot)} \to 1 | \xleftarrow{\$} \mathbb{Z}_2^{2l \times n}] - \Pr[\mathcal{D}_{\mathrm{MSLPN}}^{\widetilde{\Gamma}_{\tau,2l,n,0}(\mathbf{X},\cdot)} \to 1 | \xleftarrow{\$} \mathbb{Z}_2^{2l \times n}] \right| = \Pr\left[\bigcup_{i=1}^{q} A_i \right]$$

$$\leq \sum_{i=1}^{q} \Pr[A_i] = q\alpha'. \tag{3}$$

From Eq.(2), Eq.(3) and triangle inequality, we have proved the claim of Lemma 2

$$\left| \Pr\left[\mathcal{D}_{\mathrm{MSLPN}}^{\widetilde{\Gamma}_{\tau,2l,n,d}(\mathbf{X},\cdot)} \to 1 | \mathbf{X} \xleftarrow{\$} \mathbb{Z}_2^{2l \times n} \right] \right| \geq \varepsilon' - q\alpha'.$$

$\square$

Under the assumption that the AUTH$^{\#}$ protocol is secure against active adversaries which is proved in Theorem 1, we complete the proof that the AUTH$^{\#}$ protocol is secure against MIM attacks.

Theorem 2 (Rizomiliotis, Gritzalis [20]). *If the* $\mathrm{AUTH}^{\#}$ *protocol is* (t, q, ε)-*secure against active adversaries, the protocol is* $(O(t), q, \varepsilon')$-*secure against the General MIM adversaries, where*

$$\varepsilon' = \frac{\varepsilon + q E_s^{\mathrm{AUTH}^{\#}} \cdot \mathrm{negl}(l)}{1 - q \cdot \mathrm{negl}(l)}.$$

5   Conclusions and Open Problems

In this paper we proved that the $\mathrm{AUTH}^{\#}$ protocol is secure against active attacks under a new computational assumption, the MSLPN* assumption. We also proved that the MSLPN* assumption is probabilistic polynomial time equivalent to the LPN assumption. This result fills the gap of the security proof of the $\mathrm{AUTH}^{\#}$ protocol against MIM attacks.

Whereas the $\mathrm{AUTH}^{\#}$ protocol is secure against MIM attacks, it is insecure against a strong MIM (sMIM) attack. The sMIM attack is in the MIM attack model introduced by Lyubashevsky and Masny [15]. We describe the sMIM attack against the $\mathrm{AUTH}^{\#}$ protocol in Appendix A. Two MACs proposed by Kiltz et al. [14] imply two-pass authentication protocols which are secure against sMIM attacks. However the secret key size and computational complexity of the MACs became huge since they require hash functions. It remains an open problem to propose smaller key size two-pass authentication protocols which are secure against sMIM attacks.

Acknowledgement. The second author was supported by JSPS Grant Number KAKENHI 25280001. We thank Shota Yamada and Takashi Yamakawa for helpful discussion.

References

1. Berlekamp, E.R., McEliece, R.J., van Tilborg, H.C.A.: On the Inherent Intractability of Certain Coding Problems. IEEE Transactions on Information Theory 24, 384–386 (1978)
2. Bosley, C., Haralambiev, K., Nicolosi, A.: HB^N: An HB-like protocol secure against man-in-the-middle attacks. Cryptology ePrint Archive, Report 2011/350 (2011)
3. Bringer, J., Chabanne, H.: Trusted-HB: A Low-Cost Version of HB$^+$ Secure Against Man-in-the-Middle Attacks. IEEE Transactions on Information Theory 54(9), 4339–4342 (2008)
4. Bringer, J., Chabanne, H., Dottax, E.: HB^{++}: a Lightweight Authentication Protocol Secure against Some Attacks. In: SecPerU, pp. 28–33. IEEE Computer Society (2006)
5. Duc, D.N., Kim, K.: Securing HB$^+$ against GRS Man-in-the-Middle Attack. In: SCIS (2007)
6. Frumkin, D., Shamir, A.: Un-Trusted-HB: Security Vulnerabilities of Trusted-HB. Cryptology ePrint Archive, Report 2009/044 (2009)

7. Gilbert, H., Robshaw, M.J.B., Seurin, Y.: Good Variants of HB$^+$ Are Hard to Find. In: Tsudik, G. (ed.) FC 2008. LNCS, vol. 5143, pp. 156–170. Springer, Heidelberg (2008)

8. Gilbert, H., Robshaw, M.J.B., Seurin, Y.: HB$^{\#}$: Increasing the Security and Efficiency of HB$^+$. In: Smart, N. (ed.) EUROCRYPT 2008. LNCS, vol. 4965, pp. 361–378. Springer, Heidelberg (2008)

9. Gilbert, H., Robshaw, M.J.B., Sibert, H.: An Active Attack Against HB$^+$ - A Provably Secure Lightweight Authentication Protocol. IACR Cryptology ePrint Archive, 2005:237 (2005)

10. Hopper, N.J., Blum, M.: Secure Human Identification Protocols. In: Boyd, C. (ed.) ASIACRYPT 2001. LNCS, vol. 2248, pp. 52–66. Springer, Heidelberg (2001)

11. Juels, A., Weis, S.A.: Authenticating Pervasive Devices with Human Protocols. In: Shoup, V. (ed.) CRYPTO 2005. LNCS, vol. 3621, pp. 293–308. Springer, Heidelberg (2005)

12. Katz, J., Shin, J.S.: Parallel and Concurrent Security of the HB and HB$^+$ Protocols. In: Vaudenay, S. (ed.) EUROCRYPT 2006. LNCS, vol. 4004, pp. 73–87. Springer, Heidelberg (2006)

13. Katz, J., Smith, A.: Analyzing the HB and HB$^+$ Protocols in the "Large Error" Case. IACR Cryptology ePrint Archive, 2006:326 (2006)

14. Kiltz, E., Pietrzak, K., Cash, D., Jain, A., Venturi, D.: Efficient Authentication from Hard Learning Problems. In: Paterson, K.G. (ed.) EUROCRYPT 2011. LNCS, vol. 6632, pp. 7–26. Springer, Heidelberg (2011)

15. Lyubashevsky, V., Masny, D.: Man-in-the-middle secure authentication schemes from LPN and weak PRFs. In: Canetti, R., Garay, J.A. (eds.) CRYPTO 2013, Part II. LNCS, vol. 8043, pp. 308–325. Springer, Heidelberg (2013)

16. Munilla, J., Peinado, A.: HB-MP: A further step in the HB-family of lightweight authentication protocols. Computer Networks 51(9), 2262–2267 (2007)

17. Ouafi, K., Overbeck, R., Vaudenay, S.: On the Security of HB$^{\#}$ against a Man-in-the-Middle Attack. In: Pieprzyk, J. (ed.) ASIACRYPT 2008. LNCS, vol. 5350, pp. 108–124. Springer, Heidelberg (2008)

18. Pietrzak, K.: Subspace LWE. In: Cramer, R. (ed.) TCC 2012. LNCS, vol. 7194, pp. 548–563. Springer, Heidelberg (2012)

19. Rizomiliotis, P., Gritzalis, S.: $GHB^{\#}$: A Provably Secure HB-Like Lightweight Authentication Protocol. In: Bao, F., Samarati, P., Zhou, J. (eds.) ACNS 2012. LNCS, vol. 7341, pp. 489–506. Springer, Heidelberg (2012)

20. Rizomiliotis, P., Gritzalis, S.: Revisiting lightweight authentication protocols based on hard learning problems. In: Buttyán, L., Sadeghi, A.-R., Gruteser, M. (eds.) WiSec, pp. 125–130. ACM (2013)

A   Strong Man-in-the-Middle Attack

In this section, we sketch a strong MIM (sMIM) attack against the AUTH$^{\#}$ protocol. The sMIM attack model is introduced in [15] and implies the MIM attack model defined in Section 2.3 of this paper. We describe the sMIM security game in the AUTH$^{\#}$ protocol and define the attacker's winning condition in the game.

Setup: Generate a secret key **S** and return it to the tag and the reader.

Attack: Run the sMIM adversary who has access to the tag and the reader and let him interact with them in polynomial time. The interaction is as follows: The sMIM adversary interrupts a bit selector **v** from the reader to the tag, and sends $\mathbf{v} \oplus \mathbf{v}'$ as a perturbed bit selector to the tag. The tag sends a response $(\mathbf{r}, \mathbf{z})$. The adversary perturbs the response and sends $(\mathbf{r} \oplus \mathbf{r}', \mathbf{z} \oplus \mathbf{z}')$ to the reader. The reader outputs accept if $(\mathbf{r} \oplus \mathbf{r}', \mathbf{z} \oplus \mathbf{z}')$ is valid response, otherwise he outputs reject.

Winning Condition: we say that the adversary wins the game if at some points he makes a query to the reader such that

1. $(\mathbf{v}', \mathbf{r}', \mathbf{z}') \neq (\mathbf{0}, \mathbf{0}, \mathbf{0})$ and
2. the reader outputs accept.

We now describe a simple sMIM attack which can brake the AUTH$^{\#}$ protocol with overwhelming probability.

Step 1. Construct a vector $\mathbf{z}' \in \mathbb{Z}_2^n$ such that the i-th element of $\mathbf{z}'$ is 1 and all remaining elements are 0 for any $i \in [n]$.

Step 2. Interrupt $(\mathbf{r}, \mathbf{z})$ sent from the tag to the reader. Send a perturbed response $(\mathbf{r}, \mathbf{z} \oplus \mathbf{z}')$ to the reader.

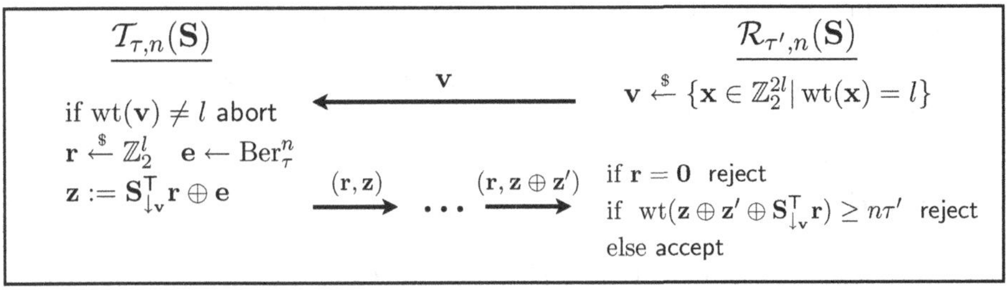

Fig. 2. Strong MIM attack against the AUTH$^{\#}$ protocol

Since added element $\mathbf{z}'$ is not zero vector, the adversary fulfills the winning condition 1. It is obvious that the random vector $\mathbf{r}$ is not zero vector with overwhelming probability. For the perturbed response $(\mathbf{r}, \mathbf{z} \oplus \mathbf{z}')$ sent from the adversary, we have

$$\mathbf{z} \oplus \mathbf{z}' \oplus \mathbf{S}_{\downarrow \mathbf{v}}^{\mathsf{T}} \mathbf{r} = \mathbf{S}_{\downarrow \mathbf{v}}^{\mathsf{T}} \mathbf{r} \oplus \mathbf{e} \oplus \mathbf{z}' \oplus \mathbf{S}_{\downarrow \mathbf{v}}^{\mathsf{T}} \mathbf{r} = \mathbf{e} \oplus \mathbf{z}'.$$

From the construction of the vector $\mathbf{z}'$, the almost all element without i-th bit of the vector $\mathbf{e} \oplus \mathbf{z}'$ follows Ber$_\tau$. Then, the hamming weight of the vector $\mathbf{e} \oplus \mathbf{z}'$ is less than the threshold $n\tau'$ with high enough probability. Therefore the adversary also fulfills winning condition 2. From the above, the AUTH$^{\#}$ protocol is insecure against the sMIM attack.

Improved Linear Cryptanalysis
of Reduced-Round MIBS

Aslı Bay[1], Jialin Huang[1,2], and Serge Vaudenay[1]

[1] EPFL, Switzerland
[2] Shanghai Jiao Tong University, China
{asli.bay,serge.vaudenay}@epfl.ch, jlhuang.cn@gmail.com

Abstract. MIBS is a 32-round lightweight block cipher with 64-bit block size and two different key sizes, namely 64-bit and 80-bit keys. Bay et al. provided the first impossible differential, differential and linear cryptanalyses of MIBS. Their best attack was a linear attack on the 18-round MIBS-80. In this paper, we significantly improve their attack by discovering more approximations and mounting Hermelin et al.'s multidimensional linear cryptanalysis. We also use Nguyen et al.'s technique to have less time complexity. We attack on 19 rounds of MIBS-80 with a time complexity of $2^{74.23}$ 19-round MIBS-80 encryptions by using $2^{57.87}$ plaintext-ciphertext pairs. To the best of our knowledge, the result proposed in this paper is the best cryptanalytic result for MIBS, so far.

Keywords: multidimensional linear cryptanalysis, lightweight block ciphers, MIBS, RFID tags, sensor networks.

1 Introduction

MIBS [ISSK09] is a lightweight block cipher suitable for constraint environments, such as RFID tags and sensor networks. MIBS was proposed by Izadi et al. in 2009; it has a simple Feistel structure and an SPN round function. The first and detailed cryptanalysis of reduced-round MIBS was realized by Bay et al. [BNV10] and they gave linear, differential and impossible differential cryptanalyses of MIBS. The best attack among them was the linear attack on the 18-round MIBS-80 with the time complexity of $2^{78.62}$ 18-round MIBS encryptions.

Linear cryptanalysis was proposed by Matsui and firstly applied to FEAL cipher [MY93] and subsequently to DES [Mat94b]. It is a known-plaintext attack and the adversary assumes that the plaintexts are independent and linearly distributed over the message space $\{0,1\}^n$. Essentially, the attack exploits linear (or affine) relations of plaintext, ciphertext and the key bits. Afterwards, Matsui [Mat94a] discovered that using two linear approximations together helps to reduce the data complexity of linear cryptanalysis. Simultaneously, Kaliski and Robshaw [JR94] introduced multiple linear cryptanalysis to reduce data complexities of Matsui's algorithms by using several approximations, but each linear approximation involves the same key bits. Then, Biryukov et al. [BCQ04] further improved this technique by using several linear approximations involving

M. Yoshida and K. Mouri (Eds.): IWSEC 2014, LNCS 8639, pp. 204–220, 2014.

different key bits. However, both in Kaliski-Robshaw's and Biryukov et al.'s techniques, the statistical independence of each linear approximations is assumed. It is shown by Murphy in [Mur06] that this assumption may not hold in general. Biryukov et al. [BCQ04] is also added an enhancement heuristically to its method by using more approximations which are linearly and statistically dependent.

Afterwards, Baignères et al. [BJV04] proposed a statistical linear distinguisher, such that statistical independence of linear approximations is not needed anymore. In their technique, the attack is modeled as a hypothesis testing problem based on the log-likelihood ratio (LLR). They showed that the efficiency of a multidimensional distinguisher is measured by the distance of its distribution to the uniform distribution. This distance is then called the capacity (see Definition 1) which is directly related to the number of samples N needed for the attack.

Hermelin et al. further analyzed this technique for extending Matsui's Algorithm 1 and Matsui's Algorithm 2 to multiple dimensions by using some statistical techniques [HCN08, CHN09, HCN09, HN10, Her10, HN11, HN12]. They studied on the goodness-of-fit problem solved by the χ^2-statistic, the LLR-statistic method and the convolution method. They showed how to use correlations of one-dimensional linear approximations to determine multidimensional probability distributions (see Lemma 2), and to compute the capacity (see Lemma 3). They verified the new techniques on the AES candidate Serpent.

Table 1. Key recovery attacks on reduced-round MIBS

#Rounds	Data	Time	Memory	Cipher	Reference	Attack type
12	2^{59} CP	$2^{58.8}$	2^{62}	MIBS-80	[BNV10]	ID
13	2^{61} CP	2^{40}	2^{24}	MIBS-64	[BNV10]	DC
13	2^{61} CP	2^{56}	2^{24}	MIBS-80	[BNV10]	DC
14	2^{40} CP	$2^{37.2}$	2^{40}	MIBS-64	[BNV10]	DC
14	2^{40} CP	2^{40}	2^{40}	MIBS-80	[BNV10]	DC
17	2^{58} KP	2^{69}	2^{58}	MIBS-80	[BNV10]	LC
18^1	$2^{63.47}$ KP	$2^{78.62}$	$2^{63.47}$	MIBS-80	[BNV10]	LC
19	$2^{57.87}$ KP	$2^{78.22}$	2^{76}	MIBS-80	Section 4	MLC
19	$2^{57.87}$ CP	$2^{74.23}$	2^{72}	MIBS-80	Section 5	MLC

Time complexity is number of reduced-round encryptions; DC: Differential Cryptanalysis; ID: Impossible Differential Attack; CP: Chosen Plaintext; KP: Known Plaintext; MLC: Multidimensional Linear Cryptanalysis

In this paper, we present a multidimensional linear attack on the 19-round MIBS-80 which outperforms the previous linear attack in terms of the number of rounds, time and data complexities. See Table 1 for the comparison of our results with the existing ones. We exploit Bay et al.'s attack by finding/using more linear approximations to reduce the data complexity. Moreover, we use Nguyen et al.'s approach to decrease time complexity of the attack, which enables us to attack on one more round.

---

[1] We put the corrected complexities compared to [BNV10] by fixing a flaw in the attack.

The rest of the paper is organized as follows. We give a brief description of MIBS in Section 2. Some mathematical background and the detailed description of the linear attack in multiple dimensions are given in Section 3. Section 4 gives our multidimensional linear attack on the 19-round MIBS-80. Section 5 proposes a chosen-message version of the attack given in Section 4 on the 19-round MIBS-80. Finally, Section 6 concludes the paper.

2 Description of MIBS

MIBS [ISSK09] is a block cipher using the conventional Feistel structure (see Fig. 1). MIBS has a 64-bit block size supporting 64-bit and 80-bit keys and iterates 32 rounds for both key sizes. The round function F of MIBS is an SPN composed of an XOR layer with a round key, a layer of 4×4-bit S-Boxes (S layer), and a linear transformation layer (P layer), in this order. The components of the encryption process involved in F are explained as follows. Note that all internal operations in MIBS are nibble-wise, that is, on 4-bit words.

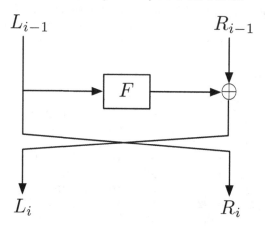

Fig. 1. The ith round of MIBS

Key addition: In each round i, $1 \le i \le 32$, the 32-bit input state s_i to the F function is XORed with the round key K_i, that is $s_i' = s_i \oplus K_i$, where "$\oplus$" denotes XOR.

S-Box layer S : After key addition, the state s_i' is split into eight nibbles and identical 4×4 S-Boxes (see Table 2) are applied in parallel.

Table 2. The S-Box of MIBS in hexadecimal notation

x	0	1	2	3	4	5	6	7	8	9	a	b	c	d	e	f
$S(x)$	4	f	3	8	d	a	c	0	b	5	7	e	2	6	1	9

Linear transformation layer P : The input $(y_1, y_2, y_3, y_4, y_5, y_6, y_7, y_8)$ is transformed into its output $(y'_1, y'_2, y'_3, y'_4, y'_5, y'_6, y'_7, y'_8)$ by

$$y'_1 = y_1 \oplus y_2 \oplus y_4 \oplus y_5 \oplus y_7 \oplus y_8;$$
$$y'_2 = y_2 \oplus y_3 \oplus y_4 \oplus y_5 \oplus y_6 \oplus y_7;$$
$$y'_3 = y_1 \oplus y_2 \oplus y_3 \oplus y_5 \oplus y_6 \oplus y_8;$$
$$y'_4 = y_2 \oplus y_3 \oplus y_4 \oplus y_7 \oplus y_8;$$
$$y'_5 = y_1 \oplus y_3 \oplus y_4 \oplus y_5 \oplus y_8;$$
$$y'_6 = y_1 \oplus y_2 \oplus y_4 \oplus y_5 \oplus y_6;$$
$$y'_7 = y_1 \oplus y_2 \oplus y_3 \oplus y_6 \oplus y_7;$$
$$y'_8 = y_1 \oplus y_3 \oplus y_4 \oplus y_6 \oplus y_7 \oplus y_8,$$

where y_i's and y'_i's are 4-bit words.

Key Schedule: For our attack purposes, we mention only the 80-bit version of the key schedule generating 32-bit round keys K_i, for $1 \le i \le 32$. Let $state^i$ denote the ith round key state and let $state^0$ denote the 80-bit secret key. Considering bit numbering in right-to-left, 80-bit key schedule is formalized in Algorithm 1. In these algorithms, "$\ggg$" means bitwise rotation to right, "$\|$" means string concatenation, and "$\sim$" indicates a sequence of bit positions. In addition, S denotes the S-Box which is the same as the S-Box (see Table 2) in the round function. In the rest of this thesis, we denote by MIBS-80 (resp. MIBS-64) the 80-bit key (resp. 64-bit key) version of MIBS. Note that the input to the ith round is denoted by (L_{i-1}, R_{i-1}), with $(L_i, R_i) = (R_{i-1} \oplus F(K_i, L_{i-1}), L_{i-1}) \in \{0,1\}^{32}$ denoting the round output. Let (L_0, R_0) and (L_{32}, R_{32}) denote a plaintext block and a ciphertext block, respectively.

Algorithm 1. The 80-bit key schedule of MIBS.

1: **for** $i = 1$ to 32 **do**
2:   $state^i = state^{i-1} \ggg 19$
3:   $state^i = S[state^i[80 \sim 77]] \| S[state^i[76 \sim 73]] \| state^i[72 \sim 1]$
4:   $state^i = state^i[80 \sim 20] \| state^i[19 \sim 15] \oplus \text{RoundCounter} \| state^i[14 \sim 1]$
5:   $K_i = state^i[80 \sim 49]$
6: **end for**

---

3 Preliminary

3.1 Mathematical Background

We denote by $\mathbb{F}_2$ the field with two elements and $\mathbb{F}_2^m$ denotes the m-dimensional vector space over $\mathbb{F}_2$. Let X be a discrete random variable in $\mathbb{F}_2^m$ and $p = (p_0, p_1, \ldots, p_{2^m-1})$ be the probability distribution of X such that $p_\eta = \Pr(X = \eta)$, where $\eta \in \mathbb{F}_2^m$. The function $f = (f_1, \ldots, f_m) : \mathbb{F}_2^n \to \mathbb{F}_2^m$ is called a vectorial Boolean function, where $f_i : \mathbb{F}_2^n \to \mathbb{F}_2$ is a Boolean function.

Definition 1. *Let* $p = (p_0, p_1, \ldots, p_\eta)$ *and* $q = (q_0, q_1, \ldots, q_\eta)$ *be two discrete probability distributions with sample space* $\mathcal{S}$. *Then, the* capacity *between* p *and* q *is*

$$C(p, q) = \sum_{\eta \in \mathcal{S}} \frac{(p_\eta - q_\eta)^2}{q_\eta}.$$

In the case where q is the uniform distribution θ, the capacity is denoted by $C(p)$. Let Y be a Bernoulli(p_0)-distributed random variable which takes values in $\{0, 1\}$ such that $\Pr(Y = 0) = p_0$. Then, the *correlation* of Y with zero is defined as

$$c(Y) = 2\Pr(Y = 0) - 1 = 2p_0 - 1. \tag{1}$$

The *bias* of Y, denoted as ε is equal to $c(Y)/2$. Let X be an m-bit random variable with probability distribution p and $a \in \mathbb{F}_2^m$. Then, we have

$$c(a \cdot X) = \sum_{\eta \in \mathbb{F}_2^m} (-1)^{a \cdot \eta} p_\eta. \tag{2}$$

The following lemma proves that the probability distribution p of m-bit random variable X, taking values from $\mathbb{F}_2^m$, is computed by the correlations of $a \cdot X$, where $a \in \mathbb{F}_2^m$.

Lemma 2. *([HCN08]) Let X be an m-bit random taking values from $\mathbb{F}_2^m$ variable with probability distribution p, then*

$$p_\eta = 2^{-m} \sum_{a \in \mathbb{F}_2^m} (-1)^{a \cdot \eta} c(a \cdot X), \quad \forall \eta \in \mathbb{F}_2^m.$$

Lemma 3. *([HCN08]) Let X be an m-bit random variable taking values from $\mathbb{F}_2^m$ and p be its probability distribution. Then, the capacity of p is*

$$C(p) = \sum_{a \in \mathbb{F}_2^m - \{0\}} c(a \cdot X)^2.$$

3.2 Matsui's Algorithm 2 in Multidimensional Linear Cryptanalysis

Let $f : \mathbb{F}_2^n \to \mathbb{F}_2^n$ be a vectorial Boolean function and binary vectors $w_i \in \mathbb{F}_2^n$ and $u_i \in \mathbb{F}_2^n$ be the binary masks such that the pairs (u_i, w_i) are linearly independent. Each one-dimensional approximation of f is defined as a function g_i such that

$$g_i(X) = w_i \cdot f(X) \oplus u_i \cdot X, \quad \forall X \in \mathbb{F}_2^n,$$

where all g_i's are the base approximations for $i = 1, \ldots, m$. Let c_i be the correlation of g_i, $i = 1, \ldots, m$, and $g = (g_1, g_2, \ldots, g_m)$ be an m-dimensional vectorial Boolean function. Let $p = (p_0, p_1, \ldots, p_{2^m-1})$ be the probability distribution of g. This p can be computed from all possible one-dimensional correlations by Lemma 2.

For an n-bit block cipher of r rounds, R^r denotes the last round of the cipher with its inverse R^{-r}, and $K_r \in \mathbb{F}_2^\ell$ denotes the last round key. K_r is also called the outer key. Let x and y' be the plaintext and ciphertext, respectively. The $(r-1)$-round m-dimensional linear approximation of the block cipher is written by

$$Ux \oplus Wy \oplus VK_{1,..,r-1},$$

where, $y = R^{-r}(y', K_r)$, $K_{1,...,r-1}$ is inner key bits, $U = (u_1, u_2, \ldots, u_m)^T$, $V = (v_1, v_2, \ldots, v_m)^T$ and $W = (w_1, w_2, \ldots, w_m)^T$ are the matrices of the masks for the texts and the inner key bits, respectively. The matrix V splits the inner key bits into 2^m equivalent classes such that $z = VK_{1,...,r-1} \in \mathbb{F}_2^m$. Furthermore, if $Ux \oplus Wy$ is distributed with p, then $Ux \oplus Wy \oplus VK_{1,...,r-1}$ is distributed with p^z, where all p^z's, $z \in \mathbb{F}_2^m$, are the permutations of each other. That is,

$$p_{\eta \oplus \alpha}^z = p_\eta^{z \oplus \alpha}, \quad \forall z, \eta, \alpha \in \mathbb{F}_2^m.$$

This implies that $C(p) = C(p^z)$, for all $z \in \mathbb{F}_2^m$. Now, we denote by $\widetilde{K_r}$ and $\widetilde{z}$ the right rth round key and the right inner key class, respectively. The aim of Matsui's Algorithm 2 for multidimensional linear attacks is to find $\widetilde{K_r}$ as well as $\widetilde{z}$. Note that we only attack on the last round key, but recovering more round keys is doable. The attack is mainly composed of four phases, namely, the *distillation phase*, the *analysis phase*, the *ranking phase* and the *search phase*.

In the distillation phase, we collect N plaintext-ciphertext pairs (x_1, y_1'), $\ldots, (x_N, y_N')$, where $x_1, \ldots, x_N$ are taken independently from the uniform distribution. By Algorithm 2, we compute the empirical probability distributions $q[K_r, \cdot]$ for eah key candidate K_r which are

$$q[K_r, \eta] = N^{-1} \#\{t : Ux_t \oplus WR^{-r}(y_t', K_r) = \eta\}, \quad \forall \eta \in \mathbb{F}_2^m.$$

Algorithm 2. Distillation phase

1: **procedure** COMPUTE $q((x_1, y_1'), \ldots, (x_N, y_N'), g_1, g_2, \ldots, g_m)$
2:     **for** $t = 1 \to N$ **do**
3:         **for** $K_r = 0 \to 2^\ell - 1$ **do**
4:             partially decrypt y_t' and obtain $y_t = R^{-r}(y_t', K_r)$
5:             **for** $i = 1 \to m$ **do**
6:                 compute $\eta_i = u_i \cdot x_t \oplus w \cdot y_t$
7:             **end for**
8:             increment the counter $q[K_r, \eta]$ corresponding to $\eta = (\eta_1, \ldots, \eta_m)$
9:         **end for**
10:     **end for**
11:     update $q[K_r, \eta]$ as $q[K_r, \eta]/N$
12: **end procedure**

Algorithm 3. Analysis phase

1: **procedure** COMPUTE CONVOLUTION(q,p)
2:    **for** $K_r = 0 \to 2^\ell - 1$ **do**
3:       compute $q[K_r, \cdot] * p$ using Fast Fourier Transform (FFT)
4:       store $G(K_r) = \max_{z \in \mathbb{F}_2^m} (q[K_r, \cdot] * p)_z$ and z' which is the index of the maximal component of $(q[K_r, \cdot] * p)$.
5:    **end for**
6: **end procedure**

In the analysis phase, we choose the convolution method [HN10, Her10], as it is efficient in terms of both time and data complexities. Let p and q be the probability distributions of two m-bit random variables, X and Y, respectively. The ith component of the convolution of p and q is defined as

$$(q * p)_i = \sum_{\eta \in \mathbb{F}_2^m} q_\eta p_{i \oplus \eta}.$$

Using the convolution method, the mark of each key candidate K_r is defined by

$$G(K_r) = \max_{z \in \mathbb{F}_2^m} (q[K_r, \cdot] * p)_z.$$

For each possible K_r, we find the maximal component of the convolution $(q[K_r, \cdot] * p)$, and record this maximal component as $G(K_r)$ together with its corresponding index z'. Because, the right key $\widetilde{K_r}$ is supposed to have the highest mark $G(K_r)$ and the right inner key $\widetilde{z}$ is recovered corresponding to $G(\widetilde{K_r})$. The detailed process of the analysis phase is mentioned in Algorithm 3.

In the ranking phase, we rank the key candidates by $G(K_r)$, and the keys are sorted in a decreasing order according to their ranking values. Under a predetermined advantage a, the right key candidate $\widetilde{K_r}$ should be within the position of $2^{\ell-a}$, where ℓ is the number of targeted key bits.

Then, the search phase, where the remaining key bits are searched and the correctness of the ranking result is verified, can be done by a number of trial encryptions according to the sorted candidate list.

3.3   Complexities of Multidimensional Linear Attacks (by the Convolution Method)

The advantage of the convolution method can be computed from the following Theorem.

Theorem 4. *[Her10] To distinguish the uniform distribution from the distributions of p^z which are close to the uniform one ($z \in \mathbb{F}_2^m$), the advantage of the convolution method for finding the last round key K_r is given by*

$$a = (\sqrt{NC(p)} - \Phi^{-1}(P_S))^2/2 - m,$$

where $P_S(> 0.5)$ *is the success probability,* N *is the amount of data required for the attack,* Φ *is the cumulative distribution function of the normal distribution,* $C(p)$ *is the capacity of* p *and* m *is the dimension of the linear approximation.*

From Theorem 4, the data complexity N of the convolution method is approximated to

$$N = \frac{a + m}{C(p)},$$

where $C(p)$ is the capacity of p, a denotes the advantage, and m is the dimension of the linear approximation.

The time complexity of the analysis phase is $m2^{m+\ell}$ operations. In the ranking phase, sorting can be done within $\ell 2^{\ell}$. In addition, the time complexity of the search phase depends on the advantage, i.e. 2^{k-a}, where k is the master key size. Algorithm 2 computes the empirical probability distributions for all keys K_r with $\mathcal{O}(mN2^{\ell})$ time complexity, in a conventional way. However, this complexity can be reduced to $\mathcal{O}(N + \lambda 2^{m+\ell})$ in [NWW11], where $\lambda > 0$ differs by the attack cases. That is, if only the last round(s) keys are attacked, then $\lambda = 4m + 3\ell$, and if both first and last rounds keys are attacked, then $\lambda = 3m + 3\ell$. This is not somewhat different from the extension of the Collard's method for reducing the time complexity of the Matsui's Algorithm 2 [CSQ07].

However, in [NWW11], they consider linear approximations having the same output masks and they compute the empirical probability distribution for both cases. In our attack, linear approximations have different input and output masks, we slightly modify their strategy to use and present as follows. Note that in our case the active S-boxes in the first and last rounds are the same for all linear approximations even with different masks.

Lemma 5. *Let* $g_a = f_1^a(x, y') \oplus f_2^a(x, K_1) \oplus f_3^a(y', K_r)$ *be all linear approximations involved in an attack, and* f_1^a, f_2^a *and* f_3^a *be boolean functions, for all* $a \in \mathbb{F}_2^m$. *Assume w.l.o.g. that* g_i*'s, for* $i = 1, \ldots, m$, *constitute* m *base linear approximations which linearly span the rest of approximations. Let* K_1 *and* K_r *denote the respective key bits in the first and last rounds. Let* x *and* y' *be the plaintext and ciphertext, respectively. Then, in the distillation phase, the probability distribution* $q[k, \eta]$ *of* $g = (g_1, g_2, \ldots, g_m)$, *where* $\eta \in \mathbb{F}_2^m$ *and* K *contains* ℓ *bits from both* K_1 *and* K_r *in total, is computed with* $\mathcal{O}(mN + (2m + 3\ell)2^{\ell+m} + 2^{\ell})$ *time complexity and* $\mathcal{O}(2^{m+\ell})$ *memory complexity.*

Proof. For the details of this proof please refer to Appendix A. The proof can also be implied by the attack procedure explained in Section 4.

4   Multidimensional Linear Cryptanalysis of Reduced-Round MIBS-80

In this section, we apply a 12-dimensional linear attack on the 19 rounds of MIBS-80 by using the convolution method [Her10].

4.1   Previous 16-round Linear Approximations

Bay et al. [BNV10] found a set of six 16-round linear approximations with 31 active S-boxes. Namely, these linear approximations are due to the six possible instantiations from the linear approximation table (LAT) (see Appendix B) of MIBS, $(w, z) \in \{(2_x, 6_x), (6_x, 2_x), (4_x, e_x), (e_x, 4_x), (8_x, d_x), (d_x, 8_x)\}$, where the symmetry $w \xrightarrow{\text{S-Box}} z$ and $z \xrightarrow{\text{S-Box}} w$ (both with the same bias 2^{-2}) is exploited. Each of these 16-round linear approximations has a bias $\varepsilon = 2^{-31}$. Since $c = 2|\varepsilon|$, their correlations are $c = 2^{-30}$. The set of 16-round linear approximations can be found in Appendix C. Note that the input mask to the ith round is denoted by $(\Gamma L_{i-1}, \Gamma R_{i-1})$. The $(i+1)$th round input mask is the ith round output mask. Values subscripted by "x" are in hexadecimal base.

4.2   Our Set of 16-round Linear Approximations

We exploit the 16-round linear approximations mentioned in Section 4.1 with 31 active S-boxes. We find 594 more by using different combinations of non-zero masks in the last round of them. Strictly speaking, we cut the first 15 rounds of these linear approximations. The total bias of each is 2^{-29}. Since the last round input mask to the function F is free to choose, there are ten possible nonzero input masks with nonzero biases for each w, that is, there are two nonzero input masks with a bias of 2^{-2} and eight input masks with a bias of 2^{-3}. The values of w's and their corresponding $\bar{y}$'s and $\bar{z}$'s (here, w, $\bar{y}$ and $\bar{z}$ form the masks together) are given in Table 3 in a group manner. Hence, we take all possible combinations of all values for $(\bar{y}, \bar{z})$ and obtain 600 linear approximations[2] depicted in Table 4. Note that the last pair of bit masks in Table 4 stands for the output masks after the swapping of half blocks in a round. These approximations are indeed generated by twelve base linear approximations. For example, one set of twelve base approximations is $(w, \bar{y}, \bar{z}) \in B = \{(2_x, 6_x, 6_x), (2_x, 6_x, b_x), (2_x, b_x, 6_x), (4_x, 9_x, e_x), (4_x, 9_x, 9_x), (4_x, e_x, 9_x), (8_x, b_x, d_x), (8_x, b_x, b_x), (8_x, d_x, b_x), (d_x, 8_x, 8_x), (d_x, 8_x, c_x), (d_x, c_x, 8_x)\}$. In detail, 24 of 600 linear approximations have biases 2^{-31}, 192 of them have biases 2^{-32} and 384 of them have biases 2^{-33}. Since, $c = 2|\varepsilon|$, they have respective correlations $c_1 = 2^{-30}$, $c_2 = 2^{-31}$ and $c_3 = 2^{-32}$. The capacity of the 12-dimensional system is lower bounded by

$$24 \times (2^{-30})^2 + 192 \times (2^{-31})^2 + 384 \times (2^{-32})^2 = 2^{-53.415}.$$

Note that we ignore the rest of $2^{12} - 601$ approximations as they have negligible correlations.

4.3   A 12-dimensional Linear Attack on the 19 Rounds of MIBS-80

We use all possible $2^{12} - 1$ (dependent and independent) linear approximations generated from the base approximations mentioned in Section 4.2. We attack on

---

[2] These approximations contain the previous ones mentioned in Section 4.1.

Table 3. Possible values for w, $\bar{y}$ and $\bar{z}$

w	$\bar{y}, \bar{z}$	bias
2_x	$6_x, b_x$	2^{-2}
	$2_x, 3_x, 4_x, 5_x, 8_x, 9_x, e_x, f_x$	2^{-3}
4_x	$9_x, e_x$	2^{-2}
	$2_x, 3_x, 4_x, 5_x, a_x, b_x, c_x, d_x$	2^{-3}
6_x	$1_x, 2_x$	2^{-2}
	$8_x, 9_x, a_x, b_x, c_x, d_x, e_x, f_x$	2^{-3}
8_x	b_x, d_x	2^{-2}
	$1_x, 3_x, 5_x, 7_x, 8_x, a_x, c_x, e_x$	2^{-3}
d_x	$8_x, c_x$	2^{-2}
	$2_x, 3_x, 6_x, 7_x, a_x, b_x, e_x, f_x$	2^{-3}
e_x	$4_x, c_x$	2^{-2}
	$1_x, 3_x, 5_x, 7_x, 9_x, b_x, d_x, f_x$	2^{-3}

19 rounds of MIBS-80 by using the convolution method [Her10] together with the (modified) Nguyen et al.'s approach [NWW11] (see Section 3.3). We recover some key bits from the last round key as well as the first and the second rounds' keys, by considering them as a combined ℓ-bit key. Note that the 600 linear approximations that we found in Section 4.2 are useful to compute the (lower bound of) capacity of the system which is used for finding the required number of the data for the attack.

We perform a key-recovery attack on 19 rounds of MIBS-80 by placing the 16-round linear approximations of 12-dimension between rounds 3 and 18. Because the capacity of the 12-dimensional linear approximation is $2^{-53.415}$, according to Theorem 4, the data requirement is $N = 2^{57.874}$ plaintext-ciphertext pairs by taking 10 bits of advantage, i.e. $a = 20$. According to Theorem 4 our attack's success probability is $P_S = 0.9$. We recover some part of the key bits from the first, second and the last rounds. We guess K_1 (except $K_{1,3}$), $K_{2,6}$, K_{19} (except $K_{19,3}$), which make 60 round key bits in total. Notice that the third S-Box of the first round is not active due to the fact that its output is not needed to compute the input to the first and the sixth S-Boxes in the second round. All four phases of the attack are explained as follows.

We call $T = P \oplus S$, composed of the S and the P layers of MIBS. Let $\alpha = 0w0w000w$, $\beta = 00\bar{y}0000\bar{z}$, where w, $\bar{y}$ and $\bar{z}$ take their values from the set B. Notice that any set of base approximations is acceptable. According to the set B, the combined coefficients (represented as 12-dimensional vectors) of the $2^{12} - 12 - 1$ approximations are also known.

Let $K' = (K_1, K_2, K_{19})$ contain 96 bits, $v = (L_0, R_0, R_{19})$ and $K' \oplus v = (K_1 \oplus L_0, K_2 \oplus R_0, K_{19} \oplus R_{19})$. Let us define $b_1 : \{0,1\}^{2^{96}} \rightarrow \{0,1\}^{2^{32}}$ such that $b_1(K' \oplus v) = K_1 \oplus L_0$. Similarly, define $b_2(K' \oplus v) = K_2 \oplus R_0$, and $b_3(K' \oplus v) = K_{19} \oplus R_{19}$. Then, the base and combined approximations are

$$h^a(P, C) \oplus g^a(K', (P, C)_\ell),$$

Table 4. A set of 16-round linear approximations, where "$*$" can be 2^{-3}, 2^{-4} or 2^{-5}, and w and z take the values as we mentioned in Section 4.1.

Round i	ΓL_{i-1}	ΓR_{i-1}	Number of active S-Boxes	Bias
1	$0w0w000w$	00000000	0	2^{-1}
2	00000000	$0w0w000w$	2	2^{-3}
3	$0w0w000w$	$00z0000z$	3	2^{-4}
4	$00z0000z$	$w0ww000w$	2	2^{-3}
5	$w0ww000w$	$z0zz000z$	2	2^{-3}
6	$z0zz000z$	$00w0000w$	3	2^{-4}
7	$00w0000w$	$0z0z000z$	2	2^{-3}
8	$0z0z000z$	00000000	0	2^{-1}
9	00000000	$0z0z000z$	2	2^{-3}
10	$0z0z000z$	$00w0000w$	3	2^{-4}
11	$00w0000w$	$z0zz000z$	2	2^{-3}
12	$z0zz000z$	$w0ww000w$	2	2^{-3}
13	$w0ww000w$	$00z0000z$	3	2^{-4}
14	$00z0000z$	$0w0w000w$	2	2^{-3}
15	$0w0w000w$	00000000	0	2^{-1}
16	00000000	$0w0w000w$	2	$*$
17	$0w0w000w$	$00\bar{y}0000\bar{z}$	-	-

where

$$h^a(P,C) = \alpha_a \cdot L_0 \oplus \alpha_a \cdot R_{19} \oplus \beta_a \cdot L_{19},$$

and

$$g^a(K',(P,C)_\ell) = g^a(K' \oplus v) =$$
$$g'^a(b_1(K' \oplus v), b_2(K' \oplus v), b_3(K' \oplus v)) =$$
$$g'^a(K_1 \oplus L_0, K_2 \oplus R_0, K_{19} \oplus R_{19}) =$$
$$\alpha_a \cdot T(T(L_0 \oplus K_1) \oplus R_0 \oplus K_2) \oplus \beta_a \cdot T(R_{19} \oplus K_{19})$$

Here, $(P,C)_\ell$ denotes the ℓ text bits interacting with the ℓ-bit attacked key bits. According to α_a and β_a, we know only 64 bits of $K' \oplus v$ involved in the computation of g^a. Thus, hereafter when we mention $g^a(K' \oplus v)$, we mean that the function g^a acts directly on these 64 bits. That is, $K' \oplus v$ actually denotes the 64 active bits. Here, K' includes the 64 active key bits in K_1, K_2 and K_{19} and v is the 64 bits of texts.

The base approximations are denoted as $h^a(P,C) \oplus g^a(K',(P,C)_\ell)$, where $a = 1,\ldots,12$. After examining the key schedule of MIBS-80, it can be verified that K_1 and K_2 share four attacked bits in common, that is $K_2[3 \sim 0] = K_1[22 \sim 19]$, where "$\sim$" indicates a sequence of bit positions. Therefore, while K' denotes the 64 key bits interacting with the text bits, K denotes the 60 key bits considering the key schedule.

Distillation Phase:

1. Collect $N = 2^{57.874}$ plaintext-ciphertext pairs (P_t, C_t), for $t = 1, \ldots, N$.
2. The table containing all empirical correlations $r[a, K]$ for each 60-bit key K can be computed as follows.
   (a) Construct $T^{2^{12} \times 2^{64}}$ in a way that for all $a \in \mathbb{F}_2^{12}$, for all $(P_t, C_t) = (L_0^t \| R_0^t, L_{19}^t \| R_{19}^t), t = 1, \ldots, N$, if $h^a(P_t, C_t) = 0$, increment the counter $T[a, (P_t, C_t)_l]$, otherwise decrement it. Afterwards, update $T[a, (P_t, C_t)_l] = T[a, (P_t, C_t)_l]/N$. The time complexity of this is $N \times 2^{12}$ computations of h^a. The memory complexity for T is $2^{m+l} = 2^{76}$ block units, and hereafter each block unit denotes a size of $\log_2 N$ bits[3]. However, this table can be generated by constructing another table $E^{2^{12} \times 2^{64}}$ in the next step to reduce its time complexity.
   (b) Build another table $E^{2^{12} \times 2^{64}}$ by

   $$E[z_1, z_2] = \#\{(P_t, C_t), t = 1, \ldots, N | (h^1(P_t, C_t), \ldots, h^{12}(P_t, C_t)) = z_1,$$
   $$\text{and } (P_t, C_t)_l = z_2\}, \text{where } z_1 \in \mathbb{F}_2^{12}, z_2 \in \mathbb{F}_2^{64}.$$

   The time complexity of this step is $12 \times N \approx 2^{61.459}$ computations of h^a, i.e. two XOR operations. As one-round encryption is equivalent to more than seven XOR operations including the cost of S-Boxes, the above complexity can be regarded as $12 \times N \times 2/7 = 2^{59.652}$ one-round encryptions. The required memory complexity for E is $2^{m+l} = 2^{76}$ block units.
   (c) Now, build the table T from tables E and H. Let $H^{2^{12} \times 2^{12}}$ be a matrix such that $H[i, j] = (-1)^{i \cdot j}, \forall i, j \in \mathbb{F}_2^{12}$. For each fixed v, (that is, for each column vector in T), we can compute

   $$T[a, v] = \sum_{z_1=0}^{2^{12}-1} (-1)^{a \cdot z_1} E[z_1, v]$$

   by the relation
   $$T[\cdot, v] = HE[\cdot, v],$$

   with the time complexity 12×2^{12} multiplications. As there are 2^{64} columns in T, the total time complexity is $12 \times 2^{64+12} \approx 2^{79.585}$ multiplications, which is equal to $3/7 \times 2^{79.585} \approx 2^{78.363}$ one-round encryptions[4]. The memory complexity for H is 2^{22} bytes[5].
   (d) We can now construct the matrix $r^{2^{12} \times 2^{64}}$ having entries $r[a, K']$ from table T as

   $$r[a, K'] = \sum_{v=0}^{2^{64}-1} (-1)^{g^a(K' \oplus v)} T[a, v].$$

---

[3] Each entry in T is at most N, thus at most $\log_2 N$ bits are needed.
[4] We assume that three XORs correspond to one multiplication.
[5] Each entry in H is either 1 or -1.

Again, the memory complexity for r is about $2^{12+64} = 2^{76}$ block units. Then, for each $a \in \mathbb{F}_2^{12}$, compute S^a from g^a. Here, S^a has the size of $2^{64} \times 2^{64}$ and $S^a[i,j] = S^a[K',v] = (-1)^{g^a(K' \oplus v)}$. The time complexity of constructing each S^a is 3×2^{64} one-round MIBS encryptions. We will compute

$$r[a, \cdot] = S^a T[a, \cdot].$$

Note that each S^a is a circulant matrix. Thus, vector $r[a, \cdot]$ is calculated with $3 \times 64 \times 2^{64}$ multiplications. The total time complexity of computing r is $2^{12} \times 3 \times 64 \times 2^{64} = 2^{83.584}$ multiplications, that is, $3/7 \times 2^{83.584} \approx 2^{82.362}$ one-round encryptions. Due to the fact that S^a is a circulant matrix, only the first row is needed to be stored. Hence, the memory complexity is 2^{57} bytes.

(e) According to the common key bits in K' brought by the key schedule, K' actually has only 60 bits required to be guessed. Thus, we select the possible 2^{60} keys in r and eliminate the wrong keys based on the key schedule. We update $r[a, K']$ to $r[a, K]$ which only contains the columns for possible keys.

3. Finally, find $q[K, \cdot]$ for only key bits $K \in \mathbb{F}_2^{60}$ from the empirical correlations $r[a, K]$, by using Lemma 2. Hence, we have

$$q[K, \cdot] = 2^{-12} H r[\cdot, K],$$

where $H^{2^{12} \times 2^{12}}$ is exploited again, i.e. $H[i,j] = (-1)^{i \cdot j}$. The time complexity of computing the row vector of $q[K, \cdot]$ is 12×2^{12} multiplications. The total time complexity of this step is $2^{60} \times 12 \times 2^{12} \approx 2^{75.585}$ multiplications, i.e. $3/7 \times 2^{75.585} \approx 2^{74.363}$ one-round encryptions. Also, $2^{12+60} = 2^{72}$ block units are needed for storing q.

The total time complexity is computed by summing up all above steps. $1/19 \times (2^{59.652} + 2^{78.363} + 2^{82.362} + 2^{74.363}) \approx 2^{78.207}$ 19-round MIBS encryptions. The total memory complexity is 2^{76} block units.

Analysis Phase: We use the convolution method [Her10] explained in Section 3.2. As mentioned before, the necessary number of data for the attack is $2^{57.874}$ plaintext-ciphertext pairs. Since we obtain the empirical probability distribution from the observed data, and we can compute the theoretical probability distributions from 600 linear approximations by Lemma 2, we can directly apply the convolution method described in Algorithm 3. Then, we obtain the right key and the right inner key class by sorting their marks. The time needed for this phase is about $m2^{m+\ell} = 2^{75.585}$ multiplications, equivalently $3/7 \times 1/19 \times 2^{75.585} \approx 2^{70.115}$ 19-round encryptions, where $m = 12$ and $\ell = 60$.

Ranking and Search Phases: As we get a 10-bit advantage, and $2^{60-10} = 2^{50}$ candidate keys kept from the analysis phase are ranked according to their maximal marks with $2^{65.907}$ time complexity. Thus, we make $2^{50+20} = 2^{70}$ trial encryptions to find the correct 80-bit secret key.

To sum up, the total time and memory complexities of the attack are the sum of complexities of all phases (the complexity of the ranking phase can be ignored), namely $2^{78.207} + 2^{70.115} + 2^{70} + 2^{65.907} = 2^{78.217}$ 19-round MIBS encryptions and 2^{76} block units, respectively.

5   The Chosen-Plaintext Version of the Attack

The time and memory complexities of the attack on the reduced-round MIBS-80 detailed in Section 4 can be reduced by fixing some plaintext bits corresponding to the active S-Boxes like in [KM01]. The main reason is that we do not need to guess the key bits corresponding to the fixed data, as any output parity of the S-Box will always be fixed, that is, it is always 0 or 1. Due to the fact that we need $2^{57.874}$ number of plaintext-ciphertext pairs for the attack, we have the freedom of fixing 4-bits of plaintexts corresponding to the one S-box. Let us consider 4 fixed plaintext bits for the first active S-Box of the first round. Hence, the number of guessed key bits becomes $\ell = 56$ bits instead of $\ell = 60$ bits. By updating the previous attack according to this method with using the same number of data, we obtain $2^{74.228}$ 19-round encryptions of time and 2^{72} block units of memory.

6   Conclusion

This paper proposes a multidimensional linear cryptanalysis on the reduced-round MIBS-80. The attack is faster than the previous linear attack, also requires less data complexity thanks to exploiting many linear approximations. As far as we know, the result proposed in this paper is the best cryptanalytic result for MIBS-80, so far.

References

[BCQ04]   Biryukov, A., De Cannière, C., Quisquater, M.: On Multiple Linear Approximations. In: Franklin, M. (ed.) CRYPTO 2004. LNCS, vol. 3152, pp. 1–22. Springer, Heidelberg (2004)

[BJV04]   Baignères, T., Junod, P., Vaudenay, S.: How Far Can We Go Beyond Linear Cryptanalysis? In: Lee, P.J. (ed.) ASIACRYPT 2004. LNCS, vol. 3329, pp. 432–450. Springer, Heidelberg (2004)

[BNV10]   Bay, A., Nakahara Jr., J., Vaudenay, S.: Cryptanalysis of Reduced-Round MIBS Block Cipher. In: Heng, S.-H., Wright, R.N., Goi, B.-M. (eds.) CANS 2010. LNCS, vol. 6467, pp. 1–19. Springer, Heidelberg (2010)

[CHN09]   Cho, J.Y., Hermelin, M., Nyberg, K.: A New Technique for Multidimensional Linear Cryptanalysis with Applications on Reduced Round Serpent. In: Lee, P.J., Cheon, J.H. (eds.) ICISC 2008. LNCS, vol. 5461, pp. 383–398. Springer, Heidelberg (2009)

[CSQ07]   Collard, B., Standaert, F.-X., Quisquater, J.-J.: Improving the Time Complexity of Matsui's Linear Cryptanalysis. In: Nam, K.-H., Rhee, G. (eds.) ICISC 2007. LNCS, vol. 4817, pp. 77–88. Springer, Heidelberg (2007)

[HCN08]   Hermelin, M., Cho, J.Y., Nyberg, K.: Multidimensional Linear Cryptanal-
          ysis of Reduced Round Serpent. In: Mu, Y., Susilo, W., Seberry, J. (eds.)
          ACISP 2008. LNCS, vol. 5107, pp. 203–215. Springer, Heidelberg (2008)
[HCN09]   Hermelin, M., Cho, J.Y., Nyberg, K.: Multidimensional Extension of Mat-
          sui's Algorithm 2. In: Dunkelman, O. (ed.) FSE 2009. LNCS, vol. 5665, pp.
          209–227. Springer, Heidelberg (2009)
[Her10]   Hermelin, M.: Multidimensional Linear Cryptanalysis. Phd thesis (2010)
[HN10]   Hermelin, M., Nyberg, K.: Dependent Linear Approximations: The Algo-
          rithm of Biryukov and Others Revisited. In: Pieprzyk, J. (ed.) CT-RSA
          2010. LNCS, vol. 5985, pp. 318–333. Springer, Heidelberg (2010)
[HN11]   Hermelin, M., Nyberg, K.: Linear Cryptanalysis Using Multiple Linear Ap-
          proximations. In: IACR Cryptology ePrint Archive, 2011/093
[HN12]   Hermelin, M., Nyberg, K.: Multidimensional Linear Distinguishing Attacks
          and Boolean Functions. Cryptography and Communications 4, 47–64 (2012)
[ISSK09] Izadi, M., Sadeghiyan, B., Sadeghian, S.S., Khanooki, H.A.: MIBS: A New
          Lightweight Block Cipher. In: Garay, J.A., Miyaji, A., Otsuka, A. (eds.)
          CANS 2009. LNCS, vol. 5888, pp. 334–348. Springer, Heidelberg (2009)
[JR94]   Kaliski Jr., B.S., Robshaw, M.J.B.: Linear Cryptanalysis Using Multiple
          Approximations. In: Desmedt, Y.G. (ed.) CRYPTO 1994. LNCS, vol. 839,
          pp. 26–39. Springer, Heidelberg (1994)
[KM01]   Knudsen, L.R., Mathiassen, J.E.: A Chosen-Plaintext Linear Attack on
          DES. In: Schneier, B. (ed.) FSE 2000. LNCS, vol. 1978, pp. 262–272.
          Springer, Heidelberg (2001)
[Mat94a] Matsui, M.: The First Experimental Cryptanalysis of the Data Encryption
          Standard. In: Desmedt, Y.G. (ed.) CRYPTO 1994. LNCS, vol. 839, pp.
          1–11. Springer, Heidelberg (1994)
[Mat94b] Matsui, M.: Linear Cryptanalysis Method for DES Cipher. In: Helleseth,
          T. (ed.) EUROCRYPT 1993. LNCS, vol. 765, pp. 386–397. Springer, Hei-
          delberg (1994)
[Mur06]   Murphy, S.: The Independence of Linear Approximations in Symmetric
          Cryptanalysis. IEEE Transactions on Information Theory 52(12), 5510–
          5518 (2006)
[MY93]   Matsui, M., Yamagishi, A.: A New Method for Known Plaintext Attack of
          FEAL Cipher. In: Rueppel, R.A. (ed.) EUROCRYPT 1992. LNCS, vol. 658,
          pp. 81–91. Springer, Heidelberg (1993)
[NWW11]   Nguyen, P.H., Wu, H., Wang, H.: Improving the Algorithm 2 in Multidimen-
          sional Linear Cryptanalysis. In: Parampalli, U., Hawkes, P. (eds.) ACISP
          2011. LNCS, vol. 6812, pp. 61–74. Springer, Heidelberg (2011)

A   Proof of Lemma 5

For the sake of understanding, we use the same notations as that of Nguyen's
paper [NWW11].

Proof. According to Lemma 2, we can compute the empirical probability distribution of m-dimensional linear approximations from their one-dimensional
empirical correlations. We now define a matrix $r^{2^m \times 2^\ell}$ composed of the correlations of all g^a's, for $a \in \mathbb{F}_2^m$ and $K \in \mathbb{F}_2^\ell$. Notice that $r[a, K] = 1$, for all
$K \in \mathbb{F}_2^\ell$ if $a = (0, \ldots, 0)$. Otherwise, we compute $r[a, K]$ by constructing a table

$T^{2^m \times 2^\ell}$. This table T is built as follows: for all $a \in \mathbb{F}_2^m$, we increment the counter $T[a, (x_t, y'_t)_\ell]$, where $(x_t, y'_t)_\ell$ denotes the ℓ-bits of plaintexts and ciphertexts interacting with attacked key bits from K_1 and K_r, if $f_1^a(x_t, y'_t) = 0$, otherwise decrement it. Then, update $T[a, K] = T[a, K]/N$.

However, the table T can be built in a more efficient way by providing another table $E^{2^m \times 2^\ell}$ which is

$$E[h_1, h_2] = \#\{(x_t, y'_t), t = 1, \ldots N | (f_1^1(x_t, y'_t), \ldots, f_1^m(x_t, y'_t)) = h_1, (x_t, y'_t)_\ell = h_2\},$$

for all $h_1 \in \mathbb{F}_2^m$, for all $h_2 \in \mathbb{F}_2^\ell$.

The time complexity of building E is mN. The memory complexity required for E is 2^{m+l} block units, here the size of each block unit is $\log_2 N$, as the possible biggest value stored in E is N. Now, we build the table T from tables E and H, where $H^{2^m \times 2^m}$ is a Hadamard matrix such that $H[i, j] = (-1)^{i \cdot j}$ for $i, j \in \mathbb{F}_2^m$. Hence, $T[\cdot, v] = HE[\cdot, v]$, for each fixed v, we have

$$T[a, v] = \sum_{h_1=0}^{2^m - 1} (-1)^{a \cdot h_1} E[h_1, v].$$

As H is a Hadamard matrix, for each column $v \in \mathbb{F}_2^\ell$, $T[\cdot, v]$ is obtained by $m2^m$ time complexity. Thus, for the whole T, the time complexity is $m2^{\ell+m}$. The memory complexity for H is 2^{2m-7} bytes.

We now write

$$r[a, K] = \sum_{v=0}^{2^\ell - 1} (-1)^{f^a(K \oplus v)} T[a, K], \qquad a \in \mathbb{F}_2^m.$$

Here, $f^a = f_2^a \oplus f_3^a$. We note that only ℓ bits from x and y' are used in f^a. Now, we define another $2^\ell \times 2^\ell$ table S^a depending on a for all $i, j \in \mathbb{F}_2^\ell$ such that $S^a[i, j] = (-1)^{f^a(i \oplus j)}$. The time complexity of constructing all S^a is 2^ℓ because S^a is a circulant matrix and the active S-Boxes in our case are the same. Hence, we get

$$r[a, \cdot] = S^a T[a, \cdot].$$

Due to the fact that S^a is a *circulant* matrix (see [CSQ07]), $r[a, \cdot]$ is computed in $3\ell 2^\ell$ operations with 2^ℓ bytes to store the first row of S^a. The total time complexity of computing r is $3\ell 2^{\ell+m}$ multiplications. Finally, by using Lemma 2, we get $q[K, \cdot] = 2^{-m} H r[\cdot, K]$ with $m2^m$ time complexity. The total time complexity of computing q is $m2^{\ell+m}$. The memory complexity for q is $2^{m+\ell}$ block units.

By summing up all above steps, the time complexity is $\mathcal{O}(mN + (2m + 3\ell)2^{\ell+m} + 2^\ell)$. Here, we use $\mathcal{O}$ notation because the exact value depends on the detailed time unit. According to the size of the used matrices, the memory complexity is $2^{m+\ell}$ block units.

B   Linear Approximation Table (LAT) of the S-Box in MIBS

	0_x	1_x	2_x	3_x	4_x	5_x	6_x	7_x	8_x	9_x	a_x	b_x	c_x	d_x	e_x	f_x
0_x	8	0	0	0	0	0	0	0	0	0	0	0	0	0	0	0
1_x	0	-2	0	2	0	-2	-4	-2	2	0	-2	0	2	0	2	-4
2_x	0	0	-2	-2	-2	2	-4	0	0	4	2	-2	-2	-2	0	0
3_x	0	2	2	0	2	0	0	2	-2	4	0	2	0	2	-2	-4
4_x	0	-2	-2	4	-2	0	0	2	0	-2	2	0	-2	0	-4	-2
5_x	0	0	-2	2	2	-2	0	0	2	2	0	4	-4	0	2	2
6_x	0	-2	4	2	0	-2	0	-2	0	2	4	-2	0	2	0	2
7_x	0	4	0	0	0	-4	0	0	-2	-2	2	-2	-2	-2	2	-2
8_x	0	2	2	4	0	2	-2	0	-2	0	0	2	2	-4	0	2
9_x	0	0	2	-2	-4	-4	-2	2	0	0	-2	2	0	0	-2	2
a_x	0	-2	0	-2	-2	0	2	-4	-2	0	2	4	0	-2	0	-2
b_x	0	0	4	0	-2	2	2	2	4	0	0	0	-2	-2	2	-2
c_x	0	0	0	0	2	-2	2	-2	2	2	-2	-2	0	-4	-4	0
d_x	0	2	0	-2	2	0	-2	0	4	-2	4	2	2	0	-2	0
e_x	0	4	-2	2	-4	0	2	-2	2	2	0	0	2	2	0	0
f_x	0	2	2	0	0	2	-2	-4	0	-2	-2	0	-4	2	-2	0

C   Previous 16-round Linear Approximations

Round i	ΓL_{i-1}	ΓR_{i-1}	Number of active S-Boxes	Bias
1	$0w0w000w$	00000000	0	2^{-1}
2	00000000	$0w0w000w$	2	2^{-3}
3	$0w0w000w$	$00z0000z$	3	2^{-4}
4	$00z0000z$	$w0ww000w$	2	2^{-3}
5	$w0ww000w$	$z0zz000z$	2	2^{-3}
6	$z0zz000z$	$00w0000w$	3	2^{-4}
7	$00w0000w$	$0z0z000z$	2	2^{-3}
8	$0z0z000z$	00000000	0	2^{-1}
9	00000000	$0z0z000z$	2	2^{-3}
10	$0z0z000z$	$00w0000w$	3	2^{-4}
11	$00w0000w$	$z0zz000z$	2	2^{-3}
12	$z0zz000z$	$w0ww000w$	2	2^{-3}
13	$w0ww000w$	$00z0000z$	3	2^{-4}
14	$00z0000z$	$0w0w000w$	2	2^{-3}
15	$0w0w000w$	00000000	0	2^{-1}
16	00000000	$0w0w000w$	2	2^{-3}
17	$0w0w000w$	$00z0000z$	-	-

Characterization of EME with Linear Mixing

Nilanjan Datta and Mridul Nandi

Indian Statistical Institute, Kolkata
nilanjan_isi_jrf@yahoo.com, mridul.nandi@gmail.com

Abstract. EME is a SPRP or strong pseudorandom permutation construction which uses a nonlinear mixing in between two encryption layers. The designers of EME have shown that the construction is not SPRP secure if the mixing layer of EME is replaced by any linear mixing over a binary field. In this paper, we complete their observation by showing SPRP-insecurity even if we have linear mixing over any non-binary prime field. We have some positive result that PRP (pseudorandom permutation) and online PRP security can be achieved for certain types of linear mixing functions. In fact, we fully characterize all those linear mixing for which (online) PRP security is achieved and demonstrate attacks for all other linear mixing functions.

Keywords: EME, SPRP, (online) PRP, Distinguishing Attack.

1 Introduction

A mode of operation is a method of constructing an encryption algorithm which can encrypt arbitrary length messages. It generally uses a blockcipher as an underlying object and possibly some algebraic operations such as finite field operations. SPRP (Strong Pseudo Random Permutation) is a strong security requirement of an encryption scheme. A chosen plaintext adaptive adversary (CPA) can make queries to the encryption oracle only. Whereas, a chosen plaintext ciphertext adaptive adversary (CCA) can make queries to both encryption and decryption oracles. For a SPRP (or PRP) secure encryption scheme, no CCA (or respectively, CPA) adversary can distinguish the construction from a random permutation. The basic known paradigms of popularly known SPRP based constructions can be described as follows:

Hash-Encrypt-Hash:
  This type of SPRP constructions consists of an Encryption layer between two layers of invertible hash. This type of constructions was first introduced by Naor-Reingold [17]. Later, similar approach is considered in constructions like PEP [5], TET [12] and HEH [19].

Hash-Counter-Hash: In this category of SPRP constructions, the first hash function layer is used to generate counter. Based on the counter, one obtains ciphertext in stream cipher mode. Finally, the ciphertext is hashed using the second hash layer. This approach is first observed in the original proposal of XCB [14].

M. Yoshida and K. Mouri (Eds.): IWSEC 2014, LNCS 8639, pp. 221–239, 2014.
© Springer International Publishing Switzerland 2014

Later, following this paradigm, various constructions like HCTR [8], HCH [6] and MXCB [16] have been proposed.

Encrypt Mix Encrypt: In this category of SPRP constructions, a nonlinear mixing layer is used in between two encryption layers. This approach was introduced by Halevi and Rogaway in CMC [9]. Later constructions like EME [10] and EME* [11] (a variant of EME which can incorporate arbitrary length messages) use this approach.

1.1 EME Encryption Scheme

EME [10] is a blockcipher mode of operation, that turns an n-bit blockcipher into a tweakable enciphering scheme that acts on strings of ℓn bits, where $\ell \in [1..n] := \{1, 2, \ldots, n\}$. So, EME is defined for all plaintext having less or equal to n blocks (n-bit strings). The mode is parallelizable, but as serial-efficient as the non-parallelizable mode CMC [9]. EME algorithm entails two layers of ECB encryption with a standard masking and a nonlinear mixing based on the blockcipher in between (see Fig. 1 below). It is proved to provide SPRP [13] security in the standard, provable security model assuming that the underlying blockcipher E_K is SPRP.

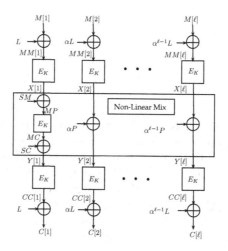

Fig. 1. EME Construction [10]. Enciphering a ℓ-block message $(M[1], M[2], \ldots, M[\ell])$ under EME. Here $L = \alpha E_K(0^n)$, $SM = \oplus_{i=2}^{\ell} X[i] \oplus T$, $P = MP \oplus MC$ and $SC = \oplus_{i=2}^{\ell} Y[i] \oplus T$, where T denotes the tweak.

1.2 Motivation

Motivation of this paper is to analyze simplified variant of EME for which the middle layer of nonlinear function is replaced by a linear function mix. We denote this as $\mathsf{EME}_{\mathsf{mix}}$ or $\mathsf{EME}_{\mathsf{mix}}^{E_K}$ where E_K is the underlying blockcipher (an illustration is given in Fig. 3 in section 3). Replacing nonlinear mixing by linear mixing actually helps to have faster and parallel implementation of the construction as the invocation of middle layer blockcipher causes a bottleneck in hardware. However, the designers of EME showed that, if nonlinear mixing is replaced by any binary linear mixing then there exists a CCA-distinguisher making only four queries which can distinguish it from a random permutation. But it seems that attack cannot be extended (i) for weaker adversaries such as CPA and/or (ii) in any underlying non-binary field (as they have exploited "characteristic 2" property of the binary field). Thus, it is an interesting problem to study how much security can be achieved from this simplified variant of EME with linear mixing when the linear mixing may be based on any non-binary field.

Online Encryption. We also note that, the given construction is meant to provide SPRP or PRP in which every block of a ciphertext depends on all blocks of corresponding plaintext. In a weaker version of an encryption scheme, called online encryption, we demand dependency between ciphertext and plaintext in an online manner. More precisely, the ith block of ciphertext only depends on the first i blocks of plaintext, not on the subsequent blocks. The advantage of an online encryption is that the ciphertext can be efficiently computed in low-end devices or platforms with limited memory. Moreover, the computation can be made in online manner. In other words, even if the last plaintext block is not received, all the ciphertext blocks except the last block can be computed and released. Whenever the last block of plaintext is reached, the final ciphertext block can be computed efficiently. This property may not hold for a general encryption scheme.

It is easy to observe that if we use linear mix function which is online computable (characterized by a lower triangular matrix) then the encryption scheme becomes an online encryption as the ECB layers are completely parallel. We have the indistinguishable security notions for these types of constructions, namely online PRP and online SPRP. Informally, we try to distinguish from the ideal function which returns all random blocks after maintaining the online property. So our problem of studying security properties can be extended to possibilities of using online linear mixing.

1.3   Our Contribution

In this paper, we obtain the following results:

1. **Positive results:** First we define two specific classes of invertible linear mixing functions Lmix (all entries in matrix representation is non-zero) and online linear mixing functions OLmix (lower triangular matrices with all entries in lower triangular part are non-zero) over any field (including binary field) in section 3. We prove that EME with any mixing function from Lmix (or OLmix) achieves PRP security (or online PRP security respectively) in section 4.

2. **Negative results:** In subsection 3.2, we show that all other (online) linear mixing functions over any field cannot provide (online) PRP security (i.e. insecure against CPA adversary). Moreover, in section 5, we show that EME with any linear mixing (even from these two classes) doesn't provide SPRP or online SPRP security, not just in the binary field (already shown by the authors of EME) but also in any other non-binary field.

Thus, we fully characterize all linear mixing in EME type constructions which can provide security. One can use this as a basic building block to construct encryption mechanism which requires PRP security, e.g., authenticated encryption [1]. Two such already known constructions are COPA [2] and ELmE [7].

2   Preliminaries

Let $\mathbb{B} := \{0,1\}^n$ be the set of all n-bit strings for a fixed integer n. In this paper an n-bit string is also called a **block**. With the canonical encoding, we equivalently view blocks as elements of the Galois field $\mathbf{GF}(2^n)$. Let α denote a primitive element of the field. Let $x := (x[1], x[2], \ldots, x[\ell]) \in \mathbb{B}^\ell$ be an ℓ-tuple. We call $\ell := \|x\|$ block-length of x. For $1 \le a \le b \le \ell$, we denote $x[a..b] := (x[a], x[a+1], \ldots, x[b])$ and $x[..b] = x[1..b]$. We denote a q-tuple $(v_1, \ldots, v_q)$ by $\tilde{v}$, where $v_i \in \mathbb{B}^+ := \bigcup_{j=1}^{\infty} \mathbb{B}^j, \forall i$.

2.1   Online Function and Permutation

An online function is a length preserving function whose i^{th} output block is determined from the first i input blocks. So, a function f is said to be an **online function** if

$$\forall i, \ (x[1..i] = x'[1..i]) \ \Rightarrow \ (f(x)[1..i] = f(x')[1..i]). \tag{1}$$

In other words, the ith block of $f(x)$ is functionally independent of $x[i+1], x[i+2], \cdots$. An online function is called an **online permutation** if the function itself is a permutation. One can easily check that f is an online permutation if and only if

$$\forall i, \ (x[1..i] = x'[1..i]) \ \Leftrightarrow \ (f(x)[1..i] = f(x')[1..i]). \tag{2}$$

We say that a tuple $(Q_1, R_1, \ldots, Q_q, R_q)$ is **online permutation compatible** if for all $s \ne s'$ and all i, $(Q_s[1..i] = Q_{s'}[1..i]) \ \Leftrightarrow \ (R_s[1..i] = R_{s'}[1..i])$.

2.2   Security Definitions

Let A be a probabilistic adversary with it's random coin r_A. Let f_K and g_L be two keyed functions. We define the distinguishing advantage of A distinguishing f_K from g_L as:

$$\mathbf{Adv}_f^g(A) = \ \Pr_{L, r_A}[A^{g_L} = 1] - \Pr_{K, r_A}[A^{f_K} = 1]$$

where the two probabilities are computed under randomness of keys L and K respectively and r_A. In this paper, we give a particularly strong definition of privacy, one asserting indistinguishability from random strings. Consider an adversary A who has access of one of two types of oracles: a "real" encryption oracle f_K or an "ideal" encryption oracle g_K (also denoted $). A real encryption oracle takes an input M and returns $C = f_K(M)$. Whereas, an ideal encryption oracle $ returns a random string R with $\|R\| = \|M\|$, for every fresh message M. Given an adversary A and an encryption scheme f_K, we define the **prf-advantage** of A by the distinguishing advantage of A distinguishing f from $. More formally,

$$\mathbf{Adv}_f^{\mathrm{prf}}(A) := \mathbf{Adv}_f^{\$}(A) = \Pr_{\$,r_A}[A^{\$} = 1] - \Pr_{K,r_A}[A^{f_K} = 1].$$

We define the maximum prf-advantage $\mathbf{Adv}_f^{\mathrm{prf}}(q, \sigma, t) = \max_A \mathbf{Adv}_f^{\mathrm{prf}}(A)$ where the maximum is taken over all algorithms A which run in time t, make queries at most q with the total number of blocks at most σ. For unbounded time adversaries (i.e $t = \infty$), we simply write $\mathbf{Adv}_f^{\mathrm{prf}}(q, \sigma) := \mathbf{Adv}_f^{\mathrm{prf}}(q, \sigma, \infty)$.

We define the **olprf-advantage** of A against f as the distinguishing advantage of f_K from the ideal online function $g_L := \$_{ol}$ which responses random string keeping the online property. In notation, $\mathbf{Adv}_f^{\mathrm{olprf}}(A) := \mathbf{Adv}_f^{\$_{ol}}(A)$. Similarly, we define maximum olprf-advantage $\mathbf{Adv}_f^{\mathrm{olprf}}(q, \sigma, t)$ and $\mathbf{Adv}_f^{\mathrm{olprf}}(q, \sigma)$ for unbounded adversary. In this paper, we study the above two security properties when we prove the security for EME. By switching lemma [3] between random function and random permutation one can extend the analysis for (online) pseudorandom permutation advantage. A more strong definition of security for an encryption scheme f_K is given by the (online) SPRP notion which is similar to the (online) PRP notion except that the adversary has the power of accessing decryption oracle as well, i.e., it is a CCA adversary. Formally,

$$\mathbf{Adv}_f^{\mathrm{sprp}}(A) = \mathbf{Adv}_{f,f^{-1}}^{\Pi,\Pi^{-1}}(A) = \Pr_{\Pi,r_A}[A^{\Pi,\Pi^{-1}} = 1] - \Pr_{K,r_A}[A^{f_K,f_K^{-1}} = 1]$$

and $\mathbf{Adv}_f^{\mathrm{osprp}}(A) = \mathbf{Adv}_{f,f^{-1}}^{\Pi_{ol},\Pi_{ol}^{-1}}(A)$ where Π and Π_{ol} denote uniform random and online uniform random permutation respectively, over the domain same as that of f_K.

2.3 View and A-Realizable

For this subsection, we consider **deterministic unbounded time adversaries**. It is well known that unbounded deterministic distinguishers are as powerful as probabilistic because a deterministic distinguisher can run with a fixed random coin for which the advantage is maximum. For more details, we refer to section 2.2, assumption 1 in [15]. We define view of a deterministic unbounded time adversary A interacting with an oracle $\mathcal{O}$ by a tuple $\tau(A^{\mathcal{O}}) := (Q_1, R_1, \ldots, Q_q, R_q)$ where Q_i is the ith query and R_i is the response by $\mathcal{O}$. It is also called $\mathcal{O}$-view. A tuple $\tau = (Q_1, R_1, \ldots, Q_q, R_q)$ is called A-realizable if it makes query Q_i after obtaining all previous responses $R_1, \ldots, R_{i-1}$. As A is assumed to be deterministic, given $R_1, \ldots, R_q$, there is a unique q-tuple $Q_1, \ldots, Q_q$ for which the combined tuple is A-realizable. Now we describe the popular **coefficient H-technique** which would be used here to bound distinguish advantages. Suppose f and g are two oracles and V denotes all possible A-realizable views while A interacts with f or g (they must have same input and output space).

Lemma 1 (Coefficient H Technique [18, 20]). *Let A be a deterministic unbounded time adversary and $V_{good} \subseteq V$ such that*

$$\forall v \in V_{good}, \quad \Pr[\tau(A^f) = v] \geq (1 - \epsilon)\Pr[\tau(A^g) = v],$$

then $\mathbf{Adv}_f^g(A) \leq \epsilon + \Pr[\tau(A^g) \notin V_{good}]$.

Proof. The given condition says that $\Pr[\tau(A^g) = v] - \Pr[\tau(A^f) = v] \leq \epsilon \times \Pr[\tau(A^f) = v]$ for all $v \in V_{good}$. Now,

$$\mathbf{Adv}_f^g(A) = \Pr[A^g = 1] - \Pr[A^f = 1]$$

$$= \sum_{v \in V} (\Pr[\tau(A^g) = v] - \Pr[\tau(A^f) = v])$$

$$= \sum_{v \notin V_{good}} (\Pr[\tau(A^g) = v] - \Pr[\tau(A^f) = v])$$

$$+ \sum_{v \in V \cap V_{good}} (\Pr[\tau(A^g) = v] - \Pr[\tau(A^f) = v])$$

$$\leq \Pr[\tau(A^g) \notin V_{good}] + \epsilon \times \sum_{v \in V \cap V_{good}} \Pr[\tau(A^f) = v]$$

$$\leq \Pr[\tau(A^g) \notin V_{good}] + \epsilon. \qquad \square$$

Note that as A is a deterministic adversary, $\Pr[\tau(A^f) = v]$ doesn't depend on A for all A-realizable views $v = (Q_1, R_1, \ldots, Q_q, R_q)$ and is given by:

$$\Pr_f[\tau(A^f) = v] = \Pr_f[f(Q_1) = R_1, \ldots, f(Q_q) = R_q].$$

The probability in the right hand side is also called interpolation probability [4]. Similar equality for g holds. When g is a random function, all Q_i's are distinct and $\|Q_i\| = \|R_i\|$ for all i, then $\Pr[\tau(A^\$) = v] = 2^{-n\sigma}$ where $\sigma := \sigma(\widetilde{Q}) = \sum_i \|Q_i\|$ denotes the number of blocks present in all queries and $\widetilde{Q} = (Q_1, \ldots, Q_q)$. Similarly, whenever v satisfies the online property (i.e. v is online permutation compatible), $\Pr[\tau(A^{\$_{ol}}) = v] = 2^{-n\sigma_{ol}}$ where $\sigma_{ol} := \sigma_{ol}(\widetilde{Q})$ denotes the size of the set of all prefixes of queries

$$\mathbb{P}(\widetilde{Q}) := \{Q_i[..j] : 1 \leq j \leq \|Q_i\|, 1 \leq i \leq q\}.$$

How to Use Coefficient H-Technique

Lemma 1 is a very useful tool to prove indistinguishability of two functions f and g under deterministic unbounded adversaries. For example, when we want to bound $\mathbf{Adv}_f^{\mathrm{prf}}(q, \sigma)$, we need to identify a set of good views V_{good} appropriately (which depends on the construction f) such that the following conditions hold.

1. $\Pr[\tau(A^\$) \notin V_{good}] \le \epsilon'$ for some small ϵ'. The computation of ϵ' is usually easy even for an adaptive unbounded time adversary A as we need to deal with random function.

2. The interpolation probability

$$\Pr_K[f_K(Q_1) = R_1, \ldots, f_K(Q_q) = R_q] \ge (1 - \epsilon)2^{-n\sigma}$$

for some ϵ. The computation of this probability is purely combinatorial as we do not need to deal with any adversary. This may not be simple as we need to count the number of functions f_K for which it gives output R_i for the input Q_i, for all $1 \le i \le q$.

After we establish both, the coefficient H-technique tells us that distinguishing probability is bounded above by $(\epsilon + \epsilon')$. Similar treatment can be applied for bounding $\mathbf{Adv}_f^{\mathrm{olprf}}(q, \sigma)$. Here we have to show that $\Pr_K[f_K(Q_1) = R_1, \ldots, f_K(Q_q) = R_q] \ge (1 - \epsilon)2^{-n\sigma_{ol}}$ as $2^{-n\sigma_{ol}}$ is the interpolation probability for a random online function $\$_{ol}$.

3 $\mathsf{EME}_{\mathsf{mix}}$: A General Form of EME with Linear Mixing

Suppose for each $i \ge 1$, mix^i is a linear function from $\mathbb{B}^i$ to $\mathbb{B}^i$ with its matrix representation $B^i = ((b_{r,s}^i))$. To any such sequence $\mathsf{mix} := \langle \mathsf{mix}^i \rangle_i$ of linear functions, we associate an encryption scheme $\mathsf{EME}_{\mathsf{mix}}$ based on a random masking key L and an underlying blockcipher E_K which is defined as below.

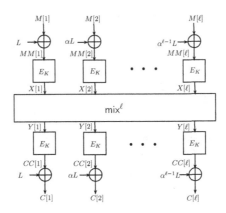

Fig. 2. Encrypt-Mix-Encrypt construction with a linear mix function mix^ℓ in the place of a nonlinear function used in EME

Algorithm EME$_{mix}$,   mix $= \langle mix^i \rangle_i$.
Input: $M = (M[1], \ldots, M[\ell]) \in \mathbb{B}^\ell$.
Key: Blockcipher key K and masking key $L \in \mathbb{B}$.
Output: $C = (C[1], \ldots, C[\ell]) \in \mathbb{B}^\ell$.

- Layer-1 (Input Masking Layer): $MM[j] = M[j] + \alpha^{j-1}L$, $1 \le j \le \ell$.
- Layer-2 (1st Encrypt Layer) : $X[j] = E_K(MM[j])$, $1 \le j \le \ell$.
- Layer-3 (Linear Mix Layer) : $Y[i] = \sum_{j=1}^{\ell} b_{i,j}^\ell \cdot X[j]$, $1 \le i \le \ell$.
- Layer-4 (2nd Encrypt Layer) : $CC[j] = E_K(Y[j])$, $1 \le j \le \ell$.
- Layer-5 (Output Masking Layer) : $C[j] = CC[j] + \alpha^{j-1}L$, $1 \le j \le \ell$.

Clearly, mix^i needs to be invertible to make the algorithm invertible. We only consider invertible linear functions (so the matrices are invertible). In case of an online encryption scheme, the sequence mix cannot be an arbitrary sequence of lower triangular matrices. To achieve online property, the elements of the matrices must be functionally independent of ℓ, the size of the mix functions. More formally, for all $i \le \ell < \ell'$ and all j, $b_{i,j}^\ell = b_{i,j}^{\ell'}$ (which is equal to 0 whenever $j > i$). In this paper, we are interested in the following two types of sequences **of linear invertible mixing functions** - Online linear mixing function OLmix and full linear mixing function Lmix (which is not online). Here $B^\ell := ((b_{i,j}^\ell))$ denotes the $(\ell \times \ell)$ matrix corresponding to mix$^\ell$.

1. **OLmix**: A sequence $\langle mix^i \rangle_i$ is said to be of type OLmix if $\forall \ell, \forall j \le i \le \ell$, $b_{i,j}^\ell = b_{i,j} \ne 0$ and for all other $i > j$, $b_{i,j} = 0$. So the layer-3 becomes $Y[i] = \sum_{j=1}^{i} b_{i,j} \cdot X[j]$,
2. **Lmix**: A sequence $\langle mix^i \rangle_i$ is said to be of type Lmix if $\forall \ell, \forall i, j \le \ell$, $b_{i,j}^\ell \ne 0$.

Examples of mix functions of types OLmix and Lmix are given as follows:

$$B_{Lmix}^\ell = \begin{pmatrix} \alpha & 1 & \cdots & 1 \\ 1 & \alpha & \cdots & 1 \\ \vdots & \vdots & \vdots & \vdots \\ 1 & 1 & \cdots & \alpha \end{pmatrix} \qquad B_{OLmix}^\ell = \begin{pmatrix} 1 & 0 & \cdots & 0 \\ (\alpha+1) & 1 & \cdots & 0 \\ \vdots & & \vdots & \vdots \\ \alpha^{\ell-2}(\alpha+1) & \alpha^{\ell-3}(\alpha+1) & \cdots & 1 \end{pmatrix}$$

One can check that these matrices are invertible. Thus $\langle B_{Lmix}^\ell \rangle$ and $\langle B_{OLmix}^\ell \rangle$ are examples of type Lmix and OLmix respectively. Note that, the matrix B_{OLmix} used in the construction ELmE [7]. Before we make security analysis we first study why we consider these two types of mix functions in the following subsection.

3.1   Necessity of Lmix (or OLmix) for Security of EME$_{mix}$

Suppose, the mix function used is not Lmix. Hence at least one entry of B^ℓ matrix is zero for some ℓ. Let $b_{i,j}^\ell = 0$. Now we have the following equation for $Y[i]$:

$$Y[i] = \sum_{k \ne j} b_{i,k}^\ell X[k]$$

Since $Y[i]$ is independent of $X[j]$, hence any two messages M_1 and M_2 with ℓ many blocks whose all blocks are same except the jth block would yield $C_1[i] = C_2[i]$ with probability one (for a random function this can happen with probability 2^{-n}). This breaks the prf security of the construction. This shows the necessity of Lmix to obtain PRP or PRF security of the construction.

Similarly, the necessity of OLmix can be shown in order to obtain OLPRP Security of the construction. Suppose, the mix function used is not OLmix. Hence at least one lower triangle entries of B matrix is zero. Assume $b^{\ell}_{i,j} = 0$, where $j \leq i$. Now we have the following equation for $Y[i]$:

$$Y[i] = \sum_{\substack{k \neq j \\ j \leq i}} b^{\ell}_{i,k} X[k]$$

Since $Y[i]$ is independent of $X[j]$, hence any two messages M_1 and M_2 (with ℓ blocks for any $\ell \geq i$) whose all blocks are same except the jth block would yield $C_1[i] = C_2[i]$. As $M_1[..i] \neq M_2[..i]$ this can happen for a random online function with probability 2^{-n}. Hence it breaks the online security.

4 Security Analysis of EME_{mix}

Let $F_{mix} := F^{L,\Pi}_{mix}$ denote the construction EME^{Π}_{mix} for which the underlying blockcipher is replaced by the uniform random permutation Π on n-bits and L is the masking key. Note that whenever mix is of type Lmix, every output block of F_{mix} depends on all input blocks, i.e. it is not an online permutation. Similarly, when mix is of type OLmix it is an online encryption. By using standard hybrid argument, we have

$$\mathbf{Adv}^{prf}_{\mathsf{EME}_{mix}}(q, \sigma, t) \leq \mathbf{Adv}^{prf}_{F_{mix}}(q, \sigma) + \mathbf{Adv}^{prp}_{E}(\sigma, \sigma, t').$$

where $t' = t + O(\sigma)$. The actual value can be determined from the underlying computational model and so we ignore these. Similarly for online prf-advantage:

$$\mathbf{Adv}^{olprf}_{\mathsf{EME}_{mix}}(q, \sigma, t) \leq \mathbf{Adv}^{olprf}_{F_{mix}}(q, \sigma) + \mathbf{Adv}^{prp}_{E}(\sigma, \sigma, t').$$

In this section, we prove the security of F_{mix} which ensures the security for EME_{mix} assuming that the underlying blockcipher is pseudorandom function or permutation. Our main results on security proof can be summarized as follows. Let A be any adversary which makes at most q queries with σ many blocks in all queries. Then the following results hold.

- A can distinguish the F_{mix} online encryption scheme from a random online function \$$_{ol}$, with probability at most $\frac{5\sigma^2}{2^n}$ where mix is of type OLmix.
- A can distinguish the F_{mix} encryption scheme from a random function \$, with probability at most $\frac{5\sigma^2}{2^n}$ where mix is of type Lmix.

The organization of the section is as follows: In section 4.1, we set up all the notations required for the formal proofs. Then, in sections 4.2 and 4.3, we prove Theorem 1 (OLPRF security of F_{OLmix}) using Propositions 1 and 2 and Theorem 2 (PRF security of F_{Lmix}) using Propositions 3 and 4. We prove all the four Propositions in section 4.4.

4.1 Notation Setup and Definitions

Collision relation. Given a tuple $v := (v_i)_{i \in \mathcal{I}}$ where $v_i \in \mathcal{I}$, we define an equivalence relation $\mathsf{Coll}(v)$ on $\mathcal{I}$, called **collision relation**, as follows: $\mathsf{Coll}(v) = \{(i, i') \in \mathcal{I}^2 : v_i = v_{i'}\}$.

Let A be an adversary which makes q queries M_i and obtains responses C_i, $1 \le i \le q$. For simplicity, we assume that all M_i's are distinct. We denote $\|M_i\| = \|C_i\| = \ell_i$. Let $\sigma = \sum_{i=1}^q \ell_i$ denotes the number of blocks. We denote $\mathcal{I} = \{(i, j) : 1 \le j \le \ell_i, 1 \le i \le q\}$, $\widetilde{M} = (M_1, \dots, M_q)$ and $\widetilde{C} = (C_1, \dots, C_q)$. We define $\gamma(\widetilde{M})$, an equivalence relation on $\mathcal{I}$:

$$\gamma(\widetilde{M}) := \{((i,j), (i',j)) \in \mathcal{I}^2 : M_i[j] = M_{i'}[j]\}$$

Similarly, we define $\gamma(\widetilde{C})$. Let $\gamma_1 = \gamma(\widetilde{M})$ and $\gamma_2 := \{((i,j), (i',j)) : M_i[..j] = M_{i'}[..j]\}$. Let the number of equivalence class of γ_i be s_i, $i = 1, 2$.

Internal Variables in the Computation of $F_{\mathsf{mix}}^{L,\Pi}(M_i)$. For notational simplicity, we denote $F := F_{\mathsf{mix}}^{L_0, \pi}$, which is the EME based on the sequence of mix function mix, a permutation π (in place of the blockcipher E_K) and the masking key $L_0 \in \mathbb{B}$. Here L_0 and π are fixed, so no randomness is assumed. While we compute $F(M_i) = C_i$, $1 \le i \le q$, we obtain the following internal variables MM_i, X_i, Y_i, and CC_i which are all ℓ_i-tuple of blocks, $1 \le i \le q$.

Definition 1 (Good Online Views). A view $v = (\widetilde{M}, \widetilde{C})$ is called **good-online view** if $\forall i, j, i', j'$, $(C_i[j] = C_{i'}[j']) \Leftrightarrow (j = j', M_i[..j] = M_{i'}[..j])$.

The condition says that we can have collision of ciphertext blocks in those positions only if those are ciphertexts of two messages with same prefixes up to that block. Clearly, for **good-online view**, we have: $s_1 \le s_2 = \sigma_{ol} \le \sigma$.

Definition 2 (Good Views). A view $v = (\widetilde{M}, \widetilde{C})$ is called **good view** if $C_i[j] \ne C_{i'}[j']$ for all $(i, j) \ne (i', j')$.

The condition says that we do not have any collision in ciphertext blocks. Let $\tau_{good, ol}$ denote set of all good online views and τ_{good} denote set of all good views. Clearly, for **good view**, we have: $s_1 \le s_2 \le \sigma$.

4.2 OLPRF Security of EME$_{\mathsf{OLmix}}$

Let mix be of type OLmix for this subsection. To obtain OLPRF security of F_{mix}, we use two properties: (1) generating good-online views for random online functions is high and (2) for any fixed good-online view, the interpolation probability is high for F_{mix}. We recall that by using coefficient H technique as described in section 2.3, we would be able to bound the online prf advantage. We formally present this two properties in the following two propositions. The proofs of these propositions are given in subsection 4.4. We recall the notation $v = (\widetilde{M}, \widetilde{C})$ where $\widetilde{M} = (M_1, \ldots, M_q)$, $\widetilde{C} = (C_1, \ldots, C_q)$, σ denotes the number of blocks in $\widetilde{M}$ and $\sigma_{ol} = \sigma_{ol}(\widetilde{M})$. The encryption scheme F_{mix} is based on an n-bit uniform random permutation Π and the sequence mix.

Proposition 1 (Obtaining a good-online view has high probability)

$$\Pr[\tau(A^{\$_{ol}}) \notin \tau_{good,ol}] \leq \frac{\sigma^2}{2^n}.$$

Proposition 2 (High interpolation probability of F_{mix}). $\forall v \in \tau_{good,ol}$ with $\sigma_{ol} = \sigma_{ol}(\widetilde{M})$, the number of distinct prefixes present in all queries,

$$\Pr_{L,\Pi}[F_{\text{mix}}^{L,\Pi}(M_1) = C_1, \ldots, F_{\text{mix}}^{L,\Pi}(M_q) = C_q] \geq (1 - \tfrac{4\sigma^2}{2^n}) \times 2^{-n\sigma_{ol}}.$$

Now we state the main theorem of the security of F_{mix} which follows directly from Coefficient H-Technique as described in section 2.3.

Theorem 1. Let mix be of type OLmix. Then, $\mathbf{Adv}_{F_{\text{mix}}}^{\text{olprf}}(q, \sigma) \leq \frac{5\sigma^2}{2^n}.$

Proof. Note that $\Pr[\tau(A^{\$_{ol}}) = v] = 2^{-n\sigma_{ol}}$. So Proposition 2 essentially says that $\forall v \in \tau_{good,ol}$, $\Pr[\tau(A^{F_{\text{mix}}}) = v] \geq (1 - \tfrac{4\sigma^2}{2^n}) \times \Pr[\tau(A^{\$_{ol}}) = v]$. By combining with Proposition 2 in Lemma 1, the proof follows. $\square$

Recall that F_{mix} denotes the construction $\text{EME}_{\text{mix}}^{\Pi}$. Now the advantage of the actual construction, when Π is replaced by the blockcipher E_K, is given by the following corollary:

Corollary 1. $\mathbf{Adv}_{\text{EME}_{\text{mix}}}^{\text{olprf}}(q, \sigma, t) \leq \frac{5\sigma^2}{2^n} + \mathbf{Adv}_E^{\text{prp}}(\sigma, \sigma, t')$, where $t' = t + O(\sigma)$.

4.3   PRF Security of EME_{Lmix}

Let mix be of type Lmix for this subsection. We use similar idea to prove PRP security of EME_{mix}. Here we use two properties: generating good views for random functions is high and the interpolation probability is high for F_{mix}. We formally present this two properties in the following two propositions. The proofs of these propositions are given in the next subsection.

Proposition 3 (Obtaining a good view has high probability)

$$\Pr[\tau(A^{\$}) \notin \tau_{good}] \leq \frac{\sigma^2}{2^n}.$$

Proposition 4 (High interpolation probability of F_{mix}). $\forall v \in \tau_{good}$,

$$\Pr_{L,\Pi}[F_{\text{mix}}^{L,\Pi}(M_1) = C_1, \ldots, F_{\text{mix}}^{L,\Pi}(M_q) = C_q] \geq (1 - \tfrac{4\sigma^2}{2^n}) \times 2^{-n\sigma}.$$

Now we state the main theorem of the security of F_{mix} which follows directly from Coefficient H-Technique as described in section 2.3.

Theorem 2. $\mathbf{Adv}_{F_{mix}}^{prf}(q, \sigma) \leq \frac{5\sigma^2}{2^n}$.

Proof. Note that $\Pr[\tau(A^\$) = v] = 2^{-n\sigma}$. So Proposition 4 essentially says that $\forall v \in \tau_{good}$, $\Pr[\tau(A^{F_{mix}}) = v] \geq (1 - \frac{4\sigma^2}{2^n}) \times \Pr[\tau(A^\$) = v]$. By combining with Proposition 3 in Lemma 1, the proof follows.   □

Similar to the previous one, we have the following corollary from Theorem 2.

Corollary 2. $\mathbf{Adv}_{EME_{mix}}^{olprf}(q, \sigma, t) \leq \frac{5\sigma^2}{2^n} + \mathbf{Adv}_E^{prp}(\sigma, \sigma, t')$, where $t' = t + O(\sigma)$.

4.4   Proof of Propositions 1-4

First we prove that generating good online views for random online functions and good views for random functions are high. In particular, we prove Proposition 1 and Proposition 3.

Proof of Propositions 1 and 3. To prove Proposition 1, we consider the view of an adaptive adversary A while interacting with a random online function. According to the definition, an online view is not a good view if $\exists i, j, i', j'$ with $C_i[j] = C_{i'}[j']$, where $M_i[..j] \neq M_{i'}[..j']$. Suppose $i < i'$ or $i = i', j < j'$. Then $C_i[j]$ is computed by $M_i[..j]$ before the computation of $C_{i'}[j']$. As $M_i[..j] \neq M_{i'}[..j']$, the outcome of $C_{i'}[j']$ is uniform and independent from $C_i[j]$. So, the probability that $C_{i'}[j']$ takes the previously computed fixed value $C_i[j]$ is $\frac{1}{2^n}$. As there are at most $\binom{s_2}{2} \leq \binom{\sigma}{2}$ pairs, Proposition 1 holds.

Similarly, for Proposition 3, we call a view to be not good if $\exists (i, j) \neq (i', j')$ with $C_i[j] = C_{i'}[j']$. With similar argument, one can show that, the probability of $C_{i'}[j]$ taking the previously computed fixed value $C_i[j]$ is $\frac{1}{2^n}$. The Proposition follows as there can be at most $\binom{s_2}{2}$ pairs and $s_2 \leq \sigma$ for good views.   □

Now we prove the high interpolation probability of EME_{OLmix} and EME_{Lmix}. In particular, we prove Proposition 2 and Proposition 4 respectively.

Proof of Propositions 2 and 4. Here we prove Proposition 2. Proposition 4 follows very similar way and so we skip it. To prove it, we need to find a lower bound on the number of elements of the set $E(\widetilde{M}, \widetilde{C}) := \{(L_0, \pi) : F_{mix}^{L_0, \pi}(M_i) = C_i, \forall i\}$. In fact, we bound on all those pairs for which $\widetilde{X} = (X_1, \dots, X_q)$ is good (defined below) in addition with the above event.

Definition 3. *We say a q tuple $\widetilde{x} = (x_1, \dots, x_q)$ with $\|x_i\| = \ell_i$ is **good** if $\mathsf{Coll}(\widetilde{x}) = \gamma_1$ and $\mathsf{Coll}(\widetilde{y}) = \gamma_2$ where $\widetilde{y} = (y_1, \dots, y_q)$ and $y_i = mix^{\ell_i}(x_i)$. Let Good denote the set of all such good tuples.*

Given any $\widetilde{x} \in$ Good (which defines $\widetilde{y}$ as in the definition) we write the set $\mathcal{L}_{\widetilde{x}}$ of all those $L_0 \in \mathbb{B}$ for which the following conditions hold:

1. $\forall((i,j),(i',j')) \notin \gamma(\widetilde{M})$, $M_i[j] + \alpha^{j-1}L_0 \neq M_{i'}[j'] + \alpha^{j'-1}L_0$,
2. $\forall((i,j),(i',j')) \notin \gamma(\widetilde{C})$, $C_i[j] + \alpha^{j-1}L_0 \neq C_{i'}[j'] + \alpha^{j'-1}L_0$,
3. $\forall((i,j),(i',j')) \in \mathcal{I}$, $M_i[j] + \alpha^{j-1}L_0 \neq y_{i'}[j']$,
4. $\forall((i,j),(i',j')) \in \mathcal{I}$, $C_i[j] + \alpha^{j-1}L_0 \neq x_{i'}[j']$

Now we prove the following main claims which are required to bound the number of pairs $(L_0, \pi) \in E(\widetilde{M}, \widetilde{C})$.

Claim: (1) $|\mathsf{Good}| \geq (1 - \frac{\sigma^2}{2^n})2^{ns_1}$ and (2) for all $\widetilde{x} \in \mathsf{Good}$, $|\mathcal{L}_{\widetilde{x}}| \geq 2^n - 3\sigma^2$.

The proof of the claim is postponed to after this proposition. Now we continue with the proof of the proposition by using the claim. Note that any pair (L_0, π) uniquely determines $\widetilde{X}$. We say that **the pair (L_0, π) is good if the corresponding $\widetilde{X}$ is good.** For any good $\widetilde{x}$, and $L_0 \in \mathcal{L}_{\widetilde{x}}$, the set of of all permutations π which satisfies the given event is same as the set

$$\{\pi : \pi(MM_i[j]) = x_i[j], \ \pi(y_i[j]) = CC_i[j]\}$$

where $\widetilde{MM}$ and $\widetilde{CC}$ are computed from L_0, $\widetilde{M}$ and $\widetilde{C}$. As there are $s_1 + s_2$ input-output for π, the number of such permutation is exactly $(2^n - s_1 - s_2)!$. So, the number of pairs (L_0, π) for which $\widetilde{X} = \widetilde{x}$ and satisfies $E(\widetilde{M}, \widetilde{C})$ is at least $(2^n - s_1 - s_2)! \times (2^n - 3\sigma^2)$. Since, there are $2^{ns_1}(1 - \frac{\sigma^2}{2^n})$ many good tuples $\widetilde{x}$ (from claim 1), the number of pairs $(L_0, \pi) \in E(\widetilde{M}, \widetilde{C})$, which are also good is at least $2^n! \times 2^{-n(s_2-1)}(1 - \frac{4\sigma^2}{2^n})$. As the total number of pairs (L_0, π) is exactly $2^n! \times 2^n$, the proposition follows. $\qquad \square$

Proof of Claim (1): Recall that $\widetilde{x} \in \mathsf{Good}$ if $\mathsf{Coll}(\widetilde{x}) = \gamma_1$ and $\mathsf{Coll}(\widetilde{y}) = \gamma_2$ which means the following 4 conditions hold for all i, i', j, j':

1. $x_i[j] = x_{i'}[j']$ if $M_i[j] = M_i[j']$.
2. $x_i[j] \neq x_{i'}[j']$ if $M_i[j] \neq M_{i'}[j']$.
3. $y_i[j] = y_{i'}[j']$ if $j = j'$, $M_i[..j] = M_{i'}[..j]$.
4. $y_i[j] \neq y_{i'}[j']$ if $M_i[..j] \neq M_{i'}[..j']$.

Total number of $\widetilde{x}$ which satisfies condition 1 is exactly 2^{ns_1} as s_1 is the number of equivalence classes of $\gamma(\widetilde{M})$ and so we can choose x-values freely for all equivalence classes. It is easy to see that condition 1 implies condition 3 (since, $M_i[..j] = M_{i'}[..j]$ implies $\forall k \leq j$, $x_i[k] = x_{i'}[k]$ and hence $y_i[j] = y_{i'}[j]$). Now we count the number of non-good (i.e., not good) tuples $\widetilde{x}$ satisfying condition 1. This can happen in two following cases.

Case-1. $\widetilde{x}$ satisfies condition 1 (and so condition 3) but doesn't satisfy condition 2. This can happen if there exists $((i,j),(i',j')) \notin \gamma(\widetilde{M})$ and $x_i[j] = x_{i'}[j']$. For any such fixed $((i,j),(i',j'))$, the number of $\widetilde{x}$ is $2^{n(s_1-1)}$, as we can choose (s_1-1) many x-values freely. The number of such (unordered) pair $((i,j),(i',j'))$ is at most $\binom{\sigma}{2}$ and so we have $\binom{\sigma}{2}2^{n(s_1-1)}$ many tuples satisfying condition 1 but not condition 2.

Case-2. $\widetilde{x}$ satisfies condition 1 but doesn't satisfy condition 4. So, $\exists((i,j),(i',j'))$ such that $y_i[j] = y_{i'}[j']$ and $M_i[..j] \neq M_{i'}[..j']$. Now, $M_i[..j] \neq M_{i'}[..j']$ can happen in one of the following 2 ways:

- $M_i[..j] = M_{i'}[..j]$ but $j \neq j'$ (so assume $j < j'$). In this case, if we write $y_i[j]$ and $y_{i'}[j']$ in terms of x-variables then

$$y_i[j] = y_{i'}[j'] \Rightarrow \sum_{k=j+1}^{j'} b_{j',k} x_{i'}[k] = 0.$$

So we need to choose $x_{i'}[k]$ freely for all $k \in \{j+1, \ldots, j'\}$ satisfying this relation. The relation is non-trivial as all $b_{j',k} \neq 0$. Hence, for any such fixed $((i,j),(i',j'))$, the number of $\widetilde{x}$ is exactly $2^{n(s_1-1)}$.

- There exists $r \leq j$ such that $M_i[r] \neq M_{i'}[r]$ and let us assume that r is the minimum such index. So,

$$y_i[j] = y_{i'}[j'] \Rightarrow b_{j,r} x_i[r] - b_{j',r} x_{i'}[r] = \sum_{k=r+1}^{j'} b_{j',k} x_{i'}[k] - \sum_{k=r+1}^{j} b_{j,k} x_i[k].$$

Again, it is a non-trivial equation as $x_i[r]$ and $x_{i'}[r]$ would be chosen freely (since $M_i[r] \neq M_{i'}[r]$) from all other x-variables involved in the equations and $b_{j,r}, b_{j',r} \neq 0$. Hence, for any such fixed $((i,j),(i',j'))$, the number of $\widetilde{x}$ is exactly $2^{n(s_1-1)}$.

As we can choose at most $\binom{\sigma}{2}$ many pairs $((i,j),(i',j'))$ in either cases, we have at most $\binom{\sigma}{2} 2^{n(s_1-1)}$ many tuples satisfying condition 1 but not condition 4. Thus, the number of good tuples is at least $2^{ns_1} - 2\binom{\sigma}{2} 2^{n(s_1-1)}$. Hence, the claim follows. □

Proof of Claim (2): If $L_0 \notin \mathcal{L}_{\widetilde{x}}$, then one of the four cases occurs:

Case 1: $L_0 = \frac{(M_i[j] + M_{i'}[j'])}{\alpha^{j-1} + \alpha^{j'-1}}$, for some $((i,j),(i',j')) \notin \gamma_1$. This occurs for at most $\binom{s_1}{2}$ cases.

Case 2: $L_0 = \frac{(C_i[j] + C_{i'}[j'])}{\alpha^{j-1} + \alpha^{j'-1}}$, for some $((i,j),(i',j')) \notin \gamma_2$. This occurs for at most $\binom{s_2}{2}$ cases.

Case 3: $L_0 = \frac{(M_i[j] + Y_{i'}[j'])}{\alpha^{j-1}}$, for some $((i,j),(i',j')) \in \mathcal{I}$. This occurs for at most $s_1.s_2$ cases.

Case 4: $L_0 = \frac{(C_i[j] + X_{i'}[j'])}{\alpha^{j-1}}$, for some $((i,j),(i',j')) \in \mathcal{I}$. This occurs for at most $s_1.s_2$ cases.

So, the size of $\mathbb{B} \setminus \mathcal{L}_{\widetilde{x}}$ is at most $3\sigma^2$ (as $s_1 \leq s_2 \leq \sigma$). Hence, the claim follows. □

5   SPRP Attack against $\mathsf{EME}_{\mathsf{mix}}$ for Any Underlying Field

In this section, we show an SPRP attack against this construction. First, we revisit the attack that authors proposed in the paper [10] to prove that the construction with linear mix doesn't provide SPRP security. We give a distinguisher D that attacks the mode, distinguishing it from a Pseudo random permutation and its inverse using only 4 queries. We recall that $A = ((a_{i,j}))$ is the inverse matrix of $B = ((b_{i,j}))$.

Revisiting SPRP Attack against EME$_{mix}$ for Binary Field

1. D queries two messages $M_1 = (M_1[1], M_1[2], M_1[3])$ and $M_2 = (M_2[1], M_1[2], M_1[3])$ where $M_2[1] \neq M_1[1]$. Let $C_1 = (C_1[1], C_1[2], C_1[3])$ and $C_2 = (C_2[1], C_2[2], C_2[3])$ be the responses, respectively.

2. Now, D queries two ciphertexts $C_3 = (C_1[1], C_2[2], C_2[3])$ and $C_4 = (C_2[1], C_1[2], C_1[3])$. Let $M_3 = (M_3[1], M_3[2], M_3[3])$ and $M_4 = (M_4[1], M_4[2], M_4[3])$ be the respective responses.

3. If $M_3[1] \neq M_4[1]$ and $\forall j > 1$, $M_3[j] = M_4[j]$; then D returns 1 (meaning the real). Else D returns 0 (i.e. the random).

Logic Behind the Attack. The main observation is that, $\forall i : Y_3[i] + Y_4[i] = Y_1[i] + Y_2[i]$ as the underlying field is binary. The authors use this property to mount the attack. The detail is given below:
$\forall j = 1, 2, 3$ we have,

$$\begin{aligned}
X_3[j] + X_4[j] &= (a_{j,1}Y_3[1] + a_{j,2}Y_3[2] + a_{j,3}Y_3[3]) + (a_{j,1}Y_4[1] + a_{j,2}Y_4[2] + a_{j,3}Y_4[3]) \\
&= a_{j,1}(Y_3[1] + Y_4[1]) + a_{j,2}(Y_3[2] + Y_4[2]) + a_{j,3}(Y_3[3] + Y_4[3]) \\
&= a_{j,1}(Y_2[1] + Y_1[1]) + a_{j,2}(Y_1[2] + Y_2[2]) + a_{j,3}(Y_1[3] + Y_2[3]) \\
&= (a_{j,1}Y_1[1] + a_{j,2}Y_1[2] + a_{j,3}Y_1[3]) + (a_{j,1}Y_2[1] + a_{j,2}Y_2[2] + a_{j,3}Y_2[3]) \\
&= X_2[j] + X_1[j]
\end{aligned}$$

Clearly for $j = 2$ and 3, $(X_2[j] = X_1[j]) \Rightarrow (X_3[j] = X_4[j])$. Similarly $(X_2[1] \neq X_1[1]) \Rightarrow (X_3[1] \neq X_4[1])$.

Now, the question raise is what about the security of EME$_{mix}$ when the underlying field is not binary. In the following two subsections, we prove that, ELE$_{mix}$ doesn't provide SPRP even in non-binary fields.

5.1 SPRP Attack for against OLmix Type mix Functions

Here we show an SPRP attack against the EME construction that uses mix function of type OLmix, over any field (not necessarily binary field).

1. D queries two messages $M_1 = (M_1[1], M_1[2], M_1[3])$ and $M_2 = (M_1[1], M_2[2], M_1[3])$ where $M_2[2] \neq M_1[2]$. Let $C_1 = (C_1[1], C_1[2], C_1[3])$ and $C_2 = (C_1[1], C_2[2], C_2[3])$ be the responses, respectively.

2. Now, D queries two ciphertexts $C_3 = (C_3[1], C_1[2], C_1[3])$ and $C_4 = (C_3[1], C_2[2], C_2[3])$ where $C_3[1] \neq C_1[1]$. Let $M_3 = (M_3[1], M_3[2], M_3[3])$ and $M_4 = (M_4[1], M_4[2], M_4[3])$ be the respective responses.

3. If $M_3[3] = M_4[3]$; then D returns 1 (meaning the real). Else D returns 0 (i.e. the random).

Main idea why the attack works. The main idea of the attack is that the value $M_3[3]$ is calculated using $C_1[2]$ and $C_1[3]$ both of whose values are dependent on the value $M_1[2]$. So, the value of $M_3[3]$ should have an influence of the value $M_1[2]$ but the effects of $M_1[2]$ via $C_1[2]$ and $C_1[3]$ cancels each other out implying the value of $M_1[2]$ has no effect in calculating $M_3[3]$. Using this observation, we mount the attack. The formal proof is as follows:

$$
\begin{aligned}
X_3[3] &= a_{3,1}Y_3[1] + a_{3,2}Y_1[2] + a_{3,3}Y_1[3] \\
&= a_{3,1}Y_3[1] + a_{3,2}(b_{2,1}X_1[1] + b_{2,2}X_1[2]) + a_{3,3}(b_{3,1}X_1[1] + b_{3,2}X_1[2] + b_{3,3}X_1[3]) \\
&= a_{3,1}Y_3[1] + (a_{3,2}b_{2,1} + a_{3,3}b_{3,1})X_1[1] + (a_{3,2}b_{2,2} + a_{3,3}b_{3,2})X_1[2] + a_{3,3}b_{3,3}X_1[3] \\
&= a_{3,1}Y_3[1] + (a_{3,2}b_{2,1} + a_{3,3}b_{3,1})X_1[1] + a_{3,3}b_{3,3}X_1[3] \quad (\text{As } a_{3,2}b_{2,2} + a_{3,3}b_{3,2} = 0)
\end{aligned}
$$

Now, we have,

$$
\begin{aligned}
X_4[3] &= a_{3,1}Y_3[1] + a_{3,2}Y_2[2] + a_{3,3}Y_2[3] \\
&= a_{3,1}Y_3[1] + a_{3,2}(b_{2,1}X_1[1] + b_{2,2}X_2[2]) + a_{3,3}(b_{3,1}X_1[1] + b_{3,2}X_2[2] + b_{3,3}X_1[3]) \\
&= a_{3,1}Y_3[1] + (a_{3,2}b_{2,1} + a_{3,3}b_{3,1})X_1[1] + (a_{3,2}b_{2,2} + a_{3,3}b_{3,2})X_2[2] + a_{3,3}b_{3,3}X_1[3] \\
&= a_{3,1}Y_3[1] + (a_{3,2}b_{2,1} + a_{3,3}b_{3,1})X_1[1] + a_{3,3}b_{3,3}X_1[3] \quad (\text{As } a_{3,2}b_{2,2} + a_{3,3}b_{3,2} = 0) \\
&= X_3[3]
\end{aligned}
$$

Note that, as $A_{(3 \times 3)}$ is the inverse matrix of $B_{(3 \times 3)}$, we have, $a_{3,1}b_{1,2} + a_{3,2}b_{2,2} + a_{3,3}b_{3,2} = 0$. Now, since A is a lower triangular matrix, so is B, which implies $b_{1,2} = 0$. Hence, the equality $a_{3,2}b_{2,2} + a_{3,3}b_{3,2} = 0$ is obtained.

5.2   SPRP Attack for Lmix Type mix Functions

Here we show an SPRP attack against the EME construction that uses mix function of type Lmix, over any field.

1. D queries four messages $M_1 = (M_1[1], M_1[2], M_1[3])$, $M_2 = (M_2[1], M_1[2], M_1[3])$, $M_3 = (M_1[1], M_3[2], M_1[3])$ and $M_4 = (M_2[1], M_3[2], M_1[3])$. Let $C_1 = (C_1[1], C_1[2], C_1[3])$, $C_2 = (C_2[1], C_2[2], C_2[3])$, $C_3 = (C_3[1], C_3[2], C_3[3])$ and $C_4 = (C_4[1], C_4[2], C_4[3])$ be the responses, respectively.

2. Now, D queries two ciphertexts $C_5 = (C_2[1], C_1[2], C_1[3])$ and $C_6 = (C_4[1], C_3[2], C_3[3])$. Let $M_5 = (M_5[1], M_5[2], M_5[3])$ and $M_6 = (M_6[1], M_6[2], M_6[3])$ be the respective responses.

3. If $M_5[3] = M_6[3]$; then D returns 1 (meaning the real). Else D returns 0 (i.e. the random).

Main idea behind the attack. The main idea of the attack is similar to the previous attack. Here, we observe that the value $M_5[3]$ is calculated using the values $C_2[1]$, $C_1[2]$ and $C_1[3]$ each of which are dependent on the value $M_1[2]$. So, the value of $M_5[3]$ should have an influence of the value $M_1[2]$ but the combined effects of $M_1[2]$ via $C_2[1]$, $C_1[2]$ and $C_1[3]$ cancels each other out implying the value of $M_1[2]$ has no effect in calculating $M_5[3]$. Using this observation, we mount the attack. The detail is given below:

$$
\begin{aligned}
X_5[3] &= a_{3,1}Y_2[1] + a_{3,2}Y_1[2] + a_{3,3}Y_1[3] \\
&= a_{3,1}(b_{1,1}X_2[1] + b_{1,2}X_1[2] + b_{1,3}X_1[3]) + a_{3,2}(b_{2,1}X_1[1] + b_{2,2}X_1[2] + b_{2,3}X_1[3]) \\
&\quad + a_{3,3}(b_{3,1}X_1[1] + b_{3,2}X_1[2] + b_{3,3}X_1[3]) \\
&= a_{3,1}b_{1,1}X_2[1] + (a_{3,2}b_{2,1} + a_{3,3}b_{3,1})X_1[1] + (a_{3,1}b_{1,2} + a_{3,2}b_{2,2} + a_{3,3}b_{3,2})X_1[2] + \\
&\quad (a_{3,1}b_{1,3} + a_{3,2}b_{2,3} + a_{3,3}b_{3,3})X_1[3] \\
&= a_{3,1}b_{1,1}X_2[1] + (a_{3,2}b_{2,1} + a_{3,3}b_{3,1})X_1[1] + (a_{3,1}b_{1,3} + a_{3,2}b_{2,3} + a_{3,3}b_{3,3})X_1[3]
\end{aligned}
$$

Now we have,

$$
\begin{aligned}
X_6[3] &= a_{3,1}Y_4[1] + a_{3,2}Y_3[2] + a_{3,3}Y_3[3] \\
&= a_{3,1}(b_{1,1}X_2[1] + b_{1,2}X_3[2] + b_{1,3}X_1[3]) + a_{3,2}(b_{2,1}X_1[1] + b_{2,2}X_3[2] + b_{2,3}X_1[3]) \\
&\quad + a_{3,3}(b_{3,1}X_1[1] + b_{3,2}X_3[2] + b_{3,3}X_1[3]) \\
&= a_{3,1}b_{1,1}X_2[1] + (a_{3,2}b_{2,1} + a_{3,3}b_{3,1})X_1[1] + (a_{3,1}b_{1,3} + a_{3,2}b_{2,3} + a_{3,3}b_{3,3})X_1[3] \\
&= X_5[3]
\end{aligned}
$$

Here also, we use the fact $a_{3,1}b_{1,2} + a_{3,2}b_{2,2} + a_{3,3}b_{3,2} = 0$.

6   Conclusion

In this paper, we characterize EME with linear mixing. In particular, we show that, the necessary as well as sufficient condition for EME with linear mixing to have the PRP and OLPRP security, is to use Lmix and OLmix type linear mixing. We also prove that EME with any linear mixing doesn't provide the strong security SPRP, even if the construction is extended to some non-binary fields. Thus our result gives a guideline that, one can have an efficient PRP or OLPRP construction using EME with efficient linear mix having Lmix or OLmix property respectively and for SPRP security based on EME construction the mixing has to be nonlinear.

Acknowledgement. This work is supported by the Centre of Excellence in Cryptology (CoEC) and R.C. Bose Centre, for Cryptology and Security, Indian Statistical Institute, Kolkata.

References

[1] – (no editor): CAESAR: Competition for Authenticated Encryption: Security, Applicability, and Robustness, http://competitions.cr.yp.to/caesar.html. Citations here: §1.3

[2] Andreeva, E., Bogdanov, A., Luykx, A., Mennink, B., Tischhauser, E., Yasuda, K.: Parallelizable and authenticated online ciphers. In: Sako, K., Sarkar, P. (eds.) ASIACRYPT 2013, Part I. LNCS, vol. 8269, pp. 424–443. Springer, Heidelberg (2013). Citations here: §1.3

[3] Bellare, M., Rogaway, P.: The security of triple encryption and a framework for code-based game-playing proofs. In: Vaudenay, S. (ed.) EUROCRYPT 2006. LNCS, vol. 4004, pp. 409–426. Springer, Heidelberg (2006). Citations here: §2.2

[4] Bernstein, D.J.: A short proof of the unpredictability of cipher block chaining (2005), http://cr.yp.to/papers.html#easycbc. Citations here: §2.3

[5] Chakraborty, D., Sarkar, P.: A new mode of encryption providing a tweakable strong pseudo-random permutation. In: Robshaw, M. (ed.) FSE 2006. LNCS, vol. 4047, pp. 293–309. Springer, Heidelberg (2006). Citations here: §1

[6] Chakraborty, D., Sarkar, P.: HCH: A New Tweakable Enciphering Scheme Using the Hash-Encrypt-Hash Approach. In: Barua, R., Lange, T. (eds.) INDOCRYPT 2006. LNCS, vol. 4329, pp. 287–302. Springer, Heidelberg (2006). Citations here: §1

[7] Datta, N., Nandi, M.: Misuse Resistant Parallel Authenticated Encryptions. To be published in ACISP 2014 (2013), http://eprint.iacr.org/2013/767. Citations here: §1.3 §3

[8] Wang, P., Feng, D., Wu, W.: HCTR: A Variable-Input-Length Enciphering Mode. In: Feng, D., Lin, D., Yung, M. (eds.) CISC 2005. LNCS, vol. 3822, pp. 175–188. Springer, Heidelberg (2005). Citations here: §1

[9] Halevi, S., Rogaway, P.: A Tweakable Enciphering Mode. In: Boneh, D. (ed.) CRYPTO 2003. LNCS, vol. 2729, pp. 482–499. Springer, Heidelberg (2003). Citations here: §1 §1.1

[10] Halevi, S., Rogaway, P.: A parallelizable enciphering mode. In: Okamoto, T. (ed.) CT-RSA 2004. LNCS, vol. 2964, pp. 292–304. Springer, Heidelberg (2004). Citations here: §1 §1.1 §1.1, §1.1, §5

[11] Halevi, S.: EME*: Extending EME to handle arbitrary-length messages with associated data. In: Canteaut, A., Viswanathan, K. (eds.) INDOCRYPT 2004. LNCS, vol. 3348, pp. 315–327. Springer, Heidelberg (2004). Citations here: §1

[12] Halevi, S.: Invertible Universal Hashing and the TET Encryption Mode. In: Menezes, A. (ed.) CRYPTO 2007. LNCS, vol. 4622, pp. 412–429. Springer, Heidelberg (2007). Citations here: §1

[13] Luby, M., Racko, C.: How to construct pseudorandom permutations from pseudorandom functions. SIAM Journal of Computing, 373–386 (1988). Citations here: §1.1

[14] McGrew, D., Fluhrer, S.: The Extended Codebook (XCB) Mode of Operation (2004), http://eprint.iacr.org/2004/278. Citations here: §1

[15] Nandi, M.: A Simple and Unified Method of Proving Indistinguishability. In: Barua, R., Lange, T. (eds.) INDOCRYPT 2006. LNCS, vol. 4329, pp. 317–334. Springer, Heidelberg (2006). Citations here: §2.3

[16] Nandi, M.: An Efficient SPRP-secure Construction based on Pseudo Random Involution (2008), http://eprint.iacr.org/2008/092. Citations here: §1

[17] Naor, M., Reingold, O.: On the construction of pseudorandom permutations: Luby-Racko revisited. Journal of Cryptology, 29–66 (1999). Citations here: §1

[18] Patarin, J.: The "Coefficients H" Technique. In: Avanzi, R.M., Keliher, L., Sica, F. (eds.) SAC 2008. LNCS, vol. 5381, pp. 328–345. Springer, Heidelberg (2009)

[19] Sarkar, P.: Improving Upon the TET Mode of Operation. In: Nam, K.-H., Rhee, G. (eds.) ICISC 2007. LNCS, vol. 4817, pp. 180–192. Springer, Heidelberg (2007). Citations here: §1

[20] Vaudenay, S.: Decorrelation: A Theory for Block Cipher Security. Journal of Cryptology, 249–286 (2003)

Exponentiation Inversion Problem Reduced from Fixed Argument Pairing Inversion on Twistable Ate Pairing and Its Difficulty

Shoichi Akagi and Yasuyuki Nogami

Graduate School of Natural Science and Technology, Okayama University,
3–1–1, Tsushima–Naka, Okayama, Okayama 700-8530, Japan
`yasuyuki.nogami@okayama-u.ac.jp`

Abstract. As one of problems that guarantee the security of pairing–based cryptography, *pairing inversion* problem is studied. Some recent works have reduced *fixed argument pairing inversion* (FAPI) problem to exponentiation inversion (EI) problem. According to the results, FAPI problem is solved if EI problem of exponent $(q^k - 1)/\Phi_k(q)$ is solved, where q, k, and r are the characteristic, embedding degree, and order of pairing group, respectively. $\Phi_k(x)$ is the cyclotomic polynomial of order k. This paper shows an approach for reducing the exponent of EI problem to $q - 1$ especially on Ate pairing. For many embedding degrees, it is considerably reduced from the previous result $(q^k - 1)/\Phi_k(q)$. After that, the difficulty of the reduced EI problem is discussed based on the distribution of correct $(q - 1)$–th roots on a small example.

Keywords: pairing inversion problem, trace, Barreto–Naehrig curve.

1 Introduction

Fixed argument pairing inversion (FAPI) problem is one of important research targets for ensuring the security of pairing–based cryptography. According to some recent papers [4], [5], most of FAPI problems have been reduced to *exponentiation inversion* (EI) problems. In detail, let q, k, and r be the characteristic, embedding degree, and group order, respectively, the exponent of the reduced EI problem is $(q^k - 1)/\Phi_k(q)$, where $\Phi_k(x)$ is the cyclotomic polynomial of order k. Since recent efficient pairing calculations [1], [10] are based on Ate pairing[6], this paper deals with a class of FAPI problems on Ate pairing together with *twist* technique such as *sextic twist* that is available for the well known Barreto–Naehrig (BN) curve [2].

Pairing is a bilinear map that has two inputs P, Q (rational points) and one output z (a finite field element). As a typical setting in the context of Ate pairing of embedding degree k, the input rational points P and Q of order r are defined on an elliptic curve over prime field $\mathbb{F}_q$ and extension field $\mathbb{F}_{q^k}$, respectively. Throughout this paper, $\mathbb{F}_q$ and $\mathbb{F}_{q^m}$ denote a prime field of characteristic q and its m–th extension field, respectively. Then, the output z is calculated as a

M. Yoshida and K. Mouri (Eds.): IWSEC 2014, LNCS 8639, pp. 240–249, 2014.

non–zero element of order r in $\mathbb{F}_{q^k}$. As one of FAPI problems defined by these three values, this paper focuses on the following problem: Find *unknown* P from *given* Q and z. [1] This paper shows that the objective P is calculated if the *correct* $(q-1)$-th root of Tate pairing[7] is obtained[2]. The idea of the reduction from $(q^k - 1)/\Phi_k(q)$ to $q - 1$ is applicable for various pairing–friendly curves of even embedding degree such as BN curve. The reduced EI problem is still difficult even though the reduction is a significant achievement. Thus, this paper discusses the difficulty of the reduced EI problem based on the distribution of correct $(q-1)$-th roots on a small example.

2   Preliminaries

This section introduces some mathematical notations since this paper considers pairing inversion problems on Ate pairing with some curves. Especially, This paper focuses on some efficient pairing–friendly curves, such as Barreto–Naehrig (BN) curve[2], Brezing–Weng (BW) curve[3] and , Freeman curve[3], with *twist* technique[10] on Ate pairing.

2.1   Pairings

In what follows, let k, q, r and t be the embedding degree, characteristic, order of pairing group and trace of Frobenius[3], respectively. The following three pairings appear in this paper.

Ate Pairing and Ate$_i$ Pairing :   Suppose the following three groups and Ate$_i$ pairing notation.

$$\begin{aligned}
\mathbb{G}_1 &= E(\mathbb{F}_{q^k})[r] \cap \mathrm{Ker}(\phi - [1]), \\
\mathbb{G}_2 &= E(\mathbb{F}_{q^k})[r] \cap \mathrm{Ker}(\phi - [p]), \\
\mathbb{G}_T &= \mathbb{F}_{q^k}^* / (\mathbb{F}_{q^k}^*)^r,
\end{aligned} \tag{1}$$

$$\alpha_i : \ \mathbb{G}_2 \times \mathbb{G}_1 \to \mathbb{G}_T. \tag{2}$$

Ate$_1$ pairing is especially called **Ate pairing**. Then, let $P \in \mathbb{G}_1$ and $Q \in \mathbb{G}_2$, Ate pairing $\alpha(Q, P)$ and Ate$_i$ pairing $\alpha_i(Q, P)$ are given as follows, where $f_{s,Q}(P)$ is generally calculated by the Miller's algorithm with loop parameter s[9].

$$\alpha_i(Q, P) = f_{q^i \bmod r, Q}(P)^{\frac{q^k - 1}{r}}. \tag{3}$$

$$\alpha(Q, P) = f_{t-1, Q}(P)^{\frac{q^k - 1}{r}}. \tag{4}$$

---

[1] Let $\mathbb{G}_1$, $\mathbb{G}_2$, and $\mathbb{G}_T$ be groups of order r such that $P \in \mathbb{G}_1$, $Q \in \mathbb{G}_2$, and $z \in \mathbb{G}_T$, this type of FAPI is often called FAPI–2 [4].

[2] The result of Ate pairing is able to be translated to that of Tate pairing, therefore, this paper mainly uses Tate pairing notations.

Note that the bilinearity of Ate$_i$ pairing holds after calculating the *final expo-nentiation* of $(q^k - 1)/r$.

An important point is that $f_{q^i,Q}(P)$ whose loop parameter is just q^i without mod r holds the bilinearity without the final exponentiation[8].

Tate Pairing :   Suppose three groups $\mathbb{G}_1$, $\mathbb{G}_2$, and $\mathbb{G}_T$ defined as Eq. (1). Then, let $P \in \mathbb{G}_1$ and $Q \in \mathbb{G}_2$, Tate pairing $\tau(Q, P)$ is defined as follows.

$$\tau(Q, P) = f_{r,Q}(P)^{\frac{q^k-1}{r}}. \tag{5}$$

In the same of Ate$_i$ pairing, the bilinearity holds after calculating the *final ex-ponentiation*.

2.2   Divisor Theorem

In what follows, let $f_{a,Q}(P)$ be denoted as $f_{a,Q}$ in brief. Let $l_{P,Q}$ and v_T be the line and vertical line passing through rational points P, Q and T, respectively, then the following relations are given[5].

$$f_{-n,Q} = \frac{1}{f_{n,Q} \cdot v_{[n]Q}}. \tag{6a}$$

$$f_{a+b,Q} = f_{a,Q} \cdot f_{b,Q} \cdot \frac{l_{[a]Q,[b]Q}}{v_{[a+b]Q}}. \tag{6b}$$

$$f_{ab,Q} = f_{a,Q}^b \cdot f_{b,[a]Q} = f_{b,Q}^a \cdot f_{a,[b]Q}. \tag{6c}$$

According to the divisor theorem, it is shown that the three pairings are easily transformed to each other[5]. Thus, for simplicity, this paper in what follows mainly uses Tate pairing notations instead of Ate pairing.

3   Pairing Inversion Problem

In the case of Ate pairing, pairing inversion problems are roughly classified into the following three types:

FAPI–1 :   Find $Q \in \mathbb{G}_2$ from given $P \in \mathbb{G}_1$ and $\alpha(Q, P) \in \mathbb{G}_T$.
FAPI–2 :   Find $P \in \mathbb{G}_1$ from given $Q \in \mathbb{G}_2$ and $\alpha(Q, P) \in \mathbb{G}_T$.
GPI   :   Find $P' \in \mathbb{G}_1$ and $Q' \in \mathbb{G}_2$ satisfies $\alpha(Q', P') = \alpha(Q, P)$ from given $\alpha(Q, P) \in \mathbb{G}_T$.

The main target of this paper is FAPI-2 problem. The previous works [4], [5] have dealt with the general cases of FAPI problems and then shown that they are reduced to EI problem of exponent $(q^k - 1)/\Phi_k(q)$. Then, another approach together with a smaller exponent, that is just $q - 1$, is proposed in the case of BN curve. After that, it is shown that the approach is applicable for not only BN curve but also BW and Freeman curves. In detail, it is generalized for even embedding degrees through the case of Freeman curve.

3.1   Proposal

An Important Relation on Ate Pairing with BN Curve :   In the case
of BN curve of embedding degree 12, let $P(x_P, y_P) \in \mathbb{G}_1$ and $Q(x_Q, y_Q) \in \mathbb{G}_2$,
it satisfies $[q^6 + 1]Q = \mathcal{O}$ since $q^6 + 1$ is divisible by the order r. Then, consider
$f_{q^6+1,Q}(P)$ as follows.

$$f_{q^6+1,Q}(P) = f_{r \cdot \frac{q^6+1}{r},Q}(P) = f_{r,Q}^{\frac{q^6+1}{r}}(P) \cdot f_{\frac{q^6+1}{r},[r]Q}(P). \tag{7a}$$

On the other hand, the following relation is also obtained.

$$f_{q^6+1,Q}(P) = f_{q^6,Q}(P) \cdot f_{1,Q}(P) \cdot \frac{l_{[q^6]Q,Q}}{v_{[q^6+1]Q}} = f_{q^6,Q}(P) \cdot (x_P - x_Q). \tag{7b}$$

Thus, a relation shown below is obtained based on the above equations since
$q^{12} - 1 = (q^6 - 1) \cdot (q^6 + 1)$.

$$\frac{f_{r,Q}^{\frac{q^6+1}{r}}(P)}{f_{q^6,Q}(P)} = \frac{\sqrt[q^6-1]{\tau(Q,P)}}{f_{q^6,Q}(P)} = x_P - x_Q. \tag{8}$$

then the target of this problem is to obtain $X = x_P$ of P. As previously introduced, the denominator $f_{q^6,Q}(P)$ and $\tau(Q, P)$ are easily obtained as elements in
$\mathbb{G}_T$ from $\alpha(Q, P)$. The above relation is furthermore improved by using higher
degree traces and norm as follows.

Trace and Norm :   First, powering both sides of Eq. (8) to $(q^6 - 1)/(q - 1)$,

$$\frac{\sqrt[q-1]{\tau(Q,P)}}{f_{q^6,Q}(P)^{(q^6-1)/(q-1)}} = (X - x_Q)^{(q^6-1)/(q-1)}. \tag{9}$$

Let the left–hand side of the above equation be c that becomes a non–zero
element in $\mathbb{F}_q$, then we have

$$(X - x_Q)^{(q^6-1)/(q-1)} - c = 0. \tag{10}$$

Since the objective X belongs to $\mathbb{F}_q$, the following relation holds.

$$\prod_{i=0}^{5}(X - x_Q^{q^i}) - c = 0. \tag{11}$$

In the case of BN curve, x_Q of $Q \in \mathbb{G}_2$ for Ate pairing belongs to the proper
subfield $\mathbb{F}_{q^6}$ [10] as previously introduced. Thus, the trace and norm of x_Q leads
to a simple relation as follows.
   Let $\mathrm{M}_{x_Q}(X) = \prod_{i=0}^{5}(X - x_Q^{q^i})$ be the minimal polynomial of x_Q that is an
irreducible polynomial of degree 6 over $\mathbb{F}_q$, it satisfies that

$$\mathrm{M}_{x_Q}(X) - c = X^6 - 3^{-1}\mathrm{Tr}\left(x_Q^3\right)x^3 + \mathrm{N}(x_Q) - c = 0. \tag{12}$$

Tr $(\cdot)$ and N$(\cdot)$ are trace and norm functions with respect to the prime field $\mathbb{F}_q$. Since x_Q is known as an input of this problem, these values are easily calculated. As shown in **App. A**, the feature of BN curve shows that the coefficients of x^5, x^4, x^2, x of $\mathrm{M}_{x_Q}(X)$ always become 0. Therefore, calculating d and e in $\mathbb{F}_q$ such that

$$\mathrm{M}_{x_Q}(X) - c = (X^3 - d)(X^3 - e) = 0 \tag{13}$$

is not difficult. Thus, this FAPI problem is reduced to a smaller EI problem of exponent $q - 1$ as shown in Eq. (9). In addition, the meaning of this problem is partially replaced to whether d or e becomes a cubic residue in $\mathbb{F}_q$. In detail, d or e needs to be a cubic residue in $\mathbb{F}_q$ such that its solution $X = x_P$ belongs to $\mathbb{F}_q$ as x–coordinate of $P \in \mathbb{G}_1$.

According to Eq. (9), if the correct $(q-1)$–th root of Tate pairing $\tau(Q, P)$ that could be inversely formulated as $\sqrt[q-1]{\tau(Q,P)} = f_{r,Q}(P)^{(q^{12}-1)/r(q-1)}$ is obtained, $X = x_P$ is obtained. Thus, it has been shown that this approach reduces EI problem on Ate pairing with BN curve to the exponent $q - 1$.

3.2 EI Problem on Ate Pairing with BW Curve

In the case of BW curve of embedding degree 8, the following relation corresponding to Eq. (8) of BN curve is first obtained.

$$\frac{f_{r,Q}^{\frac{q^4+1}{r}}(P)}{f_{q^4,Q}(P)} = x_P - x_Q. \tag{14}$$

Then, powering both sides of Eq. (14) to $(q^4 - 1)/(q - 1)$, the following relation corresponding to Eq. (9) is obtained.

$$\frac{\sqrt[q-1]{\tau(Q,P)}}{f_{q^4,Q}(P)^{(q^4-1)/(q-1)}} = (X - x_Q)^{(q^4-1)/(q-1)} = (X - x_Q)^{q^3+q^2+q+1}, \tag{15}$$

where $X = x_P$ as the target of this problem. Let the left–hand side of the above equation be $c \in \mathbb{F}_q$, as shown in **App. A**,

$$\mathrm{M}_{x_Q}(X) - c = x^4 + 2^{-1}\mathrm{Tr}\left(x_Q^2\right)x^2 + \mathrm{N}(x_Q) - c = (X^2 - d)(X^2 - e) = 0, \tag{16}$$

where $\mathrm{M}_{x_Q}(X)$ is the minimal polynomial of $x_Q \in \mathbb{F}_{q^4}$, that is an irreducible polynomial of degree 4 over $\mathbb{F}_q$. The above d and e are easily obtained as elements in $\mathbb{F}_q$ and one of them at least needs to be a quadratic residue in $\mathbb{F}_q$ since $\mathrm{M}_{x_Q}(X) - c = 0$ has a solution $X = x_P$ in $\mathbb{F}_q$.

Thus, it has been shown that this approach also reduces EI problem on Ate pairing with BW curve to the exponent $q - 1$.

3.3 EI Problem on Ate Pairing with Freeman Curve

This section deals with Freeman curve for instance. Then, the discussion supports Ate pairing using pairing–friendly curves of even embedding degree.

In the case of Freeman curve of embedding degree 10, the following relation corresponding to Eq. (8) of BN curve is first obtained.

$$\frac{f_{r,\hat{Q}}^{\frac{q^5+1}{r}}(P)}{f_{q^5,Q}(P)} = x_P - x_Q. \tag{17}$$

Then, powering both sides of Eq. (17) to $(q^5 - 1)/(q - 1)$, the following relation corresponding to Eq. (9) is obtained.

$$\frac{\sqrt[q-1]{\tau(Q,P)}}{f_{q^5,Q}(P)^{(q^5-1)/(q-1)}} = (X - x_Q)^{(q^5-1)/(q-1)} = (X - x_Q)^{q^4+q^3+q^2+q+1}, \tag{18}$$

where $X = x_P$ as the target of this problem. Let the left–hand side of the above equation be $c \in \mathbb{F}_q$ and let $\mathrm{M}_{x_Q}(X)$ be the minimal polynomial of $x_Q \in \mathbb{F}_{q^5}$, that is an irreducible polynomial of degree 5 over $\mathbb{F}_q$,

$$\mathrm{M}_{x_Q}(X) - c = 0. \tag{19}$$

Though the form of $\mathrm{M}_{x_Q}(X)$ for Freeman curve is not as simple as those for BN and BW curves, it is easily calculated. Then, $\mathrm{M}_{x_Q}(X) - c$ becomes reducible over $\mathbb{F}_q$ such that it has a solution $X = x_P$ in $\mathbb{F}_q$.

Thus, it has been also shown that this approach reduces EI problem on Ate pairing with Freeman curve, furthermore pairing–friendly curves of even embedding degree, to the exponent $q - 1$.

3.4   Difficulty of the Reduced EI Problem of FAPI–2

This section observes the difficulty of the reduced EI problem of FAPI–2 on BN curve with Eq. (9). Let the correct $(q - 1)$–th root of Tate pairing $\tau(Q,P)$ be C and let $\hat{C}$ be a $(q - 1)$–th root of $\tau(Q,P)$ such that $\hat{C} \in \mathbb{G}_3$[3]. $\hat{C}$ is easily and uniquely obtained in $\mathbb{G}_3$ since $q - 1$ and r are coprime. It is found that $C/\hat{C}$ becomes a non–zero element in $\mathbb{F}_q^*$. Thus, in other words, the EI problem is solved if $C/\hat{C} \in \mathbb{F}_q^*$ is obtained.

As a small example, let the characteristic q and the order r of BN curve be 2143 and 2089, respectively, the distribution of $C/\hat{C}$ for all rational point pairs of pairing becomes as the histogram of **Fig.** 1. According to this figure, it seems that $C/\hat{C}$'s are uniformly distributed to show the difficulty of EI problem[4].

4   FAPI–1 Problem

The previous section has dealt with the case of FAPI–2 problem on Ate pairing. The approaches are also applicable to FAPI–1 problem and it reduces EI problem

---

[3] It is one of $(q - 1)$–th roots of $\tau(Q,P)$ and explicitly determined in $\mathbb{G}_3$.

[4] Since sextic twist is available on BN curve, each number of occurrences in the histogram becomes 6 or some multiples of 6. In other words, certain six rational points associated with sextic twist have the same value of $C/\hat{C}$.

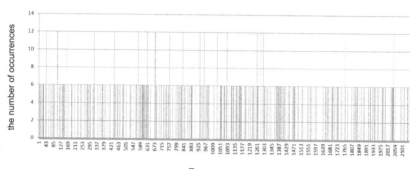

Fig. 1. Histogram of $C/\hat{C}$'s on BN curve with $q = 2143$

to exponent $q^{k/2} - 1$ at least when the embedding degree is even. In addition, when a pairing-friendly curve has another twist such as sextic twist, the exponent can be more reduced.

4.1   FAPI–1 : EI Problem on Ate Pairing with BN Curve

In the case of FAPI–1, this paper takes the same approach of the previous section. Noting that the objective of this problem is Q, $X = x_Q$ in this section. After Eq. (8), a similar approach to the previous section is usable.

Trace and Norm : In the case of FAPI–1, Eq. (10) is rewritten as follows.

$$(x_P - X)^{(q^6 - 1)/(q - 1)} - c = 0. \tag{20}$$

Since the objective X belongs to $\mathbb{F}_{q^2}$, the following relation holds.

$$\prod_{i=0}^{5}(x_P - X^{q^i}) - c = \prod_{i=0}^{5}(X^{q^i} - x_P) - c = 0. \tag{21}$$

$Q(X, Y)$ have a corresponding rational point $Q'(X', Y')$ on $E'(\mathbb{F}_{q^2})[r][10]$. Let $v \in \mathbb{F}_{q^2}$ be a cubic non residue, X is written as

$$X = v^{1/3} X'. \tag{22}$$

As shown in **App. A**, noting that $X' \in \mathbb{F}_{q^2}$, the following equation is obtained from Eq. (21).

$$X'^3 X'^{3q} + x_P{}^3(X'^3 v + X'^{3q} v^q) + x_P{}^6 - c = 0. \tag{23}$$

As shown above, this equation causes another difficult problem to solve. Therefore, a slightly different approach is needed as follows.

Trace and Norm for FAPI–1 Problem : First, powering both sides of Eq. (8) to $(q^6 - 1)/(q^2 - 1)$ not $(q^6 - 1)/(q - 1)$,

$$\frac{q^2-1\sqrt{\tau(Q,P)}}{f_{q^6,Q}(P)^{(q^6-1)/(q^2-1)}} = (x_P - X)^{(q^6-1)/(q^2-1)} = -\prod_{i=0}^{2}(X^{q^{2i}} - x_P). \quad (24)$$

Let c be the left–hand side of the above equation, as shown in **App. A**, the above equation is transformed as

$$X'^3 - v^{-1}(x_P^3 - c) = 0. \quad (25)$$

This equation has at least one solution $(X = x'_Q)$. According to Eq. (24), if the correct $(q^2 - 1)$–th root of Tate pairing $\tau(Q, P)$ is obtained, X is obtained. Thus it has been shown that this approach for FAPI–1 problem reduces it to EI problem of the exponent $q^2 - 1$.

4.2   FAPI–1 : EI Problem on Ate Pairing with BW Curve

In the case of BW curve, powering both sides of Eq. (14) to $(q^4 - 1)/(q^2 - 1)$, the following relation corresponding to Eq. (24) is obtained.

$$\frac{q^2-1\sqrt{\tau(Q,P)}}{f_{q^4,Q}(P)^{(q^4-1)/(q^2-1)}} = (x_P - X)^{(q^4-1)/(q^2-1)} = (X - x_P)^{q^2+1}, \quad (26)$$

X is written as $v^{1/2}X'$ such that $X' \in \mathbb{F}_{q^2}$ since BW curve has twist curve[10]. Then let c be the left–hand side of the above equation, in the same of **App. A**, the above equation is transformed as

$$(X - x_P)^{q^2+1} - c = \prod_{i=0}^{1}((v^{1/2}X')^{q^{2i}} - x_P) - c = vX'^2 - (x_P^2 + c) = 0,$$

$$X'^2 - v^{-1}(x_P^2 + c) = 0. \quad (27)$$

Thus, it has been shown that this approach for FAPI–1 problem can reduce EI problem to the exponent $q^2 - 1$.

4.3   FAPI–1 : EI Problem on Ate Pairing with Freeman Curve

In the case of Freeman curve, there is no need to change Eq. (17) and the following relation corresponding to Eq. (24) is obtained.

$$\frac{f_{r,\tilde{Q}}^{\frac{q^5+1}{r}}(P)}{f_{q^5,Q}(P)} = x_P - X. \quad (28)$$

Let c be the left–hand side of the above equation, the above equation is transformed as

$$X + c - x_P = 0. \quad (29)$$

This approach can reduce EI problem to the exponent $q^5 - 1$. Thus it has been shown that EI problem is reduced to the exponent $q^{k/2} - 1$ in the same way when the embedding degree k is even.

5   Conclusion and Future Works

As shown in this paper, one of FAPI problems on Ate pairing with BN curves, for example, has been reduced to EI problem of exponent $q-1$. It is considerably reduced from $(q^k - 1)/\Phi_k(q)$ of the previous works. This approach is applicable for pairing–friendly curves of even embedding degree such as Freeman curve. As one of future works, it will be extended for odd embedding degrees.

Then, the reduced EI problem that is to solve the correct $(q - 1)$–th root of Tate pairing, denoted by $\sqrt[q-1]{\tau(Q, P)}$ in this paper, will be still difficult. The difficulty has been discussed with a small example in this paper. Thus, as another future work, the size of EI problem needs to be furthermore reduced from $q - 1$ though it may need some auxiliary input.

The approach shown in this paper will be appropriately modified for the other FAPI problems and not restricted to Ate pairing.

References

1. Aranha, D.F., Karabina, K., Longa, P., Gebotys, C.H., Lopez, J.: Faster Explicit Formulas for Computing Pairings over Ordinary Curves, Cryptology ePrint Archive, Report 2010/526 (2010)
2. Barreto, P.S.L.M., Naehrig, M.: Pairing-Friendly Elliptic Curves of Prime Order. In: Preneel, B., Tavares, S. (eds.) SAC 2005. LNCS, vol. 3897, pp. 319–331. Springer, Heidelberg (2006)
3. Freeman, D., Scott, M., Teske, E.: A Taxonomy of Pairing–Friendly Elliptic Curves, IACR ePrint archive, http://eprint.iacr.org/2006/372.pdf
4. Galbraith, S.D., Hess, F., Vercauteren, F.: Aspects of pairing inversion. IEEE Transactions on Information Theory 54(12), 5719–5728 (2008)
5. Kanayama, N., Okamoto, E.: Approach to Pairing Inversions Without Solving Miller Inversion. IEEE Transactions on Information Theory 58(2), 1248–1253 (2012)
6. Hess, F., Smart, N., Vercauteren, F.: The Eta Pairing Revisited. IEEE Trans. Information Theory, 4595–4602 (2006)
7. Galbraith, S.D., Harrison, K., Soldera, D.: Implemeting the Tate pairing. In: Fieker, C., Kohel, D.R. (eds.) ANTS 2002. LNCS, vol. 2369, pp. 324–337. Springer, Heidelberg (2002)
8. Matsuda, S., Kanayama, N., Hess, F., Okamoto, E.: Optimized versions of the Ate and Twisted Ate Pairings, Cryptology ePrint Archive, Report 2007/013 (2007), http://eprint.iacr.org/2007/013.pdf
9. Miller, V.S.: The Weil Pairing, and its Efficient Calculation. Journal of Cryptology 17, 235–261 (2004)
10. Nogami, Y., Akane, M., Sakemi, Y., Kato, H., Morikawa, Y.: Integer Variable χ–Based Ate Pairing. In: Galbraith, S.D., Paterson, K.G. (eds.) Pairing 2008. LNCS, vol. 5209, pp. 178–191. Springer, Heidelberg (2008)

A   Minimal Polynomial $\mathrm{M}_{x_Q}(X)$ of x_Q over $\mathbb{F}_q$

Case of BN Curve

The minimal polynomial $\mathrm{M}_{x_Q}(X)$ of x_Q over $\mathbb{F}_q$ is given by

$$\mathrm{M}_{x_Q}(X) = \prod_{i=0}^{5}(X - x_Q^{q^i}). \tag{30}$$

When using a certain pair of $x'_Q \in \mathbb{F}_{q^2}$ and a cubic non residue $v \in \mathbb{F}_{q^2}$, x_Q is written as

$$x_Q = v^{1/3} x'_Q, \tag{31}$$

where $v^{1/3}$ belongs to $\mathbb{F}_{q^6}$ and thus x_Q also belongs to $\mathbb{F}_{q^6}$[10]. Note here that

$$v^{q^2/3} = v^{(q^2-1)/3} \cdot v^{1/3} = \epsilon v^{1/3}, \quad v^{q^4/3} = v^{(q^2-1)(q^2+1)/3} \cdot v^{1/3} = \epsilon^2 v^{1/3}, \tag{32}$$

where ϵ is a primitive third root[5] of unity in $\mathbb{F}_q$. Thus, it satisfies that $\epsilon^3 = 1$ and $1 + \epsilon + \epsilon^2 = 0$. Then, Eq. (30) is modified as

$$M_{x_Q}(X) = \prod_{i=0}^{5}(X - x_Q^{q^i}) = \prod_{i=0}^{2}(X - \epsilon^i \cdot v^{1/3} \cdot x'_Q) \prod_{i=0}^{2}(X - \epsilon^i \cdot v^{q/3} \cdot x'^q_Q),$$

$$= (X^3 - vx'^3_Q)(X^3 - v^q x'^{3q}_Q) = X^6 - (vx'^3_Q + v^q x'^{3q}_Q)X^3 + (vx'^3_Q)^{1+q}. \tag{33}$$

For the above equation,

$$\mathrm{Tr}\left(x_Q^3\right) = \sum_{i=0}^{5} x_Q^{3q^i} = \sum_{i=0}^{5}(v^{1/3}x'_Q)^{3q^i},$$

$$= \sum_{i=0}^{2}(vx'^3_Q + v^q x'^{3q}_Q) = 3(vx'^3_Q + v^q x'^{3q}_Q), \tag{34a}$$

$$\mathrm{N}(x_Q) = \prod_{i=0}^{5} x_Q^{q^i} = \prod_{i=0}^{2}(\epsilon^i \cdot v^{1/3}x'_Q)(\epsilon^i \cdot v^{q/3}x'^q_Q) = (vx'^3_Q)^{1+q}. \tag{34b}$$

Thus, ϵ is simply canceled and then Eq. (12) is obtained.

In the same way of the above, the equation

$$\prod_{i=0}^{2}(x_Q^{q^{2i}} - x_P) + c = 0, \tag{35}$$

is transformed as follows,

$$\prod_{i=0}^{2}(x_Q^{q^{2i}} - x_P) + c = \prod_{i=0}^{2}(\epsilon^i \cdot v^{1/3}x'_Q - x_P) = vx'^3_Q - x_P^3 + c = 0,$$

$$x'^3_Q - v^{-1}(x_P^3 - c) = 0. \tag{36}$$

Let $X = x'_Q$, Eq. (25) is obtained.

---

[5] Since $q - 1$ is divisible by 3, it belongs to $\mathbb{F}_q$.

Related Key Secure PKE
from Hash Proof Systems

Dingding Jia[1], Bao Li[1], Xianhui Lu[1], and Qixiang Mei[2,*]

[1] State Key Laboratory of Information Security, Institute of Information Engineering,
Chinese Academy of Sciences, Beijing, China, 100093
[2] College of Information, Guangdong Ocean University, China
{ddjia,lb,xhlu}@is.ac.cn, nupf@163.com

Abstract. In this paper we propose a framework for constructing public key encryption against related key attacks from hash proof systems in the standard model. Compared with the construction of Wee (PKC2012), our framework avoids the use of one-time signatures. We show that the schemes presented by Jia *et al.* (ProvSec2013) could fit into our framework. And we give more instantiations of the proposed framework based on the QR and DCR assumptions for affine key related functions.

Keywords: related key attack, 4-wise independent hash, subset membership problem, hash proof system.

1 Introduction

Related key attack (RKA)[9,7] means that the attacker can modify keys stored in the memory and observe the outcome of the cryptographic primitive under the modified keys. It demonstrates a realistic attack that given physical access to a hardware device, an adversary can use fault injection techniques to tamper with and induce modifications to the internal state of the device [9,7]. RKA security has been studied for a long time in block ciphers [6,21] and attracts interests in other areas in recent years, like identity based encryptions (IBE), public key encryptions (PKE), signatures, etc. [2,5].

Specifically, PKE schemes against chosen ciphertext RKA (CC-RKA) is formulated by Bellare *et al.* [2]. In a CC-RKA game for PKE, the adversary can make decryption queries with a function and a ciphertext. On receiving the query, the challenger first applies the function to the secret key and gets a modified key, then it uses the modified key to decrypt the ciphertext and return the message to the adversary.

Bellare and Cash [1] built RKA secure pseudorandom functions (PRF) from key homomorphic PRF and finger-printing under the DDH and DLIN assumptions. Bellare *et al.* [5] built RKA secure IBE from IBE that was key homomorphic and supported collision resistant identity renaming. Bellare *et al.* [2] showed

---

* This work is Supported by the National Basic Research Program of China (973 project)(No.2013CB338002), the National Nature Science Foundation of China (No.61379137, No.61272534).

M. Yoshida and K. Mouri (Eds.): IWSEC 2014, LNCS 8639, pp. 250–265, 2014.

that CC-RKA secure PKE could be achieved from RKA secure PRF and RKA secure IBE separately. Wee [25] proposed a framework for constructing CC-RKA secure PKE from adaptive trapdoor relations that were key homomorphic and finger-printing. These works have some design ideas in common: the key homomorphism property assures RKA queries can be answered as long as queries involving with the normal key can be answered; the finger-printing property, similar to collision resistant identity renaming in IBE, assures that a ciphertext is valid for a unique secret key (identity).

However, Wee [25] gave an RKA attack on the DDH based scheme given by Cramer and Shoup [10], and pointed out that the the Cramer-Shoup CCA secure constructions [12,11] could not achieve finger-printing, since the smoothness requirement in hash proof systems (HPSs) essentially stipulates that the secret key has some residual entropy given only its evaluation on a NO instance of the underlying subset membership problem, thus they achieved the CC-RKA security through "all-but-one" proof technique. Subsequently, Jia *et al.* [18] presented CC-RKA secure PKE schemes based on the DDH and HR assumptions, which seemed consistent with the paradigm of the HPS.

HPS, which is constructed from languages related to hard subset membership problems, is introduced by Cramer and Shoup [11] as an important primitive to build paradigm for CCA secure PKE schemes. After being proposed, several efforts have been made to improve the efficiency of the paradigm for CCA security, such as [20,22,16]. Researchers also proved the CCA security of a scheme by showing the scheme can fit into the corresponding paradigm [17]. Security proof for schemes through HPSs and "all-but-one" techniques are very different, thus we are interested in studying the CC-RKA security for schemes based on HPSs.

1.1 Our Contributions

We give a generic PKE construction from the projective HPS, and prove that the construction is CC-RKA secure in the standard model when the HPS satisfies the key homomorphism and computational finger-printing properties. We show that schemes in [18] fit into this paradigm, and give other efficient instantiations based on the QR and DCR assumptions.

Technical Overview. Generally, in the CC-RKA security proof, the simulator should handle two more problems compared with the CCA security proof: firstly, how to answer decryption queries under the related functions of the secret key without revealing extra information about the secret key? secondly, how to prohibit the adversary from promoting a query out of the challenge ciphertext and the key related function?

In the HPS, decryption queries are easy to answer since the simulator holds the secret key. To make the adversary gain no more information about the secret key from the decryption answers than what it can get from the public key (except for a negligible probability), we require the HPS to satisfy the key homomorphism property analogous to that in previous works [5,25]. Here key homomorphism means that there exists an efficient algorithm to compute the hash value of the input X under the modified key through the hash value of another input X' under the original secret key, where X' can be publicly computed. It assures that except for negligible probability, decryption answers are completely determined by the public key.

To prohibit the adversary from promoting a query out of the challenge ciphertext and key related functions, we consider the following two points: firstly, we hope that there is a unique secret key involving with a given ciphertext. However, as stated by Wee [25], it is impossible to fulfill the "finger-printing" property for the Cramer-Shoup framework, so we require a weaker notion called the computational finger-printing (CFP) property, which allows the existence of multi secret keys that correspond to the same hash value for a random input, but no efficient algorithm can find two of them. Secondly, we hope that no adversary can get the same hash value by modifying the input and the secret key simultaneously. Although no existing HPSs can achieve this property, we note that when Kiltz *et al.* [20] realized the CCA secure paradigm from the HPS, they used an interesting primitive called 4-wise independent hash to extract randomness. For a randomly given 4-wise independent hash function $\mathcal{H}$ and two random variables $X, \tilde{X}$ with negligible collision probability, the output $\mathcal{H}(\tilde{X})$ is close to uniformly random even $\mathcal{H}(X)$ is fixed, as long as the min-entropy of X and $\tilde{X}$ are large enough. We prevent the malleability by extending the domain of 4-wise independent hash in [20], so that the output is randomly distributed when the input is changed.

Comparison with Previous Works. Following the original theory given by Bellare and Kohoo [3], modification on the secret key is parameterized by the class of Φ functions. Let S be the secret key space, if S is closed under one operation "$+$", Φ^{lin} is used to denote the class of linear functions; if S is closed under two operations "$+$" and "$\times$", Φ^{affine} is used to denote the class of affine functions; $\Phi^{\text{poly}(d)}$ is used to denote the class of polynomial functions bounded by degree d similarly. The PRF given by Bellare and Cash [1] achieves RKA security for $\Phi = \Phi^{\text{lin}}$ under the DDH and DLIN assumptions. The IBE scheme given by Bellare, Paterson and Thomson [5] achieves RKA security for $\Phi = \Phi^{\text{poly}(d)}$ under the non-standard q-EBDDH assumption and $\Phi = \Phi^{\text{affine}}$ under the BDDH assumption. So one can get Φ-CC-RKA secure PKE for $\Phi = \Phi^{\text{lin}}$ under the DDH and DLIN assumptions by combining [2] and [1]; also one can get Φ-CC-RKA secure PKE for $\Phi = \Phi^{\text{poly}(d)}$ under the non-standard q-EBDDH assumption and $\Phi = \Phi^{\text{affine}}$ under the BDDH assumption by combining [2] and [5]. In Wee's instantiation of PKE schemes [25], they achieved Φ-CC-RKA secure for Φ being linear-shift under the factoring, BDDH and LWE assumptions. Our instantiations can achieve Φ-CC-RKA secure for Φ being affine functions under the DDH, HR, QR and DCR assumptions.

Note that compared with previous works, our construction removes the use of one-time signatures and has efficiency close to that of the CCA secure PKE construction in [20].

Related Works. Tamper resilience is also considered along with the leakage resilience security and there are schemes satisfying the corresponding security definitions [19,13]. Since in the security game they do not restrict the classes of related key deriving functions, the adversary is not allowed to make tampering queries after seeing the challenge ciphertext, so they have a different approach from ours and do not require the finger-printing property. Besides, the scheme in [19] achieved the security via key update and could only encrypt one bit. And the security model defined by Damgård *et al.* [13] bound the number of times that the adversary could make tampering queries.

Organization. The rest of our paper is organized as follows: in section 2 we give definitions and preliminaries; in section 3 we give our generic construction and security proof; in section 4 we show instantiations based on the DDH, QR and DCR assumptions; section 5 is the conclusion.

2   Definitions and Preliminaries

2.1   Notations

We use PPT as the abbreviation of probabilistic polynomial time. Let $l(X)$ denote the length of X. Let $s \leftarrow_R S$ denote choosing a random element s from S if S is a set, and assigning to s the output of S on uniformly chosen randomness if S is a PPT algorithm. Let X and Y be probability spaces on a finite set S, the statistical distance $SD(X, Y)$ between X and Y is defined as $SD(X,Y) := \frac{1}{2}\Sigma_{\alpha \in S}|\Pr_X[\alpha] - \Pr_Y[\alpha]|$, The min-entropy of a random variable X is defined as $H_\infty(X) = -\log_2(max_{x \in D}\Pr[X = x])$, wherein D is the domain of X. A function $f(n)$ is said negligible if for any polynomial $p(\cdot) > 0$, there exists an N such that for all $n > N, f(n) < \frac{1}{p(n)}$. A function $g(n)$ is said overwhelming if $1 - g(n)$ is negligible.

2.2   Security Definitions

Public Key Encryption. A public key encryption scheme consists of three polynomial time algorithms: $(Keygen, Enc, Dec)$. The key generation algorithm takes as input the public parameters and outputs a pair of keys (pk, sk), $Keygen$ $(pp) \rightarrow_R (pk, sk)$; the encryption algorithm takes as input a message m, a public key pk and outputs a ciphertext C, $Enc(pk, m) \rightarrow_R C$; the decryption algorithm Dec takes as input the ciphertext C and a secret key sk and outputs a message m or $\perp$, $Dec(sk, C) = m$ or $\perp$. For correctness it is required that $Dec(sk, Enc(pk, m)) = m$.

Φ-*CC-RKA Security.* Here we give the security definition of Φ-CC-RKA. Let PKE= $(Keygen, Enc, Dec)$ be a public key encryption scheme, the advantage of an adversary $\mathcal{A}$ in breaking the Φ-CC-RKA security of PKE is defined as:

$$Adv_{\mathcal{A},\text{PKE}}^{\Phi\text{-CC-RKA}} = \left|\Pr\left[b = b' : \begin{array}{c}(pk, sk) \leftarrow_R Keygen(pp);\\ (m_0, m_1) \leftarrow \mathcal{A}^{\mathcal{O}(sk,\cdot,\cdot)}(pk); b \leftarrow_R \{0,1\};\\ C^* \leftarrow_R Enc(pk, m_b); b' \leftarrow \mathcal{A}^{\mathcal{O}(sk,\cdot,\cdot)}(C^*, pk)\end{array}\right] - \frac{1}{2}\right|.$$

When the adversary issues queries (ϕ, C), where $\phi \in \Phi$, the oracle $\mathcal{O}(sk, \cdot, \cdot)$ responds with $Dec(\phi(sk), C)$. And after seeing the challenge ciphertext, the adversary is not allowed to make queries with $(\phi(sk), C) = (sk, C^*)$.

Definition 1 (Φ-CC-RKA Security). *A PKE scheme is Φ-CC-RKA secure if for any PPT adversary $\mathcal{A}$, $Adv_{\mathcal{A},PKE}^{\Phi\text{-}CC\text{-}RKA}$ is negligible in λ.*

Here our security definition follows the definition given by Bellare *et al.* [2].

Symmetric Encryption. A symmetric encryption scheme consists of two polynomial time algorithms: $(\mathcal{E},\mathcal{D})$. Let $\mathcal{K}_{SE}$ be the secret key space. The encryption algorithm $\mathcal{E}$ takes as input a message m and a secret key K and outputs a ciphertext χ, $\mathcal{E}(K,m) = \chi$; the decryption algorithm $\mathcal{D}$ takes as input the ciphertext χ and a secret key K and outputs a message m or $\perp$, $\mathcal{D}(K,\chi) = m$ or $\perp$. Here both algorithms are deterministic. For correctness it is required that $\mathcal{D}(K,\mathcal{E}(K,m)) = m$.

Ciphertext Indistinguishability. Let $SE = (\mathcal{E},\mathcal{D})$ be a symmetric encryption scheme, the advantage of an adversary $\mathcal{A}$ in breaking the ciphertext indistinguishability (IND-OT) of SE is defined as:

$$Adv_{\mathcal{A},\text{SE}}^{\text{IND-OT}} = \left| \Pr\left[b = b' : \begin{array}{l} K^* \leftarrow_R \mathcal{K}_{SE}; (m_0, m_1) \leftarrow \mathcal{A}; b \leftarrow_R \{0,1\}; \\ \chi^* \leftarrow \mathcal{E}(K^*, m_b); b' \leftarrow \mathcal{A}(\chi^*) \end{array} \right] - \frac{1}{2} \right|.$$

We say that SE is one-time secure in the sense of indistinguishability (IND-OT) if for every PPT $\mathcal{A}$, $Adv_{\mathcal{A},\text{SE}}^{\text{IND-OT}}$ is negligible.

Ciphertext Integrity. Informally, ciphertext integrity requires that it is difficult to create a valid ciphertext corresponding to a uniformly chosen secret key for any PPT adversary $\mathcal{A}$, even $\mathcal{A}$ is given an encryption of a chosen message with the same key before. Let $SE = (\mathcal{E},\mathcal{D})$ be a symmetric encryption scheme, the advantage of an adversary $\mathcal{A}$ in breaking the ciphertext integrity (INT-OT) of SE is defined as:

$$Adv_{\mathcal{A},\text{SE}}^{\text{INT-OT}} = \Pr\left[\chi \neq \chi^* \wedge \mathcal{D}(K^*, \chi) \neq \perp : \begin{array}{l} K^* \leftarrow_R \mathcal{K}_{SE}; m \leftarrow \mathcal{A}; \\ \chi^* \leftarrow \mathcal{E}(K^*, m); \chi \leftarrow \mathcal{A}(\chi^*) \end{array} \right].$$

We say that SE is one-time secure in the sense of integrity (INT-OT) if for every PPT $\mathcal{A}$, $Adv_{\mathcal{A},\text{SE}}^{\text{INT-OT}}$ is negligible.

Authenticated Encryption. A symmetric encryption scheme SE is secure in the sense of one-time authenticated encryption (AE-OT) iff it is IND-OT and INT-OT secure. An AE-OT secure symmetric encryption can be easily constructed using a one-time symmetric encryption and an existentially unforgeable MAC [12,4].

2.3   Hash Proof Systems

Recall the concept of hash proof system (HPS) introduced by Cramer and Shoup [11]. Let $\mathcal{X}, \mathcal{Y}, \mathcal{SK}, \mathcal{PK}$ be sets and $\mathcal{L} \subset \mathcal{X}$ be a language, in which an instance $L \in \mathcal{L}$ can be efficiently sampled with a witness $r \in \mathcal{R}$. Let Λ be a family of hash functions indexed by $sk \in \mathcal{SK}$ mapping from $\mathcal{X}$ to $\mathcal{Y}$. Let μ be a PPT function mapping from $\mathcal{SK}$ to $\mathcal{PK}$. A hash proof system $\mathbf{H} = (\Lambda, \mathcal{SK}, \mathcal{X}, \mathcal{L}, \mathcal{R}, \mathcal{Y}, \mathcal{PK}, \mu)$ is projective if for all $sk \in \mathcal{SK}$, the action of Λ_{sk} on $\mathcal{L}$ is determined by $\mu(sk)$.

That is, there are two PPT algorithms $(Priv, Pub)$ to compute $\Lambda_{sk}(L)$ for $L \in \mathcal{L}$ with witness r :

$$\Lambda_{sk}(L) = Priv(sk, L) = Pub(\mu(sk), L, r).$$

For $X \in \mathcal{X} \backslash \mathcal{L}$, it is required that there is still enough min-entropy for $\Lambda_{sk}(X)$ given $\mu(sk)$ and X.

Definition 2 (κ-entropic [20]). *The projective HPS is κ-entropic if for all $X \in \mathcal{X} \backslash \mathcal{L}$,*
$H_\infty(\Lambda_{sk}(X) | X, \mu(sk)) \geq \kappa.$

We assume that there are efficient algorithms to sample $sk \in \mathcal{SK}$ and $X \in \mathcal{X}$ uniformly at random.

Definition 3 (Subset Membership (SM) Problem). *SM problem in the HPS $\boldsymbol{H}$ is to distinguish a randomly chosen $Z_0 \in \mathcal{L}$ from a randomly chosen $Z_1 \in \mathcal{X} \backslash \mathcal{L}$. Concretely, the advantage of an adversary $\mathcal{A}$ in breaking SM is defined as:*

$$Adv_{\mathcal{A}}^{SM} = |\Pr[\mathcal{A}(\mathcal{X}, \mathcal{L}, Z_1)] - \Pr[\mathcal{A}(\mathcal{X}, \mathcal{L}, Z_0)]|.$$

We say that the SM problem is hard if for every PPT $\mathcal{A}$, $Adv_{\mathcal{A}}^{SM}$ is negligible.

HPS with Trapdoor. Following [22,20], we also require that the SM problem can be efficiently solved with a master trapdoor, which will be used not in the actual scheme but in the security proof. In fact, all known hash proof systems have such a trapdoor.

2.4   4-Wise Independent Hash Functions

Here we review the primitive called 4-wise independent hash family [20] that can be used as a randomness extractor. A simple construction of 4-wise independent hash family is shown in [20].

Definition 4 (4-wise Independent Hash Family [20]). *Let $\mathcal{HS}$ be a family of hash functions $\mathcal{H} : \mathcal{X} \to \mathcal{Y}$. We say that $\mathcal{HS}$ is 4-wise independent if for any distinct $x_1, x_2, x_3, x_4 \in \mathcal{X}$, the output $\mathcal{H}(x_1), ..., \mathcal{H}(x_4)$ are uniformly and independently random, where $\mathcal{H} \leftarrow_R \mathcal{HS}$.*

The next two lemmata state that for a 4-wise independent hash function $\mathcal{H}$ and two random variables $X, \tilde{X}$ with $\Pr[X = \tilde{X}] = \delta$ negligible that even related, the random variable $(\mathcal{H}, \mathcal{H}(X))$ and $(\mathcal{H}, \mathcal{H}(X), \mathcal{H}(\tilde{X}))$ are close to uniformly random as long as the min-entropy of X and $\tilde{X}$ are large enough.

Lemma 1 (Leftover Hash Lemma [15]). *Let $X \in \mathcal{X}$ be a random variable where $H_\infty(X) \geq \kappa$. Let $\mathcal{HS}$ be a family of pairwise independent hash functions with domain $\mathcal{X}$ and range $\{0,1\}^l$. Then for $\mathcal{H} \leftarrow_R \mathcal{HS}$ and $U_l \leftarrow_R \{0,1\}^l$,*

$$SD((\mathcal{H}, \mathcal{H}(X)), (\mathcal{H}, U_l)) \leq 2^{(l-\kappa)/2}.$$

Lemma 2 (A Generalization of the Leftover Hash Lemma [20]). *Let* $(X, \tilde{X}) \in \mathcal{X} \times \mathcal{X}$ *be two random variables having joint distribution where* $H_\infty(X) \geq \kappa, H_\infty(\tilde{X}) \geq \kappa$ *and* $\Pr[X = \tilde{X}] = \delta$. *Let* $\mathcal{HS}$ *be a family of 4-wise independent hash functions with domain* $\mathcal{X}$ *and range* $\{0, 1\}^l$. *Then for* $\mathcal{H} \leftarrow_R \mathcal{HS}$ *and* $U_{2l} \leftarrow_R \{0, 1\}^{2l}$,

$$SD((\mathcal{H}, \mathcal{H}(X), \mathcal{H}(\tilde{X})), (\mathcal{H}, U_{2l})) \leq \sqrt{1 + \delta} \cdot 2^{l - \kappa/2} + \delta.$$

The following lemma from [18] that will be used in our security proof states that for a 4-wise independent hash function $\mathcal{H}$ and two random variables $X, \tilde{X}$ with $\Pr[X = \tilde{X}] = \delta$ negligible that even related, the output $\mathcal{H}(\tilde{X})$ is close to uniformly random even $\mathcal{H}(X)$ is fixed as long as the min-entropy of X and $\tilde{X}$ are large enough.

Lemma 3. *[18] Let* $\delta \leq \frac{1}{2}, l \leq 6$, $(X, \tilde{X}) \in \mathcal{X} \times \mathcal{X}$ *be two random variables having joint distribution where* $\Pr[X = \tilde{X}] = \delta$ *and* $H_\infty(X) \geq \kappa, H_\infty(\tilde{X}) \geq \kappa$. *Let* $\mathcal{HS}$ *be a family of 4-wise independent hash functions with domain* $\mathcal{X}$ *and range* $\{0, 1\}^l$. *Then for* $\mathcal{H} \leftarrow_R \mathcal{HS}$ *and* $U_l \leftarrow_R \{0, 1\}^l$,

$$SD((\mathcal{H}, \mathcal{H}(X), \mathcal{H}(\tilde{X})), (\mathcal{H}, \mathcal{H}(X), U_l)) \leq 2^{l - \frac{\kappa - 1}{2}} + \delta.$$

3   RKA Secure PKE from Hash Proof Systems

3.1   Computational Finger-Printing and Φ-Key Homomorphism

In this section we begin by introducing two additional properties for the HPS to build RKA secure PKE. Generally speaking, computational finger-printing means that for any PPT adversary, for a randomly given X, it cannot compute two different secret keys that can get the same hash value of X. Φ-key homomorphism means that there exists an efficient algorithm T to compute the value $\Lambda_{\phi(sk)}(X)$ on input $\Lambda_{sk}(X')$ and X, where X' can be computed publicly, here we use the word "homomorphism" to indicate that the evaluation on $\phi(sk)$ can be transformed to the evaluation on sk.

Computational Finger-Printing (CFP). For a uniformly chosen $X \in \mathcal{X} \backslash \mathcal{L}$, the CFP problem is to compute $sk_1 \neq sk_2$, s.t. $\Lambda_{sk_1}(X) = \Lambda_{sk_2}(X)$. The advantage of $\mathcal{A}$ in solving the CFP problem is formally defined as

$$Adv_{\mathcal{A}}^{\text{CFP}} = \Pr[\Lambda_{sk_1}(X) = \Lambda_{sk_2}(X), sk_1 \neq sk_2 | X \leftarrow_R \mathcal{X} \backslash \mathcal{L}; (sk_1, sk_2) \leftarrow \mathcal{A}(X)].$$

Definition 5 (CFP). *We say that the CFP holds for an HPS if for all PPT algorithm* $\mathcal{A}$, $Adv_{\mathcal{A}}^{CFP}$ *is negligible in* λ.

We stipulate that "+" and "×" are two operations defined on the secret key space $\mathcal{SK}$ and $\mathcal{SK}$ is closed under "+" and "×" to define the affine functions on $\mathcal{SK}$.

Definition 6 (Φ-key Homomorphism). *We say an HPS is* Φ-key homomor-phic *if there are PPT algorithms* T_1, T_2 *such that with overwhelming probability over pp, for all* $\phi \in \Phi$, *and all* $sk, X \in \mathcal{X}$:

$$\Lambda_{\phi(sk)}(X) = T_2(pp, \phi, \Lambda_{sk}(X'), X), \quad where \quad X' = T_1(pp, pk, \phi, X).$$

3.2 The General Construction

In this part we give a general PKE construction from hash proof systems. The structure of our construction inherits that in [20]. By extending the domain of the 4-wise independent hash function to $\mathcal{X} \times \mathcal{Y}$, we can prove the Φ-CC-RKA security of the construction.

Let $\mathbf{H} = (\Lambda, \mathcal{SK}, \mathcal{X}, \mathcal{L}, \mathcal{R}, \mathcal{Y}, \mathcal{PK}, \mu)$ be a projective hash proof system with κ-entropic. Let SE be an AE-OT secure symmetric encryption scheme with secret key space $\{0,1\}^l$. Let $\mathcal{HS}$ be a family of 4-wise independent hash functions with domain $\mathcal{X} \times \mathcal{Y}$ and image $\{0,1\}^l$ and $\mathcal{H}$ is chosen uniformly random from $\mathcal{HS}$. Public parameters are set as $pp = (\mathbf{H}, \mathcal{H})$.

$Keygen(pp)$: The key generation algorithm chooses random secret key $sk \leftarrow_R \mathcal{SK}$ and computes the public key as $pk = \mu(sk)$.

$Enc(pk, m)$: The encryption algorithm samples random $L \in \mathcal{L}$ with witness r, the ciphertext $C = (C_0, C_1)$ is computed as:

$$C_0 = L, Y = Pub(pk, L, r), K = \mathcal{H}(C_0, Y), C_1 = \mathcal{E}(K, m).$$

$Dec(sk, C)$: The decryption algorithm computes the message as:

$$Y = Priv(sk, C_0), K - \mathcal{H}(C_0, Y), m = \mathcal{D}(K, C_1).$$

Correctness can be easily verified from the correctness of the symmetric encryption scheme and the projective property of the HPS. In terms of concrete security, it requires the entropy κ to be sufficiently large to assure the security of SE.

Remark. Compared with the paradigm in [20], we extend the domain of the 4-wise independent hash function to $\mathcal{X} \times \mathcal{Y}$, so that related key attacks such that $(C_0 \neq C_0^*, \Lambda_{\phi(sk)}(C_0) = \Lambda_{sk}(C_0^*))$ can be prevented.

3.3 Security Proof

Theorem 1. *If $\mathbf{H}$ is a projective HPS with the corresponding SM problem hard and satisfies the CFP and Φ-key homomorphism properties, SE is an AE-OT secure symmetric encryption scheme with secret key space $\{0,1\}^l$, $\mathcal{HS}$ is a family of 4-wise independent hash functions with domain $\mathcal{X} \times \mathcal{Y}$ and image $\{0,1\}^l$, then our PKE scheme is Φ-CC-RKA secure. In particular, for every CC-RKA adversary $\mathcal{A}$ against security of the above scheme, there exist adversaries $\mathcal{B}, \mathcal{C}, \mathcal{D}, \mathcal{F}$ with*

$$Adv_{\mathcal{A},PKE}^{\Phi\text{-}CC\text{-}RKA} \leq Adv_{\mathcal{B}}^{SM} + (q+1)2^{l-(\kappa-1)/2} + q(Adv_{\mathcal{C}}^{CFP} + Adv_{\mathcal{D},SE}^{INT\text{-}OT}) + Adv_{\mathcal{F},SE}^{IND\text{-}OT}$$

where $\kappa = H_\infty(Y)$.

First let us recall a lemma that will be used in our proof.

Lemma 4. *[12] Let S_1, S_2, S_0 be events defined on some probability space satisfying that event $S_1 \wedge \neg S_0$ occurs iff $S_2 \wedge \neg S_0$ occurs, then*

$$|\Pr[S_1] - \Pr[S_2]| \leq \Pr[S_0].$$

Proof (of Theorem 1). Suppose that the public key is pk and the secret key is sk. The challenge ciphertext is denoted by $C^* = (C_0^*, C_1^*)$. We also denote by r^*, Y^*, K^* the values corresponding with r, Y, K related to C^*. We say a ciphertext C is invalid if $C_0 \notin \mathcal{L}$. The master trapdoor mt is used to solve the SM problem.

To prove the security of our scheme, we define a sequence of games that any PPT adversary can not tell the difference between two adjacent games. Let q denote the number of decryption queries that the adversary makes during the whole game.

$Game_0$: the real security game.

$Game_1$: the same as $Game_0$ except that the challenge ciphertext is generated using the secret key. That is

$$Y^* = Priv(sk, C_0^*).$$

$Game_2$: the same as $Game_1$ except that the challenge ciphertext is invalid. That is, C_0^* is chosen uniformly from $\mathcal{X} \backslash \mathcal{L}$.

$Game_3$: the same as $Game_2$ except that the decryption oracle rejects all queries (ϕ, C) that satisfy $T_1(pp, pk, \phi, C_0) \notin \mathcal{L}$. This can be achieved with the help of the master trapdoor mt.

$Game_4$: the same as $Game_3$, except that SE encrypts m_b using a random key K^+ instead of K^*.

Let $Adv_{\mathcal{A}}^i$ denote $\mathcal{A}$'s advantage in $Game_i$ for $i = 0, 1, ..., 4$.

It is clear to see $Adv_{\mathcal{A}}^0 = Adv_{\mathcal{A}}^1$ from the projective property of HPS.

Lemma 5. *Suppose that there exists a PPT adversary $\mathcal{A}$ such that $Adv_{\mathcal{A}}^1 - Adv_{\mathcal{A}}^2 = \epsilon$, then there exists a PPT adversary $\mathcal{B}$ with advantage ϵ in solving the SM problem.*

Proof. $\mathcal{B}$ receives $D = (\mathcal{X}, \mathcal{L}, Z)$ and its task is to decide whether $Z \in \mathcal{L}$. $\mathcal{B}$ picks a random $sk \in \mathcal{SK}$, computes $pk = \mu(sk)$ and sends pk to $\mathcal{A}$.

Whenever $\mathcal{A}$ submits (ϕ, C), $\mathcal{B}$ simply runs the decryption oracle with the secret key $\phi(sk)$.

When $\mathcal{A}$ submits (m_0, m_1), $\mathcal{B}$ randomly chooses $b \leftarrow_R \{0, 1\}$, it sets $C_0^* = Z, Y^* = Priv(sk, Z), K^* = \mathcal{H}(C_0^*, Y^*), C_1^* = \mathcal{E}(K^*, m_b)$ and responds with $C^* = (C_0^*, C_1^*)$.

When $\mathcal{A}$ outputs b', $\mathcal{B}$ outputs 1 if $b' = b$ and 0 otherwise.

Note that when $Z \in \mathcal{L}$, then the above game perfectly simulates $Game_1$; when $Z \in \mathcal{X} \backslash \mathcal{L}$, the above game perfectly simulates $Game_2$.   □

Lemma 6. *Suppose that there exists a PPT adversary $\mathcal{A}$ in $Game_2$ and $Game_3$ such that it can submit a query (C, ϕ) satisfying $C_0 = C_0^*$, $\phi(sk) \neq sk, Y = Y^*$ with probability δ, then there exists a PPT adversary $\mathcal{B}$ with advantage δ in breaking the CFP property.*

Proof. $\mathcal{B}$ receives X and its task is to compute $sk_1 \neq sk_2$ such that $\Lambda_{sk_1}(X) = \Lambda_{sk_2}(X)$. $\mathcal{B}$ chooses random $sk \in \mathcal{SK}$ and computes $pk = \mu(sk)$. Then $\mathcal{B}$ sends pk to $\mathcal{A}$.

Whenever $\mathcal{A}$ submits $(\phi, C), \mathcal{B}$ simply runs the decryption oracle with the secret key $\phi(sk)$.

When $\mathcal{A}$ submits $(m_0, m_1), \mathcal{B}$ randomly chooses $b \leftarrow_R \{0,1\}$, it sets $C_0^* = X, Y^* = Priv(sk, X)$, $K^* = \mathcal{H}(C_0^*, Y^*), C_1^* = \mathcal{E}(K^*, m_b)$ and responds with $C^* = (C_0^*, C_1^*)$.

Whenever $\mathcal{A}$ submits (ϕ, C) satisfying $C_0 = C_0^*, \phi(sk) \neq sk, Y = Y^*$, which means $\Lambda_{sk}(X) = \Lambda_{\phi(sk)}(X)$. Thus $\mathcal{B}$ can solve the CFP problem with output $(sk, \phi(sk))$.   □

Lemma 7. *Assume that the symmetric encryption scheme is AE-OT secure, $\mathcal{HS}$ is a family of 4-wise independent hash functions, the CFP assumption holds, then*

$$|Adv_{\mathcal{A}}^2 - Adv_{\mathcal{A}}^3| \leq q(2^{l-(\kappa-1)/2} + Adv_{\mathcal{C}}^{CFP} + Adv_{\mathcal{D},SE}^{INT\text{-}OT}).$$

Proof. Let E be the event that a query (C, ϕ) is rejected in $Game_3$ but not rejected in $Game_2$. Then we have $|Adv_{\mathcal{A}}^2 - Adv_{\mathcal{A}}^3| \leq Pr[E]$. Let Γ^* be the random variable (C_0^*, Y^*), Γ be the random variable (C_0, Y).

Case 1: $C_0 = C_0^*$.
  - $\phi(sk) = sk$. According to the κ-entropic property, given pk and a random $C_0^* \in \mathcal{X} \backslash \mathcal{L}$, $H_\infty(\Lambda_{sk}(C_0^*)) = H_\infty(Y^*) \geq \kappa$, thus $H_\infty(\Gamma^*) \geq \kappa$, then we can get that $SD((\mathcal{H}, pk, \mathcal{H}(\Gamma^*)), (\mathcal{H}, pk, U_l)) \leq 2^{(l-\kappa)/2}$ from the leftover hash lemma. And according to the INT-OT property of the SE scheme, for a uniformly chosen $\bar{K} \in U_l$, given a valid symmetric ciphertext C_1^*, the probability that an adversary can generate a $C_1 \neq C_1^*$ s.t. $\mathcal{D}(\bar{K}, C_1) \neq \perp$ is bounded by $Adv_{\mathcal{D},SE}^{INT\text{-}OT}$, so in this case the adversary can produce a ciphertext s.t. $\mathcal{D}(K^*, C_1) \neq \perp$ with probability at most $Adv_{\mathcal{D},SE}^{INT\text{-}OT} + 2^{(l-\kappa)/2} < Adv_{\mathcal{D},SE}^{INT\text{-}OT} + 2^{l-(\kappa-1)/2}$.
  - $\phi(sk) \neq sk$ and $C_0' = T_1(pp, pk, \phi, C_0) \notin \mathcal{L}$. From Lemma 6 it can be seen that $Pr[Y = Y^*] = \delta$, hence $Pr[\Gamma = \Gamma^*] = \delta$, where δ is negligible under the CFP assumption. We have $H_\infty(Y^*) \geq \kappa$, similarly, since $C_0' \notin \mathcal{L}$, according to the κ-entropic property, $H_\infty(\Lambda_{sk}(C_0')) \geq \kappa$, and Y is determined by C_0 and $\Lambda_{sk}(C_0')$, hence $H_\infty(Y) \geq \kappa$ and $H_\infty(\Gamma) \geq \kappa$. From Lemma 3 we know:

$$SD((pk, \mathcal{H}, \mathcal{H}(\Gamma^*), \mathcal{H}(\Gamma)), (pk, \mathcal{H}, \mathcal{H}(\Gamma^*), U_l)) \leq 2^{l-(\kappa-1)/2} + \delta.$$

And according to the INT-OT property of the SE scheme, for a uniformly chosen $\bar{K} \in U_l$, given a valid symmetric ciphertext C_1^*, the probability that an adversary can generate a $C_1 \neq C_1^*$ s.t. $\mathcal{D}(\bar{K}, C_1) \neq \perp$ is bounded by $Adv_{\mathcal{D},SE}^{INT\text{-}OT}$, so in this case the adversary can produce a ciphertext s.t. $\mathcal{D}(K, C_1) \neq \perp$ with probability at most $Adv_{\mathcal{D},SE}^{INT\text{-}OT} + Adv_{\mathcal{C}}^{CFP} + 2^{l-(\kappa-1)/2}$.

Case 2: $C_0 \neq C_0^*$, and $C_0' = T_1(pp, pk, \phi, C_0) \notin \mathcal{L}$. Since $C_0 \neq C_0^*$, $\Gamma \neq \Gamma^*$. And as discussed above we have $H_\infty(Y^*) \geq \kappa$. Since $C_0' \notin \mathcal{L}$, according to the κ-entropic property, $H_\infty(\Lambda_{sk}(C_0')) \geq \kappa$, and Y is determined by C_0 and $\Lambda_{sk}(C_0')$, hence $H_\infty(Y) \geq \kappa$ and $H_\infty(\Gamma) \geq \kappa$. From Lemma 3 we know:

$$SD((pk, \mathcal{H}, \mathcal{H}(\Gamma^*), \mathcal{H}(\Gamma)), (pk, \mathcal{H}, \mathcal{H}(\Gamma^*), U_l)) \leq 2^{l-(\kappa-1)/2}.$$

According to the INT-OT property of the SE scheme, for a uniformly chosen $\bar{K} \in U_l$, given a valid symmetric ciphertext C_1^*, the probability that an adversary can generate a $C_1 \neq C_1^*$ s.t. $\mathcal{D}(\bar{K}, C_1) \neq \bot$ is bounded by $Adv_{\mathcal{D},SE}^{INT\text{-}OT}$, so in this case the adversary can produce a ciphertext s.t. $\mathcal{D}(K, C_1) \neq \bot$ with probability at most $Adv_{\mathcal{D},SE}^{INT\text{-}OT} + 2^{l-(\kappa-1)/2}$.

From the above analysis, we can see that $|Adv_{\mathcal{A}}^2 - Adv_{\mathcal{A}}^3| \leq q(2^{l-(\kappa-1)/2} + Adv_{\mathcal{C}}^{CFP} + Adv_{\mathcal{D},SE}^{INT\text{-}OT})$. □

Lemma 8. *Assume that $\mathcal{HS}$ is a family of 4-wise independent hash functions, then $|Adv_{\mathcal{A}}^3 - Adv_{\mathcal{A}}^4| \leq 2^{(l-k)/2}$.*

Proof. Since in both $Game_3$ and $Game_4$, all decryption queries are rejected except those $(\phi, (C_0, C_1))$ satisfying $C_0' \in \mathcal{L}$, and the value of $\Lambda_{\phi(sk)}(C_0) = T_2(pp, \phi, \Lambda_{sk}(C_0'), C_0)$ is completely determined by pk, ϕ and C_0, so $\Lambda_{\phi(sk)}(C_0)$ leaks no more information about sk than pk. As a result, conditioned on the decryption answers, it still holds that $H_\infty(Y^*) \geq \kappa$ and $H_\infty(\Gamma^*) \geq \kappa$. Then from the leftover hash lemma, $SD((\mathcal{H}, pk, \mathcal{H}(\Gamma^*)), (\mathcal{H}, pk, U_l)) \leq 2^{(l-\kappa)/2}$, so $|Adv_{\mathcal{A}}^3 - Adv_{\mathcal{A}}^4| \leq 2^{(l-k)/2}$. □

Lemma 9. *Suppose that there exists a PPT adversary $\mathcal{A}$ such that $Adv_{\mathcal{A}}^4 = \epsilon$, then there exists a PPT adversary $\mathcal{B}$ with the same advantage in breaking the IND-OT security of the SE scheme.*

Proof. $\mathcal{B}$ chooses random $sk \in \mathcal{SK}$, computes $pk = \mu(sk)$ and sends pk to $\mathcal{A}$.

Whenever $\mathcal{A}$ submits (ϕ, C), $\mathcal{B}$ simply runs the decryption oracle with the secret key $\phi(sk)$.

When $\mathcal{A}$ submits (m_0, m_1), $\mathcal{B}$ sends (m_0, m_1) to its challenger and receives C_1^*. Then $\mathcal{B}$ chooses random $C_0^* \in \mathcal{X} \backslash \mathcal{L}$ and responds with $C^* = (C_0^*, C_1^*)$.

When $\mathcal{A}$ outputs b', $\mathcal{B}$ outputs b'. □

4   Instantiations

In the following we give three instantiations from the DDH, QR and HR assumptions, wherein the one based on the DDH assumption is the same as that in [18], so our construction can be seen as a generalization and high level understanding of schemes in [18]. And the schemes based on the QR and DCR assumptions can be seen as applications of our general approach.

4.1   Instantiation from DDH

Decisional Diffie-Hellman Assumption (DDH). Let $\mathcal{G}$ denote a group generation algorithm, which takes in a security parameter λ and outputs a prime p and a group description G of order p.

Run $\mathcal{G}(1^\lambda)$ to get (p, G), and randomly choose $g_1, g_2 \in G, r \neq w \in \mathbb{Z}_p$. Set $Z_0 = (g_1^r, g_2^r), Z_1 = (g_1^r, g_2^w)$. The advantage of $\mathcal{A}$ is defined as

$$Adv_{\mathcal{A}}^{DDH} = \Big| \Pr[\mathcal{A}(g_1, g_2, Z_1) = 1] - \Pr[\mathcal{A}(g_1, g_2, Z_0) = 1] \Big|.$$

Definition 7 (DDH). *We say that $\mathcal{G}$ satisfies the DDH assumption if for any PPT algorithm $\mathcal{A}$, $Adv_{\mathcal{A}}^{DDH}$ is negligible in λ.*

We recall the projective HPS constructed by Cramer and Shoup [11], of which the corresponding subset membership problem is based on the DDH assumption. Run $\mathcal{G}(1^\lambda)$ to get (p, G), and let g_1, g_2 be two independent generators. Here the master trapdoor is $w := log_{g_1} g_2$ Define $\mathcal{X} = G^2$ and $\mathcal{L} = \{(g_1^r, g_2^r) : r \in \mathbb{Z}_p\}$. The value r is a witness of $L \in \mathcal{L}$. Let $\mathcal{SK} = \mathbb{Z}_p^2, \mathcal{PK} = G$ and $\mathcal{Y} = G$. For $sk = (sk_1, sk_2) \in \mathbb{Z}_p^2$, define $\mu(sk) = pk = g_1^{sk_1} g_2^{sk_2}$. For $X = (X_1, X_2) \in \mathcal{X}$, define

$$\Lambda_{sk}(X) = X_1^{sk_1} X_2^{sk_2}. \tag{1}$$

Then given $pk = \mu(sk), L \in \mathcal{L}$ and a witness $r \in \mathbb{Z}_p$, the public evaluation algorithm $Pub(pk, L, r)$ can compute $Y = \Lambda_{sk}(L)$ as $Y = pk^r$. Correctness can be easily verified by the definition of μ and eq. (1).

As stated in [20], in the above HPS, $H_\infty(\Lambda_{sk}(X)|pk, X) = log_2(|G|)$ for $X \in \mathcal{X} \backslash \mathcal{L}$.

It is easy to see that the CFP holds under the DDH assumption. For an adversary $\mathcal{B}$ which receives $D = (g_1, g_2, \hat{g}_1, \hat{g}_2)$ and its task is to decide whether D is a DDH tuple. $\mathcal{B}$ chooses random $r \neq w \in \mathbb{Z}_p$, computes $X_1 = g_1^r, X_2 = g_2^w$ and sends $X = (X_1, X_2)$ to $\mathcal{A}$. If $\mathcal{A}$ can output $sk \neq \hat{sk}$ and $\Lambda_{sk}(X) = \Lambda_{\hat{sk}}(X)$, that is, $g_1^{r sk_1} g_2^{w sk_2} = g_1^{r \hat{sk}_1} g_2^{w \hat{sk}_2}$, then one can compute a σ such that $g_2 = g_1^\sigma$, and hence decide whether D is a DDH tuple by checking whether the equation $\hat{g}_2 = \hat{g}_1^\sigma$ holds.

Here we define $\phi_{a_1,a_2,b_1,b_2}(sk_1, sk_2) = (a_1 sk_1 + b_1, a_2 sk_2 + b_2)$ and $X' = T_1(pp, pk, \phi, X) = (X_1^{a_1}, X_2^{a_2}), T_2(pp, \phi, \Lambda_{sk}(X'), X) = \Lambda_{sk}(X')X_1^{b_1} X_2^{b_2} = X_1^{a_1 sk_1 + b_1} \cdot X_2^{a_2 sk_2 + b_2}$. The correctness can be easily verified.

$Keygen(pp)$	$Enc(pk, m)$	$Dec(sk, C)$
$pp = (\mathcal{H}, p, G, g_1, g_2)$	$r \leftarrow_R \mathbb{Z}_p^*; C_{01} = g_1^r, C_{02} = g_2^r$	Parse C as (C_{01}, C_{02}, C_1)
$sk_1, sk_2 \leftarrow_R \mathbb{Z}_p$	$K = \mathcal{H}(C_{01}, C_{02}, pk^r)$	$K = \mathcal{H}(C_{01}, C_{02}, C_{01}^{sk_1} C_{02}^{sk_2})$
$pk = g_1^{sk_1} g_2^{sk_2}$	$C_1 = \mathcal{E}(K, m)$	Return $\{m, \bot\} \leftarrow \mathcal{D}(K, C_1)$
Return (sk, pk)	Return $C = (C_{01}, C_{02}, C_1)$	

Fig.1. PKE scheme $HE_1 = (Keygen, Enc, Dec)$ [18]

Instantiations from the HR assumption [23,18] can be got similarly.

4.2   Instantiation from QR

Quadratic Residuosity Assumption (QR). Let RSA_{gen} denote an RSA generation algorithm, which takes in a security parameter λ and outputs (P, Q, N, g)
such that $N = PQ, P = 2p + 1, Q = 2q + 1$ for primes P, Q, p, q. Let J_N denote
the subgroup of elements in $\mathbb{Z}_N^*$ with Jacobi symbol 1, and let QR_N denote the
unique (cyclic) subgroup of $\mathbb{Z}_N^*$ of order pq. Let g denote the generator of QR_N.

Generally speaking, QR assumption means that it is difficult to distinguish
a random element in QR_N from a random element in $J_N \backslash QR_N$. To formulate
this notion precisely, run $RSA_{gen}(1^\lambda)$ to get (P, Q, N, g), and randomly choose
$u_0 \in QR_N, u_1 \in J_N \backslash QR_N$. Master trapdoor here is (P, Q). The advantage of $\mathcal{A}$
is defined as

$$Adv_{\mathcal{A}}^{QR} = \Big| \Pr[\mathcal{A}(g, u_1) = 1] - \Pr[\mathcal{A}(g, u_0) = 1] \Big|.$$

Definition 8 (QR). *We say that RSA_{gen} satisfies the QR assumption if for
any PPT algorithm $\mathcal{A}$, $Adv_{\mathcal{A}}^{QR}$ is negligible in λ.*

We recall the projective HPS constructed by Cramer and Shoup [11,20], of
which the corresponding subset membership problem is based on the QR assump-
tion. Run $RSA_{gen}(1^\lambda)$ to get (P, Q, N, g). Define $\mathcal{X} = J_N$ and $\mathcal{L} = QR_N = \{g^r :
r \in \mathbb{Z}_{pq}\}$. The value r is a witness of $L \in \mathcal{L}$. Let $\mathcal{SK} = \mathbb{Z}_{[N/2]}^k, \mathcal{PK} = QR_N^k$ and
$\mathcal{Y} = J_N^k$. For $sk = (s_1, ..., s_k) \in \mathbb{Z}_{[N/2]}^k$, define $\mu(sk) = pk = (pk_1, ..., pk_k) =
(g^{s_1}, ..., g^{s_k})$. For $X \in \mathcal{X}$, define

$$\Lambda_{sk}(X) = (X^{s_1}, ..., X^{s_k}). \tag{2}$$

Then given $pk = \mu(sk), L \in \mathcal{L}$ and a witness $r \in \mathbb{Z}_{[N/4]}$, the public evaluation
algorithm $Pub(pk, L, r)$ can compute $Y = (Y_1, ..., Y_k) = (pk_1^r, ..., pk_k^r)$.

For $X \in \mathcal{X} \backslash \mathcal{L}, H_\infty((X^{s_1}, ..., X^{s_k})|pk, X) = k$.

The CFP can be easily deduced from the QR assumption similarly as the
analysis in [8,14]. For an adversary $\mathcal{B}$ which receives $D = (g, u)$ and its task is to
decide whether $u \in QR_N$. $\mathcal{B}$ chooses random $r \in \mathbb{Z}_{[N/4]}$, computes $X = -g^r$ and
sends X to $\mathcal{A}$. If $\mathcal{A}$ can output $sk \neq \hat{sk}$ which satisfy that $\Lambda_{sk}(X) = \Lambda_{\hat{sk}}(X)$.
Then there must exists $s_i \neq \hat{s}_i$ such that $(-g^r)^{s_i} = (-g^r)^{\hat{s}_i}$ for some $1 \leq i \leq
k$. Since with overwhelming probability g^r is a generator of QR_N, then with
overwhelming probability $s_i = \hat{s}_i \bmod pq$, so one can get the value of pq, hence
factor N and decide whether $u \in QR_N$.

Here we define $\phi_{a_1, b_1, ..., a_k, b_k}(sk) = (a_1 s_1 + b_1, ..., a_k s_k + b_k)$ and T_1 be the
identity function, $T_2(pp, pk, \phi, Y, X) = (Y_1^{a_1} X_1^{b_1}, ..., Y_k^{a_k} X_k^{b_k})$. The correctness
can be easily verified.

$Keygen(pp)$	$Enc(pk,m)$	$Dec(sk,C)$
$pp = (\mathcal{H}, P, Q, N, g)$	$r \leftarrow_R \mathbb{Z}_{[N/4]}; C_0 = g^r$	Parse C as (C_0, C_1)
for $i = 1$ to $4l$ do	$K = \mathcal{H}(C_0, pk_1^r, ..., pk_{4l}^r)$	$K = \mathcal{H}(C_0, C_0^{s_1}, ..., C_0^{s_{4l}})$
$s_i \leftarrow_R \mathbb{Z}_{[N/2]}; pk_i = g^{s_i}$	$C_1 = \mathcal{E}(K, m)$	
$pk = (pk_i), sk = (s_i)$	Return $C = (C_0, C_1)$	Return $\{m, \perp\} \leftarrow \mathcal{D}(K, C_1)$
Return (sk, pk)		

Fig. 2. PKE scheme $\text{HE}_2 = (Keygen, Enc, Dec)$. (Here we require $k = 4l$.)

4.3 Instantiation from DCR

Decisional Composite Residuosity Assumption (DCR).[24] Let RSA_{gen} denote an RSA generation algorithm, which takes in a security parameter λ and outputs (P, Q, N) such that $N = PQ, P = 2p + 1, Q = 2q + 1$ for primes P, Q, p, q. Generally speaking, DCR assumption means that it is difficult to distinguish whether a randomly chosen element in $Z_{N^2}^*$ is an Nth power. To formulate this notion precisely, run $RSA_{gen}(1^\lambda)$ to get (P, Q, N). Master trapdoor is (P, Q). The advantage of $\mathcal{A}$ is defined as

$$Adv_{\mathcal{A}}^{DCR} = \Big| \Pr[\mathcal{A}(N, r^N \bmod N^2) = 1] - \Pr[\mathcal{A}(N, r) = 1] \Big|.$$

Here r is chosen randomly from $\mathbb{Z}_{N^2}^*$.

Definition 9 (DCR). *We say that RSA_{gen} satisfies the DCR assumption if for all PPT algorithm $\mathcal{A}, Adv_{\mathcal{A}}^{DCR}$ is negligible in λ.*

We recall the projective HPS constructed by Cramer and Shoup [11], of which the corresponding subset membership problem is based on the DCR assumption. Run $RSA_{gen}(1^\lambda)$ to get (P, Q, N). Define $\mathcal{X} = G_N \cdot G_{N'} \cdot I$, where G_τ is a cyclic group of order $\tau, N' = pq, I$ is the subgroup of $\mathbb{Z}_{N^2}^*$ generated by $(-1 \bmod N^2)$, $\mathcal{L} = G_{N'} \cdot I = \{g^r\}$, here r is the witness and $g = -\zeta^N$ can be seen as a random generator of $\mathcal{L}$, where $\zeta \leftarrow_R \mathbb{Z}_{N^2}^*$.

Let $\mathcal{SK} = \mathbb{Z}_{[N^2/2]}, \mathcal{PK} = G_{N'} \cdot I$ and $\mathcal{Y} = G_N \cdot G_{N'} \cdot I$. For $sk = s \in \mathbb{Z}_{[N^2/2]}$, define $\mu(sk) = pk = g^s$. For $X \in \mathcal{X}$, define $\Lambda_{sk}(X) = X^s$.

Then given $pk = \mu(sk), L \in \mathcal{L}$ and a witness $r \in \mathbb{Z}_{[N/2]}$, the public evaluation algorithm $Pub(pk, L, r)$ can compute $Y = pk^r$.

For $X \in \mathcal{X} \backslash \mathcal{L}, H_\infty((X^s)|pk, X) = log_2(N)$.

The CFP can be easily deduced from the DCR assumption similarly as the analysis in [8,14]. For an adversary $\mathcal{B}$ which receives $D = (N, u)$ and its task is to decide whether u is an Nth power. $\mathcal{B}$ chooses random $\zeta \in \mathbb{Z}_{N^2}^*, \alpha \in \mathbb{Z}_N^*, \beta \in \mathbb{Z}_{[N/4]}$, computes $X = -(1 + N)^\alpha \zeta^{N\beta}$ and sends X to $\mathcal{A}$. If $\mathcal{A}$ can output $sk \neq \hat{sk}$ which satisfy that $\Lambda_{sk}(X) = \Lambda_{\hat{sk}}(X)$. Then there must be $(1 + N)^{\alpha sk} = (1 + N)^{\alpha \hat{sk}}$ and $(-\zeta^N)^{\beta sk} = (-\zeta^N)^{\beta \hat{sk}}$, then with overwhelming probability there is $sk = \hat{sk} \bmod pq$, thus $\mathcal{B}$ can factor N and solve the DCR problem.

Here we define $\phi_{a,b}(sk) = as + b$ and T_1 be the identity function, $T_2(pp, pk, \phi, Y, X) = Y^a X^b$. The correctness can be easily verified.

$Keygen(pp)$	$Enc(pk, m)$	$Dec(sk, C)$
$pp = (\mathcal{H}, P, Q, N, g)$	$r \leftarrow_R \mathbb{Z}_{[N/2]}; C_0 = g^r$	Parse C as (C_0, C_1)
$s \leftarrow_R \mathbb{Z}_{[N^2/2]}$	$K = \mathcal{H}(C_0, pk^r)$	$K = \mathcal{H}(C_0, C_0^s)$
$pk = g^s$	$C_1 = \mathcal{E}(K, m)$	
Return (sk, pk)	Return $C = (C_0, C_1)$	Return $\{m, \perp\} \leftarrow \mathcal{D}(K, C_1)$

Fig.3. PKE scheme $HE_3 = (Keygen, Enc, Dec)$

5   Conclusion

In this paper, we give a generic public key encryption construction secure against related key attacks from the projective HPS in the standard model, show the DDH based scheme in [18] fits our framework and give more instantiations based on other hard subset membership problems, like the QR and DCR assumptions. We require the HPS be κ-entropic and use a 4-wise independent hash function as a randomness extractor. Compared with previous works, our construction removed the use of one-time signatures, thus is more efficient.

Acknowledgments. We are very grateful to anonymous reviewers for their helpful comments. We also thank Yamin Liu for helpful discussions.

References

1. Bellare, M., Cash, D.: Pseudorandom Functions and Permutations Provably Secure against Related-Key Attacks. In: Rabin, T. (ed.) CRYPTO 2010. LNCS, vol. 6223, pp. 666–684. Springer, Heidelberg (2010)
2. Bellare, M., Cash, D., Miller, R.: Cryptography Secure against Related-Key Attacks and Tampering. In: Lee, D.H., Wang, X. (eds.) ASIACRYPT 2011. LNCS, vol. 7073, pp. 486–503. Springer, Heidelberg (2011), Also Cryptology ePrint Archive, Report 2011/252
3. Bellare, M., Kohno, T.: A Theoretical Treatment of Related-Key Attacks: RKA-PRPs, RKA-PRFs, and Applications. In: Biham, E. (ed.) EUROCRYPT 2003. LNCS, vol. 2656, pp. 491–506. Springer, Heidelberg (2003)
4. Bellare, M., Namprempre, C.: Authenticated Encryption: Relations among Notions and Analysis of the Generic Composition Paradigm. In: Okamoto, T. (ed.) ASIACRYPT 2000. LNCS, vol. 1976, pp. 531–545. Springer, Heidelberg (2000)
5. Bellare, M., Paterson, K.G., Thomson, S.: RKA Security beyond the Linear Barrier: IBE, Encryption and Signatures. In: Wang, X., Sako, K. (eds.) ASIACRYPT 2012. LNCS, vol. 7658, pp. 331–348. Springer, Heidelberg (2012)
6. Biham, E.: New Types of Cryptanalytic Attacks Using Related Keys. In: Helleseth, T. (ed.) EUROCRYPT 1993. LNCS, vol. 765, pp. 398–409. Springer, Heidelberg (1994)
7. Biham, E., Shamir, A.: Differential Fault Analysis of Secret Key Cryptosystems. In: Kaliski Jr., B.S. (ed.) CRYPTO 1997. LNCS, vol. 1294, pp. 513–525. Springer, Heidelberg (1997)
8. Boneh, D.: Twenty Years of Attacks on the RSA Cryptosystem (1999)

9. Boneh, D., DeMillo, R.A., Lipton, R.J.: On the Importance of Checking Cryptographic Protocols for Faults (Extended Abstract). In: Fumy, W. (ed.) EUROCRYPT 1997. LNCS, vol. 1233, pp. 37–51. Springer, Heidelberg (1997)
10. Cramer, R., Shoup, V.: A Practical Public Key Cryptosystem Provably Secure against Adaptive Chosen Ciphertext Attack. In: Krawczyk, H. (ed.) CRYPTO 1998. LNCS, vol. 1462, pp. 13–25. Springer, Heidelberg (1998)
11. Cramer, R., Shoup, V.: Universal Hash Proofs and a Paradigm for Adaptive Chosen Ciphertext Secure Public-Key Encryption. In: Knudsen, L.R. (ed.) EUROCRYPT 2002. LNCS, vol. 2332, pp. 45–64. Springer, Heidelberg (2002)
12. Cramer, R., Shoup, V.: Design and Analysis of Practical Public-Key Encryption Schemes Secure against Adaptive Chosen Ciphertext Attack. SIAM J. Compt. 33(1), 167–226 (2003)
13. Damgård, I., Faust, S., Mukherjee, P., Venturi, D.: Bounded Tamper Resilience: How to Go beyond the Algebraic Barrier. In: Sako, K., Sarkar, P. (eds.) ASIACRYPT 2013, Part II. LNCS, vol. 8270, pp. 140–160. Springer, Heidelberg (2013)
14. Groth, J.: Cryptography in Subgroups of $\mathbb{Z}_n^*$. In: Kilian, J. (ed.) TCC 2005. LNCS, vol. 3378, pp. 50–65. Springer, Heidelberg (2005)
15. Håstad, J., Impagliazzo, R., Levin, L.A., Luby, M.: A Pseudorandom Generator from any One-way Function. SIAM J. Comput. 28(4), 1364–1396 (1999)
16. Hofheinz, D., Kiltz, E.: Secure Hybrid Encryption from Weakened Key Encapsulation. In: Menezes, A. (ed.) CRYPTO 2007. LNCS, vol. 4622, pp. 553–571. Springer, Heidelberg (2007)
17. Hofheinz, D., Kiltz, E.: The Group of Signed Quadratic Residues and Applications. In: Halevi, S. (ed.) CRYPTO 2009. LNCS, vol. 5677, pp. 637–653. Springer, Heidelberg (2009)
18. Jia, D., Lu, X., Li, B., Mei, Q.: RKA Secure PKE Based on the DDH and HR Assumptions. In: Susilo, W., Reyhanitabar, R. (eds.) ProvSec 2013. LNCS, vol. 8209, pp. 271–287. Springer, Heidelberg (2013)
19. Kalai, Y.T., Kanukurthi, B., Sahai, A.: Cryptography with Tamperable and Leaky Memory. In: Rogaway, P. (ed.) CRYPTO 2011. LNCS, vol. 6841, pp. 373–390. Springer, Heidelberg (2011)
20. Kiltz, E., Pietrzak, K., Stam, M., Yung, M.: A New Randomness Extraction Paradigm for Hybrid Encryption. In: Joux, A. (ed.) EUROCRYPT 2009. LNCS, vol. 5479, pp. 590–609. Springer, Heidelberg (2009); Also Cryptology ePrint Archive, 2008/304
21. Knudsen, L.R.: Cryptanalysis of LOKI91. In: Seberry, J., Zheng, Y. (eds.) AUSCRYPT 1992. LNCS, vol. 718, pp. 196–208. Springer, Heidelberg (1993)
22. Kurosawa, K., Desmedt, Y.: A New Paradigm of Hybrid Encryption Scheme. In: Franklin, M. (ed.) CRYPTO 2004. LNCS, vol. 3152, pp. 426–442. Springer, Heidelberg (2004)
23. Naccache, D., Stern, J.: A New Public Key Cryptosystem based on Higher Residues. In: CCS 1998, pp. 59–66 (1998)
24. Paillier, P.: Public-Key Cryptosystems Based on Composite Degree Residuosity Classes. In: Stern, J. (ed.) EUROCRYPT 1999. LNCS, vol. 1592, pp. 223–238. Springer, Heidelberg (1999)
25. Wee, H.: Public Key Encryption against Related Key Attacks. In: Fischlin, M., Buchmann, J., Manulis, M. (eds.) PKC 2012. LNCS, vol. 7293, pp. 262–279. Springer, Heidelberg (2012)

Towards Symmetric Functional Encryption for Regular Languages with Predicate Privacy

Fu-Kuo Tseng, Rong-Jaye Chen, and Bao-Shuh Paul Lin

National Chiao-Tung University,
No.1001, Daxue Road, Hsinchu City 300, Taiwan
{fktseng,rjchen}@cs.nctu.edu.tw, bplin@mail.nctu.edu.tw

Abstract. We present a symmetric-key predicate-only functional encryption system, SP-FE, which supports functionality for regular languages described by deterministic finite automata. In SP-FE, a data owner can encrypt a string of symbols as encrypted symbols for matching. Later, the data owner can generate predicate tokens of the transitions in a deterministic finite automaton (DFA). The server with these tokens can decrypt a sequence of encrypted symbols correctly and transfer from one state to another accordingly. If the final state belongs to the set of accept states, the server takes assigned operations or returns the corresponding encrypted data. We have proven SP-FE preserves both keyword privacy and predicate privacy through security analysis and security games. However, to achieve predicate privacy, we put bounds on the length of a keyword and the number of states of a DFA. Due to these restrictions, SP-FE can only capture finite languages. Finally, we present the performance analysis of SP-FE and mention possible future work.

Keywords: symmetric functional encryption, deterministic finite automaton, regular language, predicate-only scheme, predicate privacy.

1 Introduction

Functional public-key encryption schemes [1] and many of their instances like attribute-based encryption schemes [2,3,4] and predicate encryption schemes [5,6,7] were devised to support expressive search predicates on encrypted data. However, in all of these schemes, search predicates involve only a *fixed* number of keywords from the predefined keyword universe. Processing a string of encrypted symbols representing a keyword is essential for the predicates of certain regular languages for lexical analysis and pattern matching.

However, the predicate tokens in functional encryption schemes reveal the content of the search predicates because encryption does not require a private key in the public-key setting. Adversaries can encrypt the keywords of their choices and check the ciphertexts with the delegated predicate token to learn whether the chosen keywords satisfy the search predicate encoded in the predicate token. Therefore, predicate privacy is inherently impossible to achieve in the public-key setting. Researchers started focusing on the symmetric-key setting for predicate

M. Yoshida and K. Mouri (Eds.): IWSEC 2014, LNCS 8639, pp. 266–275, 2014.

privacy with keyword-based search predicates [8,9,10]. Functional encryption for regular languages, a type of symbol-based search predicates, was considered in [11] and [12], while functional encryption for regular languages with additional *keyword privacy* and *predicate privacy* is still an open problem.

Our Contributions. We propose a symmetric-key predicate-only functional encryption scheme, SP-FE, supporting predicates of deterministic finite automata (DFA). We make use of Yoshino *et al.* scheme [10] by encrypting each symbol in the plaintext as an encrypted symbol and each symbol set of a transition as a predicate token. However, direct transformation cannot achieve both plaintext/keyword and predicate privacy because some information may reveal to the adversary: (1) The length of a plaintext, n_w, (2) the number of states of a DFA, n_Q, (3) the number of accept states, $|F|$, (4) the number of transitions, $|\delta|$, and (5) the path of the transition. Thus, we systematically add special symbols among ordinary symbols in the plaintext, while inserting dummy states, transitions and shuffling states of a DFA. These designs guarantee the adversaries cannot gain extra advantages in the challenge games. However, to achieve predicate privacy, we put bounds on the length of a string and the number of (accept) states of a DFA, thus SP-FE can only capture finite languages.

Related Works. Functional encryption schemes [1] are non-interactive public-key encryption schemes where anyone possessing a secret key sk_f can compute a function $f(x)$ of a value x from the encryption $\texttt{Enc}(x)$ without learning any other information about x. However, the predicate tokens in these functional encryption schemes may reveal the content of the underlying search predicates because encryption does not require a private key in the public-key setting. Thus predicate privacy is inherently impossible to achieve in the public-key setting. Shen *et al.* [9] was the first to consider predicate privacy in the symmetric-key setting. Blundo *et al.* [8] used the assumptions related to linear split secret sharing, while Yoshino *et al.* [10] further enhanced the efficiency by prime-order group instantiation. However, in all of these schemes, search predicates involve only a fixed number of keywords in the keyword universe. Processing a string of searchable symbols is essential for the search predicates of regular languages. The functional encryption for regular languages was devised in the public-key setting with message privacy only [11]. The functional encryption for regular languages with *keyword privacy* and *predicate privacy* is still an open problem.

2   Background and Preliminary

This section presents the background and preliminary of SP-FE.

2.1   Deterministic Finite Automata and Regular Languages

A deterministic finite automaton (DFA) is a finite state machine that accepts or rejects finite strings of symbols. A DFA M is a quintuple $(Q, \Sigma, \delta, q_0, F)$ where (1) Q is a finite set of states, (2) Σ is the input alphabet, a finite set of symbols, (3) $\delta : Q \times \Sigma \rightarrow Q$ is the transition function, where $(q, q', \sigma) \in \delta$ iff $\delta(q, \sigma) = q'$, (4) q_0 is an initial state, and (5) F is the set of final states, a subset of Q. $\square$

Given a DFA $M = (Q, \Sigma, \delta, q_0, F)$, if M accepts an string $w = w_1 w_2, \cdots, w_n$ $\in \Sigma^n$, there exists a sequence of states, a transition path, $r = r_0, r_1, ..., r_n \in Q^n$, where (1) $r_0 = q_0$, (2) $\delta(r_i, w_{i+1}) = r_{i+1}$, for $0 \leq i \leq n-1$, and (3) $r_n \in F$. A regular language is also defined as a language recognized by a DFA.

2.2   Definitions and Security Model

A symmetric-key predicate-only functional encryption scheme for DFA-based predicates consists of four algorithms: Setup, Encrypt, KeyGen, and Decrypt. In addition to a security parameter, the setup algorithm takes as input a alphabet Σ and a special alphabet Σ'. The algorithms are described as follows.

- *Setup*$(1^\lambda, \Sigma, \Sigma')$: It takes a security parameter 1^λ as input and outputs public parameters and a secret key SK. Public parameters include two parameters to decide the maximum length of an input string, N_w, the maximum number of states, N_Q, and the maximum number of transitions in a DFA, $N_\delta = N_Q^2$.
- *Encrypt*(SK, w): It takes a secret key SK and a string (of symbols) w, where $|w| \leq N_w/2$, and outputs a ciphertext CT, a string of encrypted symbols.
- *KeyGen*$(SK, M=(Q, \Sigma, \delta, q_0, F))$: It takes a secret key SK and a DFA M as input, where $|Q| \leq N_Q/2$ and outputs a TK, a string of encrypted transitions.
- *Decrypt*(TK, CT): It takes a token TK and a ciphertext CT as input, and outputs either '1' ('Accept') or '0' ('Reject') indicating that the result of the DFA M encoded in TK on the input w encrypted in CT. □

Security Model. The selective game-based security is considered in SK-FE.

- **Setup:** The challenger C runs the setup algorithm and gives public parameters to the adversary $\mathcal{A}$. $\mathcal{A}$ outputs a bit $d \in \{0, 1\}$: if $d = 0$, $\mathcal{A}$ takes up a ciphertext challenge and outputs two plaintexts w_0 and w_1. Otherwise, $\mathcal{A}$ takes up a token challenge and outputs two description of DFAs M_0 and M_1.

- **Phase 1:** $\mathcal{A}$ adaptively outputs one of the following two queries. In a ciphertext challenge, $\mathcal{A}$ issues ith ciphertext query by requesting for the ciphertext CT^i of w^i. C responds with $CT^i \leftarrow Encrypt(SK, w^i)$. Also, $\mathcal{A}$ issues jth token query by requesting a DFA M^j with the restriction that M^j accepts or rejects both w_0 and w_1 with the same number of accept states in the transition paths. C responds with $TK^j \leftarrow KeyGen(SK, M^j)$. In a token challenge, $\mathcal{A}$ issues ith ciphertext query by requesting for a string of ciphertext CT^i of w^i with the restriction that w^i is accepted or rejected by both M_0 and M_1 with the same number of accept states in the transition paths. C responds with $CT^i \leftarrow Encrypt(SK, w^i)$. Also, $\mathcal{A}$ issues jth token query by requesting for a DFA M^j. C responds with $TK^j \leftarrow KeyGen(SK, M^j)$. The restrictions are to ensure the challenge is not trivial.

- **Challenge:** The challenger C flips a random coin $b \in \{0, 1\}$. If $\mathcal{A}$ has chosen the ciphertext challenge, C gives $CT_b \leftarrow Encrypt(SK, w_b)$ to $\mathcal{A}$; otherwise ($\mathcal{A}$ has chosen the token challenge), C gives $TK_b \leftarrow KeyGen(SK, M_b)$ to $\mathcal{A}$.

- **Phase 2:** $\mathcal{A}$ continues to query CT^i and TK^j as in Phase 1.

- **Guess:** $\mathcal{A}$ outputs a guess $b' \in \{0, 1\}$ of b. The advantage of an adversary $\mathcal{A}$ in this game is defined as $Pr[b' = b] - \frac{1}{2}$.

Definition 1. *A symmetric-key predicate-only functional encryption scheme for DFA-type predicates is token indistinguishable if all polynomial-time adversaries have at most a negligible advantage in winning the above token challenge game. This property guarantees predicate privacy.*

Definition 2. *A symmetric-key predicate-only functional encryption scheme for DFA-type predicates is ciphertext indistinguishable if all polynomial-time adversaries have at most a negligible advantage in winning the above ciphertext challenge game. This property guarantees keyword privacy.*

2.3 Notation

Σ is a set of ordinary symbols used to form a keyword/plaintext w, while Σ' is a set of special symbols randomly added into w to form w'. The special symbols cannot be specified in w. The union of these two sets forms Σ''. Each symbol $w_i \in \Sigma''$ has a unique index s_i. The sizes of these three sets are σ, σ', and σ'' respectively. n_w denotes the length of w, while N_w denotes the maximum length of w', where $n_w \leq \frac{1}{2}N_w$. In addition, there are $\lceil \frac{1}{2}N_w \rceil$ groups of special symbols, whose size is from 1 to $\lceil \frac{1}{2}N_w \rceil$. A group of special symbols are added as a set in a predefined circular order starting with any one of the symbols in this group.

A predicate DFA M is denoted as $(\Sigma, Q, \delta, q_0, F)$. Redundant states are chosen from Q to form Q' and from F to form F', while duplicated transitions are included in δ to form δ'. Q' and δ' are randomized to form Q'' and δ''. The sizes of Q, Q' and Q'' are n_Q, n'_Q and $n''_Q = N_Q$ respectively, where $N_Q \geq 2n_Q$. The states in Q are marked from 0 to $n_Q - 1$, thus the number of transition in δ is $n_\delta = n_Q^2$. N_Q denotes the maximum number of states, thus the maximum number of transitions N_δ is N_Q^2. Note that we further require $|F| \leq N_Q/4$ and $|Q| \leq N_Q/2$. q_0 and F' are randomized into q'_0 and F''. δ and its matrix representation A_δ can be converted. If $A_\delta[x][y]$ is a symbol set W, where $W \subseteq \Sigma''$ and $x, y \in Q''$, there are (x, y, w_i) transitions in δ, where $w_i \in W$.

2.4 Complexity Assumption

Given a bilinear 3-factor-based composite-order group generator $\mathcal{G}$, output three groups $\mathbb{G}_i$ of distinct prime order p_i for $i = 1, 2, 3$ by the experiment:

1. $(p_1, p_2, p_3, \mathbb{G}, \mathbb{G}_T, \hat{e}) \leftarrow \mathcal{G}(1^\lambda)$,
2. $N \leftarrow p_1 p_2 p_3$, $g_1 \xleftarrow{R} \mathbb{G}_1$, $g_2 \xleftarrow{R} \mathbb{G}_2$, $g_3 \xleftarrow{R} \mathbb{G}_3$,
3. $P \leftarrow (N, \mathbb{G}, \mathbb{G}_T, \hat{e})$,
4. $D \leftarrow (g_1, g_1^{a_1}, g_2, g_2^{b_1}, g_3^{c_1}, g_3^{c_2 d}, g_3^d, g_3^{d^2}, g_1^{a_2} g_3^{c_1 d})$, where $a_1, a_2 \xleftarrow{R} \mathbb{Z}_{p_1}$,
   $b_1 \xleftarrow{R} \mathbb{Z}_{p_2}$, and $c_1, c_2, d \xleftarrow{R} \mathbb{Z}_{p_3}$, and
5. $T_0 \leftarrow g_1^{a_3} g_3^{c_2}$, $T_1 \leftarrow g_1^{a_3} g_2^{b_2} g_3^{c_2}$, where $a_3 \xleftarrow{R} \mathbb{Z}_{p_1}$ and $b_2 \xleftarrow{R} \mathbb{Z}_{p_2}$.

The advantage of an adversary $\mathcal{A}$ in distinguishing T_0 from T_1 with the parameters (P, D) is defined as $Adv_\mathcal{A} := |\Pr[\mathcal{A}(P, D, T_0) = 1] - \Pr[\mathcal{A}(P, D, T_1) = 1]|$.

Definition 3. The above complexity assumption holds for any polynomial-time adversary $\mathcal{A}$ if $Adv_\mathcal{A}$ is negligible [10].

Procedure: SymbolSetToVector(W, *mode*) [6]
Input: W, where $W \subseteq \Sigma''$, $|\Sigma''| = \sigma''$; *mode* = 0: TK, *mode* = 1: CT;
        Each symbol $w_i \in \Sigma''$ is assigned a unique index s_i.
Output: v_W

---

if (W is $\emptyset$) then $v_W = (a_{\sigma''}, a_{\sigma''-1}, \ldots, a_0) = (0, 0, \cdots, 0)$
else if (*mode* is 0) then
    $v_W = (a_{\sigma''}, a_{\sigma''-1}, \ldots, a_{d+1}, a_d, a_{d-1}, \ldots, a_0)$, where
    $f(x) = \prod_1^d (x - s_i) = a_d x^d + a_{d-1} x^{d-1} + \ldots + a_0$ and $a_{\sigma''} = \ldots = a_{d+1} = 0$.
else (*mode* is 1) then
    $v_W = (s_i^{\sigma''} \bmod N, \ldots, s_i^0 \bmod N) = (a_{\sigma''}, a_{\sigma''-1}, \ldots, a_0)$, where N is the
    order of the groups $\mathbb{G}$ and $\mathbb{G}_T$.
return v_W

Fig. 1. The procedure 'SymbolSetToVector'

2.5   The Building Block

The scheme by Yoshino *et al.* [10] provides a good starting point to construct SP-FE. It is a keyword-based predicate-only predicate encryption scheme.

- IPE.Setup(1^λ): It takes a security parameter 1^λ as input and outputs public parameters and a secret key SK.
- IPE.Encrypt(SK, x): It takes a secret key SK and a plaintext $x \in \Sigma$ and outputs a ciphertext CT.
- IPE.GenToken(SK, y): It takes a secret key SK and a description of predicate y as input and outputs a token TK.
- IPE.Check(TK, CT): It takes a token TK and a ciphertext CT as input and outputs either '1' ('Accept') or '0' ('Reject') indicating the result of the predicate y encoded in TK on the input x encrypted into CT. □

Note that disjunctive predicates are used to protect the input symbols of a transition in SK-FE. The procedure **SymbolSetToVector** is to generate the vector of an input string and that of a symbol set for a transaction (See Fig. 1).

3   SP-FE Construction

We provide main procedures of SP-FE construction. Following that, we present detailed algorithms with comprehensive explanation.

3.1   Main Procedures

We make use of Yoshino *et al.* scheme [10] by encrypting each symbol in the plaintext as an encrypted symbol and each symbol set for a transition as a predicate token. However, direct transformation cannot achieve both keyword and predicate privacy because the information can be revealed to the adversary: (1) the length of a plaintext, (2) the number of states in a DFA, (3) the number of accept states, (4) the number of transitions, and (5) the transition path. Thus, **addSpecialSymbols** adds special symbols to the plaintext, while **addStatesTransitions** inserts dummy states, transitions and shuffles states of a DFA

Procedure: addSpecialSymbols(w)
Input: w, where $w = (w_1, \ldots, w_{n_w}), w_i \in \Sigma, n_w \leq \ell$
Output: w', where $w' = (w'_1, \ldots, w'_{N_w}), w'_i \in \Sigma'', N_w = 2\ell$

Repeat 1. and 2. until $n_w = N_w$.

1. Set $pos \xleftarrow{R} \mathbb{Z}_{n_w+1}$ and $k \xleftarrow{R} \mathbb{Z}_{N_w - n_w}$
2. Insert the $(k+1)th$ symbol group at position pos with a pre-defined circular order starting from one of the symbols in the group. Set $n_w = n_w + (k+1)$.

return $w' = (w_1, w_2, \ldots, w_{N_w})$

Fig. 2. The procedure 'addSpecialSymbol'

a >< ∧a ⊣⊢ a | ♯aa⌞⌜⌝⌟a | aa <⊢⊣ ∧ > a | aa⌟⌞⌜♯⌝a | a ⊣⊢ a >< ∧a | aa♯ < ∧♯ > a | ♯aa ⊢⊣ ♯♯a

Fig. 3. The procedure 'addSpecialSymbol'('**aaa**') and its seven possible outputs

Procedure: addStatesTransitions(M)
Input: $M{=}(Q, \Sigma, \delta, q_0, F), n_Q \leq \ell$, where
$|\delta| = n_\delta, \delta = \{(u^j, v^j, w_k)\}_{j=1}^{n_\delta}; u^j, v^j \in Q$ and $w_k \in \Sigma$
Output: $M''{=}(Q'', \Sigma'', \delta'', q'_0, F'')$, where $N_Q = 2\ell$ and $|\delta''| = N_\delta = N_Q^2$

1. *Add Random Symbols*: For each row i in a DFA, each of the symbols in Σ'' should appear once and only once. If a symbol w_i of a group of special symbols of size d does not appear in the row i,
   (a) Prepare the sequence $w_i, w'_1, w'_2, \cdots, w'_d$ starting with w_i and a sequence of states $i, t_1, t_2, \cdots, t_d$, where w_i does not appear in row i and w'_j does not appear in row t_j for $1 \leq j \leq d$ and $t_j \in Q$
   (b) Include the transitions (i, t_1, w_i), (t_j, t_{j+1}, w'_j) for $1 \leq j \leq d-1$, and (t_d, i, w'_d) into δ to form δ'.
2. *Add Random States, Add Final States and Transitions*:
   (a) Randomly duplicate $(\frac{\ell}{2} - |F|)$ states from F to form F'. The new state creates a new column and copies the row of its original state as its row.
   (b) Randomly duplicate $\frac{\ell}{2}$ states from the $\frac{\ell}{2}$ states in 1. together with F' to form Q'. Denote S_i as the set of equivalent states of the state i, where $S_i \subseteq Q'$, $\cup_{i=1}^{|Q|} S_i = Q'$, and $S_i \cap S_j = \emptyset$ for any two sets.
   There are extra $\ell^2 - n_q^2$ transitions added into δ to form δ'.
3. *Shuffle Symbols within Equivalent Set*: For each row i, the transition symbols are shuffled among the columns of the equivalent states to form δ''.
4. *Shuffle States*: Randomly choose two states Q_i, Q_j. Exchange ith row with jth row, and ith column with jth column to form Q'' and δ''. Set one state in S_{q_0} as a starting state q'_0, while set F'' as the final states after exchange.

return $M''{=}(Q'', \Sigma'', \delta'', q'_0, F'')$, where $\delta''{=}\{(u^j, v^j, w_k)\}_{j=1}^{N_\delta}$

Fig. 4. The procedure 'addStatesTransitions'

accordingly to make sure the same language is accepted (See Fig. 2 and Fig. 4).

Example. In Fig. 3, ℓ is set as four. There are four groups of special symbols denoted as (1) '♯', (2) '⊢' and '⊣', (3) '<', '∧' and '>', and (4) '⌜', '⌝', '⌟' and '⌞'. We have d ordered sequences of a group of size d. For example, to insert the symbols of the third group, one of the three sequences can be chosen from:

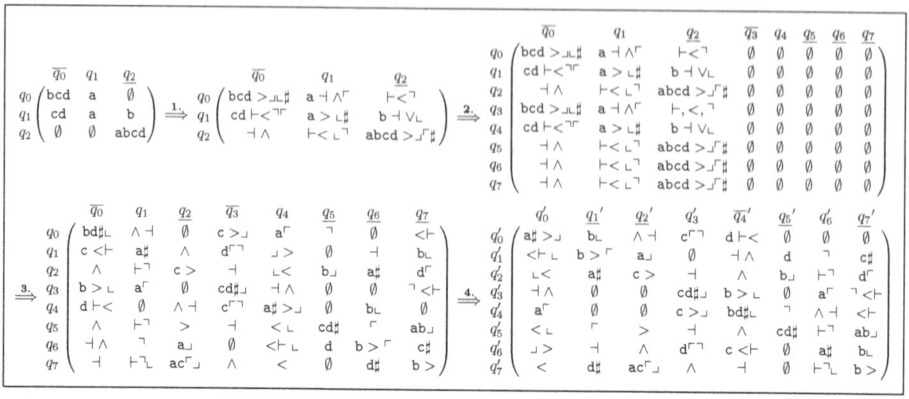

Fig. 5. The procedure 'addStatesTransitions' processing 'containing substring **ab**'. The start state is overlined, while the accepting state(s) is underlined.

'$< \wedge >$', '$\wedge >$<', and '$>< \wedge$'. In addition, one group of symbols can be nested in the other group of symbols like in the third, fourth and sixth column in Fig. 3. After the special symbols between two ordinary symbols are consumed by a DFA, their effects will be canceled out, namely, the same state will be revisited.

Example. In Fig. 5, ℓ is set as four and $\Sigma = \{a, b, c, d\}$. For each row, every symbols in Σ'' should appear once and only once. In addition, the input DFA has specified all the symbols in Σ for each row. To fill in a special symbol of a group, there is a transition path from state i back to state i again after consuming the ordered circular sequence starting from this symbol. Take symbol '$>$' as example, the sequence is '$>$', '$<$' and then '$\wedge$'. There is a transition path: $q_0 \overset{>}{\Rightarrow} q_0 \overset{<}{\Rightarrow} q_2 \overset{\wedge}{\Rightarrow} q_0$ and there are $(q_0, q_0, >)$, $(q_0, q_2, <)$, and $(q_2, q_0, \wedge)$ transitions in δ. The next step is to duplicate the set of accept states so that $|F'| = \ell/2$ and duplicate the other states so that $Q'' = 2\ell$. Therefore, there are three equivalent sets: $S_{q_0} = \{q_0, q_3\}$, $S_{q_1} = \{q_1, q_4\}$, and $S_{q_2} = \{q_2, q_5, q_6, q_7\}$. For the third step, the symbols of one equivalent set in one row can be redistributed. Take q_2 row as example. '$\dashv$' is moved from q_0-column into q_3-column, while '$\llcorner$' is moved from q_1-column into q_4-column. Finally, exchange state 0 with state 4 and state 1 with 6 by interchanging q_0-row with q_4-row, q_0-column with q_4-column, q_1-row with q_6-row, and q_1-column with q_6-column. Set the start state q_0' from $S_{q_0}' = \{q_3', q_4'\}$ as q_4' and hide the others. Set the set of final states F'' as $\{q_1', q_2', q_5', q_7'\}$.

3.2 Main Algorithms

SP-FE consists of four probabilistic polynomial-time algorithms (See Fig. 6). In SP-FE.Setup, the user executes IPE.Setup to obtain a SK and system parameters. In SP-FE.Encrypt, the user executes **addSpecialSymbols** on input w to produce w'. Then the user calls to **symbolSetToVector** and IPE.Encrypt for each of the symbols in w' to produce a CT. In SP-FE.GenToken, the user executes **addStatesTransitions** on the search predicate M to produce M''. Then the user calls to **symbolSetToVector** and IPE.GenToken for each of the

SP-FE.Setup(1^λ):	SP-FE.Encrypt($SK, w = w_1, \ldots, w_{n_w}$):
$SK \leftarrow$ IPE.Setup($1^\lambda, \Sigma, \Sigma'$)	$w' \leftarrow$ **addSpecialSymbols**(w), where $|w'| = N_w$
Set ℓ, where $N_w = 2\ell, N_Q = 2\ell, N_\delta = N_Q^2$	**for** ($i = 1$ to N_w) **do**
return SK	$\quad x_i \leftarrow$ **symbolSetToVector**($w'_i, 1$)
	$\quad CT_i =$ IPE.Encrypt(x_i); $CT = CT \cup CT_i$
	end of for
	return $CT = \{CT_i\}_{i=1}^{N_w}$
SP-FE.GenToken($SK, M = (\Sigma, Q, \delta, q_0, F)$):	SP-FE.Decrypt(CT, TK):
$M'' \leftarrow$ **addStatesTransitions**(M), where	$q_c = q'_0$, where q_c is current state
$\quad M'' = (\Sigma'', Q'', \delta'', q'_0, F''), |Q''| = N_Q, |\delta''| = N_Q^2$	**for** ($i = 1$ to N_w) **do**
for($r = 1$ to N_Q) **do**	$\quad$ **for all** $(q_c, j, TK_{q_c,j}) \in \delta''$, where $j \in Q''$ **do**
$\quad$ **for**($c = 1$ to N_Q) **do**	$\quad\quad$ **if** (IPE.Check($CT_i, TK_{q_c,j}$) == 1) **then**
$\quad\quad (r, c, y_{r,c}) \leftarrow$ **symbolSetToVector**($A_{\delta''}[r][c], 0$)	$\quad\quad\quad q_c = j$, ***break inner for-loop***
$\quad\quad TK_{r,c} = (r, c,$ IPE.GenToken($SK, y_{r,c}$))	$\quad\quad$ **end of if**
$\quad\quad TK = TK \cup TK_{r,c}$	$\quad$ **end of for**
$\quad$ **end of for**	**end of for**
end of for	**if** ($q_c \in F''$) **then return** 1
return TK	**else return** 0

Fig. 6. The main construction SK-FE

transitions in δ'' to produce a token TK. In SP-FE.Decrypt, the server executes IPE.Check on input CT_i and $TK_{q_c,j}$ to test a transition $(q_c, j, TK_{q_c,j})$ in δ''. The server obtains the next state j if IPE.Check($CT_i, TK_{q_c,j}$) returns '1' and set the current state q_c as j. The server continues to check CT_{i+1} with the transitions in δ'' starting with q_c. If the final state q_c is in F'' after checking CT_{N_w}, the plaintext w' satisfies the DFA in M''.

3.3 Correctness

If a keyword w is accepted (or rejected) by a DFA M, the corresponding w' is accepted (or rejected) by the DFA M''. On the one hand, one group of special symbols with a predefined circular order can be added and possibly nested in the other group of symbols in **addSpecialSymbols** (See Fig 2, Step 2). On the other hand, a group of special symbols are filled in a DFA is the same circular order in **addStatesTransitions** (See Fig 4, Step 1). We have prepared a sequence $w_i, w'_1, w'_2, \cdots, w'_d$ starting with w_i and a valid sequence of states $i, t_1, t_2, \cdots, t_d$. The corresponding transitions $(i, t_1, w_i), (t_j, t_{j+1}, w'_j)$ for $1 \leq j \leq d - 1$, and (t_d, i, w'_d) are added into M''. Every time a series of special symbols between two ordinary symbols are processed by a DFA, their effects are canceled out, namely, the same state after DFA's processing the former ordinary symbol is revisited just before the latter ordinary symbol is encountered. Therefore, w is recognized by a DFA M if and only if the special symbols are ignored in w' and the transitions of special symbols are removed in M''.

4   Analysis

We describe a sequence of hybrid security games to demonstrate that SP-FE achieves both keyword privacy and predicate privacy.

4.1   Security Analysis

Proof Sketch. The proof uses a sequence of hybrid games where a challenge token is encrypted with one vector in the first subsystem and with another vector in the second subsystem. Let $(\boldsymbol{w}, \boldsymbol{z})$ denote a token encrypted by vector $\boldsymbol{w}$ in the first subsystem and by vector $\boldsymbol{z}$ in the second subsystem. Try to prove the challenge token associated with $\boldsymbol{w}$ corresponding to $(\boldsymbol{w}, \boldsymbol{w})$ is indistinguishable from that associated with $\boldsymbol{z}$ corresponding to $(\boldsymbol{z}, \boldsymbol{z})$. A sequence of hybrid games demonstrates $(\boldsymbol{w}, \boldsymbol{w}) \simeq (\boldsymbol{w}, \boldsymbol{0}) \simeq (\boldsymbol{w}, \boldsymbol{z}) \simeq (\boldsymbol{0}, \boldsymbol{z}) \simeq (\boldsymbol{z}, \boldsymbol{z})$. In addition to the distribution of ciphertexts and tokens, the distribution of the transition path should be protected. The distribution of transition paths should be computationally indistinguishable; otherwise, the adversary can gain extra advantages in breaking the security game. However, because there are at least $N_w/2$ symbols added into the input string of length at most $N_w/2$ and $N_Q/2$ states inserted into a DFA with at most $N_Q/2$ states, the distribution of transition path are computationally hidden because there are at least extra $N_w/2 \geq n_w$ random transitions in the transition path. Finally, the information n_w, n_Q, F and δ, supplemented into N_w, N_Q and δ'', is computationally hidden from the adversary (See Fig 4). As the space is limited, we give these proofs in the full version of our paper [13].

Theorem 1. *If $\mathcal{G}$ satisfies Assumption 1, SP-FE is token indistinguishable.*

Theorem 2. *If $\mathcal{G}$ satisfies Assumption 1, SP-FE is ciphertext indistinguishable.*

Corollary 1. *If $\mathcal{G}$ satisfies Assumption 1, SP-FE is selective secure, namely, SP-FE achieves both keyword privacy and predicate privacy.*

4.2   Performance Analysis

The performance of SP-FE is as follows: SP-FE.Encrypt requires N_w number of SK-PE.Encrypt. SP-FE.GenToken costs N_Q^2 number of SK-PE.GenToken. SP-FE.Decrypt takes $\frac{1}{2}N_Q$ number of SK-PE.Check in average for each transition. For the performance of SK-PE, SK-PE.Encrypt $(8\sigma''+2) \cdot T_{add}+(13\sigma''+3) \cdot T_{sm}$, while SK-PE.GenToken takes $(8\sigma''+2) \cdot T_{add}+(13\sigma''+3) \cdot T_{sm}$. SK-PE.Check takes $(2\sigma''+2) \cdot T_{pairing}$. T_{add}, T_{sm} and $T_{pairing}$ denote the time for the point addition in $\mathbb{G}$, the scaler multiplication in $\mathbb{G}$ and the embedded pairing function. On the other hand, a plaintext w of length n_w is encrypted as N_w symbols. The size of the ciphertext is $N_w \cdot (2\sigma''+2) \cdot |\mathbb{G}|$, while that of the token is $N_\delta \cdot (2\sigma''+2) \cdot |\mathbb{G}|$ plus the description of the DFA, where $|\mathbb{G}|$ is the size of the element in $\mathbb{G}$.

5   Conclusions

In this paper, we proposed a symmetric-key predicate-only functional encryption scheme SP-FE, which supports functionality for regular languages. SP-FE is proven to guarantee keyword privacy and predicate privacy. In addition, SP-FE can be extended to a full-fledged functional encryption scheme by the technique from [6] to further manage messages. For future work, we would like to relax the restrictions in SP-FE to support predicates of more expressive languages.

Acknowledgments. This research is supported by National Science Council, Taiwan under contract No. 102-2221-E-009-084-, and Delta Electronics, Inc. under contract No. 103C005.

References

1. Boneh, D., Sahai, A., Waters, B.: Functional encryption: Definitions and challenges. In: Ishai, Y. (ed.) TCC 2011. LNCS, vol. 6597, pp. 253–273. Springer, Heidelberg (2011)
2. Bethencourt, J., Sahai, A., Waters, B.: Ciphertext-policy attribute-based encryption. In: Proceedings of the 2007 IEEE Symposium on Security and Privacy, SP 2007, pp. 321–334. IEEE Computer Society, Washington, DC (2007)
3. Goyal, V., Pandey, O., Sahai, A., Waters, B.: Attribute-based encryption for fine-grained access control of encrypted data. In: Proceedings of the 13th ACM Conference on Computer and Communications Security, CCS 2006, pp. 89–98. ACM, New York (2006)
4. Ostrovsky, R., Sahai, A., Waters, B.: Attribute-based encryption with non-monotonic access structures. In: Proceedings of the 14th ACM Conference on Computer and Communications Security, CCS 2007, pp. 195–203. ACM, New York (2007)
5. De Caro, A., Iovino, V., Persiano, G.: Fully secure hidden vector encryption. In: Abdalla, M., Lange, T. (eds.) Pairing 2012. LNCS, vol. 7708, pp. 102–121. Springer, Heidelberg (2013)
6. Katz, J., Sahai, A., Waters, B.: Predicate encryption supporting disjunctions, polynomial equations, and inner products. In: Smart, N.P. (ed.) EUROCRYPT 2008. LNCS, vol. 4965, pp. 146–162. Springer, Heidelberg (2008)
7. Lewko, A., Okamoto, T., Sahai, A., Takashima, K., Waters, B.: Fully secure functional encryption: Attribute-based encryption and (Hierarchical) inner product encryption. In: Gilbert, H. (ed.) EUROCRYPT 2010. LNCS, vol. 6110, pp. 62–91. Springer, Heidelberg (2010)
8. Blundo, C., Iovino, V., Persiano, G.: Predicate encryption with partial public keys. In: Heng, S.-H., Wright, R.N., Goi, B.-M. (eds.) CANS 2010. LNCS, vol. 6467, pp. 298–313. Springer, Heidelberg (2010)
9. Shen, E., Shi, E., Waters, B.: Predicate privacy in encryption systems. In: Reingold, O. (ed.) TCC 2009. LNCS, vol. 5444, pp. 457–473. Springer, Heidelberg (2009)
10. Yoshino, M., Kunihiro, N., Naganuma, K., Sato, H.: Symmetric inner-product predicate encryption based on three groups. In: Takagi, T., Wang, G., Qin, Z., Jiang, S., Yu, Y. (eds.) ProvSec 2012. LNCS, vol. 7496, pp. 215–234. Springer, Heidelberg (2012)
11. Waters, B.: Functional encryption for regular languages. In: Safavi-Naini, R., Canetti, R. (eds.) CRYPTO 2012. LNCS, vol. 7417, pp. 218–235. Springer, Heidelberg (2012)
12. Goldwasser, S., Kalai, Y.T., Popa, R.A., Vaikuntanathan, V., Zeldovich, N.: How to run turing machines on encrypted data. In: Canetti, R., Garay, J.A. (eds.) CRYPTO 2013, Part II. LNCS, vol. 8043, pp. 536–553. Springer, Heidelberg (2013)
13. Tseng, F.K., Chen, R.J., Lin, B.S.P.: Towards symmetric functional encryption for regular languages with predicate privacy. Cryptology ePrint Archive, Report 2014/407 (2014), http://eprint.iacr.org/

Framework for Efficient Search and Statistics Computation on Encrypted Cloud Data

Sanjit Chatterjee and Sayantan Mukherjee

Department of Computer Science and Automation,
Indian Institute of Science, Bangalore, India
{sanjit,sayantan.mukherjee}@csa.iisc.ernet.in

Abstract. Storing data in untrusted cloud, keeping it confidential and allowing search and other operations on the encrypted data without revealing any meaningful information is currently an area of major interest in cryptology. Various new encryption paradigms are proposed to address the problem. Hidden Vector Encryption (HVE) is one such approach that supports different kinds of queries (e.g. search, comparison etc.) as a conjunctive normal form. In this paper we present a framework for efficient searching and computing simple statistics on the encrypted database based on the functionality of HVE. We revisit the work of Tseng et al. from IWSEC'13 and identify certain limitations of their methodology. In this paper we propose several new encodings for different attribute classes that overcome the limitations of the previous work to a great extent. Our technique, not only increases the span of queries allowed but also improves the efficiency of most of the queries than in the work of Tseng et al.

Keywords: database privacy, search on encrypted data, hidden vector encryption, efficient encoding for searchable queries.

1 Introduction

With the increase of amount of data available to any user, the idea of *Cloud Storage* was projected as a probable way to resolve the issue of storage. To keep the data confidential, any conventional *secure encryption scheme* (public key encryption (PKE) and secret key encryption (SKE)) would have been satisfactory. If PKE or SKE is used, the user needs to download whole encrypted dataset from *cloud service provider*, decrypt it, compute the function and send the dataset back to *cloud service provider* after encrypting it once again. Therefore using conventional *secure encryption scheme* is not scalable if the dataset is very large.

Generalization of the notion of identity-based encryption (IBE) [1] has been used to compute different types of functions securely. To solve the problem of searching over the encrypted text, public key encryption with keyword search (PEKS) [2] was constructed. To allow *fine grained access control* over the ciphertext, predicate encryption (PE) [3] was constructed. Hidden vector encryption

M. Yoshida and K. Mouri (Eds.): IWSEC 2014, LNCS 8639, pp. 276–285, 2014.

(HVE) [4,5,6] is one such predicate encryption that implements *equality predicate function* efficiently. Using HVE as a basic building block, a framework was proposed in [7] to search and compute statistics efficiently.

Related Work: In [4, Section 6], some applications using HVE were described. They proposed *searchable encryption* for Comparison, Range and AND queries. But their construction does not allow NOT, CNF or DNF queries. In contrast, the framework presented in [7] allows AND, OR, NOT and Range queries. But the mechanism of both Range and OR queries were rather inefficient [7, Table 5]. Further, their implementation of NOT query [7, Table 7], prevents one to incorporate it in association with another query (e.g. $(x_i = a \wedge x_j \neq b)$ is not allowed in [7]). Also the framework in [7] does not support CNF or DNF query.

Contribution: In this work, we construct a framework that uses HVE as a black box to search in the encrypted domain efficiently. To do so, we propose to classify the attributes based on their properties. For different classes of attributes, we define different encodings and propose suitable methods to search in the encrypted domain. Our framework is more efficient in terms of the number of trapdoors generated than [7] as shown in Table 3. In this proposed framework, the span of queries allowed is significantly improved than in [7] as shown in Table 4.

Organization of the Paper: The notion of searchable encryption, query types and attribute classification are briefly described in Section 2. In Section 3 we present the transformations used in our framework and algorithms to process them. In Section 4 application of our proposed framework and its effectiveness is briefly described. Section 5 concludes this paper identifying some possible future directions.

2 Preliminaries

In this section we present the notion of searchable encryption, an overview of the framework in terms of entities communicating and different attribute classes.

2.1 Searchable Encryption

The notion of Searchable Encryption [4] was formulated to simulate the computation of predicate function (f) on plaintext and predicate value in encrypted domain. Searchable Encryption is defined by four randomized algorithms: Setup_{SE}, $\mathsf{Encrypt}_{SE}$, KeyGen_{SE} and Test_{SE}. HVE [4] is a searchable encryption defined by four randomized algorithms: Setup, Encrypt, KeyGen and Test. For $x = (x_1, \ldots, x_l) \in \{0,1\}^l$ and $y = (y_1, \ldots, y_l) \in \{0, 1, *\}^l$, the predicate function of HVE is $P_y^{HVE}(x) = 1 \iff \forall j \, (y_j \neq * \Rightarrow y_j = x_j)$. Boneh et al. constructed a searchable encryption system in [4, Section 6] based on the existence of secure HVE over Σ_{01}^{nw} as described next, in an informal way. Setup_{SE} and Test_{SE} were designed to be same as Setup and Test of HVE respectively. $\mathsf{Encrypt}_{SE}$ encodes the attribute value (x) to attribute vector x and encrypts x using Encrypt of HVE. KeyGen_{SE} encodes the predicate value (y) to predicate vector y and creates trapdoor(s) from y using KeyGen of HVE.

2.2   System Model

The system model we consider, is similar to the system model described in [7]. There are two system entities:

- Client: The *sender clients* gather the data, encrypt it using suitable searchable encryption mechanism and send the encrypted data to the CSP. Some dedicated *receiver clients* will be there to ask CSP to perform search queries by sending proper trapdoor(s) constructed using KeyGen of the searchable encryption mechanism.
- Cloud Service Provider(CSP): CSP keeps all the encrypted data received from the clients in a table, provides a framework for searching and returns the output to the *receiver clients*. CSP is considered to be honest-but-curious. Every *client* and CSP has an authenticated channel to communicate. On search query from a *receiver client*, CSP sends back the indices of satisfying tuples which it finds using Test of the searchable encryption mechanism.

Achieving functionalities similar to plaintext database query mechanism (e.g. comparison, range, composite (AND, OR)[1], normal form query etc) is the basic requirement of the framework.

Query-Type – Different types of query allowed in our framework will be marked by: *T0, T1, T2, T3, T4, EQ0, EQ1, DC* to identify the way they will be processed. The query marked by *DC* will only be used to create trapdoor for $(* * \cdots *)$. Rest of the query-types will be described when we define the transformations in later sections.

2.3   Attribute Classes

An entity (or tuple) in relational database system represents real world object and attribute represents the property of the entity [8]. The *attribute vector* $(\tilde{x}_i)$ for attribute (x_i) will be of length $|dom(x_i)|$ where $dom(x_i)$ denotes the domain of x_i.

We classify the attribute set $(x_1, \ldots, x_l)$ by *comparability* and *uni/multi-value* of the intra-domain elements. We call an attribute x_i *comparable* if $(dom(x_i), \leq)$ is a totally-ordered set. Attributes that have a single value for a particular entity, are called *uni-value* attributes whereas attributes that are not *uni-value* are called *multi-value* attributes. For example, *age* is a uni-value comparable attribute; *permanent address* is uni-value incomparable attribute whereas *allotted projects* is a multi-value incomparable attribute.

3   Proposed Transformations

In this section, we analyze different types of queries and corresponding predicate functions allowed in each of the attribute classes. For different attribute classes,

---

[1] AND-query(I)/OR-query(I) and AND-query(II)/OR-query(II) stands for composite query on single attribute and multiple attribute respectively.

we describe different encodings to construct attribute vector $(\tilde{x})$ and predicate vector $(\hat{y})$ from attribute (x) and predicate (y) values respectively. The attribute vector $(\tilde{x})$ will be encrypted into ciphertext using Encrypt of HVE. For each of the attribute classes, we briefly describe algorithms to convert the predicate vector $(\hat{y})$ to sub-predicate vector(s) $(\{\tilde{y}\})$ which in turn will be converted into trapdoor(s) using KeyGen of HVE.

The searchable encryption mechanism we construct, uses HVE in a generic way. As our framework needs to provide security in terms of *attribute hiding* and *key-confidentiality* [6, Section 2.2], we use HVE construction of [6]. Once the network administrator generates MSK using Setup$_{SE}$, it needs to send MSK to other clients as we used HVE constructed in private key setting. The sender and receiver clients perform the ciphertext and trapdoor generation respectively and CSP tries to find a match of tuple for given trapdoor as mentioned in Section 2.2.

We follow the convention that possible attribute values of x_i (i.e. elements of $dom(x_i)$) are indexed and the bijection $I : dom(x_i) \rightarrow [1, \ldots, |dom(x_i)|]$ computes the corresponding index of an attribute value. For comparable attribute class, I is order-preserving. For example, x_1 in Table 1 has 4 possible values (i.e. $50, 60, 70$ and 80) and $I(50) = 1, I(60) = 2, I(70) = 3$ and $I(80) = 4$. We also follow the convention that not-mentioned indexes of attribute and predicate vectors are implicitly assigned 0. For example, $\forall k \in [1, \ldots, |dom(x_i)|], k \neq I(x_i)$, $\hat{y}[k] = 1$ means $\hat{y} = (1 \cdots 101 \cdots 1)$ where 0 is present only at $I(x_i)^{th}$ index.

3.1 Uni-Value Comparable Attribute

As the attribute class is comparable we need to allow basic comparison (e.g. greater-or-equal-to, range etc) in the encrypted domain.

3.1.1 Attribute Vector Generation
The attribute value $(x_i = a)$ is encoded into attribute vector $(\tilde{x}_i)$ defined as $\forall j \in [1, \ldots, |dom(x_i)|], j \leq I(a), \tilde{x}_i[j] = 1$.

3.1.2 Predicate Vector Generation
As mentioned in Section 2.2, different queries are identified by different query-types. The predicate vector for comparison and range queries will be marked by *T0*.

Composite Query: Composite queries are achievable in case of *uni-value comparable attribute*. The predicate vector for AND/OR-Query(I) will be marked by *T0*. For OR-Query(II) and AND-Query(II), we mark the predicate vector by *T1* and *T2* respectively.

Normal Form Query: Normal Form queries are supported in our framework unlike [7] for *uni-value comparable attribute* class. The CNF-predicate vector will be marked by query-type *T2*.

DNF-queries are processed in a different way. Suppose for attribute x_i and x_j, we want to find out if there is any tuple that satisfies $((x_i\rho_1 a \wedge x_j\rho_2 b) \vee (x_i\rho_3 c \wedge x_j\rho_4 d))$ where $\rho_1, \rho_2, \rho_3, \rho_4$ are all order relations (e.g. $(x_i = a \wedge x_j = b) \vee (x_i \geq c \wedge x_j \leq d)$). We generate sub-predicate trapdoors for both $(x_i = a \wedge x_j = b)$ and

$(x_i \geq c \wedge x_j \leq d)$, find out the tuples that satisfy any of these two queries and then perform a set union of the satisfying tuple indices. Here we note that for every attribute class, the procedure to generate predicate vector for DNF-query is same (as described above).

3.1.3   Algorithms

We follow the convention that by X_i we identify attribute on which the query is made and by $\hat{Y}_i$ we identify the corresponding predicate vector. Each query can have several attributes $(X_1, \ldots, X_z)$.

For each attribute X_i in the given query:

- If $dom(X_i)[j]$ doesn't satisfy the query, we assign $\hat{Y}_i[j] \leftarrow 0$.
- If $dom(X_i)[j]$ satisfies the query,
  - If $(\hat{Y}_i[j-1] = 1$ or $*)$, we assign $\hat{Y}_i[j] \leftarrow *$.
  - Otherwise we assign $\hat{Y}_i[j] \leftarrow 1$.

Once the predicate vector (of the form $(\hat{Y}_1, \hat{Y}_2, \ldots, \hat{Y}_z)$) is constructed, we need to construct trapdoors for query-type $T0$, $T1$ and $T2$. Query-type $T0$ is a restricted version of query-type $T1$ where only one attribute is concerned (i.e. $z = 1$). We now describe the intuitive idea of generating sub-predicate trapdoors for query-type $T1$ and $T2$. In both the cases we first initialize a $\Sigma_{j=1}^{z}|dom(X_j)|$ length vector $spv \leftarrow (* * \cdots *)$.

For query-type $T1$, k is initialized to 0. For each attribute X_i:

- If $f_o \geq k$ is the minimum index such that $\hat{Y}_i[f_o] = 1$, we assign $spv[f_o + \Sigma_{j=1}^{i-1}|dom(X_j)|] \leftarrow 1$.
- If $f_z > f_o$ is the minimum index such that $\hat{Y}_i[f_z] = 0$,
  - We assign $spv[f_z + \Sigma_{j=1}^{i-1}|dom(X_j)|] \leftarrow 0$.
  - If $l_z \geq f_z$ is the minimum index such that $\hat{Y}_i[l_z + 1] = 1$, we update toggle-searching start index $k \leftarrow l_z + 1$.
- We generate trapdoor of spv using KeyGen of HVE.
- Then we reinitialize spv and go to first step with updated value of k.

For query-type $T2$, we design a recursive procedure that generates sub-predicate vector for each of the attributes $X_1, X_2, \ldots, X_z$ separately and concatenates them to generate one sub-predicate vector for the query. We run KeyGen of HVE on the concatenated sub-predicate vector to get back corresponding sub-predicate trapdoor. Keeping the sub-predicate vectors same for attributes $X_1, X_2, \ldots, X_{z-1}$ it finds the next sub-predicate vector for attribute X_z and appends it to the concatenation of the sub-predicate vectors for attributes $X_1, X_2, \ldots, X_{z-1}$. In this way it generates all the sub-predicate vectors and corresponding sub-predicate trapdoors.

3.2   Uni-Value Incomparable Attribute

As the attribute class is uni-value, each tuple takes exactly one attribute value. We propose our encoding based on this observation.

3.2.1 Attribute Vector Generation

The attribute value $(x_i = a)$ is encoded into attribute vector $(\tilde{x}_i)$ defined as $\tilde{x}_i[I(a)] = 1$.

3.2.2 Predicate Vector Generation

For *uni-value incomparable attribute* there will neither be any comparison query (except eq-predicate and NOT-query) nor range query.

Comparison Query: The predicate vectors for the comparison queries will be marked by *T3*. The eq-predicate vector, for $(x_i = a)$ will be $\hat{y}_i$ such that $\hat{y}_i[I(a)] = 1$. There is an exception with this kind of representation which we will discuss during OR-predicate construction. The NOT-predicate vector, for $x_i \neq a$ will be $\hat{y}_i$ such that $\forall j \in [1, \ldots, |dom(x_i)|], j \neq I(a), \hat{y}_i[j] = *$.

Composite Query: The AND-predicate vector will be marked by query-type *T3*. The AND-predicate vector for $(x_i = a \wedge x_j = b)$ query (AND-Query(II)) will be $(\hat{y}_i, \hat{y}_j)$ where $k \in \{i, j\}$, $\hat{y}_k[I(x_k)] = 1$.

The AND-predicate vector for $(x_i = a \wedge x_j \neq b)$ we define as $(\hat{y}_i, \hat{y}_j)$ where $\hat{y}_i[I(a)] = 1$ and $\forall l \in [1, \ldots, |dom(x_i)|], l \neq I(b), \hat{y}_j[l] = *$.

Our framework forms a single sub-predicate vector for OR-Query(I) which is a major efficiency improvement over [7, Table 5]. The OR-predicate vector for $(x_i = a \vee x_i = b)$ query (OR-Query(I)) is $\hat{y}_i$ such that $\hat{y}_i[I(x_i)] = *$. This kind of OR-predicate vector will be marked by *T3*.

The OR-predicate vector for $(x_i = a \vee x_j \neq b)$ query (OR-Query(II)) we define as $(\hat{y}_i, \hat{y}_j)$ and mark it by *T4* where

$$\hat{y}_i[l] = \begin{cases} * & \text{if } l = I(a) \\ 0 & \text{otherwise} \end{cases} \qquad \hat{y}_j[l] = \begin{cases} 0 & \text{if } l = I(b) \\ * & \text{otherwise} \end{cases} \qquad (1)$$

Normal Form Query: We mark the CNF-predicate vectors by query-type *T3*. For attribute x_i and x_j, the predicate vector of $((x_i = a \vee x_i = b) \wedge (x_j = c \vee x_j = d))$ will be $(\hat{y}_i, \hat{y}_j)$ where $k \in \{i, j\}$, $\hat{y}_k[I(x_k)] = *$.

3.2.3 Algorithms

We create a predicate vector for i^{th}-attribute from query as described in Section 3.2.2. We create trapdoor for predicate vectors marked by *T3* using KeyGen of HVE directly on the predicate vector. In case of *T4* marked predicate vector, we consider one attribute at a time to convert them into sub-predicate vectors (spv) and execute KeyGen of HVE on each of the spv. For example, the spvs for $(x_i = a \vee x_j \neq b)$ are $\langle \hat{y}_i, * * \cdots * \rangle$ and $\langle * * \cdots *, \hat{y}_j \rangle$ from Equation (1).

3.3 Multi-value Incomparable Attribute

Construction of predicate vector is similar to [7, Section 4.1]. We made some modifications to correct a few results of [7, Table 7] and to allow more queries. For example, predicate vector for *Q0* [7, Section 4.2] is not correct as AND-query of two attribute values (a, b) should be satisfied by tuples that take those two and some more values. We use query-type *EQ0* and *EQ1* to represent *equality(inclusive)* and *equality(atleast)* respectively. For example, we mark predicate vector of query $(x_i = a \wedge x_i = b)$ by $EQ0$. The predicate vector for query $(x_i = a \vee x_i \neq b)$ will be marked by $EQ1$ as the tuples that satisfy the query should not have $(x_i \neq a$ and $x_i = b)$.

3.3.1   Algorithms

Similar to Section 3.1.3, here we use X_i and $\hat{Y}_i$ as attribute and predicate vector respectively to describe our algorithms briefly.

We initialize $\forall i \in \{1, \ldots, z\}$, $\forall j \in [1, \ldots, |dom(X_i)|]$, $\hat{Y}_i[j] \leftarrow *$. For each literal of the query of the form $(X_i, dom(X_i[j])) \in R$ where $R \in \{=, \neq\}$:

- If R is $=$, we assign $\hat{Y}_i[j] \leftarrow 1$.
- If R is $\neq$, we assign $\hat{Y}_i[j] \leftarrow 0$.

Once the predicate vector (of the form $(\hat{Y}_1, \hat{Y}_2, \ldots, \hat{Y}_z)$) is constructed

- for query-type $EQ0$, we generate the trapdoor by running KeyGen of HVE on the predicate vector.
- for query-type $EQ1$, for each $\hat{Y}_i[k] = b$ where $b \in \{0, 1\}$, we first construct a vector $spv = (* * \ldots * b * * \ldots *)$ of length $\Sigma_{j=1}^{z} |dom(X_j)|$ where $spv[k + \Sigma_{j=1}^{i-1} |dom(X_j)|] = b$. Then we generate trapdoor(s) from spv-s using KeyGen of HVE.

3.4   Mixed Attribute Query

In this section, we will be considering queries that span through different types of attributes. As an example, $(x_i = a \vee x_j = b)$ is *mixed attribute query* iff x_i and x_j belong to different attribute classes.

For *mixed attribute query* $= \{clause_1, \ldots, clause_n\}$, the basic idea is to create predicate vector according to the rule specified for each of the concerned attribute types. As an example, for above mentioned query, the predicate vector constructed will be $\langle$predicate vector for $x_i = a$, predicate vector for $x_j = b\rangle$ where predicate vector for $x_i = a$ and $x_j = b$ will be constructed according to the rule specified for attribute type x_i and x_j respectively. The sub-predicate vector(s) generation also respects the class of the attribute.

If the clauses are connected using $\vee$, we construct sub-predicate vectors following the similar idea that we used for query-type $T1$. As an example, for $((x_i = a \vee x_i = b) \vee (x_j = c \vee x_j = d))$, the sub-predicate vectors will be $\langle$sub-predicate vector for $(x_i = a \vee x_i = b), (* * \cdots *)\rangle$ and $\langle(* * \cdots *),$ sub-predicate vector for $(x_j = c \vee x_j = d)\rangle$ where $(* * \cdots *)$ part will be marked by DC.

If the clauses are connected using $\wedge$, we construct sub-predicate vectors following the similar recursive idea that we used for query-type $T2$. As an example, $((x_i \neq a \vee x_i = b) \wedge (x_j = c \vee x_j \neq d))$, the sub-predicate vectors will be $\langle spv_{ia}, spv_{jc}\rangle$, $\langle spv_{ia}, spv_{jd}\rangle$, $\langle spv_{ib}, spv_{jc}\rangle$ and $\langle spv_{ib}, spv_{jd}\rangle$ where spv_{kf} denotes sub-predicate vector for literal $(x_k \rho f)$ where $\rho \in \{=, \neq\}$.

After constructing all the sub-predicate vectors, we use KeyGen of HVE to generate sub-predicate trapdoors.

4 Application of the Proposed Framework

We present the usefulness of our framework in terms of searching and computing statistics. We also provide comparison between [7] and our framework.

4.1 Counting Responses

In [7], a simple way of counting the responses and sampling the data has been discussed. In our framework, receiver client generates sub-predicate vector(s) (and corresponding sub-predicate trapdoors using KeyGen of HVE) from the query as described in Section 3. The receiver client sends the sub-predicate trapdoors to the CSP. To find out the tuple indices that satisfy the query, CSP runs Test of HVE and sends the satisfying tuple indices back to the receiver client. Once all such tuple indices are available to the receiver client, it computes the frequency distribution of the attribute. One such example is shown in Table 2 when the plaintext dataset looks like Table 1. We show the encoded table entries for few transaction results in Table 1 where x_1, x_2 are *uni-value comparable attributes*; x_3, x_4 are *uni-value incomparable attributes* and x_5, x_6 are *multi-value incomparable attributes*.

Table 1. Example of Transaction Records (encoded according to attribute classes)

	x_1				x_2			x_3			x_4			x_5			x_6		
row-id	50	60	70	80	30	35	40	cash	credit	debit	cycle	car	bike	bread	butter	egg	tea	coffee	beer
1	1	1	0	0	1	1	1	0	1	0	0	1	0	1	1	0	0	1	1
2	1	0	0	0	1	0	0	1	0	0	1	0	0	1	0	1	1	0	0
3	1	1	1	1	1	0	0	1	0	0	0	0	1	0	1	1	1	0	1
4	1	1	0	0	1	1	0	0	1	0	1	0	0	1	1	0	0	1	0
5	1	1	1	0	1	1	0	0	0	1	1	0	0	1	0	0	1	0	0
6	1	1	1	1	1	0	0	0	0	1	1	0	0	1	0	0	0	1	1
7	1	1	1	0	1	1	1	1	0	0	0	1	0	1	1	0	0	1	0
8	1	1	0	0	1	1	0	0	1	0	1	0	0	1	0	1	1	0	1

Table 2. Frequency Table (for $i = 1^{st}$ attribute)

Query	Query-Type	Frequency $(f_{i,j})$	Cumulative Frequency	Sub-Predicate Vector Used
$x_1 = 50$	{T0,DC,DC,DC,DC,DC}	Counting$(x_1 = 50) = 1$	1	$(10\ast\ast\ast\ast\ast\ast\ast\ast\ast\ast\ast\ast\ast\ast\ast)$
$x_1 = 60$	{T0,DC,DC,DC,DC,DC}	Counting$(x_1 = 60) = 3$	4	$(\ast10\ast\ast\ast\ast\ast\ast\ast\ast\ast\ast\ast\ast\ast)$
$x_1 = 70$	{T0,DC,DC,DC,DC,DC}	Counting$(x_1 = 70) = 2$	6	$(\ast\ast10\ast\ast\ast\ast\ast\ast\ast\ast\ast\ast\ast\ast)$
$x_1 = 80$	{T0,DC,DC,DC,DC,DC}	Counting$(x_1 = 80) = 2$	8	$(\ast\ast\ast1\ast\ast\ast\ast\ast\ast\ast\ast\ast\ast\ast)$

4.2 Comparison

In this section we provide a representative comparison between the framework proposed in [7] and our proposed framework with respect to both efficiency and span of queries. We increase the efficiency by decreasing the number of trapdoors generated as that will reduce communication cost and the number of runs of Test of

Table 3. Efficiency comparison between [7] and our framework

Attribute Class	Query	No of Trapdoors	
		Framework of [7]	Our Framework
Uni-value Comparable Attribute	Range Query	n	1
	AND-Query	1	1
	OR-Query	n	$n/2$
Uni-value Incomparable Attribute	AND-Query	1	1
	OR-Query	n	1
Multi-value Incomparable Attribute	AND-Query	1	1
	OR-Query	n	n

HVE. We show the comparison of trapdoors constructed (worst case) in both the cases in Table 3 where domain cardinality of the considered attribute class is n.

To be precise, for a predicate vector (corresponding to OR-Query on uni-value comparable attribute) of hamming weight h and t-many $\langle 10 \rangle$ toggles, the client needs to construct h-many trapdoors in [7] and t-many trapdoors in our framework where t is usually much smaller than h.

We notice that the way NOT-query is implemented in [7, Table 7] does not allow one to construct any composite predicate involving NOT. Some of the new functionalities that we achieve are shown in Table 4. For example, to search if somebody has bought *egg* and did not buy *beer*, we use 7th query of the Table 4; 10th query of the Table 4 finds if someone has bought *bread* or *butter* and *tea* or *beer*; 12th query of the Table 4 searches if somebody of *age*=35 has spent 50$ paid by *cash* and rode a *bike*.

Table 4. Representative instances of new functionalities achieved in our framework

No	Query	Sub-Predicate Vectors	
1	$x_1 \geq 60$	(*1***************)	
2	$x_1 \neq 60 \wedge x_1 \neq 70$	(10***************)	(***1************)
3	$x_1 \geq 50 \wedge x_1 \neq 60$	(10***************)	(**1*************)
4	$x_1 \neq 60 \wedge x_2 \neq 30$	(10**0***********) (10***1***********)	(**1*0***********) (**1**1**********)
5	$x_3 = $ cash $\wedge x_4 \neq $ car	(*******100*0*****)	
6	$x_3 \neq $ cash $\wedge x_4 \neq $ car	(*******0***0*****)	
7	$x_5 = $ egg $\wedge x_6 \neq $ beer	(************1**0)	
8	$x_1 = 60 \vee x_6 \neq $ beer	(*10*************) (**************0)
9	($x_5 = $ bread $\wedge x_5 = $ butter) $\vee$ ($x_6 = $ tea $\wedge x_6 = $ beer)	(***********1*1***) (**************1*1)
10	($x_5 = $ bread $\vee x_5 = $ butter) $\wedge$ ($x_6 = $ tea $\vee x_6 = $ beer)	(***********1**1***) (***********1***1) (***********11**) (**************1**1)
11	$x_1 = 50 \wedge (x_3 = $ cash $\vee x_3 = $ credit)	(10*******0********)	
12	$x_1 = 50 \wedge x_2 = 35 \wedge x_3 = $ cash $\wedge x_4 = $ bike	(10**1*0100001******)	
13	$x_1 = 50 \wedge x_2 = 35 \wedge (x_4 = $ car $\vee x_4 = $ bike)	(10**1*0***0*******)	
14	$x_1 \neq 60 \wedge x_2 = 40 \wedge (x_3 = $ debit $\wedge x_4 \neq $ car)	(10****1001*0*******) (**1***1001*0*******)

4.3   Computing Statistics

As we have decreased the number of trapdoors required for query, that efficiency is inherited while processing queries for statistics computation.

In Section 4.1 we showed the way to get back frequency distribution for each value in the $dom(x_1)$. Using these frequencies, we can easily compute *descriptive statistics* like [7]. As an example, the population mean attribute x_1 in the Table 1 will be $\Sigma_{j=1}^{|dom(x_1)|} dom(x_1)[j] * f_{1,j}/|F| = (50*1+60*2+70*1+80*1)/5 = 64$ where $|F|$ is the number of tuples stored in the database.

To compute *inferential statistics*, the receiver client needs to get random tuples of the database. The receiver client generates k random indices using random number generator, forwards those k indices to CSP, who in turn gives back the encrypted tuples indexed by those indices (here like [7] we also assume the local storage available to receiver client is sufficient to store k-many encrypted tuples. Once it gets back the encrypted tuples, the receiver client considers them as a sample database and creates a table like Table 2 in a similar fashion. Using the frequencies counted for the sampled data, we can compute *inferential statistics*.

5 Conclusion

In this paper, we critically evaluate the framework of [7] and we proposed to process queries based on attribute class distinction. This led us to improve the query complexity of original scheme. We also have increased the number of queries accommodated. For future work, we identify predicate function 'OR' as a barrier to achieve more efficient CNF or DNF query processing. We would also like to incorporate data-mining techniques (e.g. association rule mining, clustering etc) efficiently in encrypted cloud.

References

1. Boneh, D., Franklin, M.: Identity-based encryption from the weil pairing. In: Kilian, J. (ed.) CRYPTO 2001. LNCS, vol. 2139, pp. 213–229. Springer, Heidelberg (2001)
2. Boneh, D., Di Crescenzo, G., Ostrovsky, R., Persiano, G.: Public key encryption with keyword search. In: Cachin, C., Camenisch, J.L. (eds.) EUROCRYPT 2004. LNCS, vol. 3027, pp. 506–522. Springer, Heidelberg (2004)
3. Goyal, V., Pandey, O., Sahai, A., Waters, B.: Attribute-based encryption for fine-grained access control of encrypted data. In: Proceedings of the 13th ACM Conference on Computer and Communications Security, pp. 89–98. ACM (2006)
4. Boneh, D., Waters, B.: Conjunctive, subset, and range queries on encrypted data. In: Vadhan, S.P. (ed.) TCC 2007. LNCS, vol. 4392, pp. 535–554. Springer, Heidelberg (2007)
5. Iovino, V., Persiano, G.: Hidden-vector encryption with groups of prime order. In: Galbraith, S.D., Paterson, K.G. (eds.) Pairing 2008. LNCS, vol. 5209, pp. 75–88. Springer, Heidelberg (2008)
6. Blundo, C., Iovino, V., Persiano, G.: Private-key hidden vector encryption with key confidentiality. In: Garay, J.A., Miyaji, A., Otsuka, A. (eds.) CANS 2009. LNCS, vol. 5888, pp. 259–277. Springer, Heidelberg (2009)
7. Tseng, F.-K., Liu, Y.-H., Chen, R.-J., Lin, B.-S.P.: Statistics on encrypted cloud data. In: Sakiyama, K., Terada, M. (eds.) IWSEC 2013. LNCS, vol. 8231, pp. 133–150. Springer, Heidelberg (2013)
8. Elmasri, R.A., Navathe, S.B.: Fundamentals of Database Systems, 3rd edn. Addison-Wesley Longman Publishing Co., Inc., Boston (1999)

Author Index